CLARENDON ANCIENT HISTORY SERIES

*General Editors*

BRIAN BOSWORTH     MIRIAM GRIFFIN

DAVID WHITEHEAD    SUSAN TREGGIARI

The aim of the CLARENDON ANCIENT HISTORY SERIES is to provide authoritative translations, introductions, and commentaries to a wide range of Greek and Latin texts studied by ancient historians. The books will be of interest to scholars, graduate students, and advanced undergraduates.

# CURTIUS RUFUS

*Histories of Alexander the Great*
*Book 10*

Introduction and Historical Commentary by
J. E. ATKINSON

Translated by
J. C. YARDLEY

**OXFORD**
UNIVERSITY PRESS

# OXFORD
## UNIVERSITY PRESS

Great Clarendon Street, Oxford OX2 6DP

Oxford University Press is a department of the University of Oxford.
It furthers the University's objective of excellence in research, scholarship,
and education by publishing worldwide in

Oxford New York

Auckland Cape Town Dar es Salaam Hong Kong Karachi
Kuala Lumpur Madrid Melbourne Mexico City Nairobi
New Delhi Shanghai Taipei Toronto

With offices in

Argentina Austria Brazil Chile Czech Republic France Greece
Guatemala Hungary Italy Japan Poland Portugal Singapore
South Korea Switzerland Thailand Turkey Ukraine Vietnam

Oxford is a registered trade mark of Oxford University Press
in the UK and in certain other countries

Published in the United States
by Oxford University Press Inc., New York

© J. E. Atkinson and J. C. Yardley 2009

The moral rights of the authors and have been asserted
Database right Oxford University Press (maker)

First published 2009

British Library Cataloguing in Publication Data

Data available

Library of Congress Cataloging in Publication Data

Data available

Typeset by SPI Publisher Services, Pondicherry, India
Printed in Great Britain
on acid-free paper by
the MPG Books Group

ISBN 978–0–19–955762–2
ISBN 978–0–19–955763–9 (Pbk.)

1 3 5 7 9 10 8 6 4 2

# Preface

Curtius Rufus' *Histories of Alexander the Great* Book 10 justifies a special edition, as it includes the fullest account of events in Babylon immediately after Alexander's death. This is not to say that Curtius' account is therefore the best guide to what really happened at that time, but the fullness of Curtius' version does set it apart and calls for separate treatment. It also covers some key events in the last 18 months of Alexander's life, including the 'reign of terror' and the mutiny of the Macedonian troops; and it gives Curtius' final assessment of Alexander's qualities and failures.

Curtius draws attention to similarities between the events in Babylon and the situation in Rome before the accession of the new emperor, whoever he may be; he is also careful to point out where the comparison stops. Thus Curtius intended his text to be seen as of some relevance to the readers of his day. Throughout the work there is evidence of Roman colouring, but Book 10 has special significance in this regard, and indeed has to be studied by anyone interested in looking for evidence of Curtius' dates. So the historical problems are not limited to the period which is the subject of Curtius' history.

While Curtius has been variously dated to periods from the time of Augustus' establishment of the Principate through to the fourth century, most scholars treat him as a writer of the first century, or possibly of the early second century. I must declare that in my view the emperor eulogized in 10. 9. 1–5 is Claudius, but in this commentary I have tried to be even-handed, recognizing that there is a strong counter-view that Curtius wrote early in the reign of Vespasian, and that other emperors are serious possibilities.

This work has generally been located somewhere between Livy and Tacitus in linguistic, literary, and historiographical terms, and it therefore has some importance as a Latin text of the first century. Thus I have noted, or transmitted from earlier studies, usages, intertextual references, and common motifs that link Curtius with other writers of the period, such as Valerius Maximus, Velleius Paterculus, Seneca, Lucan, and Silius Italicus, as well as Livy and Tacitus.

The *Histories* is a literary work, and this book provides ample scope for demonstrating the literary nature of Curtius' historiography. Rutz, MacL Currie, Baynham and others have shown what can be achieved by looking at Curtius' narrative style. I have therefore sought to marry this approach with the more historical approach.

The major sources on Alexander the Great are well covered by commentaries in English, with Bosworth's commentary on Arrian (2 volumes in print, and the third in progress) and Brunt's well annotated edition of Arrian in the Loeb series, Hamilton's *Plutarch Alexander*, C. B. Welles's edition of Diodorus, Bk. 17 (with the more limited scope of the traditional Loeb edition), and Heckel's commentary on Yardley's translation of Justin in their *Justin, Epitome of the Philippic History of Pompeius Trogus*, vol. 1: *Books 11–12*. I have published commentaries on Curtius Books 3 to 4 and 5 to 7.2, and the remainder is covered in the second volume of my edition of Curtius for the Fondazione Lorenzo Valla/Mondadori series on Greek and Latin authors, but that is in Italian and the commentary on Book 10 is on a much smaller scale than what is offered here. Otherwise there is not a generally available commentary in English on Book 10: Dempsie's admirable commentary has unfortunately not made the transition from its appearance as a thesis for the University of St Andrews to a published version. His work complements this volume in that he places greater emphasis on issues of textual problems, language, and literary parallels.

The translation is an adaptation of John Yardley's version in the Penguin series, and I am very grateful to him for allowing me to use his work and for his assistance in some rephrasing to suit the needs of this commentary. Some adaptation was also necessary because he, under instructions from the Penguin series editor, had used the Budé text produced by Bardon (1965), while I have worked to the critical edition which I produced for Mondadori. I based my version on Müller's edition of 1954, which is generally regarded as superior to Bardon's text, but is less accessible. The text used here does not reflect the numerous textual emendations proposed by Dempsie (1991) and (1995), but they are generally of more concern to the student of Latin and palaeography than to the historian, and would not materially affect this commentary. W. S. Watt was more inclined to venture emendations that had a bearing on the historical meaning, and we were able to exchange ideas over a period of time. It was also my good fortune to be able to seek advice from Michael Winterbottom on textual and linguistic matters. I was further sensitized to the problems of interpretation by collaboration with Tristano Gargiulo, while he was engaged in translating the Latin text—and then my commentary—into Italian. By the end of that exercise we were notching up several Email messages per day, and my admiration for the skill of the translator grew even stronger.

The Commentary is intended to meet the requirements of the Series to serve senior undergraduates, graduate students and scholars. As a function of the first degree is to awaken interest in research and to introduce research methodology, it is indeed hoped that this volume will be useful at the undergraduate level. It therefore errs on the side of fullness to serve as a stand-alone edition (as opposed to a volume in a series of commentaries on the author), and, where appropriate and possible, as a one-stop reference work for the 'hit-and-run' user.

It is hoped that the references and bibliography provide an adequate introduction to the scholarly debate on the various issues raised by the text. Further references can be picked up from Holger Koch's excellent survey of a century of Curtian scholarship (1899–1999), and from surveys in *Aufstieg und Niedergang der römischen Welt*, Teil II, Band 32.4 and 34. 4, by Rutz (1986) and Atkinson (1998*b*) respectively. On historical matters the bibliography can be supplemented from i.a. Bosworth (2002), Roisman (2003), and Heckel (2006), and of course by judicious use of the Web.

My greatest debt of gratitude is to Ernst Badian, who got me interested in Alexander studies as an undergraduate in Durham, and who generously acted for the University of Cape Town as my doctoral supervisor, and later enabled me to spend a period of sabbatical leave at Harvard. My work must also reflect the influence of my first Head of Department, in what was then the University College of Rhodesia and Nyasaland, Tom Carney, whose wide range of research interests, analytical techniques, and sheer industry were a powerful challenge and inspiration. Over the years I have been fortunate to have had, at various times or over extended periods, encouragement and advice, not to mention a wealth of offprints, from a great number of scholars working in the field of Alexander and related studies, including Elizabeth Baynham (best known for her monograph on Curtius, and the local organizer of the highly successful symposium on Alexander studies held in Newcastle, NSW, in 1997), Edmund Bloedow, Ernst Fredricksmeyer, Jon Gissel, Waldemar Heckel, Simon Hornblower, Diane Spencer, Shapur Shahbazi, Adrian Tronson, the late Ursula Vogel-Wiedemann, Gerhard Wirth, Ian Worthington, and John Yardley (to whom I am very grateful for his work on the Latin of Trogus, Justin, and Curtius, and also for his role in organizing a stimulating symposium on Alexander in Ottawa).

I must also thank my colleague at UCT, David Wardle, who has been an ever reliable guide to current scholarship on the early Roman Empire, and a very sharp and critical reader of whatever drafts I have tried out on him.

I am very grateful to Miriam Griffin and David Whitehead, who as editors of the Clarendon Ancient History Series, looked at and commented on sections of this work. Most of all I must express my deepest gratitude to Brian Bosworth for his special role in initiating this project and guiding me to its fruition. Though over the years we have disagreed on many points of interpretation, the influence of his amazing range of publications and the depth of his scholarship will be apparent on almost every page of this commentary.

As ever it should not be assumed that those I have thanked for looking at my work approve of the style and content of all that appears here. I carry the responsibility for any errors, omissions, oddities, and obscurities that remain.

At the institutional level I am indebted to Alex d'Angelo, the Head of the Humanities Section of the UCT Library, who is indeed an information scientist, but has still remained a librarian, and a very helpful one. I am also very grateful to the staff of the library of the Institute of Classical Studies in London, who have given me ready assistance in the precious periods of time when I have been able to work there.

My wife Valerie, appropriately née Alexander, has had to cope with her great namesake for most of our married life, and from typewriter and waxed stencils to Pentium whatever and USBs. No doubt she will be pleased to see the back of him now that, from the Cape, we have delivered him, if not to Cairo, at least to Memphis. I am very grateful to her for her patience and practical assistance over the years.

J.A.

*University of Cape Town*
*Rondebosch, S. Africa*
*April 2008*

# Contents

# Abbreviations

| | |
|---|---|
| AC | *L'Antiquité classique* |
| AClass | *Acta Classica* |
| AHB | *Ancient History Bulletin* |
| AJA | *American Journal of Archaeology* |
| AJAH | *American Journal of Ancient History* |
| AJP | *American Journal of Philology* |
| Anc. Soc. | *Ancient Society* |
| Anc. W | *Ancient World* |
| ANRW | *Aufstieg und Niedergang der römischen Welt, II. Teil: Principat*, ed. H. Temporini and W. Haase (Berlin, 1974–) |
| AO | R. Develin, *Athenian Officials 684–321* BC (Cambridge, 1989) |
| APF | J. K. Davies, *Athenian Propertied Families, 600–300* BC (Oxford, 1971) |
| AUMLA | *The Journal of the Australasian Language and Literature Association* |
| BCH | *Bulletin de corrrespondance hellénique* |
| BJRL | *Bulletin of the John Rylands Library* |
| BMCR | *Bryn Mawr Classical Review* |
| BMCRE | H. Mattingly, *Coins of the Roman Empire in the British Museum*. Vol. i (1923), ii (1930), iii (1936, reprinted with alterations 1966) (London) |
| BNP | *Brill's New Pauly: Encyclopaedia of the Ancient World* (Leiden, 2002–) |
| C&M | *Classica et Mediaevalia* |
| CA | *Classical Antiquity* |
| CAH | *Cambridge Ancient History* |
| CHI | *The Cambridge History of Iran*. Vol. ii, ed. I. Gershevitch (Cambridge, 1985) |
| CID | J. Bousquet, *Corpus des inscriptions de Delphes*. Vol. ii (Paris, 1989) |

| | |
|---|---|
| *CIL* | *Corpus inscriptionum Latinarum* (1863–) |
| *CJ* | *Classical Journal* |
| *CP* | *Classical Philology* |
| *CQ* | *Classical Quarterly* |
| *CR* | *Classical Review* |
| *EMC* | *Echos du Monde Classique/Classical Views* |
| *FD* | *Fouilles de Delphes* (1902–) |
| *FGrH* | F. Jacoby, *Die Fragmente der griechischen Historiker* (Berlin and Leipzig, 1923–). References are given to the ancient authors according to Jacoby's numbers. Thus, for example, *FGrH* 137, F. 30 refers to fragment 30 of the author numbered 137, Cleitarchus. |
| *FHG* | C. Müller, *Fragmenta historicorum graecorum.* 5 vols. (Paris, 1878–) |
| *G&R* | *Greece and Rome* |
| *GCN* | E.M. Smallwood, *Documents Illustrating the Principates of Gaius, Claudius and Nero* (Cambridge, 1967) |
| *GHI* | M. N. Tod, *A Selection of Greek Historical Inscriptions.* Vol. ii: *From 403 to 323* BC (Oxford, 1948) |
| *GRBS* | *Greek, Roman and Byzantine Studies* |
| *Hist* | *Historia* (Wiesbaden) |
| *HSCP* | *Harvard Studies in Classical Philology* |
| *IG* | *Inscriptiones Graecae.* 1st edn. (Berlin, 1873–), 2nd edn. (Berlin, 1913–) |
| *IGBulg* | G. Mihailov, *Inscriptiones Graecae in Bulgaria repertae* (1958–70) |
| *IGRPP* | R. Cagnat (ed.), *Inscriptiones Graecae ad res Romanas pertinentes* (Paris, 1901–27) |
| *ILS* | H. Dessau, *Inscriptiones Latinae Selectae* (Berlin, 1892–1916) |
| *JHS* | *Journal of Hellenic Studies* |
| *JRS* | *Journal of Roman Studies* |
| *Kleine Pauly* | *Der Kleine Pauly, Lexicon der Antike,* ed. K. Ziegler. 5 vols. (Stuttgart, 1964–75) |
| *LEC* | *Les Études classiques* |

| | |
|---|---|
| *MDAI(A)* | *Mitteilungen des deutschen archäologischen Instituts, Athenische Abteilung* (1876–) |
| *MIL* | *Memorie dell'Istituto Lombardo, Accad. di Scienze e Lettere, Classe di Lettere* |
| *OCD*[3] | S. Hornblower and A. Spawforth (eds.) *The Oxford Classical Dictionary*, 3rd edn. (Oxford, 1996) |
| *OGIS* | W. Dittenberger *Orientis Graeci Inscriptiones Selectae*, 3rd edn. (Leipzig, 1903–5; reprinted Hildesheim, 1960) |
| *PACA* | *Proceedings of the African Classical Associations* |
| *PAPhS* | *Proceedings of the American Philosophical Society* |
| *PCPS* | *Proceedings of the Cambridge Philological Society* |
| *PDAR* | E. Nash, *Pictorial Dictionary of Ancient Rome*, 2 vols. Revised edn. (London, 1968; second edn., 1989) |
| *PP* | *La Parola del Passato* |
| *R&O* | P. J. Rhodes and R. Osborne, *Greek Historical Inscriptions, 404–323 BC* (Oxford, 2003) |
| *RAL* | *Rendiconti della reale academia dei Lincei*. 7th series (1925–) |
| *RE* | A. F. von Pauly, et al. (eds.) *Paulys Real-Encyclopädie der classischen Altertumswissenschaft* (Stuttgart, 1894–1972) |
| *REA* | *Revue des études anciennes* |
| *RFIC* | *Rivista di filologia e di istruzione classica* |
| *RhM* | *Rheinisches Museum für Philologie* |
| *RHR* | *Revue de l'histoire des religions* |
| *RPh* | *Revue de philologie, de littérature et d'histoire anciennes* |
| *RSC* | *Rivista di studi classici* (Turin) |
| *SEG* | *Supplementum epigraphicum graecum.* (Leiden, 1923–) |
| *SIG* | *Sylloge Inscriptionum Graecarum*, ed. W. Dittenberger. 3rd edn. (Leipzig, 1915–24) |
| *SO* | *Symbolae Osloenses* |
| *TAPA* | *Transactions of the American Philological Association* |
| *WJA* | *Würzburger Jahrbücher für die Altertumswissenschaft* |
| *WS* | *Wiener Studien* |
| *YCS* | *Yale Classical Studies* |
| *ZPE* | *Zeitschrift für Papyrologie und Epigraphik* |

# Introduction

## 1. LEVELS OF SIGNIFICANCE

Curtius' *Histories of Alexander* is the earliest surviving full-scale account of his reign and campaigns, and it is written in Latin. Thus it has special value even though the first two of the ten books have been lost. It is a monograph, whereas the earlier account of Alexander's reign in Diodorus Siculus Book 17 forms a chapter in a universal history, as did the account of Pompeius Trogus,[1] which is known to us through the epitome of Books 11 and 12 of his *Philippic History* written by Justin, probably in the latter half of the second century. Curtius' account is more on the scale of our key source, Arrian's *Anabasis of Alexander,* which is generally taken to have been written some time after Curtius;[2] and, being history, Curtius' work differs in design and intent from Plutarch's biography of Alexander, written probably in Trajan's reign.

These five texts—two in Latin and three in Greek—are commonly referred to as our 'primary' sources, as a group distinct from the wide range of authors, like Polybius, Strabo, and Pliny the Elder, who made discrete references to historical details garnered from first-generation sources, or, like Valerius Maximus, the Senecas and Livy, at 9. 17–19, who used Alexander, in whatever context, as an *exemplum.*[3] Of

---

[1] Diodorus may have completed his work by about 30 BC, whereas Trogus seems to have written during the last two decades of the first century BC.

[2] Many assume that Arrian wrote the *Anabasis* during Hadrian's reign, or even after 138, but Bosworth (1988*b*), 16–37 argues strongly for composition towards the end of Trajan's reign.

[3] Add purveyors of anecdotal material, like Athenaeus and Lucian. Baynham (2003), esp. 3–17, offers a general introduction.

more immediate relevance to Book 10 is a Latin text of the fourth or fifth century, the *Metz Epitome*, which concludes with a section labelled *The Last Days and Testament of Alexander* (*Liber de morte testamentumque Alexandri Magni*). This appears to be based on an account written for political purposes within fifteen years of Alexander's death. It provides a salutary reminder of how history can be bedevilled by conspiracy theories. Much of Curtius' account of Alexander's last days has not survived, but he was sceptical about the allegations of murder (10. 10. 14–18). This might add credibility to his account of the events immediately after Alexander's death, but there is ongoing debate about whether he crossed the boundary between narration and fictionalizing.

Caution is necessary for another reason, because at 10. 9. 1–6 Curtius makes specific reference to the political situation in Rome at the time of composition of this closing section of his work. If this means that Curtius intended the *Histories* to be a text for his time, we have all the more reason to expect to find other passages in his work that reflect his experience of Roman politics and society. Furthermore Alexander the Great was not a value-free historical figure in the early Roman Empire, as emulation or imitation of Alexander became an intermittent motif of imperial propaganda, and critics developed the negative image of the great man as a counter to the exploitation of the heroic myth. Hence, as Curtius was writing in an unfree society, it must be a working assumption that the *Histories* may at significant points have a metatextual level of meaning.

## 2. CURTIUS, THE AUTHOR AND HIS DATES

A biographical entry for Quintus Curtius Rufus is of necessity very brief and highly speculative, since we lack the first two books of the *Histories* and hence more importantly the preface, in which Curtius, if he followed the convention of ancient historiography, would have provided some information about his identity and the context in which he wrote. Furthermore we have no direct references to the author in other texts. In the surviving books Curtius is sparing in direct references to the Roman world of his day, and none of them is decisive. The most direct occurs in Book 10, where he uses the turmoil in Babylon after Alexander's death to introduce a eulogy of the new emperor, whose accession has either averted civil war or has put a swift end to a developing civil war (10. 9. 1–6). The uncertainty as to whether Curtius means civil war averted or swiftly terminated has allowed commentators to offer contexts ranging from 25–23 BC and the foundation of the Augustan Principate (Korzeniewski 1959) to the emergence of Constantine as sole emperor (Pichon 1908). Most, however, favour either the accession of Claudius in AD 41 or Vespasian's *coup d'état* in 69. Others consider that Curtius was eulogizing Tiberius (Devine 1979), Nero (Verdière 1966), Galba (Milns 1966), Titus (Barzano 1985), Trajan (Bosworth (1983a), esp. 151–4[4] and Rüegg (1906), 115–16), Septimius Severus (Bourazeli 1988), or Alexander Severus (Fears 1974a, 1976a and b, 2001).

The crucial passage (10. 9. 1–6) clearly indicates that Curtius wrote when the Principate was well established and had been facing a succession crisis, and thus it must have been written, *pace* Korzeniewski, no earlier than AD 14 and the accession of the second emperor, Tiberius. Curtius inserts his eulogistic reference to the new emperor at the point in the narrative where the Macedonian infantry and cavalry forces have reached a compromise and have come together, so averting a physical confrontation. This prompts the thankful note that Rome has been spared the trauma of civil war (some would say 'of further civil war'), and the narrative resumes with the judicial murders of the leaders of the infantry faction, and the killing of Meleager. Of course Curtius was not to know what would happen much beyond the accession of the new emperor, but he certainly knew that the compromise in Babylon did not mean lasting peace, as the history of the Successors was one of a succession of murders and wars among the rivals for power. So Curtius' point was that it was a good omen that Rome had found a new leader at a matching point of compromise, and he could hope that the accession would bring lasting peace and not lead into anything like the wars of the Successors. Thus many argue that Curtius' eulogy of the new

---

[4] But, as is noted below, Bosworth (2004), 566 now inclines towards a Vespasianic date.

emperor best suits the accession of Claudius in AD 41 (Mützell (1841), esp. pp. lxi–lxix, following many earlier scholars, and followed by many more, including Atkinson (1980), esp. 25–35, Bödefeld (1982), 10–20, Hamilton (1988), Martin (1987) and Baynham (1998), esp. 206–9, duly spelling out the caveats).

If Curtius knew of the revolt initiated by the governor of Dalmatia, L. Arruntius Camillus Scribonianus, in 42 (Suet. *Claud.* 13. 2 and 35. 2; Dio 60. 15), he chose to play it down, and, in any case, the revolt ended within five days. But some consider the revolt of Scribonianus a serious obstacle to dating Curtius' eulogy to Claudius' reign, unless he wrote before that revolt, which is described by Suet. *Claud.* 13. 2 as civil war, and as a civil war that spread throughout the world according to Calpurnius Siculus *Ecl.* 1, esp. 49–50, according to the interpretation of Wiseman (1982). Thus Wiseman, esp. 67 n. 95, supports the case for dating Curtius' eulogy to the early period of Nero's reign.

The case for Galba as the new emperor (Milns (1966), esp. 494–6) is vitiated by Curtius' prayer for long life for the ruling dynasty, as this worn out veteran was childless; and the same might apply to Trajan (98–117), who though fit for further military adventures, was without an heir.

If Curtius 10. 9. 1–6 is taken to refer to a new emperor who has terminated actual civil war, then the strongest candidate is Vespasian (69–79), and the prayer for the dynasty conveniently fits the prospect of a new Flavian dynasty, as the emperor had two sons, Titus and Domitian, old enough for consideration for the succession. It is argued that Curtius' phraseology better suits the suppression of civil war, and there is emphasis on the extent to which ideograms and phraseology used by Curtius reflect Flavian propaganda, eulogy and literature (Stroux (1929), Instinsky (1962), Scheda (1969), Grilli (1976), Rutz (1981) and (1983*a*), Barzano (1985), and Fugmann (1995)). Rutz (1983*a*) takes J.C. Rodriguez's study of Curtius' language to show that Curtius wrote in the first century, but later than Seneca, and thus probably in Vespasian's reign). Parallels are noted in the commentary on 10. 9. 1–6.

A problem is that phrases coined by imperial propagandists were continued or recycled, thus many expressions associated with the Claudian principate, such as *libertas*, *pax* (peace) and *salus* (well-being),[5] resurface in Vespasian's reign. Little significance may attach to ideograms which feature in Julio-Claudian propaganda and in Curtius, but do not resurface in Vespasian's propaganda,[6] but greater weight attaches to what appears in Curtius and post-Julio-Claudian propaganda. Thus a Flavian date for the eulogy much depends on the parallel noted between Curtius' phrase 'our empire is not merely recovering (*revirescit*), but even flourishes', and the slogan ROMA RESURGENS which first appears as a slogan on coins of Vespasian (*BMCRE* ii. 87, no. 425; 121, nos. 565–6 etc.). But this comparison is weakened by appearances of the key verb *revirescere* in earlier contexts (*Auct. ad Her.* 3. 34. 35 and Val. Max. 4. 8. 4).

A similar problem arises over intertextual references. Thus, for example, Curtius' phrase on 'the night which was almost our last' (10. 9. 3) has a parallel in Tacitus' introduction of the year 69 as almost the last for the Roman state (*Hist.* 1. 11. 3), and both passages seem to echo Livy 6. 17. 4. It is possible that both authors independently echoed Livy, and even possible that Tacitus was influenced by Curtius (Bosworth (2004), 554). But the parallel is hardly enough to strengthen the case that Curtius has in mind the events of 18–20 December 69, and in particular the night of 19/20 December (*pace* Fugmann (1995), 241–2).

It remains to ask whether the positioning of the eulogy in Curtius' narrative adds support to the case for a date in Vespasian's reign. At 10. 9. 19 Curtius comments that the judicial murder of Meleager's lieutenants, followed by the killing of Meleager, marked a forewarning and the beginning of civil wars. This suggests that the preceding eulogy was referring to civil war averted, and not to the violence of 68–9. Then there is the puzzle of the uniqueness of Curtius' presentation of Philip Arrhidaeus, Alexander's mentally-challenged half-brother. There may also be significance in the positioning of the eulogy in the narrative before Arrhidaeus loses his moral authority and becomes a pawn of Perdiccas. It is at least an attractive idea that Curtius was aware that some readers would approach his text with the preconception that the problem with Arrhidaeus was not unlike

---

[5] All feature with similar political connotations in Curtius' *Histories*: for example, *libertas* at 10. 7. 11, *pax* at 10. 8. 23, and *salus* at 10. 9. 3.

[6] e.g. *moderatio* (6. 6. 1) and *constantia* (5. 7. 1).

Augustus' problem with the gangling adolescent Claudius (Suet. *Claud.* 3–4).

Minor indications of Curtius' dates have been sought in his passing comments on, for example, the Nasamones and archery in his own day. At 4. 7. 19 Curtius refers to the Libyan tribe of the Nasamones as making a living by looting ships, and it is suggested that this reflects the propaganda generated by Domitian to justify his action against the tribe in 86 (Bosworth (1983a), 152–3; Dio 67. 4. 6, reporting that Domitian announced to the Senate that he had forbidden the Nasamones to exist). But Curtius' brief reference is obviously much closer to what Lucan wrote in the early 60s at *Pharsalia* 9. 438–44. Thus there is no compelling reason to put Curtius later than 86.

More problematic is Curtius' note that in his day archery was a widely practised skill (7. 5. 42). In Domitian's day archery could still be regarded as a recreational activity rather than a military skill (Suet. *Dom.* 19. 1, though see *Titus* 5. 2), and Bosworth (1983a), 152 argues that Curtius' comment would better suit the later (Trajanic) context, as there had been a significant development of units of auxiliary archers during the Flavian period and in Trajan's reign, and by Hadrian's reign training in archery was instituted in cavalry exercises (Arr. *Tact.* 44. 1).[7] Altheim (1948), 157–9 takes the point to support his case for dating Curtius to the reign of Septimius Severus. But an earlier date is quite possible: archers certainly feature in Germanicus' army in AD 16 (Tac. *Ann.* 2. 16. 3 and 17. 4–6), and Curtius was not to know whether this skill would be further developed by the Romans.

On a related point Korzeniewski (1959), 45–50 argues that Curtius' careful glossing of the term cataphract cavalry at 3. 11. 15 and 4. 9. 3 should antedate the creation in the Roman army of the first unit of Gallic and Pannonian cataphract cavalry, probably in Trajan's reign (*CIL* xi. 5632).[8] Thus on the issue of archery and cataphract cavalry the evidence has been taken to fit contexts from 25–23 BC (Korzeniewski) to the reign of Trajan or later.

---

[7] But by Caracalla's day the Roman army could still not match the Parthians in their skill as mounted archers (Herodian 4. 10. 3).

[8] Roman troops had confronted cataphract cavalry at the battle of Tigranocerta in 69 BC (Plut. *Lucullus* 26–8) and at Carrhae in 53 BC (Plut. *Crassus* 25. 8).

Curtius' references to the Parthians at 4. 12. 11, 5. 7. 9 and 8. 1 and 6. 2. 12 imply that he wrote earlier than the final demise of the Parthian empire, and thus no later than 226/7, and probably before Septimius Severus' campaign of AD 197/8 (Atkinson (1980), 23). Curtius' allusion to the Euphrates as the boundary between east and west at 10. 5. 12 may even point to a date no later than Vespasian's operations beyond the river. Nevertheless, some argue for a Severan date for Curtius: so Steele (1915) and especially Fears (2001), 450, who holds to his earlier position and suggests that Curtius wrote after the assassination of Caracalla in 217,[9] in the reign of Elagabalus, because Caracalla had been the worst type of imitator of Alexander.[10] But when Alexander Severus (222–35) became emperor, and the image of Alexander was refurbished,[11] Curtius had to revise his work and so created a laudatory obituary (10. 5. 26–36), somewhat at odds with the preceding narrative, and added a panegyric of the new emperor. Fears (1974*a*) meets the argument concerning the references to the Parthians by contending that, whereas after *c.*226/7 the Sassanids were generally referred to as *Persae*, yet Ammianus Marcellinus, writing as late as *c.*400, could substitute Parthian for Persian. It is true that Ammianus very occasionally, and perhaps for stylistic variation, refers to the Sassanid Persians as Parthians, but this does not increase the probability that Curtius would have referred consistently to the Sassanids as Parthians. Furthermore the argument should centre on what Curtius says about the Parthians, and not just about the terminology.

Then it is argued that Curtius' 'new star' (10. 9. 3) need not have a Julio-Claudian or Flavian reference, but might allude to the 'star' which appeared to mark the birth of Alexander Severus (SHA *Alex. Sev.* 13. 5; Steele (1915), 423, Griset (1964), 163). So Bourazeli (1988), 258–9, finds in a speech attributed to Alexander an endorsement of

---

[9] Herodian 4. 13. 8; Dio 78. 5. 4.

[10] Caracalla began to promote an image of himself as a new Alexander while in Thrace in 214 (Herodian 4. 8. 1). N. Hannestad, *Roman Art and Imperial Policy* (Aarhus Univ. Press, Højbjerg, 1984), 284 for his portraiture in Alexander guise.

[11] On which see J. M. Blasquez, 'Alejandro Magno, modelo de Alejandro Severo', in *Neronia IV: Alejandro Magno, modelo de los emperadores romanos* (Brussels, 1990), 25–36.

the Severan policy of extending Roman citizenship to all free-born inhabitants of the Roman empire, which was formalized in the *Constitutio Antoniniana* of 212, but Bourazeli misses the point that in its context the generous openness does not stand to Alexander's credit (commentary at 10. 3. 14).

Wirth (on Curtius in *Kleine Pauly* i. 1350) approaches the issue from the angle of Curtius' sources and suggests that Curtius made acquaintance with Ptolemy's history because he had read Arrian's *Anabasis*, and was likewise able to echo passages of Arrian's *Indica*. Thus Curtius must have written later than the mid-second century. Wirth further claims that Curtius' prose rhythm and sentence construction are consistent with such a date.[12] Wirth's first line of argument is, however, spoilt by the fact that Strabo, the elder Pliny and Plutarch managed to find Ptolemy without Arrian to show them the way.

The weight of historical, literary, and linguistic evidence may not be heavy, but still seems to be adequate to make a Severan or later date for Curtius most improbable. It is true that it was fashionable from the fourth century to emulate the style of first century authors,[13] but, if Curtius was a late author, he would have to be credited with an exceptional record of consistency in avoiding vocabulary and forms that were current in his own day, and rare or not attested in first century texts. My survey of linguistic and terminological evidence and of the evidence on prose rhythm and *clausulae* favours a first century date for Curtius.[14] On balance I still favour a Claudian date for the completion of Book 10, but, as noted earlier, the case for a Vespasianic date has steadily gained support, not least from Bosworth's conclusion that, as Tacitus had clearly read Curtius before he wrote the *Agricola*, early in 98, then Curtius must have predated Trajan's accession, and a Vespasianic date for Curtius is 'perhaps . . . the most likely' (Bosworth (2004), 566). But Bosworth's case hinges largely on the argument that Curtius' *Histories* was a recent enough text for Tacitus to make allusions to it that would be readily picked up, and yet this

---

[12] He refers to the Silver Latin era, though when it was fashionable to use this label, it was usually taken to end c. 150, a *terminus* which Wirth clearly sees as artificial.

[13] E. Norden, *Die antike Kunstprosa*, 6th edn. (Darmstadt, 1971), ii. 576–86.

[14] Atkinson (1980), esp. 43–8.

means a gap of nearly thirty years between Curtius' completion of his *magnum opus* and Tacitus' composition of the *Agricola*. Intertextual allusions to Curtius in the *Annals* would imply an even greater gap between the two works. Thus the intertextual references are not a fatal objection to a Claudian date.

## 3. POSSIBLE IDENTIFICATION WITH OTHER KNOWN CURTII

In the absence of direct external evidence on the author, the challenge is to build a profile from clues provided by the text itself. Of course we can not know whether Curtius creates an authorial *persona* that was a fiction, or more aspirational than real, but if we take the evidence at face value, we should at least still allow for the fact that Curtius was writing in an un-free society and thus might not wish to be too open about his own opinions. The Principate was an authoritarian system which required reality to be accommodated to the myths of autocracy and empire. Curtius was familiar enough with dissimulation as an instrument of government,[15] and makes frequent reference to the *species* (guise, pretence, pretext) that was presented as reality.[16] Thus I am predisposed to believe that Curtius, as an intellectually engaged member of society, was something of an ironist, but used irony lightly enough to be able to deny any hostile intent. The 'real' Curtius was probably not too different from the image he created for himself in the *Histories*.

Curtius identifies himself as a Roman in the disdain which he feels towards barbarians (as at 3. 2. 6; 4. 1. 30, 7. 8; 6. 6. 1–9; 7. 8. 10; 8. 13. 7)[17] and Greeks (as at 3. 1. 2, 4. 5. 11 and 8. 5. 7–8), and, as we have noted, in his view of the Parthian empire. His perception of the

---

[15] The noun *dissimulatio* appears at 6. 7. 32, 7. 2. 9 and 10. 9. 8 and there are 8 appearances of the verb *dissimulare*.

[16] Examples in this book are 10. 6. 21, 9. 9, and 10. 7. The noun is used some 53 times in the work as a whole, admittedly not always with so sinister a connotation (as e.g. at 10. 5. 1).

[17] Curtius can also damn with faint praise, as at 9. 1. 24.

transition of power to the new emperor is that of someone at the centre of the crisis, and thus of someone with a Roman perspective. His use of the first person in mentioning the 'night that was almost the last we had' (10. 9. 3) suggests that he saw himself as one of the ruling class. Barzano (1985), 119 takes Curtius' expressions for men of the lowest social class (*ultima plebs* (6. 8. 10) and *infima plebs* (10. 7. 1))[18] as further evidence of Curtius' noble status, but I still incline to the alternative view that his conservatism has the smack of the 'new man' (*novus homo*, the first member of his family to hold a curule magistracy, and in particular the consulship).[19] For despite that mark of the *arriviste*, dedication to traditionalism, Curtius at the same time appears to support a meritocratic system that will allow the good man to rise on merit (5. 2. 4). But he had disdain for lower order functionaries who have power without status (e.g. 7. 1. 35).

There was a Roman senator by the name of Quintus Curtius Rufus, who rose to the rank of suffect consul in AD 43, thus, early in Claudius' reign.[20] He had served as an official on the staff of the quaestor in the province of Africa, and must have held the quaestorship himself after he reached the minimum age of 25. At this point he became a senator, and Badian (1964), 263 suggests that this might have happened before the death of Augustus.

Certainly Curtius the senator had the support of the emperor Tiberius for his next appointment to a praetorship. He stood as a candidate among men from noble families (Tac. *Ann.* 11. 21. 2), which means that he must have been a 'new man'. This is also clear from the comment attributed to Tiberius that Curtius appeared to

---

[18] Cf. 4. 10. 7 on the fickleness and superstition of the masses. It is of course true that there was a technical distinction in Rome between those *plebs* who fell below the category of recipients of the corn dole (the *plebs sordida* of Tac. *Hist.* 1. 4. 4 and 3. 74. 2), and those who were in a less precarious situation as recipients of the corn dole, and/or handouts from their patrons, the group styled less dismissively the *plebs integra* or *frumentaria* (Chilver (1979), 48–9; Sallust *or. Cottae* 5 and Suet. *Nero* 12. 1). In the commentary at 10. 2. 10 attention is drawn to the different line on these labels taken by Yavetz.

[19] For background on the development of controlled admission into the nobility see T. P. Wiseman, *New Men in the Roman Senate, 139 BC–AD 14* (Oxford, 1971).

[20] Evidence on the career of the senator is reviewed by Atkinson (1980), 50–7. The date of the consulship has been established by G. Barbieri. 'I consoli dell'anno 43 dC', *RAL* 30 (1975), 153–7, followed by P. A. Gallivan, 'The *fasti* for the reign of Claudius', *CQ* 28 (1978), 407–25.

be his own creation (in other words a self-made man: Tac. *Ann.*
11. 21. 2), which echoes Cicero's description of his own status as a
'new man' (*novus homo*) at *Phil.* 6. 17 and *Planc.* 67. There was some
gossip that Curtius was the son of a gladiator, a charge that Tacitus
was too much of a gentleman to investigate, but too snobbish to
pass over.

After the consulship Curtius was presently awarded the governorship of Germania Superior, probably in the period 46–7.[21] Finally he
attained one of the two most prestigious governorships open to ex-
consuls, the governorship of Africa. There would have been a gap
after his governorship in Germany, and a gap of ten years or more
between the consulship and the governorship of Africa (or Asia) was
normal. Thus he probably went to North Africa sometime after 53,
and Weidemann (1982), 184–8 hazards 58–59. By then he was an old
man and died in office (Tac. *Ann.* 11. 21. 3; Pliny *Ep.* 7. 27. 2–3).

A hint of the senator's origins may be provided by a cadastral
record of AD 77 from Orange in Provence, which attests a Q. Curtius
Rufus as a local chief magistrate (a *duovir*). On the strength of this,
Salviat (1986) has boldly suggested that the senator's family came
from Valentia in the territory of the Cavares (cf. Pliny *HN* 3. 34 and
36 with Mela 2. 75 and Strabo 4. 1. 11. 185).

While there is a natural hesitation about the tidying up of history,
it remains an attractive possibility that the historian was the new man
senator who became consul in 43 (Atkinson (1980), 56–7, Salviat
(1986), Syme (1982), 197–8). If he was a senator in Tiberius' reign,
Curtius might well have been present at the trial of M. Terentius for
treason in AD 32, which might just explain the parallels between
Tacitus' account of M. Terentius' speech in his own defence and
our Curtius' version of the speech which Amyntas made in his
defence in 330 (Curtius 7. 1. 18–40, and esp. 26–8, with Tac. *Ann.*
6. 8. 1–3).[22] And, if the historian became a senator before the death
of Augustus, as suggested above, and witnessed the proceedings of
the Senate when Tiberius was recognized as the new emperor, this

---

[21] Tac. *Ann.* 11. 20. 3 and 21. 2, with two inscriptions from Vindonissa in
Germania Superior: *CIL* xiii. 5204 and 11514; on the date, Atkinson (1980), 53–5.
[22] Wiedemann (1870), 244–6, Sumner (1961), 33 ff., Devine (1979), 150 ff.,
Atkinson (1994), 250–5. It is of course possible that Curtius and Tacitus drew on
some earlier account of the trial, perhaps that of Aufidius Bassus; and Bosworth

could explain Curtius' interest in that other succession debate after Alexander's death.

Tacitus characterized the consular as 'subservient though surly towards his superiors', arrogant towards his inferiors and awkward among his peers (*Ann.* 11. 21. 3).[23] The historian certainly knew that some flattery of the emperor was expected of him (10. 9. 1–6), but was well aware of the insidious effect of flattery (3. 2. 10, 7. 4. 9, 8. 5. 6 and 8. 21). One can see why Tacitus was interested enough in the consular Curtius to provide an obituary: Curtius was like himself a 'new man', and both probably came from Gaul. His interest would have been compounded if this was the Curtius to whose *Histories* Tacitus made numerous inter-textual references in his own writings. The obituary would then have been as close as Tacitus came to giving recognition to a text which had attracted his attention and challenged his own cleverness.

If the historian was indeed a 'new man', whether or not the consul of 43, he was perhaps making a statement by venturing to write history. Men of equestrian rank, especially those who travelled and saw service as civil or military bureaucrats, were more likely to produce technical manuals, like Columella and Julius Graecinus on agriculture, Pomponius Mela on geography, and of course Pliny the Elder on 'natural history'.[24] If Curtius had held the praetorship under Tiberius, and had served as a provincial governor, then he would have felt himself qualified at least to understand the memoirs of those who had participated in the campaigns of Alexander,[25] and thus to be qualified to write history.

---

(2004), 564–6 adds considerable strength to the case that Tacitus may have been influenced by Curtius. Incidentally, Bosworth in that article takes a less certain line about dating Curtius' *Historiae* to the early part of Trajan's reign, but is firm in rejecting a Claudian date, while being more open to a Vespasianic context.

[23] The first phrase is as translated by R. Syme, *AJP* 79 (1958), 22.

[24] Cf. M. Beagon, *Roman Nature* (Oxford, 1992), 5–8 and J. F. Healy, *Pliny the Elder on Science and Technology* (Oxford, 1999), 2. Admittedly Pliny went on to tackle a general history of his era (*HN Preface*, 20). Julius Graecinus' father was from Fréjus and held high office as an equestrian procurator, but Graecinus gained membership of the Senate and rose to the rank of praetor (Tac. *Agr.* 4. 1). Aufidius Bassus wrote history and apparently remained an *eques* to the end of his life, but it is suggested that it was only ill health that held him back from a senatorial career (Syme (1958), i. 274–6).

[25] Cf. Polybius 12. 28a. 6–10, who attacks Timaeus for his naïve faith in the assembling of second-hand reports, and for his lack of direct experience of military matters, which disqualified him from meaningfully interrogating participants.

Those who date Curtius 10. 9. 1–6 to the reign of Vespasian or some later emperor of course exclude equation of the historian with the consul, but can allow the possibility that the historian was a member of a later generation of the family: thus Bosworth (1983*a*), 153 suggests that he was the consul's grandson. It may be prudent not to make the suggestion that, if the historian was the consul's grandson, he might just have adopted the authorial *persona* of his famous grandfather.

There is another historical Q. Curtius Rufus to consider, the one whom Suetonius includes in his list of rhetoricians, and, from what we know of those named either side of Curtius, he can be dated to the period between the latter part of Augustus reign and the early years of Nero's reign. Kaster (1995), 336–7, in his commentary on Suetonius *De grammaticis et rhetoribus*, finds it perfectly plausible that the *Histories* was written by this rhetor as the work has been generally recognized as 'steeped in school-rhetoric',[26] and he considers it no less plausible that the senator had started out as a rhetor, as Suetonius comments that some rhetors rose to gain membership of the Senate and to hold curule magistracies (25. 3).

Curtius seems to make a passing claim to some distinction as a rhetorician[27] in the way he introduces a speech supposedly delivered by a Scythian envoy to Alexander: 'What they are reported to have said before the king is perhaps foreign to our way of thinking and our character, since we have enjoyed more cultivated times and intellects, but, though their oratory could be criticized, my accurate reporting should not' (7. 8. 11 translated by Yardley). It is of course quite possible that Curtius really did render into Latin what he found in his source,[28] and chose to highlight this case as evidence of his veracity as a transmitter of source material, but it is more likely that the speech was at least in part a Curtian confection,[29] as much of it clearly belongs to the declamatory tradition in which

---

[26] Dosson (1886), 241–6, Schanz–Hosius (1935), 598–9, Leeman (1963), i. 255–6, Milns (1966), 503 ff.

[27] Though Miriam Griffin would scale this down to 'some knowledge of oratory'.

[28] So Pearson (1960), 222, attributing the original to Cleitarchus on the basis of echoes in Frags. 40, 43 and 48; cf. Baynham (1998), 89, who also notes Heckel's idea that Hegesias may have been a contributory source.

[29] Tarn, ii. 94 takes the speech to be a Curtian invention.

Alexander was urged to curb his desire to extend his empire.[30] A direct link between Curtius' rhetoric and a declamatory exercise is noted by Leeman (1963), 256 with regard to Curtius 9. 4. 17–18, which he says is so close to Seneca *Suas.* 1. 1 that Curtius must have read Seneca's text. This *suasoria* fell in the category identified by Quintilian *Inst.* 3. 8. 16 as having to do with the question whether Alexander should campaign beyond the Ocean.[31] Curtius alludes to this exercise not only in the passage mentioned, but also in 9. 2. 8–34, and 9. 3. 1–15, with references to the Ocean at 2. 26 and 3. 14. More on Curtius and rhetoric in Sections 8 and 10 below.

If a Claudian date for Curtius is established from other evidence, then there is no compelling reason to reject the possibility that the historian was the same as the rhetor mentioned by Suetonius, though the reader may balk at this further attempt to tidy up history and roll three characters into one.

## 4. CURTIUS' *HISTORIES OF ALEXANDER* AND ITS GENRE

Significantly Curtius was not writing contemporary history, and thus could not claim to be in the mainstream of Thucydidean historiography. He could not collect first-hand evidence and could not interrogate participants and witnesses.[32] He could not pretend to report what was actually said on any occasion,[33] and he could not explore the personality and motives of the characters in the story. He was not therefore able to engage in *historia* in its strict sense.[34] His account of causes of events has to be generally speculative, and his presentation of speeches, feelings, and motives depends largely on imaginative reconstruction, where he goes beyond what he found in his sources.

[30] Cf. Sen. *Suas.* 1, *Controv.* 7. 7. 19; Woodman (1983) on Vell. Pat. 2. 46. 1; Hammond (1983), 143.

[31] More precisely Quintilian alludes to this big question by reference to the argument from possibility or feasibility: Will Alexander find territory beyond the Ocean?

[32] Thuc. 1. 22. 1; Polybius 12. 28a 8–10; Wiseman (1993), 143.

[33] Wiseman (1993) here cites Polybius 36. 1. 7.

[34] As defined by Polybius 3. 31. 7–13 and 32. 6 and Cic. *De Or.* 2. 63.

At a deeper level his history offered no grand model, such as Polybius' concept of *anacyclosis* to explain the cyclical development of constitutional systems, thus it was not what Polybius called pragmatic history; and, although we do not have Curtius' preface in which he might have set out his ambition for the project, it seems unlikely that he offered an approach to the analysis of human interactions that would have predictive value, such as Thucydides claimed for his work (1. 22. 4).[35] Curtius perhaps comes closest to the Thucydidean notion at 10. 9. 1, where he says that 'destiny was already bringing civil war upon the Macedonian nation; for a throne is not to be shared and several men were aspiring to it.' The opening clause is not an expression of some religious belief, but means that civil war was destined to visit the Macedonians, because it will always be true that monarchy cannot be shared. In other words 'fate' in this case is what may be predicted from some knowledge of what has resulted from similar circumstances on every occasion in the past.[36]

At the same time, he was not writing 'universal' history, in the sense of history that spanned the centuries, such as Herodotus pioneered. The surviving text of Curtius has nothing on the sequence of world empires as we have it in Herodotus, Daniel 2. 31–45 and 7. 1–14, and then Trogus, among others.[37] And so in tackling the subject of Alexander's campaigns, Curtius chose not to follow the models of 'universal' historiography adopted by Diodorus, Timagenes and Trogus, but kept rather to the scope one might expect of at least some of the first-hand chroniclers of the period, including Ptolemy. In geographical terms Curtius' sweep is broad, but only as determined by Alexander's itinerary, and Curtius does not digress to provide potted histories region by region. Though Curtius did not follow the Herodotean model of universal history, he may have been

---

[35] A separate point would be that Curtius appears to reject Stoic determinism and the Epicurean notion of the power of random chance (*tyche*): Curtius 5. 11. 10.

[36] Rolfe ad loc. compares Tac. *Ann.* 13. 17: the reaction of ordinary people to the violent storm at the funeral of the murdered Britannicus was that it was a sign of the gods' anger, though people recognized that the principate was indivisible. Curtius makes no reference to the gods.

[37] Herodotus has the sequence Assyrian, Median, Persian, to which Daniel adds the Graeco-Macedonian monarchies. The Roman empire was added by Dionysius Halicarnassus, and also by Trogus (cf. J. 42. 5. 11–12); Atkinson (2000*b*).

influenced by Herodotus in his working of various passages.[38] He also chose not to follow Livy and Dionysius Halicarnassus in writing monumental history in celebration of Roman imperialism.

Curtius' *Histories* was also not biography, which was recognized as a genre distinct from history, as explained by Nepos *Pelopidas* 1. 1 and particularly Plut. *Alex.* 1.[39] McQueen (1967) offers a useful survey of the elements in Curtius which belong to history rather than biography, including the lengthy accounts of battles, sieges, and speeches, ethnographic and geographical detail, and episodes where Alexander is not featured or plays only a minor role.[40] The second half of Book 10 deals with events after Alexander's death and thus is not the material of biography. On the other hand Curtius includes numerous scenes that are of no great historical significance, but look like the sort of apocryphal tales that Plutarch would admit as revealing something of Alexander's character, like Alexander's embarrassment when he discovered that he had given offence by using Darius' table as a footstool (5. 2. 13–15), or his tolerance in allowing an exhausted foot-soldier to rest in his special chair (8. 4. 15–17).[41] To the same category might belong the tale of Bagoas' entrapment of Orxines (10. 2. 22–38).

Curtius' work belongs more to the genre of the monograph as defined by Polybius,[42] and as represented by Sallust's *Bellum Jugurthinum* and *Bellum Catilinae*, and, though direct influence of Sallust on Curtius is evasive, Curtius may have followed Sallust in his emulation of Thucydides' approach to political commentary and epigrammatic style.[43] Progression in historiography in antiquity tended to be dialectic, hence it is not surprising that Curtius chose

[38] Argued by e.g. Blänsdorf (1971), and Heckel (1979) and (1980). My reservations, summarized in (1998*b*), 3466, have been challenged by Ballesteros-Pastor (2003).

[39] Quintilian 3. 7. 10–17 sets out the model for the related genre of the *encomium* as a type of epideictic oratory; McQueen (1967), 19–20.

[40] As for example on events in Greece, with Agis' last stand at Megalopolis (7. 2. 18–34).

[41] McQueen (1967), 18–19 lists other examples to illustrate these points.

[42] Polybius 1. 4. 3; cf. 7. 7. 6, 16. 14. 1 and 29. 12. 2–4; Cic. *Fam.* 5. 12. 2–7.

[43] I have noted possible Thucydidean echoes at 6. 1. 8–10 (with Thuc. 7. 71. 1–4) and 6. 3. 11 (with Thuc. 1. 141. 1). The influence of Sallust on Curtius was claimed in particular by Wiedemann (1872), 756–760 and Bolaffi (1949), 195–6. See further n. 80 below.

the monograph in reaction to the Augustan fashion of universal history. He also chose not to focus on Roman history and follow the annalistic tradition, and so did not take the path of an Aufidius Bassus, who wrote a *German War* and a general history, nor a Servilius Nonianus, consul in 35 and honoured as a writer in an obituary by Tacitus (*Ann.* 14. 19).[44] He distanced himself too from Velleius Paterculus, a senator, who wrote a potted history of Rome in two books with heavy emphasis on the period of Augustus and Tiberius.[45] In choosing to write on Alexander, Curtius was perhaps concerned to produce 'Alexander—the history', to counter the plethora of representations in non-historical texts and historical texts on other subjects, but in doing this he was not opting for a value-free subject, as is discussed in Section 8.

## 5. THE STRUCTURE OF BOOK 10

Curtius clearly worked with an overall structure in mind, as can be seen by the way Book 10 balances Book 5. He reaches the end of the first half of his work with the death of Darius, while the last book obviously ends with the death of Alexander. Curtius holds back the story of Agis' revolt and his death to the beginning of Book 6, even though he believed it to have been over before the battle of Gaugamela in 331 (6. 1. 21). In the structure of the second half of the work this means that Book 6 opens with a focus on Antipater and his troubles with the Greeks. Book 10 then features the flight of Harpalus to Athens, and another challenge faced by Antipater from the Greeks. But more importantly, Antipater is a key figure in the closing chapter of the work, where Curtius deals with the tradition that Antipater organized the killing of Alexander by poison, and then goes on with a programmatic reference to the campaign of Antipater and his son

---

[44] Bassus: Sen. *Ep.* 30; Quint. 10. 1. 103; Tac. *Dial.* 23; ill health may have kept him from advancing to a senatorial career: note 24 above. Servilius: Sen. *Suas.* 6. 18 and 23, Pliny *HN* 6. 27, Quint. 10. 1. 102, and Suet. *Tib.* 61. 6 may refer. On both see Syme (1958), i. 274–8.

[45] And for that matter too Valerius Maximus: Atkinson (1980), 40; Baynham (1998), 24–6.

Cassander to maintain dominance in Macedonia and Greece (10. 10. 18–19). Book 6 introduces another theme to be developed through the second pentad, Alexander's submission to the temptations of oriental luxury and the delights of despotism. The irony was that with the death of Darius—and also the failure of Greek resistance—Alexander fell victim to the allure of the culture of his Persian enemy. This caused dissent and disorder among his troops (6. 2. 15–21), a theme that is developed at greater length in the corresponding section of Book 10.

Throughout the work Curtius gives careful attention to the structuring of individual episodes[46] as well as of each book as a whole, and this can be seen in the final book too. Book 10 opens at the stage in the narrative when Alexander, who had been forced to turn back at the river Hyphasis in 326, emerges from the disastrous march through the Gedrosian desert at the end of 325. Curtius can now focus on what he does best, political drama,[47] as he deals with the consequences of Alexander's setbacks in three fields: the satrapies, Greece and Macedonia (with the fall-out from Harpalus' flight from Babylon to Athens), and Alexander's own army.

The lengthy treatment of the mutiny at Susa (or rather Opis) in 10. 2–4 serves to highlight the dramatic reversal in the troops' attitude to Alexander with his death. The speeches of the mutinous troops and Alexander allow an overview of the record of Philip and Alexander. Then Sisygambis' lament for Alexander's passing (10. 5. 21–23) introduces Curtius' own obituary of Alexander. This obituary and his eulogy of the new emperor are both presented as digressions (10. 6. 1 and 9. 7). It further seems that, on what followed the death, Curtius structured his narrative around the eulogy of the new Princeps, and the eulogy was not therefore just an afterthought. Events in Babylon after Alexander's death were not strictly necessary to the story of Alexander, but were necessary for the eulogy. For the eulogy

---

[46] Holzberg (1988) well illustrates Curtius' skill in structuring a story by his analysis of Curtius 3. 5. 1–6. 20 on Alexander's sickness in Tarsus and the risk he took in trusting his doctor, Philip; cf. Gissel (1995) on the trial of Philotas, and (1999) on the siege of Tyre. Atkinson (1980) offers analyses section by section of Curtius' structuring of Books 3 and 4.

[47] There was a time when Livy and Curtius Rufus were recommended as models for political writers: L. Kajanto, 'Johannes Scheffer on the *imitatio veterum*', Arctos 24 (1990), 73–84.

contains the counter-factual element: what if our emperor had not emerged to put an end to the threat of destructive civil war? What happened in the Macedonian case was known; what would have happened in the Roman case could only be imagined. Hence the final chapter is also peppered with anticipatory references to events of the period of the Successors, beyond what happened in Babylon, and these references further offer the possibility of a continuation.[48]

## 6. CURTIUS' SOURCES[49]

Curtius was careful to indicate that he had read more than one source, and was not simply adapting a single text, as Justin was to do with his epitome of Pompeius Trogus' *Philippic History*. Nor was he simply offering an adaptation in Latin of a Greek text. This is shown by passages where he names sources or alludes to rival traditions. It is no surprise that Curtius twice refers directly to Cleitarchus (9. 5. 21 and 8. 15, and like Cleitarchus he gives his work the title *Histories* (plural)), since Cleitarchus was for readers of the late Republic and early Empire the most popular writer on Alexander— and consequently disdained by intellectuals with pretensions.[50] But Cleitarchus had the merit of being a first generation Alexander historian, who may have completed his work by about 310 BC, and probably published before Ptolemy completed his magisterial memoirs.[51] There are passages where Curtius seems to be in harmony with statements attributed to Cleitarchus. For example on 7. 8. 12 ff.,

---

[48] D. S. Levene, 'Sallust's *Jugurtha*: an 'historical' fragment', *JRS* 82 (1992), 53–70 demonstrates Sallust's care to avoid closure at the end of the *Jugurtha*.

[49] For a general introduction to the sources on Alexander, Bosworth (1988a), 1–15, reprinted in Worthington (2003a), 7–16; Baynham (2003).

[50] In general on Cleitarchus see Pearson (1960), 212–42; Prandi (1996), with the major review article by Bosworth (1997). Prandi (1996), 14–22 and 52–60 amply demonstrates that Cleitarchus was well known to writers of the late Republic and early Empire. Cleitarchus' influence also extended to Jewish literature (Burstein (1999), 105–12).

[51] The case for dating Cleitarchus' work to around 310 BC was convincingly established by Badian (1965); cf. Bosworth (1997) and Prandi (1996), 71 and n. 71 for further references.

Pearson (1960), 222 cites parallels in Cleitarchus Frags. 40, 43, and 48. Cleitarchus was adequate for Diodorus' purposes, and it is generally accepted that he was Diodorus' main source for Book 17.[52] Thus we can track passages where Curtius appears to be in tandem with Diodorus and assume that Cleitarchus was the common source;[53] divergences may well then indicate that Curtius was using, as he himself says, other sources too. Here of course one has to limit the comparison to differences that are more than compositional.[54]

For events in Babylon after Alexander's death Curtius' account has to be set against what little Diodorus has to offer in Book 18. This commentary follows the line that Diodorus switched from Cleitarchus to Hieronymus as his main source for Book 18, and that Curtius continued to base his account on Cleitarchus to the end of his work. Hieronymus was the preferred source for the other major writers on that period, namely Plutarch, especially for the *Life of Eumenes*, and Arrian for his *History of the Successors*.

Cleitarchus seems to have been associated with the Ptolemaic court in Alexandria and to have been a willing promoter of Ptolemy's cause. Hence, as noted above, he gave credit to Ptolemy for saving Alexander's life at the city of the Malli (9. 5. 21), leaving Ptolemy in modesty to put the record straight. Ptolemy might have been less pleased to see the prominence given in Cleitarchus' account to Thais' incitement of Alexander to destroy Persepolis (cf. Curtius 5. 7. 1–12), but perhaps Ptolemy had long since rejected Thais and Cleitarchus thought that she was now fair game. Curtius' treatment of these two episodes clearly indicates that Cleitarchus wrote before Ptolemy, and not to contradict him.[55] At 10. 5. 4 and 10. 10. 20 Curtius follows

[52] Strongly argued by Hamilton (1977), but the 'unitarian' theory is resolutely resisted by Hammond (1983), who presents Diyllus as Diodorus' second, and hardly less significant source—a line that is treated sceptically in reviews by S. Hornblower, *CR* 34 (1984), 261–4, Badian (1985*a*), and Atkinson (1985*a*), 216.

[53] A lengthy catalogue of points at which Curtius runs tandem to Diodorus, and in some cases to Justin too, is offered by Schwartz (1901), cols. 1873–4, expanded by Hamilton (1977). Significant parallels include that between Curtius 10. 2. 4 and D.S. 17. 109. 1, where both incorrectly date the exiles decree after Harpalus' flight to Athens, and Curtius expressly presents it as a punitive measure.

[54] e.g. Curtius 5. 6. 1–8 runs parallel with Diodorus 17. 70. 1–6, and the differences can be accounted for as compositional (Atkinson (1994), 110–12). This general point is well emphasized by Bosworth (1997) in his review article on Prandi (1996).

[55] Cf. Bosworth (1997).

what must be the Alexandrian tradition that Alexander wished to be taken to Egypt for burial, and he ignores the tradition established by Hieronymus that in 321 Ptolemy hijacked the hearse as it was bound for Macedonia. It seems likely that Curtius here followed Cleitarchus, and not Hieronymus.[56] We might likewise credit Cleitarchus with transferring from Ptolemy to Peithon the blunt attack on the proposal that Philip Arrhidaeus be recognized as king after Alexander's death (Curtius 10. 7. 4, against J. 13. 2. 11–12, who names Ptolemy). In this case Cleitarchus' motive would have been to clear Ptolemy of the charge of being hostile or disloyal to the man they all finished up by recognizing as their titular king.

Ptolemy himself is mentioned by Curtius as a source, and there are cases where agreement between Curtius and Arrian indicates that Curtius took information from Ptolemy, as for example at 3. 11. 3 (with A. 2. 9. 1), 5. 3. 12–15 (with A. 3. 17. 6, unlike D.S. 17. 67), 7. 10. 10 (with A. 4. 7. 2), 10. 2. 24 (with A. 7. 9. 6 and Plut. *Alex.* 15.2). On the other hand, there are cases where Curtius is at odds with Arrian or omits detail given by Arrian, when Ptolemy can reasonably be expected to have had information from his own experience: so, for example, at Curtius 3. 11. 16 (contrast A. 2. 11. 8), 3. 12. 13 ff. (contrast A. 2. 12. 6 ff.), 4. 8. 1–6 on Alexandria and the settlement of Egypt (contrast A. 3. 1. 5–2. 2, and 5. 2–7), 5. 4 on the battle for the Persian Gates (no mention of Ptolemy though he was involved: A. 3. 18. 9). It has been customary to posit that Ptolemy, when he came to write his memoirs, may have suppressed details that did credit to men with whom he clashed after Alexander's death, and favoured those who sided with him. Thus we might expect from Ptolemy negative treatment of characters like Perdiccas, Aristonus,[57] and Polyperchon.[58] This in

[56] References at 10. 10. 20. There is admittedly a problem, in that Diodorus likewise makes no mention of any unilateral move by Ptolemy at 18. 28. 2–3, although the whole of that book is based principally on Hieronymus.

[57] Aristonus supported Perdiccas after Alexander's death: A. *Succ.* 2 and F10. 6, and opposed Ptolemy's plan at Babylon (Curtius 10. 6. 16 ff.). Curtius picked up his role in saving Alexander's life at the Mallian city from Cleitarchus or Timagenes (9. 5. 15 –18). Arrian mentions Aristonus as one of the Bodyguards at 6. 28. 4, immediately naming Aristobulus (and not Ptolemy) as his source. Roisman (1984), 382 notes that this only shows that Aristobulus did record this detail, and not that Ptolemy suppressed the information.

[58] Ptolemy sided with Cassander against Polyperchon from 319 (D.S. 18. 55. 2), and Bosworth (2002), 41–2 finds this significant as indicating the source of Curtius'

turn means that if, for example, Curtius features Perdiccas in the battle for the city of the Memaeceni (7. 6. 16–24), and Arrian, who used Ptolemy as one of his two main sources, left him out (A. 4. 2. 2ff.), then it is likely that Curtius was here not using Ptolemy.[59] Conversely we may have evidence that Ptolemy omitted detail that damaged the reputations of men to whom he was indebted: thus for example, Craterus in Curtius' account played a despicable role in helping to set Philotas up for summary conviction on a charge of treason—or more accurately, misprision of treason (6. 8. 17 and 11.12 ff.), but Arrian has nothing on Craterus at this point in the narrative, though he is mentioned positively as a commander of a section of the army in Areian territory (A. 3. 25. 6–8). Thus on Craterus' involvement in the action against Philotas Ptolemy was probably silent, as Craterus had been on his side against Perdiccas (D.S. 18. 29–37); and Curtius was here not following Ptolemy. Similarly, when Curtius offers detail to the credit of Polyperchon, which is missing in Arrian's account, the difference may be that Arrian was following Ptolemy and Curtius was not.[60] The same point might be argued about Polemon.[61] But Roisman (1984) objects that this approach to source analysis, using templates of presumed political relationships, is based on a cyclical argument and a presumption that Ptolemy wrote with a propagandist intent. Thus, as Roisman complains, Ptolemy's treatment of those whom he favoured or damned is taken to indicate the date of composition of his work, and the date of composition helps to define what might have been his attitude to the various characters at that time. It is true that the pattern of political relationships in the period of the Successors was

line that Arrhidaeus had the capacity to act directly in the political scene in Babylon in 323.

[59] The same applies at Curtius 9. 1. 19, when compared with A. 5. 24. 6.

[60] Curtius 4. 13. 7 (Polyperchon stands out in support of Parmenion's advice to Alexander before the battle of Gaugamela), 5. 4. 20, and 8. 5. 22–6. 1 (Polyperchon ridicules the performance of *proskynesis* by Persians to Alexander, and is arrested; not in A. 4. 12. 2); Atkinson (1998*b*), 3463; on Polyperchon's record from 323, Heckel (2006), 226–31. Atkinson (1980), 415 adds the cautionary note that Ptolemy should not be treated as the only source possibly hostile to Polyperchon: others might have included Antigonus' associates Nearchus and Medeius.

[61] In 321/0 he was sent to challenge Ptolemy's hijacking of Alexander's hearse (A. *Succ.* 1. 25). He is presented more positively by Curtius at 7. 1. 10 ff. than by A. 3. 27. 1–3 on the same episode.

kaleidoscopic;[62] we do not have a firm indication of when Ptolemy wrote his memoirs; and we are dependent on secondary sources, and so cannot be sure that an omission by Arrian or Curtius, for example, reflects an omission by Ptolemy or whichever other primary source. *In fine* arguments about Ptolemy's political intentions in what he wrote have to be treated with caution.

Timagenes was surely used by Curtius not only on the matter of Ptolemy's supposed role in the assault on the Mallian city (cited at 9. 5. 21). His influence may perhaps be seen at 3. 1. 22 and 6. 1 and 4. 8. 9. The quest for fragments of Timagenes is complicated because Curtius clearly read and echoed the history of Trogus,[63] and Trogus probably used Timagenes as an important source.[64] Thus it is difficult to be sure how far Curtius may have consulted Timagenes directly.[65] Furthermore, whereas it is fairly easy to build up an image of Ptolemy's concerns, there is far less agreement on the characteristics of Timagenes' work, especially with regard to Alexander. I take Livy's dismissive comment on lightweight, anti-Roman Greeks to be directed at Timagenes among others, and to suggest that Timagenes was positive in his attitude to Alexander.[66] This in turn means that, if Trogus used Timagenes, he did so without necessarily following the bias in Timagenes' account. Thus, for example, Trogus must have presented Parmenion and Philotas as the innocent victims of

---

[62] Roisman (1984), 380 argues, for example, that Ptolemy's hostility to Perdiccas may only have begun in the latter half of 321.

[63] Dosson (1886), 146–7, Atkinson (1980), 59–61, Yardley (2003), 92–3; parallels include Curtius 3. 10. 3 with J. 11. 9. 7, Curtius 3. 10. 9 with J. 11. 13. 11, Curtius 4. 10. 18 with J. 11. 12. 6, Curtius 4. 14. 20 with J. 17. 2. 3, Curtius 6. 1. 7–8 with J. 28. 4. 2.

[64] The old orthodoxy that Trogus simply reworked Timagenes is now seen as too simplistic, but it remains highly likely that Timagenes was a significant influence on Trogus: cf. Heckel and Yardley (1997), esp. 30–4. J. Malitz, *Die Historien des Poseidonios* (Munich, 1983), 56 is hesitant about accepting that Trogus used Timagenes, but accepts Curtius' claim to have consulted Timagenes.

[65] Thus Prandi (1996), 140–4 argues that Curtius picked up Cleitarchus' material via Timagenes, and so used Timagenes heavily, but still allows that Curtius must have read Trogus.

[66] Atkinson (2000*b*), 314–17, noting that, as the progression in historiography tended to be dialectic, Trogus probably distanced himself from Timagenes' lines of bias. Thus if Timagenes was biased in favour of Alexander, one might expect Trogus to be more critical, as is indicated by his favourable treatment of Parmenion. Bosworth (1997) considers it not possible to ascribe any particular line to Timagenes because of the inadequacy of the evidence.

Alexander's jealousy and paranoia (cf. J. 12. 5. 3–4), but if Timagenes was the great admirer of Alexander he would not have taken that line. Curtius, though predisposed to be critical of arbitrary judicial actions, followed a tradition that Parmenion and Philotas were found to have erred into treasonable action (6. 9. 4 and 13 and 11. 21 ff. and 39). Curtius may have taken this mitigatory line from either or both of Cleitarchus (cf. D.S. 17. 80. 1) and Timagenes.[67] But Curtius in the next book tells how after the execution of Philotas the troops' attitude changed from hatred of him to pity (7. 1. 1–4). This leads into a lengthy account of how Alexander set up the murder of Parmenion. The Mafioso style killing and use of Parmenion's own officers to commit the deed made his own troops mutinous and those in Alexander's camp restive (7. 2. 13–35). They now wondered if the confession extracted from Philotas under extreme torture was indeed the truth (7. 2. 34). Then in 10. 1. 1–6 Curtius picks up again the hostile line that the troops bitterly resented the liquidation of Parmenion. Unfortunately the coverage of the demise of Parmenion in the other sources does not allow any meaningful comparative study. The flow of Curtius' narrative, if anything, tells against the idea that he switched sources on Parmenion from the beginning of Book 7. Curtius could allow a character to take different values as the needs of each new episode dictated,[68] and in this case he heightens the drama by building up a picture of how the troops came to believe that Philotas was guilty, and uses the break between books to mark the gap before the reversal in their attitude to Philotas.

Because of the high incidence of passages where Curtius appears to be in tandem with Diodorus, Curtius has also been credited by some with using other sources who feature more in the debate on Diodorus' sources, and especially Diyllus and Duris. Thus it has been argued that

---

[67] Curtius' source would not have been Ptolemy, as A. 3. 26. 1–4, following Ptolemy, indicates that there was no formal charge against Parmenion. He adds the rationalization that Alexander may have thought it improbable that Parmenion was not party to his son's plot, or considered it too dangerous to leave the father free after the execution of his son (A. 3. 26. 4).

[68] As has been argued by some with regard to characters in Seneca's tragedies, and as can be seen in Tacitus' *Annals* with the treatment of characters like Germanicus and Agrippina. In a different way Curtius may have changed the image of the officer in charge of Gaza, 'Betis' (4. 6. 7), by dropping the reference to him as a eunuch (A. 2. 25. 4).

Diodorus used Diyllus for Book 17 on Greek affairs to supplement his Alexander source(s): so in particular Tarn, ii. 78, 83 and 105, and Hammond (1983). Hammond relies heavily on the argument that if Diodorus used Diyllus for books either side of Book 17 (as at 16. 14. 5 and 76. 6, and 21. 5), then he probably also had him to hand for Book 17. Hammond then assigns passages in Diodorus 17 to Cleitarchus and Diyllus according to his characterization of their style and attitude towards Alexander, an approach rightly criticized by Badian (1985*a*). Hammond goes on to argue that if Diyllus was Diodorus' major source on Greek affairs in the time of Alexander, then Curtius probably used him likewise. But the fragments of Diyllus are very few and provide no direct evidence that Curtius used him.

With a similar line of reasoning to Hammond's, Schubert (1922), esp. 43 concluded that Diodorus and Curtius both drew on Duris, and in particular on his multi-volume *Macedonica* or *Histories*, written from *c.*280 BC.[69] Fontana (1955), esp. 171 ff. and 182–5 even argues that Duris was Diodorus' main source for Book 17.[70] In commenting on the text of Curtius I have challenged attributions to Duris at at 3. 3. 11 and 11. 4; and Kebric (1977), 65 notes that while Curtius' references to Prometheus at 7. 3. 21–22 and to Alexander's near drowning in the Indus at 9. 4. 14 echo fragments of Duris, the matching passages in Diodorus 17. 83. 1 and 97. 3 respectively suggest rather that Diodorus and Curtius were both following Cleitarchus. Then Curtius at 6. 5. 24 ff. on the visit of the Amazon queen gives a story which Duris rejected as a fiction (Plut. *Alex.* 46. 2). Thus again there is no strong argument for identifying Duris as one of Curtius' sources.

Book 10 raises the issue of other sources behind the story of Alexander's death and the tradition that there was a conspiracy led by Antipater to poison the king. There was a document known as the Royal Journal or *Ephemerides*, which recorded the events of the last twelve days or so of Alexander's life. This circulated in antiquity, probably in more than one version or edition, since the extracts provided by Plutarch and Arrian do not precisely tally. Some believe

---

[69] It covered Graeco-Macedonian history from 370/369 (D.S. 15. 60. 6) to at least the death of Lysimachus in 281 (Frag. 55 = Pliny *HN* 8. 143).

[70] Kebric (1977), 45–6 more plausibly argues that Duris probably used Cleitarchus for his account of Alexander's reign.

that what we have constitutes an extract from an official journal that was maintained throughout Alexander's campaigns. But there is no secure evidence that it was available as a source for any other episode in Alexander's life. It is most probable that this record of Alexander's last days was produced *ad hoc*, probably by those with a personal interest in averting any charge of foul play. The issue of the *Ephemerides* is of only marginal concern to the study of Book 10 as a part, if not most of the section on Alexander's last days has not survived. But, as Curtius deals with the tradition that a plot to poison Alexander could be traced back to Antipater (10. 10. 5 and 14–17), attention has to be given to the more substantial texts of the *Alexander Romance* and what may be a continuation of the *Metz Epitome*, the *Book on the death of Alexander* (*Liber de morte*). As is argued in the commentary, this tradition was probably laid down in about 308 to further Ptolemy's interests. The original was therefore probably written only after Cleitarchus had completed his work. Curtius did not need the *Romance* nor the *LM* to pick up the story that Antipater and his family were alleged to have organized the poisoning of Alexander, and there is nothing in Curtius to suggest that he must have used that family of texts.

It would seem that we can safely assume that Curtius did consult directly the three authors he names, Cleitarchus, Ptolemy, and Timagenes, and there appear to be intertextual references to Trogus. Beyond that there is evidence that he might have consulted other primary sources, including Nearchus and Onesicritus.[71] They are both referred to at 10. 1. 10–15, but Curtius here appears to be following Cleitarchus. At 10. 6. 10–12 the reference to Heracles the son of Barsine may come directly, or indirectly from Nearchus. At 9. 10. 3 Nearchus and Onesicritus are treated as of equal rank, which may come from Onesicritus, as Nearchus was his superior (A. *Ind.* 18. 9–10). But Onesicritus was not Curtius' source for 3. 6. 1. However, we can probably accept that he sampled the eulogistic verse churned out for Alexander by the poetasters: Curtius' dismissal of Agis as the purveyor of the most execrable poetry after Choerilus (Curtius 8. 5. 8; cf. 3. 1. 2) looks like a personal comment.[72]

---

[71] Atkinson (1980), 63–4.
[72] Agis is mentioned by Plut. *Mor.* 60b–c and A. 4. 9. 9. Choerilus had been panned by Horace *Epist.* 2. 1. 232–4 and *Ars P.* 357. Pearson (1960), 78 notes Porphyrion's

Other less substantial sources have been suggested to explain various perceived strands in Curtius' *Histories*. Tarn, ii. 91–122 in particular broke from the conventional approach to posit that Curtius used an extensive list of sources (pp. 115–16), and that this list included three putative traditions. First there was some lost source from which Curtius derived information on Macedonian institutions and customs (Tarn ii. 106–7). The slicing of a loaf of bread at the marriage feast (8. 4. 27) might be so explained, but the other cases he cites are insubstantial.[73] In Book 10 he alludes to the judicial process (10. 4. 1, picking up from 6. 8. 25, which is complicated by a textual crux), to supposed procedures for meetings of the army assembly or council of officers (10. 6. 1–4 and 10. 1), and the institution of the Pages (10. 5. 8, picking up from 8. 6. 2–6). But on Macedonian institutions there is little of substance, and nothing that he could not be reasonably be expected to have picked up from his narrative sources. His brief reference to the lustral ceremony involving a slaughtered dog (10. 9. 12) may similarly have come from one of his main sources, and in any case the ritual was known to Romans from earlier accounts (Poybius 23. 10. 17 and Livy 40. 6. 1–5, admittedly with rather different detail).

Tarn also posited as a source a compilation of the memoirs of Greek mercenaries. But this imagined source appears to have muddled or omitted some things which mercenaries should have known,[74] and in any case Tarn imagines that the source dried up with the death of Darius, and so it would not be relevant to the study of Curtius Book 10. Tarn's third nameless source is the Peripatetic tradition, loyal to the memory of Aristotle and Callisthenes, and thus hostile to Alexander for betraying his teacher Aristotle by succumbing to luxury and allowing himself to become an oriental tyrant.[75]

reference to the apocryphal tale of Alexander's comment that he would far prefer to be Homer's Thersites than Choerilus' Achilles.

[73] References in Atkinson (1998*b*), 3461.

[74] Tarn's theory revived an idea of Kaerst (1927), i. 544, and was in turn developed by Wolf (1964), though Wolf saw the mercenaries' contribution as absorbed into Cleitarchus' history rather than a free-standing work. Tarn's case has been dismantled by e.g. Brunt (1962) and Pearson (1960), 78–82; cf. my commentaries on 3. 8. 15 and 11. 11; 4. 1. 27–40, and 5. 8. 1–4.

[75] Tarn, ii. esp. 96–9.

The idea that there was a well defined Peripatetic line on Alexander was rigorously challenged by Badian (1958*a*), esp. 153–7 and Mensching (1963). Curtius' final assessment of Alexander (10. 5. 26–36) has many echoes of Stoic texts, but again it can be said that there was no single Stoic line on Alexander.[76]

In conclusion, much will fall into place if we assume that Curtius read, as he says he did, the Greek authors Cleitarchus, Ptolemy, and Timagenes, and perhaps other primary sources, and that he read Trogus' Latin *Philippica*, if only to provide him with a benchmark for his own more ambitious history. Curtius' dates, whether Claudian or Vespasianic, preclude the possibility that Curtius read Plutarch and Arrian.

## 7. CURTIUS AND OTHER WRITERS OF THE EARLY PRINCIPATE[77]

Echoes in Curtius of other Latin writers have a bearing on Curtius' dates, and say something about the influences on Curtius from outside the range of historical sources which he used. They may also say something about Curtius' literary pretensions.

As Roman drama preceded Roman historiography, and as there was a strong tradition of presenting Roman history as drama, Curtius may well have come under the influence of what Wiseman styles 'docu-drama'.[78] A possible echo of Ennius *Trag.* 411–12 is noted at 10. 9. 1, but this and other possible echoes of Ennius, and likewise of Naevius, whether from their tragedies or their historical epics, could have come from an intermediary source,[79] and, at the higher level, Curtius would have found dramatic writing as a feature of his Hellenistic sources.

---

[76] Fears (1974*b*) usefully interrogates the thesis developed by J. Stroux, 'Die stoische Beurteilung Alexanders', *Philologus* 88 (1933): 222–40. A Stoic view was that the defects in Alexander's character were there from the start, but latent.

[77] Cf. Atkinson (1998*b*), 3465–8.

[78] Wiseman (1993), 133–5 and 141, citing on 'docu-drama' Livy 5. 21. 8–9, Ovid *Fasti* 4. 326, and Plut. *Romulus* 8. 7.

[79] Cf. Curtius 5. 1. 8 with Ennius *Annales* 184–5 (Skutsch) and Cic. *Off.* 1. 38, and Rutz (1984), 155–6, dealing with the influence of Livy.

Sallust may have had some influence on Curtius in terms of his approach to historiography, but little evidence of intertextual referencing has been adduced, and that is generally weak.[80] Similarly there is no clear evidence that Curtius was influenced by Julius Caesar's *Commentaries*,[81] and similarities in phraseology can just as well be attributed to the requirements of the military situation to be described.

The influence of other Latin writers becomes clearer from the start of the Principate, and again the first to be mentioned is a verse author, as Curtius does consciously echo Vergil,[82] but the greater influence was clearly Livy. This is readily intelligible because of Livy's foray into counterfactual history on the subject 'What if Alexander had had to confront the might of Rome?' (Livy 9. 17–19).[83] Echoes of Livy's digression can be seen, for example, in Curtius 3. 12. 18–20, 6. 2. 1–5 and 6. 1–3, and 10. 5. 26–37 (cf. Section 5 supra). Of course the corruptive force of success on Alexander's character was a rhetorical *topos*, so echoes of Livy in unrelated passages are perhaps more telling. Thus, for example, within the obituary on Alexander Curtius seems to echo Livy's obituary on Cato,[84] and more tellingly, Curtius' comment on Ptolemy as being 'hardly likely to detract from his own glory' (9. 5. 21) seems to echo Livy's comment on Cato as 'surely not one to detract from his own heralded achievements' (34. 15. 9).[85] On

[80] Bolaffi (1949), 195–6 finds Sallustian influence in Curtius, in particular at 4. 14. 9–25, but the influence of Livy here is more obvious. Curtius' description of native huts in the Hindukusch may owe something to Sall. *Jug.* 18. 8. But the evidence is generally thin: Rutz (1986), Atkinson (1998*b*), 3466. Wiedemann (1872), 756–760 provides a list of possible Sallustian echoes. Ballesteros-Pastor (2003), 34–6 suggests links between the speech of the Scythian in Curtius 7. 8. 12–30 and Sallust *Hist.* 4. 69 [M], the *Letter of Mithradates*.

[81] Rutz (1986), 2339–40 admits the possibility of an echo of Caesar *BGall* 7. 19 and *BCiv* 1. 72 in Curtius 3. 10. 3.

[82] Balzer (1971) devotes a full thesis to the subject. Examples have been noted at 3. 2. 16; 4. 8. 8 and 13. 14; 8. 14. 27; 9. 4. 18; other parallels are listed by Steele (1915), 410.

[83] Morello (2002) examines this passage, with an emphasis on counterfactuals and apologetics.

[84] Links are noted between Curtius 10. 5. 27 and 32 and Livy 39. 40. 4, 10 and 11.

[85] A point well made by Baynham (1998), 75–6. At pp. 20–25 Baynham offers a fine introduction to the general topic of the influence of Livy on Curtius. Earlier studies of the subject include Dosson (1886), 276–7, Steele (1915), 404–9 and (1919), 43–6, Braccesi (1987), 237–9 and Rutz (1983*b*) and (1986), 2340–1. Numerous echoes of Livian phraseology are noted in this commentary, starting at 10. 1. 2.

the appointment of Abdalonymus as king of Sidon (Curtius 4. 1. 15–26), Rutz (1986), 2341 suggests a reminiscence of the tale in Livy 3. 26. 7–12 of how the Senate appealed to Cincinnatus in 458 BC to leave his smallholding and go to Rome to assume the dictatorship;[86] and Baynham (1998), 22 links Alexander's taunt to Cleitus as he kills him (8. 1. 52) to Romulus' taunt as he kills Remus (Livy 1. 48. 7). In this book, Curtius' account of the mutiny at Opis (10. 2. 15–29) seems to include intertextual references to Livy's version of Scipio Africanus' address to the Roman troops, camped on the river Sucro, who had mutinied.[87]

There is no real evidence that Curtius was in any way influenced by Velleius Paterculus or Valerius Maximus.[88] Where Curtius and Valerius Maximus tackle the same episode they have little in common beyond the core material: thus, for example, on Alexander's sickness in Cilicia, Curtius 3. 5–6 and Valerius Maximus 3. 8. ext. 6 each has more in common with Justin—and hence presumably Trogus—than he does with the other.[89] Unsurprisingly the most common cross references are probably to the Elder Seneca and his nephew. Curtius could hardly avoid echoing phrases and topics that featured in the declamatory exercises.[90] In this book links between Curtius and Seneca's essays and especially the books on *Anger, Clemency,* and *Benefits,* are prominent in the final assessment of Alexander (10. 5. 26–37).[91] The generally accepted range of dates for Curtius all allow

---

[86] Burstein (2007) deals with this episode, but focuses on the core detail that Abdalonymus was a gardener, which Burstein argues was a fiction imported by Cleitarchus.

[87] E. Burck, in *Wege zu Livius* (Darmstadt, 1967), 435; Rutz (1983b). At 10. 2. 27 I note another parallel at Livy 45. 37.

[88] Velleius and Curtius both echo Julio-Claudian propaganda themes such as *pax* (peace) and *salus* (well-being) (Vell. Pat. 2. 103 and 110. 1), and Tiberius looks after the common soldier (Vell. Pat. 2. 114) as did Alexander (Curtius 8. 4. 15–17), but such links are inconsequential. Wardle (2005) provides a well researched survey of Valerius Maximus' references to Alexander, with special attention to the subject of ruler cult.

[89] Seel (1956), 92–3, Atkinson (1980), 168–9 and (1998b), 3467–8 for other references.

[90] Bardon (1947b), 125 notes parallels between Curtius 7. 8. 12 and Seneca *Suas.* 1.5, between Curtius 9. 4. 18 and Seneca *Suas.* 1. 1 and 2; cf. Curtius 4. 14. 20 with Seneca *Suas.* 2. 3. Other references to the elder Seneca are made in this commentary at 10. 1. 42, 5. 6, 12, 30 and 36, and see W. A. Edward, *The Suasoriae of the Elder Seneca* (Cambridge, 1928), 83 ff.

[91] Other parallels are listed in Atkinson (1980), 41, Steele (1915), 412 and Schanz–Hosius (1935), 598–9.

that Curtius read the Elder Seneca, but if a Claudian date is accepted, then Curtius can not have read what the younger Seneca wrote in the reign of Nero, including the *Clementia* and the *Epistles*. If Curtius wrote his brief eulogy of the new emperor early in Claudius' reign, then he wrote this at roughly the same time as Seneca wrote the *Consolatio ad Polybium*, and, if phraseology in Curtius 10. 9. 3 and 4 reads like phraseology in the *Consolatio* (*Dial.* 11. 13. 1), then we cannot tell whether either was influenced by the other. Fears (1976*a*), 217 goes further in identifying contradictions between Curtius and Seneca as part of his case for dating Curtius much later, and indeed in the third century. But Seneca's essays are better taken as giving some idea of the literary scene at the time when he and Curtius were writing.

In terms of language Curtius has many links at various points with Pomponius Mela's work on geography, as they use very similar phraseology. Since the verbal echoes often apply to different geographical or other details,[92] the evidence points to literary influence and not to dependence of one on the other for material substance. If Mela wrote or completed his work in AD 43–4, it becomes problematic to decide whether Mela was influenced by Curtius or vice versa. Parroni (1978), in his review of Giacone's edition of Curtius, extends the list of parallels and opines that it is more likely that Curtius was influenced by Mela. The same problem arises over the numerous links between Curtius' *Histories* and Lucan's *Pharsalia*. Hosius compiled a substantial list of parallels and concluded that Lucan drew literary inspiration from Curtius, but not material detail.[93] But Pichon would not accept the implication that Curtius wrote in Claudius' reign, and argued rather that Lucan and Curtius, a much later writer than Lucan in Pichon's view, drew common inspiration from Livy.[94] With a similar concern to uphold a late date for Curtius, Fears (1976*a*) rejects attempts to trace the influence of Curtius on several passages in Silius Italicus' *Punica*, which he began writing sometime before 93.[95]

---

[92] Compare Curtius 3. 4. 6 with Mela 2. 58, Curtius 3. 13. 5 with Mela 1. 64, Curtius 6. 5. 24 with Mela 1. 105, and Curtius 8. 9. 19 with Mela 3. 51.

[93] C. Hosius, 'Lucan und seine Quellen', *RhM* 48 (1893), 380 ff., esp. 383–92.

[94] R. Pichon, *Les sources de Lucain* (Paris, 1912), esp. 254 ff.

[95] For references on the debate over Lucan and Silius Italicus see Atkinson (1980), 41–2.

There is now a growing consensus that parallels between Curtius and Tacitus[96] point to Tacitus' being the later writer, and to his familiarity with Curtius' *Historiae*. This case is fully considered by Bosworth (2004), who concludes that Tacitus' intertextual references to Curtius point to the *Histories* being a recently published, and hence fashionable text. Of immediate relevance are the connections which he establishes between Curtius 10. 3. 4 and Tac. *Agric.* 2. 3, Curtius 10. 5. 7 and Tac. *Ann.* 3. 4. 1, Curtius 10, 9. 1 and Tac. *Ann.* 13. 17. 1, Curtius 10. 9. 3 and Tac *Hist.* 1. 11. 3, and the way Tacitus subverts Curtius' encomium (as Bosworth sees it) of Alexander to deal with Germanicus. But the last mentioned parallelism may strengthen the case for setting Curtius closer to the time of Germanicus.

Syme (1987), 111 gave some recognition to Curtius' place in the literary history of the early Principate by characterizing his style as sub-Livian and pre-Tacitean.

## 8. TRUTH AND THE HISTORICAL VALUE OF CURTIUS' *HISTORIES*

Curtius Book 10 has been a critical text in the larger debate about the commitment of historians in antiquity to the pursuit of truth. The general question is whether historians were dedicated to a higher order of truth than was required of a forensic orator when he moved from the points at law to set out the facts at issue in his *narratio*. The case study here features Curtius' account of events in Babylon after the death of Alexander. McKechnie (1999) represents the extreme position that Curtius' narrative is no more than historical fiction, a line which Bosworth has consistently contested, especially in his important article (2003) on the veracity of historians in antiquity.[97]

---

[96] The pioneering work was done by Walter (1887), who collected some 600 parallels between passages in Curtius and Tacitus; cf. Alfonsi (1967) and Lund (1987). Links with Tacitus can be found in this book at i.a. 10. 3. 4 (says Lund), 7. 5 and 9. 1

[97] This can be contextualized in the larger debate among historians on the degree of tolerance that is allowed to rhetoric, imaginative reconstruction and narrative.

Errington (1970) and Schachermeyr (1970) are among those who have taken Curtius as a serious source for the events in Babylon.

At the level of literary theory the debate on the meaning of truth as the guiding principle of historiography has focused on Cicero's exploration of the issues in *De Or.* 2. 51–64 and on his letter to L. Lucceius in 55 BC (*Fam.* 5. 12), when he urged Lucceius to work into his history a sympathetic treatment of Cicero, the political figure, or, preferably, to embark on a separate monograph on his consulship of 63. Cicero *De Or.* 2. 63 includes in the requirements of historiography comment on the characters' intentions (*consilia*), and the consequences (*eventus*), as well as an account of the events themselves. Elsewhere Cicero includes explanations of causes and effects as elements of *inventio*, and of *narratio* (Cic. *Part. Or.* 31–2, *Inv. Rhet.* 1. 9 and 29, *ad Herenn.* 16), and *inventio* meant the elaboration of material to make the case more convincing. *Inventio* was supposed to produce material that was true, or having verisimilitude, or even false so long as it was convincing (Cic. *Inv. Rhet.* 1. 9 and 46, *Auct. ad Her.* 1. 13 and 16).[98] Then Cicero has Atticus say in *Brutus* 42 that it is permitted for rhetors (practitioners) to tell lies in their stories so that they can speak more cleverly. The point is made that the concession to lie is only made for orators when they are engaging in the elaboration of their story (*inventio*), and is not intended to apply to historians. But Atticus goes on to illustrate his point by referring to the story of Themistocles' death by poison as given by the orator Stratocles and our Cleitarchus, the historian. Thus, as Wiseman (1993), 133 notes, Cicero is not making a distinction between history and oratory. But he may be making a distinction between history in the style of Thucydides and historiography of

---

Thus writers like Leroy Ladurie (whom one can cite as representative of the *Annales* school of history and as a representative of 'new history'), Richard Cobb and Simon Schama have caused distress to others by their style of historiography, and Hayden White has horrified some by his treatment of history as a branch of rhetoric. Of relevance here is A. Momigliano's reaction to Hayden White's approach to historiography: 'He has eliminated the research for truth as the main task of the historian' (in Momigliano, *Settimo contributo alla storia degli studi classici e del mondo antico* (Rome, 1984), 49, quoted by Simon Hornblower, 'Narratology and Thucydides', in S. Hornblower (1994), 133).

[98] Woodman (1988), 85–7.

a more rhetorical nature (such as Cicero wanted from Lucceius),[99] and he goes on in *Brutus* 44 to make the distinction between scrupulous historians and those who take liberties. In any case, the creative process/practice preceded, or operated independently of, prescription; and the problem of characterizing many historical works in terms of genre illustrates the point that there was no job demarcation to keep writers in defined roles. Thus there were grey areas between rhetorical exercises and history, and between history and fiction.[100]

Bosworth takes a clear stand in his *OCD*[3] entry on Curtius Rufus by stating that the historian 'did not manufacture fact'. This requires some amplification, first with regard to what constitutes a fact. At the high level, key events covered in Book 10 can certainly be taken as historical, including Harpalus' flight to Athens, Alexander's decree on the return of the exiles, his death in Babylon, and the settlement in Babylon that gave recognition to Arrhidaeus as king. The question is then how far down in the level of detail can one go before there is reasonable doubt about historicity. Thus, for example, when the cavalry demanded as the price of a reconciliation with the infantry the surrender of dissident infantry leaders, did it really happen, as Curtius says, that Arrhidaeus manipulated the infantrymen into agreeing to further negotiation by offering his abdication as an alternative? No other source mentions this manoeuvre and Curtius is alone in representing Arrhidaeus as an articulate and independent role-player in these events.[101] Similarly we have no external confirmation of the intervention of the unknown soldier in the debate (10. 7. 1), nor of the comings and goings of various groups and individuals during the on-going debate (10. 7. 10, 13–14, 17, etc.). Such scenes might pass the test of verisimilitude, and one comes

---

[99] It may be added that when Cleitarchus alluded to the death of Themistocles, he was not dealing with contemporary history, and Cicero's criticism does not therefore necessarily mean that Cleitarchus took similar liberties when dealing with Alexander and contemporary history.

[100] Baynham (2003), 27–9 offers a judicious introduction to the positions that have been taken with regard to the reliability of our literary sources.

[101] Bosworth (2002), 40–2 argues that this line came from a source in Ptolemy's camp, and was not therefore a Curtian invention. To the same end Sharples (1994) argues that the particularity of Curtius' account with regard to the role of Arrhidaeus arose from his concomitant use of some source, other than Hieronymus.

back to the matter of faith, whether a historian, tackling non-contemporary history, would have taken fewer liberties than a forensic orator or a rhetorician in embellishing a story.

This then raises the array of questions relating to Curtius' attitude to his sources. Curtius knew that sources could differ on points of 'fact', as on Ptolemy's supposed role in the assault on the Mallian city, and as an historian he had to adjudicate between rival versions. Thus he would have known that for some details attestation by a single source might be a minimum and sufficient requirement for a claim to historicity. But his respect for the sources, where we can check, does not guarantee that he had some source authority for a detail we can not check, as with Arrhidaeus' offer of abdication.

Curtius at 9. 1. 34 and 10. 10. 12 notes that he feels obliged to repeat what he has found in his source(s), but is sceptical about its historical value. This was something of a convention of historiography, starting with Herodotus (1. 5. 3, 2. 123. 1, 5. 45. 2, and 7. 152. 3); cf. Sallust *Iug.* 17. 7, Livy *Praef.* 6, Valerius Maximus 1. 8. 7, Pliny *HN* 17. 93, Tac. *Germ.* 3. 3, though Seneca passes the cynical comment that lying historians attach this *caveat* to an arbitrarily chosen item as a device to get the surrounding lies accepted.[102] Curtius tries a different device to win trust in his judgement of the sources at 5. 6. 9, where he introduces a surprising detail with the line, 'but unless we are going to be sceptical about other matters, we must accept the tradition' (that some 12,000 talents of treasure were seized in Persepolis). Thus he is saying that the evidence for this detail is no weaker than that for many other matters. By implication he takes a sceptical attitude to the reliability of the credibility test. Tarn, ii. 92 is thus surely wrong to take this and 9. 1. 34 to show that Curtius is completely lacking in historical principle. Curtius' statement here is defensible, whether it is a rhetorical device to win the reader's trust, or a more general profession of awareness that the truth can be difficult to establish.

A concern to arrive at the truth might be seen in Curtius' rejection of determinism (5. 11. 10) noted above, his dismissal of omens and dreams, and his criticism of superstition. There are references to the inevitability of fate,[103] but these represent the commonplace notion of

---

[102] Seneca *QN* 4. 3. 1, with Wiseman (1993), 135.
[103] As at 4. 6. 17, 5. 12. 11, 8. 9. 32–33, 9. 6. 19 and 10. 5. 36.

personal destiny, rather than expressions of faith in the Stoic concept of *fatum*. Similarly there are references to *fortuna, sors* (one's lot)[104] and the gods, but these are generally literary commonplaces or in statements attributed to characters in the story, as in Darius' speech to his troops before the battle of Gaugamela, when the king suggests that the gods are giving the Persians a wake-up call (4. 14 20).

Curtius shows concern for serious history in the way he rationalizes material and excludes irrelevant, exotic detail. For example, he prunes the myth concerning the wagon at Gordium back to the simple reference to it as the wagon which Midas' father, Gordius is reputed to have driven (3. 1. 14). And on the city of Nysa he limits himself to a note that the locals claimed to be descended from Dionysus, and that Greeks used the name of the mountain, Meros, as licence to lie that Dionysus was concealed in the thigh (Gk. *meros*) of Jupiter (8. 10. 12). He does not buy into the tradition that Alexander's corpse showed no sign of putrefaction after a week (10. 10. 12) and he is sceptical about the tradition that Alexander was poisoned (10. 10. 14–18).

Cascon Dorado (1990), recognizing that Alexander had his admirers in the Julio-Claudian house, credits Curtius with a concern to avoid giving offence and yet to accommodate the traditional image of Alexander as a ruler turned into a tyrant by the corruptive force of success. Thus his strategy was to demythologize the Alexander legend, and he did this first by dealing more extensively with the episodes that reflected badly on Alexander. In this way Curtius sets out the political context of each episode, and puts criticism of Alexander into the mouths of Alexander's opponents (p. 258). Thus Curtius deals with these crises in a pragmatic rather than moralizing way, to make the story more real. Curtius did not allow the evidence of failure or abuse of power to blot out Alexander's qualities. Again in the interest of historical reality Curtius demythologizes by paying due regard to external factors, including the calibre of Alexander's generals, and the failure or bad luck of his enemies.[105]

---

[104] As at 4. 10. 26, 5. 12. 8, and 7. 4. 35.

[105] Cascon Dorado (1990), 262–4 gives as examples of theses two categories first 3. 7. 10, 11. 13; 4. 16. 31; 8. 1. 3, and secondly 3. 2. 17; 4. 15. 29–30; 5. 1. 39; 8. 10. 18; 9.10. 27.

Curtius often adds considerable detail, but it can be patchy and is therefore probably more to add verisimilitude to the history rather than to provide a comprehensive resource. Thus, for example, at 4. 8. 4–5 Curtius gives an account of Alexander's arrangements for the administration of Egypt which I have characterized as incomplete, misleading and inaccurate when checked against A. 3. 5 (discussion at (1980), 364–7).[106] In ladling in the detail at various points Curtius may be following the lead of Cleitarchus (Bosworth (2003), 176 on Cleitarchus' Stoffreichtum). But where Curtius includes such detail he seems to apply the test of relevance, as he does for example in the few brief references to earlier kings of Persia.[107]

Some fictionalizing by Curtius is suspected where other sources are silent on the detail or there are contradictions. Thus Gunderson (1982) suggests some fabrication of detail relating to Polydamas and Parmenion and in the story of Nabarzanes' gift of the eunuch Bagoas to Alexander. In the story of the battle of Gaugamela Curtius alone says that Parmenion sent Polydamas to Alexander for fresh orders after Mazaeus detailed troops to ransack the Macedonian baggage camp (Curtius 4. 15. 5–8). This uncorroborated scene adds to the characterization of Parmenion as a commander who irritated Alexander by his extreme caution, and it serves to introduce Polydamas, who is wanted later for the story of his despicable role in the murder of Parmenion (7. 2. 11–33). Gunderson takes as an indication of fictional elaboration Curtius' reference to Polydamas as a young man at 7. 2. 11, whereas J. 12. 12. 8 counts him among the veterans in 324. Certainly it suits the flow of the story in 7. 2 for Polydamas to be introduced as a youth, whose intimidation by Alexander offsets the preceding story of Amyntas' brave defence of his errant young brother, Polemon (7. 2. 1–10).

Gunderson (1982), 191 similarly argues that there is fiction in Curtius' story of Bagoas' plot against Orxines (10. 1. 25–38), for Curtius says that Alexander learnt from Bagoas of the riches that

---

[106] Cf. 4. 12. 5–13, a catalogue which is inaccurate and includes some anachronisms, but the mistakes were probably picked up from Curtius' source; 8. 3. 16–17 (from Aristobulus), 8. 13. 1–4 and 14. 15. Lists and strings of detail have always been a feature of oral tradition, and of course carried over into the tradition of epic, as in *Iliad* 2.

[107] e.g. on Darius I Curtius 3. 10. 8, 4. 1. 10 and 5. 6. 1.

had been in Cyrus' tomb before Orxines allegedly plundered it. This is at odds with Aristobulus' statement that Alexander had visited the tomb himself when he first took Persepolis in 330 (*FGrH* 139, F. 51 = Strabo 15. 3. 7. 730; A. 4. 29. 4–11). Gunderson (1982), 183–4 also questions Curtius' tale that Nabarzanes gave Bagoas to Alexander.[108]

Curtius includes errors of fact on matters of geography (as at 7. 3. 3–4), chronology (as at 4. 1. 34 ff. and 3. 20, and 9. 6. 21) and orientation (for example left for right at 4. 15. 2). He lets in some anachronisms (as at 5. 10. 3–9, 7. 5. 13 and 10. 1. 17–19), and contradictions (as between 3. 12. 13 and 4. 10. 24, and between 4. 10. 15 and 18). There are some mistakes common to the genre, including perhaps misreading of the Greek,[109] inaccurate transcriptions (9. 10. 29 with A. 7. 4. 1), and faulty memory, as at 5. 7. 12, where the Macedonian officer Socrates (Curtius 4. 5. 9, A. 1. 12. 7) has been turned into 'Plato the Athenian'.[110] Plato may have inspired another Curtian oddity that we should attribute in this case to literary imagination rather than inaccurate copying. On Alexander's approach to Persepolis he was met by a column of Greek prisoners of war who had been mutilated and enslaved by the Persians. He offered to repatriate them, and Curtius offers a debate between Euctemon, arguing for acceptance, and Theaetetus arguing that they have nothing to gain by leaving Persepolis (5. 5. 10–20). D.S. 17. 69. 5–7 confirms that there was a tradition that such a debate took place. Curtius' Theaetetus is not attested by any other source, and his speech is developed from Stoic philosophy, Roman values, and Roman institutions, and it must be a Curtian concoction. Curtius may also have invented the character Theaetetus, with an allusion to his homonym's wretched circumstances as described in Plato's

---

[108] Gunderson also notes (pp. 186–7, 195) that Curtius misrepresents the significance of the council of Bactrian hyparchs convened at Zariaspa (Curtius 7. 6. 14–15 with A. 4. 1. 5).

[109] A misreading of a Greek numeral at 4. 4. 16, for example, is claimed by Levi (1977), 160. Steele (1919), 51 suggests a similar error at 3. 7. 5, when read with A. 2. 5. 9. Atkinson (1980), 365–6 finds another possible misreading of a Greek source at 4. 8. 4. Then there is the notorious case of the place name Arvae (6. 4. 23), which Steele, pp. 50–1, took to arise from a misunderstanding of the Greek participle *aras* ('setting off'), as found at A. 3. 23. 6.

[110] Berve, ii. p. 429.

*Theaetetus* 142b–c and 144c–d.[111] He is paired by Curtius with Euctemon, whose name, meaning 'well-off' provides a nice irony. This case is somewhere between elaboration and fictionalizing.

So far the historiographical issues, but it remains to consider in what ways Curtius' Roman context may have interfered with his pursuit of the truth and with his presentation of the history of Alexander. First of all Rome under the Principate was not a free society, not least for those of the social class to which Curtius apparently belonged. The Principate meant domination by one man, who commanded legal and military means of coercion, and, of more immediate relevance, immense power of patronage. The eulogy of the new emperor (10. 9. 1–6) makes that point, and the focus in the *Histories* on political issues and Alexander's treatment of those who dared to stand up to him shows that Curtius was well aware of what it meant to be in the officer class under an autocrat. Curtius gives the point of view of one of his class.

Then the figure of Alexander was not value-free in the Roman political scene. At one level the image of Alexander had remained as a rallying point for Greeks and Macedonians during the Hellenistic period. So, for example, Antiochus III exploited his link with Alexander's family in 192, before he went to war with Rome (Livy 35. 47. 5–8). Next there is the circumstantial evidence that Rome banned the use of Alexander style coins in 168 BC after the third Macedonian War.[112] Thirdly we have Livy's word that Greeks were using the Alexander myth to challenge the notion of Rome's invincibility (Livy 9. 18. 6). But of greater relevance is the intermittent imitation or emulation of Alexander as a feature of Roman politics, at least from when Pompey chose to promote the image of himself as a new Alexander.[113] In the late Republic this was not a particularly

---

[111] So Atkinson (1994), 107–10, but Professor Badian suggested to me that Curtius may have found the name Euctemon in his source and took Theaetetus from a list of great mathematicians, where both names occurred.

[112] A. Giovannini, in *Alexandre le Grand* (1976), 211–13. For more extensive coverage of this whole topic see C. Bohm, *Imitatio Alexandri im Hellenismus* (Munich, 1989).

[113] Sallust *Hist.* 3. 88[M] = McGushin (1994), F84; Plut. *Pomp.* 2. 1–2, 46. 1–2, Dio 37. 21. 3; Spencer (2002), 17–19; cf. Wirth (1976), with the comments of Badian in the same volume (pp. 215–16), rejecting as myth Scipio Africanus' supposed imitation of Alexander. B. Tisé, *Imperialismo romano e imitatio Alexandri* (Galatina,

significant phenomenon,[114] but it became more overt in the Principate. Thus Germanicus invoked the image of Alexander when he addressed the citizens of Alexandria in the winter of 18/19, and referred to 'the debt owed to the hero and founder [Alexander] by all those who share his aspirations' (*Acta Alexandrinorum, POxy.* 25 (1959), no. 2435, recto lines 19–21). On his death he was likened to Alexander (Tac. *Ann* 2. 73. 1–3). Caligula more blatantly advertised his admiration for Alexander.[115] Nero raised a new legion of Italian six-footers for an expedition to the Caspian Gates, and called the unit the phalanx of Alexander the Great (Suet. *Nero* 19. 2); and his visit to Lake Alcyon in Corinthian territory and his plan to build a canal seem to have been a conscious appeal to the image of Alexander.[116] Thus, if Curtius completed his work after Caligula's death or after Nero's demise, the recent Alexander imitator(s) must have influenced his approach to the subject of the historical Alexander.[117]

Throughout the *Histories* Curtius' experience of the political world of the Roman Principate appears close to the surface, and culminates in his eulogy of the new emperor in 10. 9. 1–6. Obviously Curtius worked with the problem that faces any historian writing about a different society and an earlier age, in that the vocabulary available to the historian will in many cases fail to match the connotations of the terminology being represented. Thus, for example, the Latin terms *amicus* and *socius* (friend and ally) had precise legal connotations in interstate agreements that would not have been quite the same for the Greek terms *philoi* and *symmachoi*. Roman associations appear in the distinction between military power exercised and power delegated (5. 1. 1, 6. 3. 2 and 9. 6. 9) and in the distinction between a power

2002) argues that T. Quinctius Flamininus was the first Roman to imitate Alexander, but I have argued against this in *CR* 54 (2004), 569–70.

[114] As is well argued by Green (1979).

[115] Suet. *Calig.* 51. 3 and 52 with Dio 59. 17. 3; Wardle (1994), 112, 118 and 341.

[116] Pausanias 2. 37. 5 and 2. 1. 5, with Susan E. Alcock, 'Nero at play?' in *Reflections of Nero: Culture, History and Representation*, ed. J. Elsner and J. Masters (London, 1994), 104 and 108 n. 24. K.R. Bradley, *Suetonius' Life of Nero* (Brussels, 1978), 284–5 does not accept the suggestion that Nero adopted the 'crimped' hairstyle (Suet. *Nero* 51) in imitation of Alexander.

[117] I am assuming that Curtius predated Trajan, and, in any case, while Trajan expressed respect for Alexander, he did not overtly imitate Alexander: Wirth (1976), 197–200.

(*potestas*) attached to office in constitutional law and the less well defined concept of authority arising from seniority (*auctoritas*: 6. 8. 25). The army assembly is labelled a *contio* (first in Book 10 at 2. 18), though it did not have the same legal definition as the Roman popular assembly. Similarly Curtius uses the vocabulary of Roman ruler cult (as at 3. 7. 3 and 6. 11. 7). Callisthenes is referred to as 'the champion of public freedom' (*vindex publicae libertatis*: 8. 5. 20), which echoes Augustus' outrageous claim that he had carried out his *coup d'état* as the champion of freedom (*libertas*), which was the basic principle of the Republican constitution.[118] In this case Curtius was clearly invoking memories of the Roman Revolution. The reader of a modern translation will be largely immune to this Roman interference, but it has some bearing on the question of Curtius' success in dealing with the age of Alexander on its own terms.

For all the problems that challenge one's trust in Curtius, there is evidence enough for him to be taken seriously as a source on Alexander, as in the passages where he is more accurate than Diodorus (as at 4. 1. 15–26 with D.S. 17. 46. 6–47. 6, and 9. 7. 1–11 with D.S. 17. 99. 5), or offers material omitted by Arrian (as at 5. 6. 11–19), or preserves a precise formulation (as at 6. 6. 2 on Alexander *isotheos*, as Badian (1996) explains). Thus it would be rash to discard Curtius' account of the political scene in Babylon after Alexander's death as fiction, but there can be no certainty about where to draw the dividing line between the tradition followed by Curtius and his embellishment of it.

## 9. JUDGING ALEXANDER

It is commonly said that attempts at judging Alexander fail because the criteria used are anachronistic. On this view the fallacy of modernizing leads away from an understanding of the value system in

---

[118] *Res Gestae divi Augusti* 1. 1: 'I successfully championed the freedom of the Republic when it was oppressed by the domination of a faction'. The phrase had been a slogan of the Populares, the reformist wing of the Senate in the late Republic. The key modern study of this ideal remains Ch. Wirszubski, *Libertas as a Political Idea at Rome during the Late Republic and Early Principate* (Cambridge, 1950).

which the historical Alexander operated, and by which he would have been judged, and thus this path will lead to inappropriate character-ization. Thus, for example, Cartledge (2004), 308 concludes a brief review of the diversity of modern interpretations of Alexander's record with the comment, 'Roisman rightly injects a note of sanity by establishing the moral code of honour according to which Alexander would have acted'. Indeed there can be no doubt that the historian has to be concerned to discover the modes of thought that shaped the action decisions and judgements of the characters in the relevant historical situation. But Cartledge's endorsement of Rois-man's approach is misleading, as Roisman (2003) focuses on the vertical axis of honour[119] to show how Alexander was concerned to become, and remain, supreme by virtue of 'his personal worth, his office and his ultimate control over the resources and symbols of his empire'(p. 321). It is not a 'moral' code, and Cartledge's introduction of the term shifts the focus from what Roisman styles the heroic (or Homeric) code, and seems a rather coy way of avoiding giving offence to readers who might be Alexander enthusiasts.[120]

But nothing is going to stop writers, teachers, politicians, film-makers, and whoever, from using the Alexander legend to make whatever point they wish, and there is no guarantee that champions of value-free scholarship (if such a thing exists) will get closer to revealing the true nature (if such a thing exists) of the historical Alexander.

Curtius' final assessment of Alexander is generally recognized as more of a eulogy than his history of Alexander's campaigns would lead one to expect. But the damning criticisms are there, folded into the centre (10. 5. 33–4), and of course Curtius has already demonstrated in the structure of Book 10 that mounting hostility to Alexander among his own men could be turned around, and like many an autocrat, Alexander was perhaps never so revered as at the moment of death. Curtius' positive obituary mirrors the reaction of his troops. And being Roman, Curtius knows that the funeral eulogy has a programmatic element. Curtius praises qualities that he would

---

[119] The vertical axis refers to prestige or eminence won in a competitive environ-ment, while the horizontal axis has more to do with the respect to which each member of a peer group may claim entitlement.

[120] I deal with this whole subject more fully in a separate paper: Atkinson (2007).

like to see in the new emperor hailed in 10. 9. 1–6, and warns him off enforced ruler cult, the adoption of alien cultural practices, homicidal paranoia, and alcohol abuse. As the obituary serves this secondary, Roman purpose, we should therefore not focus on it rather than on the way Curtius presents Alexander throughout the *Histories*. Curtius was a political animal, and so gives significant weight to the political episodes, as noted several times above. He was surely no monarchist, but had to live with the reality that supreme power rested with one man. Like Seneca in the *Clementia*, Curtius wished to urge the emperor to exercise power with a sense of responsibility and to remember his humanity. It is not only in the obituary that Curtius strikes a balance between criticism of Alexander and favourable comments. Content analysis of the *Histories* shows, for example, that with regard to his use of abstract nouns applied to Alexander in respect of qualities and vices and weaknesses, the positive occurrences account for some 54 per cent of the total, whereas the positive terms applied to his officers, subjects, and enemies represent of the order of 41 per cent;[121] and the total number of such positive attributions to Alexander is higher than the number of such references to others.[122] One may read into the pattern of judgements that Curtius blamed Alexander's officers in particular for failing to stand up to Alexander when they should have spoken out. In other words they did not assert their right and responsibility to exercise their freedom of speech (*libertas*).[123] But, to return to the point, with the

---

[121] The percentages are based on the respective ratios of 93:80 and 98:140. It is perhaps significant that for Alexander, 'vices' just outbalance virtues in books 7 to 9, but virtues outnumber vices in Book 10 (17:9).

[122] The ratio is about 93:80. I count 'vices missing' as virtues.

[123] Curtius deals with this theme also by presenting favourably those who took risks in giving wise advice, whether on the Persian or the Macedonian side: e.g. with regard to Darius' ill-judged refusal to accept Charidemus' advice at 3. 2. 10–19, the advice of Darius' Greek mercenaries at 3. 8. 1–11, and Gobares' stand against Bessus at 7. 4. 1–19. But frank advice had to be given diplomatically, and not as in Cleitus' intemperate confrontation with Alexander (8. 2. 2). Curtius is further critical of yes-men and flatterers, for example, at 4. 5. 11 and 7. 31; 8. 8. 21 and 10. 1. 25 ff. At the same time, as Bödefeld (1982), esp. 66–72 notes, Curtius presents the resistance to Alexander in far stronger terms than does Arrian. Bödefeld compares the speeches attributed to Callisthenes (8. 5. 14–19) and more especially Hermolaus (8. 7. 1–6) with the attacks of Philo and Seneca on Caligula (Philo *Leg.* 117, 119; Seneca *Ben.* 2. 12. 2, *Cons. Marc.* 20. 3, *Ira* 3. 17. 1 ff.). 10. 1. 39–42 indicates that Alexander was by the end of 325 beyond taking sensible advice.

obituary and indeed with the very last line of the book Curtius gives the impression of following the precept that one should speak no ill of the dead, at least at surface level.[124]


## 10. CURTIUS' LANGUAGE AND LITERARY VALUE

One suspects that Curtius' prime concern was to create a literary work rather than to establish a reputation as a serious historian. This does not mean that he did not wish to be taken seriously as a historian, but that he would have preferred to be recognized as serious writer, whatever the value of his contribution to history. This point may be more readily appreciated if the closing section of the *Historiae* is set against the final section of Josephus' *Antiquities* (20. 259–68), in which he reviews his achievement, ticking off his historiographical checklist, and announces his future projects. The same applies to the end of the *Jewish War*, which is similarly self-congratulatory (7. 454–5), but commendably briefer. The ending of the *Histories* is more literary. Furthermore, as noted in the section on genre, Curtius does not include in his work reflective passages on historical method, such as characterize the work of Polybius, and there is no grand model of history such as Polybius' concept of *anacyclosis* (the cycle of constitutions).

Literary intent can be seen for example in Curtius' structuring of his narrative. As noted in the section on the structure of Book 10, there is an overall structural design,[125] starting with the division of the work into two pentads. Curtius is careful about the way he closes each book, rounding off one series of stories, but also preparing for the opening motifs of the following book.[126] To do this he abandons annalistic structuring, and can separate events that belong

---

[124] There may be some irony in the obituary, as at 10. 5. 35 where he says that, while Alexander owed most to his manly qualities (*virtus*), he owed rather more to good luck or Fortuna, which might remind some of the radio commercial which hailed a certain brand of (unremarkable?) cider as 'excellent with snails, and much better without'.

[125] This is disputed by Porod (1987), but Porod does call for greater attention to the way Curtius constructs individual episodes (as at p. 167).

[126] Cf. Rutz (1986), 2333–6.

together, or transpose episodes for compositional reasons. Thus, for example, a book division separates Alexander's liquidation of Philotas and his move to kill Parmenion before he could learn of his son's death (7. 2. 11–34); and the execution of Astaspes, the satrap of Carmania (9. 10. 29) is separated from the purge of other Persians, Greeks, and Macedonians in Carmania (10. 1. 1–9). Similarly Curtius anticipates the story of the arrest and detention of the Lyncestian Alexander to include it in the latter part of the lost Book 2, and he holds over to the beginning of Book 3 the commission of Cleander to recruit mercenaries in the Peloponnese.[127]

Curtius' literary pretensions must be reflected in the speeches which he created.[128] The speech which Curtius attributes to the Scythians and which he introduces with a dismissive comment about its unsophisticated and dated style (7. 8. 11) must represent a claim by Curtius to be considered a sophisticated and modern writer. The scene was a set-piece of historical texts, where the noble, uncorrupted 'barbarian' warns the aggressor not to invade without just cause, nor to rely on brute force, nor to push his luck.[129] The influence of Herodotus is marked, starting with Curtius' claim to be copying the speech faithfully.[130] Echoes of fragments from Cleitarchus suggest that Curtius took the core detail from Cleitarchus, but the more overt intertextual references in this potpourri of clichés and aphorisms must be to the declamatory exercises, as represented by Seneca *Suasoriae* 1.[131] There are also echoes of Sallust's 'Letter of Mithradates',[132] and also of Trogus, and there may be a note of humour here if Curtius introduced

---

[127] Atkinson (1980), 77–9.

[128] Helmreich (1927) offers the most thorough analysis of Curtius' speeches; cf. Bardon (1947c), esp. 203–5 and for a specific example Gissel (1995); all notice the strong influence of the schools of rhetoric. Schanz–Hosius (1935), 599–600 goes too far in stating that Curtius is 'no historian, but only a rhetorician'.

[129] Ballesteros-Pastor (2003), 27 notes among parallel scenes, Justin 9. 2. 1–2 with Plut. *Mor.* 174f, D.S. 21. 12. 2–6, Hdt. 2. 102–110 and D.S. 1. 53–58.

[130] Bosworth (1996a), 150 matches this claim with Hdt. 2. 123. 1 and 130. 2, 7. 152. 1–3, but recognizes that the speech 'must be largely his own composition'. Then at pp. 148–51 Bosworth notes other parallels between Curtius' version of the speech of the Scythian and Hdt. 1. 206–7, 3. 21. 2–3; cf. Baynham (1998), 87–9 and 123, and Ballesteros-Pastor (2003), esp. 26–31.

[131] Helmreich (1927), 211–20, Wilhelm (1928), 39–50.

[132] Ballesteros-Pastor (2003), 34–6, noting several passages in the *Letter* to be found in Sall. *Hist.* 4. 69[M] = F67 in the translation by McGushin (1994), 47–51.

the speech with the apology for its unsophisticated style, and then went on to mimic Trogus.

Tarn, ii. 94–5 pays Curtius a rare compliment in his praise of the speech attributed to Amyntas, speaking in his own defence in 330 (7. 1. 18–40). Tarn comments that this shows what Curtius could do, if he 'could be bothered', and Tarn contrasts this speech with that of Philotas in 6. 10, which he dismisses as 'rhetoric of the worst school type'. Curtius' own contribution to the speech of Amyntas is hard to determine, since no other source offers a version to provide an idea of the core material. But, as noted earlier, there are similarities to Tacitus' version of M. Terentius' defence against a charge of treason (*maiestas*) in AD 32 (Tac. *Ann.* 6. 8. 1–3), and Curtius seems to strengthen that association by having Alexander use the formulation for recording a vote in a senatorial hearing (7. 2. 8), and then admit that, without a thorough investigation of the charges laid against Amyntas, he might have engaged in dissimulation (7. 2. 9), a term that was well entrenched in Roman political discourse, and was presumably recognized as a defining element of Tiberius' principate long before Tacitus, Suetonius, and Dio laid down the tradition with which we are familiar.[133] The Roman associations which Curtius wove into this speech would have served to attract the reader's attention to his own display of rhetoric.

By contrast with the speech attributed to Amyntas, the speech which Curtius gives to Alexander in the context of the Opis mutiny (10. 2. 15—29) is not a great piece of work, and is a travesty of the core material available to Curtius, from what we can learn from Arrian's version (7. 9. 1—10. 7).[134] Curtius could have done better, and did not, presumably for a reason—to characterize Alexander in this final stage or to heighten the seriousness of this clash between Alexander and his troops. Thus it may be that his literary purpose here took precedence over any wish to show off his rhetorical talent.

[133] e.g. Tac. *Ann.* 1. 4. 3, 6. 1; 4. 71. 3; 6. 50. 1 and 51. 3, Suet. *Tib.* 24, 65. 1, Dio 57. 1. 1, 7. 1; 58. 3 and 6; Syme (1958), 422–3.

[134] Bosworth (1988*b*), 113 concludes that 'neither in its shape nor in its detailed content can [Arrian's version] bear any relation to what was actually said by Alexander', but he does accept that there was a core tradition behind the versions of Curtius and Arrian.

Curiously enough, Curtius uses connecting particles and conjunctions to introduce new sentences seldom enough to give them special force when they do appear.[135] There are two problems to be noted here: first, the translator has to contend with the fact that the connectors may have different values in different contexts. Thus for example, Curtius uses *sed* (but, however) with a strong adversative force, as at 10. 2. 4 and 9. 1, but in other contexts the conjunction is used variously to mark an antithesis, to reinforce, or to supplement, and the synonym *ceterum* can be used with resumptive force. Then should the translation mirror the function of the connector? The more serious issue is whether the translator should signal where the author has moved from asyndeton to syndeton. It would be worth investigating whether there is a pattern of syndeton being more intense where argument takes precedence over substance, and Curtius may be out to lure the reader into following his line of argument.

In Curtius there is no shortage of examples of the full range of literary devices. He is generous in distributing *sententiae*, pithy generalizations on psychology or human situations, such as the pair in 5. 4. 31: necessity can sharpen up even cowardice, and desperation is often the cause of hope[136] (and in this book cf. 10. 10. 8). For his use of imagery there is an example at 10. 7. 11 with the extended simile relating to the political instability of crowds.[137]

In fine we have in Curtius' *Historiae*, a serious historical study—'Alexander the history'—which claimed to be taken seriously as a work of literature, and was, at least for the readers of his own era, a text for its time.

---

[135] Pinkster (1990), 245 provides some comparative statistics for Cicero, Livy, and Seneca, showing Livy with the lowest, and Seneca with the highest incidence of asyndeton, the ratios of asyndeton to syndeton being respectively 42:57 and 107:41.

[136] The latter echoes Vergil *Aen.* 2. 354. Other examples include 4. 1. 20, 10. 10, and 16. 17; 8. 4. 11; 9. 9. 12 and the last line of Book 9, 10. 29.

[137] For a comprehensive review of issues relating to Curtius' style of writing see Rutz (1986).

# Translation

## 1

**1.1** There arrived at about this time Cleander, Sitalces, Heracon, and Agathon, the men who had assassinated Parmenion on the king's orders. **1.2** Five thousand infantry and 1,000 cavalry came with them, but there also came from the province which they had governed men who brought charges against them. Grateful as Alexander was for their services in the matter of the assassination, this could not compensate for all the crimes they had committed. **1.3** For after plundering everything in the secular sphere, they had not even refrained from what was sacred: virgins and women of the highest breeding had been sexually assaulted and were bemoaning the physical abuse they had suffered. **1.4** The greed and lust of these men had made the barbarians abhor the Macedonian name. **1.5** Worst of all was the lust-crazed Cleander, who had raped a virgin of noble birth and then given her to his slave as a concubine.

**1.6** What preoccupied the majority of Alexander's friends was not so much the atrocities of which these men were openly accused as the recollection that they had been responsible for Parmenion's murder, a fact which could secretly help their defence before the king. They were delighted now that Alexander's wrath had recoiled upon those who had been the instruments of that wrath and that no power which someone gains by crime is of long duration. **1.7** After examining the case, Alexander announced that one charge had been overlooked by the prosecutors, and the most important one at that, namely the defendants' assumption that he would not survive. For, he said, men wishing or believing that he would safely return from India would never have ventured upon such crimes. **1.8** So he clapped them in irons and moreover ordered the execution of 600 common soldiers responsible for putting their barbarous decisions into effect. **1.9** On the same day the men brought in by Craterus as ringleaders of the Persian insurrection were also put to death.

**1.10** Shortly afterwards Nearchus and Onesicritus arrived, the men whom Alexander had instructed to proceed some way into the Ocean. **1.11** They brought reports based partly on hearsay and partly on their own observation. There was an island lying at the mouth of the river, they said, which was rich in gold but without horses. (These, they had discovered, the inhabitants would buy for a talent each from men who ventured to transport them from the mainland.) **1.12** The sea was full of monsters, they claimed, brought in on the incoming tide, their bodies the size of large ships. Deterred from following the ships by a strident shout, these would submerge themselves, producing a mighty roar from the water, as when ships have been sunk.

**1.13** Their other information they had taken on trust from the natives, including the assertion that the Red Sea derived its name not, as was generally believed, from the colour of its waters but from a king Erythrus; **1.14** and that there was an island not far from the mainland thickly planted with palm trees and with a high column standing approximately in the middle of the wood; this, they said, was a monument to king Erythrus, and it bore writing in the script of that race. **1.15** They added that vessels carrying food-traders and merchants had crossed to the island, their pilots following up reports of gold, and they had never been seen again.

**1.16** Eager to know more, Alexander told them to resume a course close to land until they put in at the mouth of the Euphrates, after which they were to go up river to Babylon. **1.17** His ambitions knowing no bounds, Alexander had decided that, after the subjugation of the entire eastern seaboard, he would head from Syria towards Africa, because of his enmity towards the Carthaginians. Then, crossing the Numidian deserts, he would set his course for Gades, where the Pillars of Hercules were rumoured to be; **1.18** afterwards, he would go to Spain (which the Greeks called 'Hiberia', after the river Hiberus). Then he would skirt past the Alps and the Italian coastline, from which it was a short passage to

Epirus. **1.19** Accordingly, Alexander instructed his governors in Mesopotamia to cut timber on Mt Libanus, transport it down to the Syrian city of Thapsacus, and there lay down keels for 700 ships. These were to be all septiremes, which were to be transported to Babylon. The kings of Cyprus were instructed to furnish bronze, hemp, and sails.

**1.20** While he was thus engaged, Alexander was brought letters from the kings, Porus and Taxiles, informing him that Abisares had died after an illness, and Alexander's governor, Philip, of a wound (but those who had inflicted it had been punished). **1.21** Alexander therefore replaced Philip with Eudaemon—he was the commanding officer of the Thracians—and assigned Abisares' kingdom to Abisares' son.

**1.22** They next came to Parsagada, city of a Persian tribe, whose satrap was Orsines, a man pre-eminent among all the barbarians for his nobility and wealth. **1.23** He traced his lineage from Cyrus, the former Persian king, and his wealth was partly inherited from his ancestors and partly amassed by himself during his long tenure of the satrapy. **1.24** Orsines met Alexander with all manner of gifts, which he intended to give not only to the king but to his friends as well. With him were herds of horses, already broken in, chariots trimmed with silver and gold, expensive furniture, fine jewels, heavy gold vessels, purple garments, and 3,000 talents of silver coin. **1.25** However, it was his great generosity that occasioned the barbarian's death. For although he had honoured all the king's friends with gifts greater than they could have wished for, he paid no court to the eunuch Bagoas, who by now had gained Alexander's affection through putting his body at his service. **1.26** He was advised by certain people that Bagoas stood no lower in Alexander's affections than anyone else. In reply Orsines said that he paid his respects to the king's friends, not his whores, and that it was not the Persian custom to regard as men those who allowed themselves to be sexually used as women.

**1.27** When he heard this, the eunuch directed the power gained from his shameful self-degradation against the life of an innocent man of supreme distinction. He furnished the most worthless of Orsines' people with false accusations, telling them to divulge these only when he gave the order. **1.28** Meanwhile, whenever no one else was in earshot, he filled the king's credulous ears, but concealed the reason for his rancour so that his charges would carry more weight. 1.29 Though not yet under suspicion, Orsines was already losing Alexander's favour. In fact, he was being tried in secret, ignorant of the unseen danger, and the unconscionable male whore did not forget his scheming even when he was submitting to the shame of the sexual act, for, whenever he had roused the king's passion for him, he would accuse Orsines on one occasion of greed, on another even of rebellion.

1.30 The time had now come for the lies to destroy the innocent man, and fate, whose decrees are inevitable, was approaching fulfilment. For it chanced that Alexander ordered the opening of Cyrus' tomb, wishing to pay funeral honours to the corpse of Cyrus buried in it. 1.31 He had believed the tomb to be full of gold and silver, as had been commonly rumoured among the Persians, but he found nothing more than Cyrus' mouldering shield, two Scythian bows and a scimitar. 1.32 Alexander set a golden crown on the sarcophagus in which the body lay, and draped it with his own cloak, expressing surprise that so famous a king who possessed such great wealth should have received no more expensive a burial than if he had been one of the common people. 1.33 The eunuch was at Alexander's side. 'What's surprising about kings' sepulchres being empty,' he said, looking at the king, 'when satraps' houses cannot hold all the gold taken from them? 1.34 Speaking for myself, I had never set eyes on the tomb before, but I was told by Darius that 3,000 talents were buried with Cyrus. 1.35 That explains Orsines' generosity towards you: unable to keep his loot with impunity, he wanted to curry favour with you by giving it away.'

1.36 Bagoas had already roused Alexander to anger when the men he had charged to assist his undertaking came up. Bagoas on one side, and those he had suborned on the other, filled the king's ears with false accusations, 1.37 and, before he could even suspect that charges were being laid against him, Orsines was clapped in irons. Not satisfied with seeing an innocent man executed, the eunuch seized him as he went to his death. Looking at him, Orsines said: 'I had heard that women once were rulers in Asia but this really is something new—a *eunuch* as king!' 1.38 Such was the end of the most noble of Persians, a man who was not only innocent but who had also shown the king exemplary kindness.

**1.39** Phradates was also executed at this time on suspicion of having had designs on the throne. Alexander had begun to be quick to order summary execution and also to believe the worst of people. **1.40** Of course, success can alter one's nature, and rarely is a person sufficiently circumspect with regard to his good fortune. For, shortly before, this same man had been unable to condemn Alexander Lyncestes despite the evidence of two witnesses; **1.41** he had also, against his own inclinations, acquiesced in the acquittal of prisoners of lesser consequence, simply because the others thought them innocent; he had given back kingdoms to defeated enemies. **1.42** At the end of his life, however, his degeneration from his former self was such that, though earlier possessed of unassailable self-control, he followed a male whore's judgement to give some men kingdoms and deprive others of their lives.

**1.43** At about this same time, Alexander received a letter from Coenus concerning events in Europe and Asia while he was himself engaged in the conquest of India. **1.44** Zopyrion, who governed Thrace, had been lost with his entire army with the sudden onset of stormy weather and squalls while he was on an expedition against the Getae. **1.45** On learning of this set-back, Seuthes had driven his subjects, the Odrysians, to rebellion. Thrace had almost been lost and not even Greece ... [The text breaks off at this point.]

## 2

**2.1** So, with thirty ships, they crossed to Sunium (a promontory in the territory of Attica), having decided to make for the port of Athens from there. **2.2** On learning this, the king was equally incensed with Harpalus and the Athenians. He ordered a fleet to be mustered for an immediate strike on Athens. **2.3** But, while he was privately considering this plan, a letter arrived. Harpalus, it said, had entered Athens and had won the support of leading citizens by bribery, but soon an assembly of the people was held which ordered him to leave the city. He had succeeded in reaching his Greek troops, with whom he crossed to Crete, only to be treacherously murdered at the instigation of a friend of his.

2.4 Pleased with the news, Alexander dropped his plan of crossing to Europe. However, he ordered the restoration of exiles (except those with the blood of citizens on their hands) by all the cities which had expelled them. 2.5 The Greeks dared not disobey his order, despite their belief that it constituted the first step towards the collapse of their laws, and they even restored what remained of their property to the condemned men. 2.6 Only the Athenians, champions of everybody's liberty, and not just their own, were reluctant to tolerate such a mishmash of classes and individuals, for they were used to being ruled by laws and ancestral customs, and not the orders of a ruler. 2.7 Accordingly they barred the exiles from their territory, and were prepared to suffer anything rather than admit what was once the scum of their city and subsequently the scum of their places of exile.

2.8 Sending his older soldiers home, Alexander ordered a force of 13,000 infantry and 2,000 cavalry to be selected for him to keep back in Asia. He believed he could hold Asia with an army of modest proportions because he had deployed garrisons in a number of places and populated the recently established cities with colonists who were hardly looking to start trouble. 2.9 However, before choosing the men he would keep back, he ordered all the troops to declare their debts; for he had discovered that many were deeply in debt, and he had decided to discharge their obligations himself even though these derived from their own extravagance. 2.10 The men thought they were being put to a test to make it easier for Alexander to tell the wastrels from the thrifty, and so they let time slip by without doing anything. Alexander was well aware that it was embarrassment rather than insubordination that stopped them acknowledging their debts, so he had tables set at points throughout the camp and 10,000 talents put out on them. 2.11 With that an honest disclosure was finally made by the men and, from all that money, what remained was a mere 130 talents! Yes, that army which had defeated so many rich nations nevertheless took from Asia more prestige than booty.

2.12 Now when it was discovered that some were being sent home and others held back, the men assumed that Alexander was going to fix the royal seat permanently in Asia. Beside themselves and oblivious of military discipline, they filled the camp with mutinous comments and attacked the king with more abuse than ever before. Then they all together proceeded to demand demobilization, as they displayed their scarred faces and grey heads. 2.13 Neither reprimands from their officers nor their own respect for the king restrained them. Alexander wished to address them, but they prevented him with their mutinous shouting and soldierly truculence, as they publicly declared their refusal to take a step in any direction save homewards. 2.14 At last silence fell, more because they thought Alexander had experienced a change of heart than because they themselves could change, and they awaited his reaction.

2.15 'What does this sudden uproar mean,' asked Alexander, 'and such violent and wild disorder? I am afraid to speak. You have openly flouted my authority and I am a king on sufferance. You have not left me the right of addressing you, encouraging you, advising you or even watching you. 2.16 I decided to send some men home and take others with me shortly afterwards—and I see as much opposition from those who are going to leave as from those with whom I have decided to follow the advance party. 2.17 What is going on? You all join the uproar, but for different reasons. I should dearly like to know whether the complaints about me are coming from those leaving or those being kept back.'

2.18 You would have thought the shout they all raised together came from a single mouth, so concerted was the answer 'We all complain' from the whole gathering. 2.19 'No,' said Alexander, 'you cannot make me believe that you all have these grounds for complaint which you indicate; most of the army is not involved since I have discharged more than I am going to retain. 2.20 There must be some deeper problem which is turning all of you against me. For when has a king been abandoned by his entire army? Not even slaves run away from their masters in a single body, but among them there is still some sense of shame at leaving those whom the rest have deserted. 2.21 But I am forgetting your wild uproar, and I am trying to cure incurables! Yes, I abandon all the hope I had conceived in you, and I have decided to treat you not as my soldiers—for that you have now ceased to be—but as thoroughly ungrateful hirelings. 2.22 The prosperity all around you has begun to unbalance you. You have forgotten the circumstances which, through my kindness to you, you were able to leave behind—though heaven knows you deserve to grow old in them, since you find adversity easier to cope with than prosperity. **2.23** Look! Men who a short while ago were tribute-paying subjects of Illyria and Persia are now turning up their noses at Asia and at the spoils from all its nations! For men who recently went half-naked under Philip, purple robes are not good enough! They cannot stand the sight of silver and gold, and long instead for their old wooden bowls, their wickerwork shields, their rusty swords! **2.24** This was the smart equipment you had when I took you on, together with a debt of 500 talents, when the entire royal assets were no more than sixty talents—such was the basis for the great achievements to come, the basis on which I nonetheless established, if I may be forgiven for saying so, an empire comprising most of the world! **2.25** Are you sick of Asia, where your glorious achievements have made you the equals of the gods? You hasten to desert your king and go into Europe, though most of you would not have had the money for the trip if I had not discharged your debts— with plunder from Asia, of course! **2.26** And you feel no shame at carrying around the spoils of conquered nations in your deep bellies and nevertheless wishing to return to your wives and children, though few of you can display to them the prizes of victory! The rest of you have pawned even your weapons on your way to fulfilling your hopes!

**2.27** 'Yes, fine soldiers I shall lose—soldiers who are concubines to their own bed-wenches (that is all you have left of your great riches, and on them you spend money!). So those who are leaving me—let the roads be open for them! Get away from here quickly. Along with the Persians I shall cover your rear as you go. I am keeping no one back. Get out of my sight, you most ungrateful of citizens. **2.28** Happily will your parents and children welcome you when you return without your king: out they shall come to meet the deserters and runaways! **2.29** Yes, I shall triumph over your desertion of me and make you pay for it wherever I am, bestowing honour and preference upon those whom you leave behind with me. Apart from that, you will soon know how strong an army is without its king, and also what power I have on my own.'

**2.30** Furious, he leaped down from the dais and plunged into the midst of the armed men. He had taken note of those who had been most outspoken, and these he seized one by one. They dared not offer resistance, and Alexander handed thirteen of them over to his bodyguard to be kept in custody.

3

3.1 Who would have believed that a mass meeting fiercely hostile moments before could be paralysed with sudden panic 3.2 at the sight of men being dragged off for punishment whose actions had been no worse than the others? 3.3 They were terror-stricken, whether from deep respect for the royal name (because people living under a monarchy regard kings as gods), or from respect for Alexander personally; or perhaps it was because of the confidence with which he so forcefully exerted his authority. 3.4 At all events they were the very model of submissiveness: when, towards evening, they learned of their comrades' execution, so far from being infuriated at the punishment, they did everything to express individually their increased loyalty and devotion. 3.5 For when the next day they were denied an audience with Alexander, who admitted only his Asiatic soldiers, they filled the entire camp with lugubrious cries, claiming they would die on the spot if the king persisted in his anger. 3.6 Alexander, however, who was always determined to carry his plans through to the end, ordered the foreign troops to be mustered, with the Macedonians confined to their camp. When the foreign soldiers had assembled in large numbers, he had an interpreter called and gave the following address:

3.7 'When I was crossing from Europe to Asia, I hoped to annex to my empire many famous peoples and large numbers of men. I was not wrong in believing the reports I had heard of these men. 3.8 But there is more than that: I am looking upon soldiers who are courageous and unfailing in their loyalty to their kings. 3.9 I had believed everything here to be swamped in luxury and, through excessive prosperity, submerged in self-indulgence. But, by Hercules, your moral and physical strength makes you just as energetic as anyone in the performance of your military duties; and yet, brave men though you are, your dedication to loyalty is no less than your dedication to courage. 3.10 I make this statement now for the first time, but I have long known it to be true. For that reason I have made a selection of younger soldiers from among you and have integrated you into the main body of my troops. You have the same uniform and the same weapons. Your obedience, however, and your readiness to follow orders far surpass everybody else's.

**3.11** 'That is why I married the daughter of the Persian Oxyartes, feeling no hesitation about producing children from a captive. **3.12** Later on, when I wished to extend my bloodline further, I took Darius' daughter as a wife and set the pattern for my closest friends to produce children by our captives, my intention being that by this sacred union I might erase all distinction between conquered and conqueror. **3.13** So you can believe that you are my soldiers by family, not conscription. Asia and Europe are now one and the same kingdom. I give you Macedonian arms. Foreign newcomers though you are, I have made you established members of my force: you are both my fellow-citizens and my soldiers. **3.14** Everything is taking on the same hue: it is no disgrace for the Persians to copy Macedonian customs, nor for the Macedonians to imitate the Persians. Those who are to live under the same king should enjoy the same rights.'.... [The text breaks off at this point.]

4

**4.1** 'How long are you going to indulge in this self-gratification,' he asked, 'with such executions, and executions of a foreign kind at that? Your own men, your own citizens, are being dragged off to punishment without trial—led off by their own captives! If you judge that they have deserved death, at least change the executioners.'

**4.2** The advice he was given was well-intentioned, had Alexander only been able to take the truth! Instead his anger had risen to frenzy. He repeated the command, since those previously ordered had momentarily hesitated: the prisoners were to be hurled into the river, still in their bonds. **4.3** Not even this punishment could goad the men to mutiny. Instead, they came in companies to the officers and Alexander's friends with the request that he order the execution of any he decided were tainted by association with the former crime.

They offered up their persons to his anger, urging him to slaughter them ... [Another gap in the text is marked.]

5

5.1 Tears welled up as they looked at him, and they appeared not as an army visiting its king but one attending his funeral. 5.2 The grief was especially intense among those at his bedside. Alexander looked at them and said: 'After my death will you find a king worthy of such men?'

5.3 It's incredible to tell and hear, but he maintained the same posture which he had adopted before admitting the men until he had received the last salute from the whole army. He then dismissed the rank and file and, as though released from all life's obligations, collapsed in exhaustion. 5.4 He bade his friends draw near since, by now, even his voice had started to fail, and then took his ring from his finger and handed it to Perdiccas. He also gave instructions that they should have his body transported to Hammon. 5.5 When they asked him to whom he bequeathed his kingdom, he answered, 'To the best man', but added that he could already foresee great funeral games for himself provided by that issue. 5.6 When Perdiccas further asked when he wished divine honours paid to him, he said he wanted them when they themselves were enjoying good fortune. These were Alexander's last words; he died moments later.

5.7 At first the sounds of lamentation, weeping and the beating of breasts echoed throughout the royal quarters. Then a sad hush fell, enveloping all in a still silence like that of desert wastes, as they turned from grief to considering what would happen now. 5.8 The young noblemen who formed his customary bodyguard could neither suppress their bitter anguish nor confine themselves to the vestibule of the royal quarters. They wandered around like madmen, filling such a large city with the sound of their mournful grieving, forgoing no kind of lament that sorrow suggests in such circumstances. 5.9 Accordingly, those who had been standing outside the royal quarters rushed to the spot, barbarians and Macedonians alike, and in the general grief conqueror and conquered were indistinguishable.

The Persians recalled a master of great justice and clemency, the Macedonians a peerless king of outstanding valour; together they indulged in a kind of contest in mourning.

5.10 Expressions of indignation as well as grief could be heard—indignation that, through the envy of the gods, a man of such vigour had been removed from the world when he was in the bloom of his young life and fortune. They pictured for themselves his energy and his expression as he led the men into battle, laid siege to cities, scaled walls, or made presentations for gallantry before the assembled army. 5.11 The Macedonians then regretted having refused him divine honours, and admitted they had been disloyal and ungrateful in robbing him of a title his ears should have heard. And then, after long declaring their veneration for their king and bemoaning his loss, their pity focused on themselves. 5.12 They had passed from Macedonia beyond the Euphrates, and they could see that they were cut off among enemies who balked at the new regime. Lacking a definite heir to Alexander and to his throne, they saw that individuals would try to appropriate to themselves their collective power. 5.13 Then they had premonitions of the civil wars which actually followed: once more they would be obliged to shed their blood not to win dominion over Asia but to have a king. Their old scars must burst under fresh wounds. 5.14 Ageing and weak, having recently requested a discharge from their legitimate king, they would now face death to win power for someone who might be an obscure henchman!

5.15 While such considerations occupied their minds, night came on to increase their terror. The soldiers kept watch under arms, and the Babylonians maintained a lookout from their walls or from the roofs of their own houses, in the expectation of gaining clearer information. 5.16 No one dared to light lamps, and then, since they were unable to use their eyes, their ears strained after noises and voices. Often they would be gripped by irrational fear and go rushing along dark alleyways, suspected and worried in turn as they ran into each other.

5.17 The Persians had their hair shorn in traditional fashion and wore garments of mourning. Together with their wives and children they grieved with genuine feelings of regret, not for a man who had recently been their conqueror and enemy, but for one who had been a superlatively just king over their nation. They were people accustomed to living under monarchy, and they admitted they had never had a worthier ruler. 5.18 Nor was grief confined to the area within the city walls; tidings of the great tragedy had spread to the neighbouring countryside and then to most of Asia this side of the Euphrates. 5.19 They quickly reached Darius' mother too. She ripped off the clothes she wore and assumed the dress of mourning; she tore her hair and flung herself to the ground. 5.20 Next to her sat one of her two granddaughters who was in mourning after the recent loss of her husband, Hephaestion, and the general anguish reminded her of her personal grief. 5.21 But Sisigambis alone felt the woes that engulfed her entire family: she wept for her own plight and that of her granddaughters. The fresh pain had also reminded her of the past. One might have thought that Darius was recently lost and that at the same time the poor woman had to bury two sons. She wept simultaneously for the living and the dead. 5.22 Who would look after her girls, she wondered? Who would be another Alexander? This meant a second captivity, a second loss of royal status. On the death of Darius they had found a protector, but after Alexander they would certainly not find someone to guard their interests.

5.23 Amid such reflections, Sisigambis was reminded of how her eighty brothers had all been butchered on the one day by the most barbarous of kings, Ochus, and how the slaughter of so many sons was augmented by that of their father; of how only one child remained of the seven she had borne, and how even Darius' prosperity had been short-lived and served only to make his death more cruel. 5.24 Finally, she surrendered to her sorrow. She covered her head, turned away from her granddaughter and grandson, who fell at her knees to plead with her, and withdrew simultaneously from nourishment and the daylight. Five days after deciding on death, she expired. 5.25 Her end provides firm evidence for Alexander's gentle treatment of her and his fairness towards all the captives: though she could bear to live on after Darius, she was ashamed to survive Alexander.

5.26 To be sure, it is obvious to anyone who makes a fair assessment of the king that his strengths were attributable to his nature and his weaknesses to fortune or his youth. [The following were surely all natural qualities:] 5.27 incredible mental energy and an almost excessive tolerance of fatigue; courage exemplary not just in comparison with kings but even with men possessing this virtue and no other; 5.28 generosity such that he often granted greater gifts than even the gods are asked for; clemency towards the defeated (returning so many kingdoms to men from whom he had taken them, or giving them as gifts); 5.29 continuous disregard for death, which frightens others out of their minds; a burning desire for glory and fame reaching a degree which exceeded due proportion but was yet pardonable in view of his youth and great achievements. 5.30 Then there was his devotion to his parents (he had taken the decision to deify Olympias and he had avenged Philip); 5.31 then, too, his kindness towards almost all his friends, goodwill towards the men, powers of discernment equalling his magnanimity and an ingenuity barely possible at his age; 5.32 control over immoderate urges; a sex-life limited to the fulfilment of natural desire; and indulgence only in pleasures which were socially sanctioned. These were all surely gifts of his own nature.

5.33 The following are attributable to fortune: putting himself on a par with the gods and assuming divine honours; giving credence to oracles which recommended such conduct and reacting with excessive anger to any who refused to worship him; assuming foreign dress and aping the customs of defeated races for whom he had had only contempt before his victory. 5.34 But as far as his explosive temperament and fondness for drink were concerned, these had been quickened by youth and could as easily have been tempered by increasing age. 5.35 However, it must be admitted that, much though he owed to his own virtues, he owed more to Fortune, which he alone in the entire world had under his control. How often she rescued him from death! How often did she shield him with unbroken good fortune when he had recklessly ridden into danger! 5.36 She also decided that his life and his glory should have the same end. The fates waited for him to complete the subjection of the East and reach the Ocean, achieving everything of which a mortal was capable.

5.37 Such was the king and leader for whom a successor was now sought, but the burden was too great to be shouldered by one man. So it was that his reputation and the fame of his achievements distributed kings and kingdoms almost throughout the world, with those who clung on even to the tiniest fraction of his enormous estate being regarded as men of great distinction.

6

**6.1** Now at Babylon, which is where I began my digression, Alexander's bodyguards summoned his principal friends and the army officers to the royal quarters. These were followed by a crowd of the rank and file, all anxious to know to whom Alexander's estate would pass. **6.2** Many officers were unable to enter the royal quarters because they were prevented by the milling crowds of soldiers, and this despite a herald's announcement forbidding access to all except those called by name—but this order, having no authority, was ignored. **6.3** At first loud weeping and wailing broke out afresh, but then their tears stopped and silence fell as they wondered what was going to happen now.

**6.4** At this point Perdiccas presented the royal throne in full view of the assembly. On this lay Alexander's diadem, robe, and arms, and Perdiccas set upon it the ring the king had given him the previous day. The sight of these objects once more brought tears to the eyes of all and rekindled their grief. **6.5** 'For my part,' said Perdiccas, 'I return to you the ring handed to me by Alexander, the seal of which he would use on documents as symbol of his royal and imperial authority. **6.6** The anger of the gods can devise no tragedy to equal this with which we have been afflicted; and yet, considering the greatness of Alexander's achievements, one could believe that such a great man was merely on loan from the gods to the world so that, when his duty to it was complete, they might swiftly reclaim him for their family. **6.7** Accordingly, since nothing remains of him apart from the material which is excluded from immortality, let us perform the due ceremonies to his corpse and his name as soon as possible, bearing in mind the city we are in, the people we are among and the qualities of the leader and king of whom we have been deprived.

**6.8** 'Fellow soldiers, we must discuss and consider how we can maintain the victory we have won among the people over whom we have won it. We need a leader: whether it should be one man or more is up to you. But you must realize this: a mass of soldiers without a chief is a body without a soul. **6.9** This is the sixth month of Roxane's pregnancy. We pray that she produces a male who, with the gods' approval, will assume the throne when he comes of age. Meanwhile, decide how many leaders you want and who they should be.' So spoke Perdiccas.

**6.10** Nearchus then said that, while nobody could express surprise that only Alexander's blood-line was truly appropriate for the dignity of the throne, **6.11** to wait for a king not yet born and pass over one already alive suited neither the inclinations of the Macedonians nor their critical situation. The king already had a son by Barsine, he said, and he should be given the crown. **6.12** Nobody liked Nearchus' suggestion. They repeatedly signalled their opposition in traditional fashion by beating their shields with their spears and, as Nearchus pressed his idea with greater insistence, they came close to rioting. **6.13** Then Ptolemy spoke. 'Yes, a son of Roxane or Barsine really is a fitting ruler for the Macedonian people! Even to utter his name will be offensive for Europe, since he will be mostly a captive. **6.14** Is that what defeating the Persians will have meant for us—being slaves to their descendants? Their legitimate kings, Darius and Xerxes, failed to achieve that with all their thousands of troops and their huge fleets! **6.15** This is what I think. Alexander's throne should be set in the royal quarters and those who used to be consulted by him should meet there whenever a decision affecting the common good has to be made. A majority decision should stand, and these men should be obeyed by the generals and officers.' **6.16** Some agreed with Ptolemy, fewer with Perdiccas.

Then Aristonus rose to speak. When Alexander was asked to whom he was leaving his kingdom, said Aristonus, he had expressed the wish that the best man be chosen, and yet he had himself adjudged Perdiccas to be the best by handing him the ring. **6.17** For Perdiccas was not the only person who had been sitting at the king's deathbed, he continued—Alexander had looked around and selected the man to give the ring to from the crowd of his friends. It followed that he wished supreme power to pass to Perdiccas. **6.18** The assembly had no doubt that Aristonus' opinion was correct; everyone called for Perdiccas to step forward and pick up the king's ring. Perdiccas wavered between a burning desire to take it and a sense of decency, and he thought that the more diffident he was in seeking what he expected to be his the more insistently they would press it upon him. **6.19** So he hesitated, and for a long time was uncertain how to act, until finally he went back and stood behind those who had been sitting next to him.

6.20 Encouraged and reassured by Perdiccas' hesitation, Meleager, one of the generals, now said: 'May the gods forbid that Alexander's fortune and the supreme rank of such a great kingdom should end up on such shoulders! The men certainly will not tolerate it. I am not talking about those of better birth than this fellow, merely about men who do not have to suffer anything against their will. 6.21 In fact, it makes no difference whether your king be Roxane's son (whenever he is born) or Perdiccas, since that fellow is going to seize the throne anyway by pretending to act as regent. That is why the only king he favours is one not yet born, and in the general haste to resolve matters—a haste which is as necessary as it is understandable—he alone is waiting for the months to elapse, already predicting that a male has been conceived! Could you doubt that he is ready to find a substitute? 6.22 God in Heaven, if Alexander had left us this fellow as king in his stead, my opinion would be that this is the one order of his that should not be obeyed. 6.23 Well, why *not* run off and loot the treasure chests? For surely it is the people who are heirs to these riches of the king.' 6.24 So saying he burst through the soldiers, and the men who had made way for him as he left proceeded to follow him to the plunder they had been promised.

7

7.1 By now there was a dense crowd of soldiers around Meleager as the meeting had degenerated into a mutinous uproar. Then a man of the lowest class, who was unknown to most of the Macedonians, spoke as follows: 7.2 'What's the point of fighting and starting a civil war when you have the king you seek? You are forgetting Philip's son, Arrhidaeus, brother of our late king Alexander: recently he accompanied the king in performing sacrifices and ceremonies, and now he is his sole heir. How has he deserved this? What act of his justifies that he be stripped even of this universally recognized right? If you are looking for someone just like Alexander, you'll never find him; if you want his next of kin, there is only this man.' 7.3 On hearing this, the gathering fell silent, as if at an order. Then they shouted in unison that Arrhidaeus should be summoned and that the men who had held the meeting without him deserved to die.

7.4 Then Pithon began to speak through his tears. This was when Alexander was most to be pitied, he said, for he had been cheated out of the enjoyment and support of such good citizens and soldiers, men who in thinking only of their king's glorious name and memory were blind to all other considerations. 7.5 He was obviously attacking the young man who was being assigned the throne, but his derogatory remarks generated more animosity against himself than disdain for Arrhidaeus, because as the men felt sorry for the latter they also began to favour him. 7.6 Accordingly, with persistent cheers, they declared that the only man they would entertain as king was the one born to the expectation of that position, and they ordered that Arrhidaeus be summoned. 7.7 Out of antagonism and hatred for Perdiccas, Meleager promptly brought him into the royal quarters, and the men saluted him as king under the name 'Philip'.

7.8 This was the voice of the rank and file, but the prominent men felt differently. Pithon began to follow Perdiccas' strategy, designating Perdiccas and Leonnatus, both of royal birth, as guardians for Roxane's future son. 7.9 He subjoined that Craterus and Antipater should direct affairs in Europe. Then an oath of allegiance to the king born of Alexander was exacted from each of them. 7.10 Meleager, who, with good cause, was frightened of being punished, had withdrawn with his men. Now he once more came storming into the royal quarters, dragging Philip with him and shouting that Philip's robust youth justified the hopes they had as a body conceived in their new king just a little earlier. They should give Philip's offspring a chance, he declared, for he was son and brother in respect of two kings, and their own judgement should count for more than anything.

7.11 No deep sea, no vast and stormy body of water produces waves as violent as the emotions of a mob, particularly in the first flush of a freedom that is to be short-lived. 7.12 A few wished to confer supreme command on Perdiccas, whom they had recently chosen, but more were for Philip whom they had overlooked. But neither their support nor their opposition in respect of anything could last long and, regretting their decision one moment, they regretted their regret the next. Finally, however, their favour inclined towards royal stock. 7.13 Arrhidaeus had left the meeting, cowed by the authority wielded by the generals and, with his departure, his support among the common soldiers was hushed rather than weakened. So he was called back and he donned his brother's robe, the one which had been set on the throne. 7.14 Meleager put on a cuirass and took up his arms to act as the new king's escort. He was followed by the phalanx, the men beating on their shields with their spears and ready to glut themselves with the blood of those who had aspired to a throne to which they had no claim. 7.15 They were pleased that the strength of the empire would remain in the same house with the same family, and they thought a ruler of royal blood would defend the power he inherited. They were used to showing respect and veneration for the royal name, they reasoned, and this was assumed only by a man born into royal power.

7.16 In terror, Perdiccas ordered the chamber in which Alexander's body lay to be locked. With him were 600 men of proven valour, and he had also been joined by Ptolemy and the company of the Royal Pages. 7.17 But for soldiers numbering many thousands it was not difficult to break the locks. The king had also burst in, a crowd of attendants led by Meleager packed around him. 7.18 In a rage, Perdiccas called aside any who wished to protect Alexander's corpse, but the men who had broken into the room proceeded to hurl javelins at him, keeping their distance. Eventually, after many had been wounded, the older soldiers removed their helmets so that they could be more easily recognized and began to beg the men with Perdiccas to stop fighting and to surrender to the king and his superior numbers. 7.19 Perdiccas was the first to lay down his arms, and the others followed. Meleager then urged them not to leave Alexander's body, but they thought he was looking for a way to trap them, so they slipped away through another part of the royal quarters and fled towards the Euphrates. 7.20 The cavalry, composed of young men from the best families, went with Perdiccas and Leonnatus in large numbers, and these were in favour of leaving the city and pitching camp in the plains. 7.21 Perdiccas, however, had no hope that the infantry would also follow him, and so he remained in the city in order not to seem to have broken away from the main body of the army by pulling out the cavalry.

8

**8.1** But Meleager kept on warning the king that his claim to the throne should be strengthened by Perdiccas' death and that, if the latter's undisciplined spirit was not crushed, he would bring off a coup. Perdiccas well remembered how he had treated the king, he said, and no one could give true allegiance to someone he feared. **8.2** There was acquiescence rather than positive approval on the king's part, so Meleager interpreted his silence as an order and sent men to summon Perdiccas in the king's name, instructing them to kill him if he hesitated to come. **8.3** When Perdiccas was informed that the attendants had come, he stood at the threshold of his quarters, a total of sixteen Pages from the royal retinue with him. He berated the messengers, time and again calling them 'Meleager's lackeys', and the determination which showed in his expression so terrified them that they fled in panic. **8.4** Perdiccas told the Pages to mount their horses and came with a few friends to Leonnatus so that he could resist any violence offered him with a stronger force.

**8.5** The next day the Macedonians thought it deplorable that Perdiccas' life had been endangered, and they decided that Meleager's reckless behaviour would be punished by force of arms. **8.6** Meleager, however, saw a revolt coming . . . [a *lacuna* in the text is assumed] he went to the king and proceeded to ask him if he had himself given the order for Perdiccas' arrest. The king answered that, yes, he had given the order, at Meleager's prompting—but the uproar among the men was uncalled for since Perdiccas was still alive. **8.7** When the meeting had been dispersed, Meleager was terrified, especially in view of the secession of the cavalry, and he was at a loss what to do, having fallen into the very danger he had shortly before been planning for his enemy. He spent some three days brooding over plans which he kept changing.

**8.8** In fact, the royal quarters still looked as they had before: national ambassadors had audiences with the king, generals presented themselves and the vestibule was crowded with attendants and soldiers. **8.9** But a deep, spontaneous melancholy betokened their sheer desperation. Mutually suspicious, they did not dare to approach or converse with each other; they kept their thoughts to themselves and the comparisons they made between their new king and the old aroused their longing for the one they had lost. 8.10 Where, they would ask, was the man whose authority and whose auspices they had followed? They had been left behind, they would say, among hostile and fierce tribes who would seize the earliest opportunity to avenge all their past defeats. 8.11 While such reflections were preying on their minds, news arrived that the cavalry led by Perdiccas had taken control of the plains around Babylon and had blocked the transport of grain to the city. 8.12 As a result, there were food shortages at first, then outright famine, and the troops in the city began to think they should either reach an accord with Perdiccas or decide the issue in battle.

8.13 It transpired that the people in the countryside were seeking refuge in the city, fearing that their farms and villages would be plundered, while the townspeople, running out of provisions, were leaving the city—each group believing the other's situation safer than their own. 8.14 Fearing a riot among these, the Macedonians met in the royal quarters and expressed their various opinions. They decided that a deputation should be dispatched to the cavalry to discuss ending the disagreement and laying down their arms. 8.15 The Thessalian Pasas, Amissus the Megalopolitan, and Perilaus were accordingly sent by the king. They delivered the messages given to them by him, and returned with the reply that the cavalry would lay down their arms only if the king put in their hands those responsible for the rift.

8.16 When this message was brought back, the soldiers took up arms on their own initiative, and the uproar brought Philip from the royal quarters. 'This disturbance is unnecessary,' he said. 'Those who stay calm will take the prizes from those who fight each other. 8.17 Remember, too, that you are dealing with your fellow-citizens and that to deprive them abruptly of any hope of reconciliation is to rush into civil war. 8.18 Let us see if they can be appeased by a second deputation. In fact, since the king's body is still unburied, I think everyone will come together for his funeral. 8.19 Personally, I should prefer to relinquish this power rather than shed the blood of citizens while exercising it, and, if there is no other hope of achieving an agreement, I beg and entreat you to choose a better man than me.'

**8.20** Tears welling up in his eyes, he removed the crown from his head, holding it out in his right hand for anyone claiming to deserve it more to take. **8.21** Such a restrained address excited high hopes for his character, which until that day had been eclipsed by his brother's fame. So all began to insist that he act on his plan. **8.22** Arrhidaeus sent the same men back to ask now that they accept Meleager as a third general, a request which was readily granted, since Perdiccas wished to isolate Meleager from the king and felt that, on his own, Meleager would be no match for the two of them. **8.23** So, when Meleager and the phalanx came out to the rendezvous, Perdiccas went forward to meet him at the head of his cavalry squadrons. The two forces greeted each other and united, with harmony and peace now strengthened between them for ever, so they thought.

9

**9.1** But destiny was already bringing civil wars upon the Macedonian nation: for a throne is not to be shared, and several men were aspiring to it. **9.2** Thus their forces first came into conflict, then split up and, when they burdened the body with more heads than it could support, the limbs started to weaken, and an empire that might have stood firm under a single man collapsed while it rested on the shoulders of a number. **9.3** So it is with justification that the people of Rome acknowledge that they owe their salvation to their emperor, who shone out as a new star in the night that was almost our last. **9.4** It was his rising, I declare, and not the sun's, that brought light back to a darkened world at a time when its limbs lacked their head, and were out of harmony and in turmoil. **9.5** How many were the torches he then extinguished! How many the swords he sheathed! How violent the storm he scattered, suddenly clearing the skies! So our empire is not merely recovering, but even flourishes. **9.6** May I not tempt providence, but the line of this same house will prolong the conditions of this age—for ever, I pray, but at least for a long duration.

**9.7** But let me return to the narrative from which my reflections on our national prosperity diverted me. Perdiccas rested his only hope of survival on Meleager's death, believing that the latter's vanity and unreliability, his readiness to attempt a coup and his bitter enmity to himself, all called for a pre-emptive strike against him. **9.8** But with deep dissimulation he well concealed his plan so as to catch Meleager off his guard. He covertly induced individuals among the troops under his command to complain publicly (while he gave the impression of knowing nothing of it himself) that Meleager had been made Perdiccas' equal. **9.9** When their comments were reported to him, Meleager was furious, and told Perdiccas what he had learned. Perdiccas, appearing alarmed at this unexpected turn, began to express astonishment and displeasure and to put on a show of distress. Finally, they agreed that the men responsible for such mutinous talk should be arrested. **9.10** Meleager thanked Perdiccas and embraced him, commending him for his loyalty to him and his goodwill. **9.11** They then discussed the matter and devised a way to take out the guilty. They decided there should be a traditional purification ceremony for the army, and their former dissension provided a plausible reason for this. **9.12** The customary purification of the soldiers by the Macedonian kings involved cutting a bitch in two and throwing down her entrails on the left and right at the far end of the plain into which the army was to be led. Then all the soldiers would stand within that area, cavalry on one side, phalanx on the other.

**9.13** On the day they had set aside for this ceremony the king had positioned himself, along with his cavalry and elephants, opposite the infantry commanded by Meleager. **9.14** When the cavalry column was already on the move, the infantry suddenly panicked in the expectation of some offensive tactic, in view of the recent discord, and for a while they were in two minds about withdrawing into the city, the flat ground being favourable to the cavalry. **9.15** Fearing that they might be prematurely impugning their comrades' good faith, however, they held back, ready to fight if put under attack.

By now the columns were coming together and only a small space separated the two lines. **9.16** The king began to ride towards the infantry with a single squadron and, at Perdiccas' urging, he demanded for execution the instigators of the discord, although he had a personal obligation to protect them, and he threatened to attack them with all his squadrons plus his elephants if they refused. **9.17** The infantry were stunned by this unforeseen blow, and

Meleager lacked ideas and courage as much as they did. The safest course in the circumstances seemed to be to await their fate rather than provoke it. **9.18** Perdiccas saw that they were paralysed and at his mercy. He picked out from the main body some 300 men who had followed Meleager at the time when he burst from the first meeting held after Alexander's death, and before the eyes of the entire army he threw them to the elephants. All were trampled to death beneath the feet of the beasts, and Philip neither stopped it nor sanctioned it. **9.19** It seemed that he would claim as his own only those designs of which the outcome demonstrated their soundness.

This proved to be both an omen and the commencement of civil wars for the Macedonians. **9.20** Meleager, who all too late saw the treachery of Perdiccas, remained passive in the column on that occasion because he was not himself the target of violence. **9.21** Presently, however, he abandoned all hope of safety when he perceived that it was the name of the man he had himself made king that his enemies were using to engineer his destruction. He sought refuge in a temple where, failing to gain protection even from the sanctity of the place, he was murdered.


10


**10.1** Perdiccas led the army into the city and convened a meeting of the leading Macedonians. It was there decided that the empire should be apportioned as follows. The king would hold supreme power, with Ptolemy becoming satrap of Egypt and of the African peoples subject to Macedon. **10.2** Laomedon was given Syria and Phoenicia; Philotas was assigned Cilicia; Antigonus was instructed to take charge of Lycia, Pamphylia, and Greater Phrygia; Cassander was sent to Caria, and Menander to Lydia. Lesser Phrygia, which is adjacent to the Hellespont, they designated as the province of Leonnatus. **10.3** Cappadocia and Paphlagonia fell to Eumenes, who was charged with defending that region as far as Trapezus and with conducting hostilities against Ariarathes, the only chieftain refusing allegiance to Macedon. **10.4** Pithon was ordered to take command of Media; Lysimachus of Thrace and the Pontic tribes adjoining it. It was decided that the governors of India, the Bactrians and Sogdians and the other peoples living by the Ocean or the Red Sea should all retain command of their respective territories. Perdiccas was to remain with the king and command the troops following him.

10.5 Some have believed that the distribution of the provinces was prescribed by Alexander's will, but I have ascertained that this report, though transmitted by our sources, is without foundation. 10.6 In fact, whatever possessions each held after the division of the empire, he would have firmly established as his own dominion—if a boundary could ever stand in the way of unbridled ambition. 10.7 For men who recently had been subjects of the king had individually seized control of huge kingdoms, ostensibly as administrators of an empire belonging to another, and any pretext for conflict was removed since they all belonged to the same race and were geographically separated from each other by the boundaries of their several jurisdictions. 10.8 But it was difficult to remain satisfied with what the opportunity of the moment had brought them: initial possessions are disdained when there is hope of greater things. So they all thought that expanding their kingdoms was an easier matter than taking possession of them had been in the first place.

10.9 It was now the seventh day that the king's body had been lying in the coffin while everybody's attention had been diverted from the obsequies to forming a government. 10.10 Nowhere are more searing temperatures to be found than in the area of Mesopotamia, where they are such as to cause the deaths of many animals caught on open ground—so intense is the heat of the sun and the atmosphere, which bakes everything like a fire. 10.11 Springs are infrequent and are craftily concealed by the natives who keep them for their own use, while strangers are kept ignorant of them. 10.12 What I report now is the traditional account rather than what I believe myself: when Alexander's friends eventually found time to attend to his corpse, the men who had entered the quarters saw that no decay had set into it and that there was not even the slightest discoloration. The vital look that comes from the breath of life had not yet vanished from his face. 10.13 So it was that, after being instructed to see to the body in their traditional fashion, the Egyptians and Chaldeans did not dare touch him at first since he seemed to be alive. Then, praying that it be lawful in the eyes of god and man for humans to touch a god, they cleaned out the body. A golden sarcophagus was filled with perfumes, and on Alexander's head was placed the insignia of his rank.

10.14 Many believed his death was due to poison, administered to him by a son of Antipater called Iollas, one of Alexander's attendants. It is true that Alexander had often been heard to remark that Antipater had regal aspirations, that his powers exceeded those of a general, that he was conceited after his famous Spartan victory and that he claimed as his due all the things that Alexander had granted him. 10.15 There was also a belief current that Craterus had been sent with a group of veterans to murder Antipater. 10.16 Now it is well known that the power of the poison produced in Macedonia is such as to consume even iron, and that only an ass's hoof is resistant to the fluid. 10.17 (They give the name 'Styx' to the source from which this deadly venom comes.) This, it was believed, was brought by Cassander, passed on his brother Iollas, and by him slipped into the king's final drink. 10.18 Whatever credence such stories gained, they were soon scotched by the power of the people defamed by the gossip. For Antipater usurped the rule of Macedon and of Greece as well, 10.19 and he was succeeded by his son, after the murder of all who were even distantly related to Alexander.

10.20 Alexander's body was taken to Memphis by Ptolemy, into whose power Egypt had fallen, and transferred from there a few years later to Alexandria, where every mark of respect continues to be paid to his memory and his name.

# Commentary

## BOOK 10

**1. 1–9.** *Alexander executes satrapal officials accused of abuse of power and disloyalty*

*Sources*: D.S. 17. 106. 2; J. 12. 10. 8; A. 6. 27. 3–5, who does not mention Agathon and does not recall the role of Cleander and Sitalces in the killing of Parmenion; Plut. *Alex.* 68. 3.

*Bibliography*: Hamilton (1973), 128–30. Badian (1961) presents these events as part of a 'reign of terror', which began after Alexander emerged from the disastrous march through the Gedrosian desert. Higgins (1980) argues that Badian goes beyond the evidence. Bosworth (1988a), 146–8 and 241. Bosworth (1996a), 23–4 takes the story of Apollodorus, who survived the purge (A. 7. 18. 1–3), as adding to the picture of 'a court in terror'.

Curtius uses the book division to switch from Alexander's cruelty (*crudelitas*) to Persians, exemplified by the execution of the Persian, Astaspes (9. 10. 29–30), to his actions against officers charged with various offences. Curtius here emphasizes juridical terminology. This opening scene establishes the dominant theme of the book, which is Macedonian politics.

**1. 1. at about this time.** Curtius resumes the narrative with Alexander still in Carmania (A. 6. 27. 3), thus somewhere between Bampur (west of Iran Shahr) and Kahnu (see on 1. 10–15), and this would have been mid-winter 325/4 BC, and not before late December 325 (Brunt (1983), 500).

Cleander, Sitalces, Heracon and Agathon, the men who had assassinated Parmenion. In late 330 Parmenion's son, Philotas, the commander of the Companion Cavalry, was executed for failing to pass
on information of a conspiracy that was being hatched against
Alexander. Curtius deals with that drama at length in 6. 7–11
(Atkinson (1994), 212–46). Whether or not the 'conspiracy' was
contrived to entrap Philotas, as Badian (1960), 330–1 famously
suggested, the sources make it clear that Alexander was keen to be
rid of Philotas. Badian (2000a), 64–9 now expresses willingness to
accept that there may indeed have been a conspiracy, but argues
forcefully that a plot against Philotas was initiated by Craterus in
Egypt and taken up by Alexander, as Plut. *Alex.* 48. 4–49. 1 attests.
With the removal of Philotas accomplished, Alexander went for his
prime target, sending Polydamas to Ecbatana with secret orders to
Cleander and other senior officers in Media to kill Parmenion,
Alexander's 'chief of staff' (C.R. 7. 2. 19 ff.). A. 3. 26. 3 differs from
Curtius in naming these officers serving under Parmenion as Clean-
der, Sitalces, and Menidas. Heracon may have taken over Menidas'
position when the latter was sent off to Macedon to collect reinforce-
ments (A. 4. 18. 4), and when Heracon transferred to Susiana
(A. 6. 27. 5), Agathon may have replaced him in Media.

For Cleander see on 1. 5–7. Sitalces was possibly the son of the
Odrysian king Cersobleptes (Heckel (2006), 251; see on 1. 45),
and originally served Alexander as the commander of the Thracian
javelineers (A. 1. 28. 4). Agathon, son of Tyrimmas, was probably
Macedonian (Berve ii. no. 8), but served as the commander of the
Thracian cavalry (A. 1. 14. 3 and 3. 12. 4; Heckel (2006), 7). Heracon
may have started as a commander of mercenaries (Heckel (2006),
138).

1. 2. there also came from the province . . . men who brought charges
against them. Both troops and satrapal natives laid charges against
the four officers (cf. A. 6. 27. 4), but it is improbable that Cleander
and his fellow officers led their troops to Carmania in the expectation
that they faced trial and execution (cf. Bosworth (1988a), 147).

services in the matter of the assassination. The Latin phrase, *caedis
ministerium*, is developed in 1. 6 as *irae ministros* (instruments of that
wrath), and the first seems to be an intentional echo of Livy 45. 31. 2

(cf. 42. 15. 3). Another, probably conscious, Livian echo in this passage is the uncommon word he uses for raped in 1. 5, *constupra-tam*: cf. Livy 29. 17. 15, which precedes a hostile description of Scipio Africanus, a Roman Alexander (on which concept see Spencer (2002), though Spencer focuses on the generally favourable image of Scipio, when he was compared with Alexander).

**1. 3. they had not even refrained from what was sacred.** Cleander and Sitalces were found guilty of plundering temples and vandalizing tombs in Media, and Heracon was judged guilty of plundering 'the temple' in Susa (A. 6. 27. 4–5). There was a tradition that Parmenion tore down temples to Jason (J. 42. 3. 5). The reference to Jason probably arose from a Greek-speaker turning the Median word for temples, *Āyazanas, into Iasonia (Shahbazi (2003), 26–7, attributing the idea to J. Markwart). It is possible that this negative reference to Parmenion comes from a tradition counter to that which blackened the names of Parmenion's killers. Hence I would suggest that Justin derived his hostile reference to Parmenion from Timagenes, while Curtius here is closer to Trogus' version.

**1. 4. made the barbarians abhor the Macedonian name.** In Persia, if not Media, there was indeed a rebellion against Macedonian rule: Curtius 9. 10. 19; A. 6. 26. 3. But there is also an ironic level of meaning in the way Curtius expresses himself: Alexander was worried about what barbarians thought of the Macedonians. For the contrast, Livy relates how Pleminius' outrageous behaviour against Locrians raised concern in Rome because the Locrians were 'friends and allies' (Livy 29. 19. 7, a technical formula in Roman diplomacy). Curtius could have avoided the stark juxtaposition of the labels Macedonian and barbarian, but clearly chose this antithesis to fore-shadow the following scenes in which Macedonians complain about his discrimination in favour of Persians.

**1. 5–7.** *The removal of Cleander*

Cleander and Coenus were probably brothers, since each was 'the son of Polemocrates' (A. 1. 24. 1–2; Heckel (1992), 340; (2006), 85). In late 334 Cleander was commissioned to collect mercenaries from the Peloponnese (Curtius 3. 1. 1 with 4. 3. 11; A. 1. 24. 2 with 2. 20. 5), and was in command of the mercenaries at the battle of Gaugamela

(A. 3. 12. 2). Then in 330 he was left in Ecbatana under Parmenion's command. Badian (1961), 22–3 suggests that the family of Polemocrates, as members of the aristocracy of Elimiotis, had links with the family of Harpalus, which would not have done Cleander any good after 325 (see on 2. 1–3).

Coenus had married Parmenion's daughter (Curtius 6. 9. 30), and was thus compromised when Parmenion's son Philotas fell from favour. To save his skin Coenus took a leading role in denouncing Philotas (Curtius 6. 8. 17, 9. 30–31, 11.10–11). A cynical view of Coenus' motive is surely justified (cf. Heckel (1992), 60–2, against Schachermeyr (1973), 327, who would rather emphasize Coenus' loyalty to his king). But at the Hyphasis (Beas) it was Coenus who argued the case for abandoning any further advance into India (Curtius 9. 3. 3–15; A. 5. 27. 2–9). Shortly afterwards Coenus died of some disease (A. 6. 2. 1; Curtius 9. 3. 20, with the adverb *forte*—'as it happened'). Modern scholars have generally insinuated that Coenus was in fact eliminated (Badian (1961), 20, Bosworth (1996*a*), 117, Worthington (1999*b*), 44); and Badian (1961), esp. 23 ff. also argues that in killing Cleander Alexander was further punishing Coenus' family. But Holt (1999*a*) (in the version reprinted in Worthington (2003*a*), esp. 319–21) vigorously attacks this willingness to go beyond the evidence on Coenus' death. So this may not be the time to raise the possibility that Alexander used Coenus to provide a justification for turning back at the Hyphasis. But that is a very plausible scenario, as is well argued by Spann (1999).

Curtius, it is true, does not say that Alexander was in any way the cause of Coenus' death, but he was sure that the reason for the execution of Cleander went deeper than his anger at the outrageous treatment of a young Persian lady of an aristocratic family. Curtius here identifies three levels of meaning in this case: at the most public level, Cleander was charged with abuse of his power; at a deeper level this was held to have arisen from a treacherous belief that Alexander would not return from India. But Curtius understood that at a third level Alexander had no wish to remain beholden to the agent of a judicial killing, and was willing to sacrifice Cleander to the resentment of those who were appalled by the murder of Parmenion. But if ordinary troops thought that they would win a moral victory by seeing Cleander executed, and Parmenion's death thus avenged,

Alexander gave them cause to think again by ordering the execution of '600' of the troops brought by Cleander and the others (1. 8). Alexander's camp became the killing-fields.

**1. 5. the lust-crazed Cleander:** Curtius uses the noun *furor*, which must here refer to sexual obsession, as in Catullus 50. 11, Vergil *Aen.* 4. 433, and Seneca *Phaedra* 96, 178, and 184.

**1.7. one charge had been overlooked . . . the defendant's assumption that he would not survive.** Possibly an echo of a charge made against the Praetorian Prefect, Macro, by Caligula after the latter recovered from his major illness (Dio 59. 10. 6–7; Philo *Legatio ad Gaium* 61). Roisman (2003), 283–6 would argue that the Graeco-Roman agonistic ethos forced Alexander to be resolute in defending the honour and respect that he had won: on this view honour mattered more than Realpolitik.

There is an intratextual reference here to 9. 9. 23, where it is Alexander who, being desperately sick, despairs of survival: the same phrase (*desperatio salutis*) occurs in both passages.

**1. 8. he clapped them in irons.** A. 6. 27. 4–5 records the execution of Cleander and Sitalces and the acquittal for the time being of Heracon.

**ordered the execution of 600 common soldiers.** The massacre of 600 soldiers is not recorded by the other sources, and in Curtius' account it foreshadows the killing of Meleager's supporters (9. 15–19). The number 600 may not reflect a precise count, since in Latin *sescenti* (600) was one of the conventional expressions for a great number.

**1. 9. Craterus.** He is more fully introduced at 7. 9 below. Sometime before Alexander set off from Patala for Gedrosia, Craterus had been sent off with a large section of the army to Carmania on a northerly route through Arachosia and Drangiana (A. 6. 17. 3).

**ringleaders of the Persian insurrection.** This picks up the story from 9. 10. 19, where the leaders of the rebellion in Persia are identified as 'Ozines' and Zariaspes. A. 6. 27. 3 in this context names only Ordanes. Briant (1996), 761 suggests that the Persian resistance movement was betrayed by Median nobles who were collaborators.

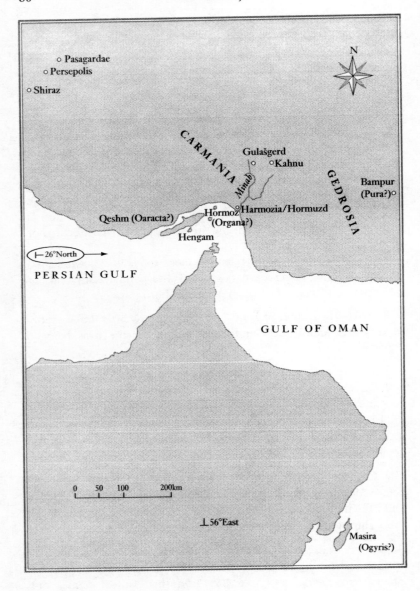

**1. 10–15.** *Nearchus and Onesicritus report on their discoveries*

*Sources*: D.S. 17. 106. 4–7; Plut. *Alex.* 68. 1; A. 6. 28. 5; *Ind.* 34–36.

*Bibliography*: Badian (1975*b*); Bosworth (1988*a*), 150–2; Brunt (1983), 518–23.

While Alexander was in Carmania Nearchus landed at the mouth of the river Anamis at a place called Harmozia (A. *Ind.* 33. 1–2), and from there he travelled inland to meet Alexander (A. *Ind.* 34, giving Nearchus' version; cf. *Anab.* 6. 28. 5, which may also be from Nearchus (Badian (1975*b*), 166), otherwise from Ptolemy: Brunt (1983), 189). Nearchus added fantasy to the basic narrative, by making his search for Alexander's camp an epic adventure, by exaggerating the rapture with which Alexander welcomed him, and by presenting the sacrifices to the gods, the Dionysiac revels and the games Alexander's way of giving thanks for Nearchus' return and honouring his achievement (*Ind.* 36. 3): Badian (1975*b*), 160 ff. But the Bacchic procession and games preceded Nearchus' arrival (Curtius 9. 10. 24–8; Plut. *Alex.* 67; and perhaps too A. 6. 28. 1–3), or were in progress when he arrived on the scene (D.S. 17. 106. 4). Without Nearchus' heroic embellishments, it appears that he did land at a port in Carmania and travel inland to meet Alexander, quite possibly in the area of Kahnu (below). He was then sent back down to the sea to continue his voyage, and some time later he rejoined Alexander's camp on Alexander's final approach to Susa (A. *Ind.* 42. 7–8; Pliny *HN* 6. 100, who puts it 6 months after Alexander set out from Patala. Patala was at the apex of the Indus delta (A. 6. 18. 2), possibly around Bahmanabad, *c.*20 km. ESE of Shahdadpur: Wilhelmy (1968), 258–63. Alexander left Patala before Nearchus (Strabo 15. 2. 5. 721), and Nearchus left around the end of September (A. *Ind.* 21. 1). Thus, as Brunt (1983), 466 suggests, Alexander probably left Patala in early September). It would have taken a good two months to move the army from the area of Kahnu (see Map, p. 80) to Susa, which they would have reached in March, if Pliny is right in stating that it was six months after Alexander's departure from Patala. Thus Nearchus' meeting in Carmania with Alexander would have been late December 325, or early in 324 (Brunt (1983), 480–1 and 500; Welles (1963), 429 suggests the spring of 324).

D.S. differs from the other sources in stating that Nearchus met Alexander in a city on the Carmanian coast called Salmous (17. 106. 4). Welles (1963), 429 suggests that Diodorus conflated the meeting with Alexander at the inland city in Carmania with Nearchus' arrival by boat at Susa and second meeting with Alexander. It is possible that he simply made a mistake in putting Salmous on the coast (so Högemann (1985), 72). Salmous has been identified as Gulašgerd or the Kahnu Oasis (Goukowsky (1981), 54–9; Högemann (1985), 72 n. 1). Nearchus thus probably landed, as Arrian states, at the site of ancient Harmozia/Hormuzd, on the river Minab, and travelled up the Minab and Jaghin to reach Kahnu. But Potts (1989) finds this identification of Salmous at odds with the toponymic evidence provided by Arab geographers, and the itinerary provided for Alexander's route into Carmania improbable; and Badian (1975*b*), 165–6 concludes that Diodorus should not be presumed to have got the facts wrong. Potts (1989) 589, goes further, by arguing that, if there really was a meeting, Salmous was somewhere on the coast, as D.S. states, but in the territory of Gedrosia, and not Carmania. But this interpretation puts D.S. too far out of line with Curtius and the other sources.

Only Curtius mentions Onescritus in this context, and Nearchus recorded that he was accompanied by Archias (A. *Ind.* 34. 6; Archias is further attested in another context at A. 7. 20. 7). Furthermore Curtius includes in Nearchus' report items which in Nearchus' own account were only encountered after the rendezvous in Carmania (see on 1. 14 and 15). There is evidence that Onesicritus was among Curtius' sources (Atkinson (2000*a*), 551 on Curtius 9. 10. 3), thus Curtius may have got this detail directly or indirectly from Onesicritus. But despite the points of difference between D.S. and Curtius, they may have shared a source: their references to the whales cohere, and Curtius' reference to an island where horses could be sold for a talent each (1. 11) can be linked with a fragment of Cleitarchus (*FGrH* 137, F29 = Pliny *HN* 6. 198).

**1. 11. an island...which was rich in gold.** Perhaps a reference to the island called Chryse at the mouth of the Indus (Pliny *HN* 6. 80). D.S. 17. 106. 6 comments on the ocean tides, which may be associated with Curtius' tale of tidal penetration of the Indus delta (9. 9. 9–26).

**1. 12. The sea was full of monsters...their bodies the size of large ships. Deterred...by a strident shout, these would submerge themselves, producing a mighty roar...as when ships have been sunk.** Close to D.S. 17. 106. 7: a common source can be assumed, and that was not Nearchus, whose account emphasized the spouting of the whales and his use of trumpets to scare them off (A. *Ind.* 30. 1–6; Strabo 15. 2. 12. 725), details not in Curtius and Diodorus. In Latin terms for whales included *cetus*, *ballaena* and *orca*, but the Elder Pliny also used the same word as Curtius, *belua* (monster), in places in his account of whales (as at *HN.* 9. 4, 6 and 12, where the subject is killer whales (*orcae*) attacking other whales (*ballaenae*)).

Nearchus claimed that the whales were up to 25 fathoms (*c.*45 m.) in length (A. *Ind.* 30. 9; cf. Pliny *HN* 9. 7), and Pliny *HN* 9. 4 repeats a claim that in the Indian Ocean whales could reach the size of four iugera (*c.*1 ha.). Curtius avoids a specific length, but for a Roman a 'big ship' could match Nearchus' 45 m.: Lucian *Navigium* 5–6 describes an unusually large cornship 120 cubits long (*c.*55 m.), and wrecks from the first centuries BC and AD include two ships of *c.*40 and 73 m. respectively (Casson (1971), 214–15), but Lucian was writing satire, not a technical manual, and most of the wrecks in Casson's list are much smaller. The classical trireme was also about 35 m. long (J. Morrison and R. Williams, *Greek Oared Ships* (Cambridge, 1968), 285). Curtius is deliberately vague, so as not to seem too credulous, and whales were not unknown in the Mediterranean. Pliny *HN.* 9. 14–15 mentions a killer-whale that found its way into the harbour at Ostia. Literary and archaeological evidence on whales in the classical period is reviewed by J. K. Papadopoulos and D. Ruscillo, 'A *ketos* in early Athens: an archaeology of whales and sea monsters in the Greek world', *AJA* 106 (2002), 187–227.

**1. 13. Their other information they had taken on trust from the natives.** This echoes Herodotus 2. 99. 1, where he moves from what he can report from autopsy to the record of what people said.

**the Red Sea derived its name . . . from a king Erythrus.** The 'Red Sea' (*mare rubrum*) was variously applied to the Indian Ocean (as at 8. 9. 6 and 14, and in the *Periplus Maris Erythraei.* and [Tibullus] 3. 8. 17–20), the Arabian Sea (as here), and either of its two inlets, the Persian Gulf (as at 5. 1. 15, with D.S. 2. 11.2; and Curtius 6. 2. 12, with Atkinson (1994), 171–2, on Curtius' dates) and the Red Sea (as at 4. 7. 18, with D.S. 3. 38. 4–5, and Strabo 16. 4. 2–4. 768). The range of usages of the term is analysed by S. E. Sidebotham, *Roman Economic Policy in the Erythra Thalassa* (Leiden, 1986), 182–6. Curtius avoids the myths relating to Erythras (for which see Strabo 16. 4. 20. 779. Pliny *HN* 6. 107 and Mela 3. 8. 72 give the variants but decline to adjudicate). Here and at 8. 9. 14 Curtius treats Erythras as an historical figure, as did Nearchus (Strabo 16. 3. 5. 766; cf. A. *Ind.* 37. 3).

**1. 14. There was an island ... with a high column ...: this ... was a monument to king Erythrus.** Nearchus and Orthagoras identified the island as Ogyris (Strabo 16. 3. 5. 766; A. *Ind.* 37. 2 has Organa), and reported that it was about 2,000 stades (*c.*360 km.) south of the Carmanian coast. Thus it has tentatively been identified as Masira (*RE* XVII, coll. 2080 ff.). From Strabo and Curtius it is clear that Nearchus did not land on Ogyris. Arrian's summary of Nearchus at *Ind.* 37. 2–3 is highly confused, but Arrian and Strabo both indicate that Nearchus learnt about Erythras' island after he left the Carmanian harbour and reached the island of Oaracta (which was 800 stades long (*c.*145 km.): A. *Ind.* 37. 2; and thus probably to be identified as Qeshm, which is about 110 km. long). The island which Nearchus bypassed—the Organa of A. *Ind.* 37. 2—to get to Qeshm must then be Hormoz.

**1. 15. vessels carrying food-traders and merchants had crossed to the island ... and they had never been seen again.** Possibly an allusion to the island which, according to Nearchus, was sacred to Poseidon and closed to humans (A. *Ind.* 37. 4). As it was *c.*40 stades (*c.*7 km.) off the coast of Oaracta, it might be identified as Hengam (Brunt (1983), 415).

**1. 16–19.** *Alexander's plans for further exploration and conquest*

*Sources:* D.S. 17. 107. 1; J. 12. 13. 1–2; A. 6. 28. 6, 7. 1. 1–3 and 19. 3–6; *Ind.* 36. 4–8; Strabo 16. 1. 11. 741.

*Bibliography:* Badian (1968), esp. 191–4; Bosworth (1988*a*), 152 and 168–70; Schachermeyr (1954), 131–40; Wirth (1972); Worthington (2004), 181–2 and 205–6.

On the immediate orders to Nearchus (1.16) Curtius agrees with Diodorus 17. 107. 1, and therefore is presumably still following Cleitarchus.

The historical background to 1. 17–19 is that Alexander did order the construction of ships at Thapsacus and did issue orders that they were to be sailed down to Babylon (cf. A. 7. 19. 3–4; Plut. *Alex.* 68. 2; Strabo 16. 1. 11. 741). Arrian and Strabo give as their authority for this detail Aristobulus, and they add that, according to Aristobulus, Alexander's purpose was to punish the Arabs for not voluntarily surrendering to him. Part of this plan was to establish colonies around the Persian Gulf (A. 7. 19. 5). Plut. *Alex.* 68. 2 seems to confirm Curtius' statement that the order for the construction of ships for assembly at Babylon was issued while Alexander was in Carmania. Quite separately, Alexander issued orders for the construction of 1,000 ships for operations in 'the west', and specifically to assist in a campaign to destroy Athens (J. 13. 5. 7). Justin indicates that this order was given after Alexander heard that the Athenians and Aetolians had launched what is known as the Lamian War. It seems reasonable to accept that there were plans for two such fleets (cf. Hauben (1976), 93 n. 104; Wirth (1972), 636 n. 133).

The picture is complicated by the tradition that, after Alexander's death, Perdiccas read out to the troops in Babylon a memorandum purporting to be Alexander's plans for the future, the so-called Last Plans. These included a campaign to win control of the North African territory as far as the Pillars of Heracles, and then Spain (D.S. 18. 4. 4; A. 7. 1. 2). Arrian adds that in some accounts Alexander also had plans to take his fleet into the Black Sea and the Sea of Azov, and other accounts mentioned Sicily and the Iapygian promontory (A. 7. 1. 3). Arrian clearly signals that the reference to Sicily and Italy did not come from his primary sources, and nor did the following explanation that Alexander's plans were motivated by his concern about the growing power of Rome. Badian (1968) has demonstrated that Perdiccas may well have read out a document, such as Diodorus gives, though what he read out may have been substantially forged. The document would have had to appear credible to the troops, but fantastic enough to secure their rejection as a working agenda. It is not clear whether Diodorus took his information on the Last Plans from Cleitarchus or Hieronymus, who was probably his major source for Book 18.

Curtius here mixes factual material on the fleet assembled at Thapsacus with references to the African element of the Last Plans, an element which is also reflected in rhetorical passages in Arrian, 4. 7. 5, 5. 26. 2 and 27. 7. He was not following Aristobulus, but may have taken some details from Cleitarchus' account. The reference to the Alps and Italy in 1. 18 appears to be another anachronism (cf. Tarn ii. 386 ff.), and should not be attributed to Cleitarchus. Curtius may here reflect the influence of Trogus (cf. J. 24. 4. 4; J. 12. 13. 1 mentions proactive diplomatic approaches to Alexander from the Spains (cf. Curtius 1.18), Gaul, Sicily, Sardinia and some communities in Italy), or the rhetoric of Livy 9. 17. 9 ff. Curtius and Diodorus 18. 4. 4 did not follow the tradition that Alexander planned to circumnavigate Africa (an extravagance noted by A. 7. 1. 2 and Plut. *Alex.* 68. 2). And presumably in a rationalizing spirit, Curtius chose to omit the story that Alexander planned to conquer and colonize Arabia to force the Arabs to recognize him as their third god, beside Uranus and Dionysus, and so acknowledge that he had equalled Dionysus' achievements (A. 7. 20. 1; Strabo 16. 1. 11. 741, giving Zeus rather than Uranus as the first deity, and citing Aristobulus as his source). Curtius may have been reluctant to accept that the conquest of Arabia might have been motivated by rivalry with Dionysus, but scholars are now more prepared to take the idea seriously: Högemann (1985), 120–35; Worthington (2004), 181–2 and 205–6; Roisman (2003), 293, and more cautiously Bosworth (1988a), 169. Bosworth (1996a), 152–3 emphasizes that the formal pretext for military action in Arabia was the more secular complaint that the Arabs had failed to send envoys and mark his presence as reason and protocol demanded (A. 7. 19. 9; Strabo 16. 1. 11. 741).

Curtius' scepticism about Alexander's divine pretensions, if that was his concern, is understandable, but the virtual exclusion of the subject of Arabia seems cavalier. He chose instead to use Nearchus' report and the ship-building order for compositional reasons to introduce Alexander's bizarre imperialist ambitions.

There was a parallel tradition that Julius Caesar had made grand plans for further imperialist adventures, with a mix of elements that were historical, including an expedition against the Parthians, and elements of fantasy, with return from Asia via Hyrcania, Scythia, and Germany (Plut. *Caes.* 58; Braccesi (1991), esp. 14–17). Other Roman resonances are noted at 1. 17.

**1. 17. his ambitions knowing no bounds.** Curtius thus falls into line with those who saw, and indeed see, the Last Plans as a reflection of Alexander's megalomania and increasing detachment from reality, though Curtius avoids mentioning the more fantastic plans. The phraseology here echoes Lucretius 1. 74.

**after the subjugation of the entire eastern seaboard.** This is Curtius' only reference to Alexander's plans for the conquest of Arabia. As noted above, recent writers have given support to the tradition that Alexander put it about that he was concerned to force the Arabs to accept him as a god alongside Uranus and Dionysus (A. 7. 20. 1; Strabo 16. 1. 11. 741, with Zeus instead of Uranus). Wirth (1972), esp. 635–9, unfortunately now sounding too much like a spin doctor, argues that after the return from India Alexander switched to a strategy of consolidation and economic development, which would in its turn bring about political unity and the opportunities for further expansion.

On the extent of Achaemenid interest in, and control over, Arabia, there are papers by J-F. Salles and D. F. Graf in *Achaemenid History IV* (Leiden, 1990); C. Tuplin, 'Darius' Suez Canal and Persian imperialism', in *Achaemenid History VI* (Leiden, 1991), esp. 274–8, claims that direct control in Arabia was very limited. Ogyris/Masira (1. 14 above), to which the Persian noble Mithropastes went in exile (Strabo 16. 767), was 'in terms of official Achaemenid surveillance, rather off the beaten track' (Tuplin, p. 277).

**because of his enmity to the Carthaginians.** Cf. D.S. 18. 4. 4; A. 5. 27. 7 and 7. 1. 2. Alexander was hostile to Carthage because of its support for its mother city Tyre (4. 2. 10 ff., and especially 4. 3. 19–26; cf. D.S. 17. 41. 1–2 and J. 11. 10. 12–14; A. 2. 24. 5), and, if we can believe Curtius, he even declared war on Carthage (4. 4. 18). There was a tradition that after Alexander's capture of Tyre, and while Parmenion was still operational, thus in the period 332—330/329, the Carthaginians sent an envoy to ascertain Alexander's intentions with regard to the city (J. 21. 6). This tradition can be traced back at least to Ennius' *Annales*, and Ennius and Trogus (i.e. ap. J. 21. 6) may have derived this from Timaeus (O. Skutsch, *The Annals of Q. Ennius* (Oxford, 1985), 379–80, on frag. 213. J-L. Ferrary, *Philhellénisme et impérialisme: aspects idéologiques de la conquête romaine du monde hellénistique* (Rome, 1988), esp. 585–8, deals with the significance which Alexander's supposed plans for Carthage had for Agathocles and later Scipio Aemilianus in the defence of their actions against Carthage.

**the Pillars of Hercules.** Alexander himself fostered the image of himself as emulating Heracles, for this theme was established as early as in Callisthenes' account of Alexander's visit to Siwah (Strabo 17. 1. 43. 814). Heracles' association with the Straits of Gibraltar was obviously drawn into the mythmaking around the North African campaign in Alexander's Last Plans. Megasthenes accepted the myths associated with the travels of Heracles, and also recorded traditions that Nebuchadnezzar and the Ethiopian seventh-century prince Taharka campaigned as far west as the Pillars of Hercules (*FGrH* 715, Fl. 11 = Strabo 15. 1. 6. 686–7). Bosworth (1996*c*), 113–27, esp. 122 notes the obvious influence of Alexander on these myths, as admirers created or embellished legends to provide 'record[s] of achievement for him to emulate and surpass' (cf. Bosworth (1996*a*), 126–7).

When imitation or emulation of Alexander became a theme of eulogy or denigration of members of the Julio-Claudian dynasty, and reference was made to plans for world dominion (e.g. Plut. *Caesar* 58. 6–8; *Res gestae divi Augusti* esp. 26–33; Vergil *Aeneid* 6. 791–807, with Spencer (2002), 195 and 138–54, and P. J. Davis, *Ovid and Augustus* (London, 2006), 44 and 142, n. 127; Orosius 6. 21. 19 ff., cf. J. 43. 1. 1–2 and 44. 5. 8 with Cresci Marrone (1993), 266), rivalry with Hercules became a feature of the texts, for example as at Seneca *Benef.* 1. 13. 1–3, with Spencer (2002), 75 ff. Of immediate relevance is the reference in Tacitus *Germ.* 34. 2 to the northern pillars of Hercules, which only the Oceanus stopped Tiberius' brother Drusus from exploring (Rives (1999), 263–4 offers commentary; cf. Lucan 3. 277–9).

A. A. Lund (1987), 53–4 makes a good case for believing that Tacitus had this passage in mind when he wrote *Germ.* 34. 2: in particular it seems that Curtius' *fama vulgaverat* (rumour/tradition had spread it abroad) was inappropriately adjusted into the perfect tense by Tacitus, when the present tense would have better suited his immediate context. Echoes of Curtius in Tacitus have a bearing on Curtius' dates (see Introduction, section 7).

**1. 18. Spain, which the Greeks called 'Hiberia' after the river Hiberus.** Cf. J. 44. 1. 2. Curtius' gloss on the name shows that he has broken away from whatever Greek source he was using. Curtius assumes the connotation of Hiberia that was established by Polybius' day (Polybius 3. 37. 10 with the commentary by Walbank (1970), 369–70; Strabo 3. 4. 19. 166. At one stage Iberia had denoted the territory between the Ebro (Hiberus) and the Pyrenees.).

**1. 19. Alexander instructed his governors … to cut timber on Mt Libanus, transport it … to … Thapsacus, and there lay down keels for 700 ships.** As noted above, Alexander was building up two fleets: a Mediterranean fleet of notionally 1,000 vessels (D.S. 18. 4. 4; J. 13. 5. 7), and an Indian Ocean fleet, to be based initially at Babylon, and again to be made of 1,000 warships (A. 7. 19. 4, citing Aristobulus; Strabo 16. 1. 11. 741. Courtney (1993), 318, in his commentary on lines by Albinovanus Pedo, notes that Germanicus was said to have had a fleet of 1,000 ships (Tac. *Ann.* 2. 6. 2), as did Alexander at Curtius 9. 3. 22). In abridging the narrative, Curtius has given the objectives set for the Mediterranean fleet and omitted the plans for the Indian Ocean fleet. It is possible that he covered the build-up of the Mediterranean fleet in the lacuna at the end of chapter 1, in which case he is alluding back to this subject at 10. 2. 4. Still, at this point he can be accused of sloppy editing. Arrian and Strabo show that some of the ships were prefabricated in Phoenicia (and Cyprus according to Strabo), and taken to Thapsacus for assembling. This tradition is quite credible (Bosworth (1988*a*), 152–3).

**Thapsacus.** Possibly Meskene (Atkinson (1980), 170–1, *pace* Brunt (1976), 486–7, who argues for Jerablus).

**all septiremes.** But A. 7. 19. 3 states that Phoenician vessels reassembled at Thapsacus covered a range from quinqueremes to triaconters, thus at least some of the vessels which sailed downstream from Thapsacus were not septiremes. Tarn ii. 386 ff. identified this reference to septiremes as an anachronism, since this type of warship was not invented before 315 BC. Now Antigonus was building up a large fleet in 315 (D.S. 19. 62. 7–8), so that when his son Demetrius engaged Ptolemy's fleet at Salamis, Cyprus, in 306/5, Demetrius' fleet included septiremes, which are indicated as his largest ships (D.S. 20. 50. 2–3; the date is problematic, but not an issue here). The list of polyremes available to Antigonus by 315 appears to have included 'nines' and 'tens' (D.S. 19. 62. 8, if the text is sound).

Thus Demetrius' septiremes were not the biggest that Antigonus had built, and the concept of a septireme came into being no later than 315; indeed Schachermeyr (1954), 336–7 argues that in the Hellenistic period Alexander was believed to have developed plans for even bigger ships (cf. Pliny *HN* 7. 208). Giant polyremes or supergalleys were not just a myth in the Hellenistic period, as historical, epigraphical and papyrological texts show (evidence reviewed by Casson (1971), 137–40). It is possible that after the reference to 700 ships, Curtius (or a later copyist) turned the description of the warships from quadrireme, or whatever, into *sept*ireme, but there is no compelling reason to reject this as part of the tradition. Quite how a septireme was configured is a matter of speculation: a trireme did not denote a ship with three men to an oar, and a septireme could certainly not mean seven men to an oar; but, while a trireme can be defined as a ship with 3 banks of oars, it does not follow that a septireme involved oars at seven levels.

**the kings of Cyprus.** Cf. on ships built for Alexander on Cyprus, Strabo 16. 1. 11. 741.

**1. 20–1.** *The Indian satrapies*

*Sources*: A. 6. 27. 2.

*Bibliography*: Brunt (1983), 471–4; Bosworth (1983*b*) and (1988*a*), 238–40.

In this section Curtius reverts to what we might call the rubric of administrative problems sorted out by Alexander. He was not here following Arrian's source: contrast A. 6. 27. 2, who *inter alia* sets this episode before Alexander reached Carmania.

**1. 20. letters from the kings Porus and Taxiles.** They are last mentioned at 9. 3. 22, where Curtius indicates that they were confirmed as client kings in their territories after Alexander turned back at the Hyphasis and arrived back at the 'Acesines' (9. 3. 20). But the critical settlement of the Indian satrapies seems rather to have been made after Alexander marched back from the Acesines to the Hydaspes, on which he founded the cities of Nicaea and Bucephala (A. 5. 29. 5, Strabo 15. 1. 28. 698, whereas Curtius sites these on the Acesines at 9. 3. 23). Back on the Hydaspes, thus early in 325, Alexander proclaimed Porus 'king of the Indian territory so far acquired' (A. 6. 2. 1), and this meant paramount chief of the nations between the Hydaspes and the Hyphasis (Hydaspes: A. *Succ.* F.1. 36; Strabo 15. 1. 29. 698; the Hyphasis: A. 5. 29. 2). In the settlement after Alexander's death, Porus was confirmed in his dominion (*dynasteia*), as were Taxiles and many other kings in their territories (D.S. 18. 6. 2), which Diodorus then covers by the term satrapies (6. 4); and in the subsequent settlement at Triparadeisos the territory of 'Porus the king' is specifically identified as a satrapy (A. *Succ.* F.1. 36). Taxiles' position may well have been reconfirmed in 325, when Alexander defined Porus' position. But the difference was that Taxiles operated as a king within a satrapy, administered by Philip (A. 5. 8. 3). This satrapy stretched from the Indus to the Hydaspes, and later in 325 was extended south to the junction of the Indus and the Acesines.

**Abisares had died after an illness.** Abisares ruled a large area north of Taxila and stretching east beyond the Hydaspes. He had submitted to Alexander (cf. 8. 13. 1 and 14. 1; 9. 1. 7; A. 5. 8. 3; 20. 5–6; D.S. 17. 90. 4; Strabo 15. 1. 28. 698, with a scathing comment on an incredible story which Onesicritus peddled about Abisares' pet snakes: Bosworth (1995), 177–8 and 260–1). He was allowed to remain in command of his territory, with the title of satrap, if A. 5. 29. 5 can be believed. A. 5. 29. 4 refers to Abisares as ill in 326.

**Alexander's governor, Philip, <had died> of a wound.** Philip, son of Machatas, was the brother of Harpalus, whose flight Curtius covers in what survives of the next chapter. Heckel (2003*a*), 220 comments that, until Harpalus' flight, Philip had still been trusted despite his family's links with the group around Antigonus (Heckel explains that Antigonus was a close associate of Antipater, and thus in the group which Alexander needed after his accession (pp. 200–1); but Antigonus was, along with other members of the 'Antipatrid–Antigonid' group sidelined in the first two years of the war, Antigonus by his appointment in 333 as satrap of Phrygia (p. 210)). Alexander was cautious of Philip, for in 326 he put him out of the way, in what was a high-risk situation, as he appointed Philip as satrap of the area between the Indus and the Hydaspes (Jhelum), which included Taxiles' kingdom (A. 5. 8. 3; 6. 15. 2). Heckel (1992), 332 raises a suspicion: 'His sudden death, corresponding roughly to the time of

Harpalus' misadventures, evokes certain suspicions about Alexander's role in the man's murder.' But, on the usual interpretation, the murder of the satrap by native mercenaries was a warning to Alexander, and as he now planned to campaign further west, against the Arabs, he decided to relinquish direct control of the satrapies beyond the Indus. Philip's satrapy was handed over to Taxiles, its southern limit later fixed as the junction of the Acesines (Chenab) and the Indus (A. 6. 27. 2 with D.S. 18. 3. 2 and Dexippus' digest of Arrian in *FGrH* 100, F 8), and its eastern boundary beyond the Hydaspes.

**1. 21. Alexander... replaced Philip with Eudaemon... commanding officer of the Thracians.** Curtius erroneously names 'Eudaemon' as satrap, but Eudamus (to give him the more correct form of his name) was rather the *strategos* left to support Taxiles until such time as Alexander should make a substantive appointment of a satrap (A. 6. 27. 2; Heckel (2006), 120). Before this appointment he was the commanding officer of the Thracians. After Alexander's death, Eudamus killed Porus and operated as a war-lord. In 317 he chose to join Eumenes, taking with him 500 cavalry, 300 infantry, and 120 elephants (D.S. 19. 14. 8).

It was probably in the immediate context of Alexander's plans for India in 324 that he extended Porus' satrapy to the Indus delta to incorporate the satrapy which Peithon, s. of Agenor, had controlled (A. 6. 15. 4; D.S. 18. 39. 6; *FGrH* 100, F8 with Bosworth (1983*b*)). The background was that Peithon was originally appointed in 325 as the satrap of the territory from the junction of Acesines and Indus down to Patala and the sea (A. 6. 17. 4 and 20. 2, with a garbled reference in J. 12. 4. 20). Bosworth argues from Dexippus (*FGrH* 100, F.8) and D.S. 18. 3. 3 on the settlement of 323, and D.S. 18. 39. 6, on the settlement of Triparadeisos, that Peithon was transferred to the satrapy that ran along the Cophen valley from the Hindu Kush to the Indus. Philip had been given responsibility for this area after the satrap, Nicanor, was killed late in 326 (A. 5. 20. 7). Thus the context for the switch of Peithon from the lower Indus to the Cophen valley would have been after the murder of Philip, and probably also in early 324. Porus was allowed to take over the lower Indus 'satrapy'. This reconstruction is convincing, and means that with the area between the Indus and the Hyphasis, and from the Acesines down to the sea under 'native rule',

Alexander's control of the Indian satrapies was more illusion than reality. But that is not Curtius' concern.

**1. 22–38.** *Bagoas engineers Orxines' death*

*Sources:* A. 6. 29. 1–30. 2; Plut. *Alex.* 69. 1–3.

*Bibliography:* Badian (1958*a*) and (1996), 22–4; Bosworth (1988*a*), 153–4; Egge (1978), 149–58; Gunderson (1982), esp. 190–6; Tarn ii. 321 ff.

The clash between Bagoas and Orxines (Curtius' Orsines) echoes that between Cleon and Callisthenes in 8. 5. 7 ff., and in some ways it foreshadows the episode after Alexander's death, when Perdiccas manipulates Philip Arrhidaeus into killing Meleager (10. 9. 7 ff.). Tarn ii. 93 and 320 ff. argues from the differences between Arrian and Curtius on the death of Orxines that Curtius, with moralizing intent, developed this tale from a libellous fiction which he took over from the Peripatetic tradition, and which can be traced back to Dicaearchus (cited by Athenaeus 13. 603a–b). But Badian (1958*a*), 147 ff. shows that Bagoas did exist, while 'the Peripatetic portrait of Alexander' is a modern invention. Gunderson (1982), 189–96 agrees with Badian about the reality of Bagoas, but suggests that Badian, from his 'moralist position' (p. 196), gave unwarranted credence to Curtius' portrayal of Bagoas' scheming against Orxines, and used the episode to mark a stage in Alexander's degeneration and the reign of terror. But Gunderson would emphasize the significance of Aristobulus' report that Alexander had inspected the tomb of Cyrus on his first visit to Pasargadae and that the satrap was not responsible for the pillaging of the tomb (Strabo 15. 3. 7. 730). Orxines was put to death for crimes that included robbery from tombs, if not Cyrus' tomb (A. 6. 30. 2). Thus, Gunderson comes to the wholesome conclusion that Orxines was punished because Alexander was justifiably and pragmatically concerned to root out corruption and to protect the population of Persia from the abuse of power by a vicious satrap. More recently, Badian (1996), 22–4 presents the desecration of Cyrus' tomb as a mark of Persian resistance to Alexander's plans for assuming the kingship of Asia.

Egge (1978), 149–58 reviews the source problems and concludes that Curtius can not be taken to have drawn this story from

Cleitarchus (p. 232, noting Diodorus' silence on the subject). Though Aristobulus stated that Orxines was not guilty of pillaging of Cyrus' tomb (Strabo 15. 3. 7. 730), Curtius could not have taken the Bagoas story from a source as biased in favour of Alexander as was Aristobulus. Plutarch's source was not Aristobulus, as he reports that the tomb robber was a Macedonian, Poulamachos, who was duly put to death (*Alex.* 69. 3). Thus Curtius was obviously not using Plutarch's source. Hammond (1983), 157 treats Curtius' version as of a piece with the tale of Nabarzanes' gift of Bagoas to Alexander in 6. 5. 22–3, and confidently attributes both to Cleitarchus. It is not impossible that Curtius picked up material by Cleitarchus indirectly from Trogus (cf. Prandi (1996), 139 and 142), but direct use of Cleitarchus for the core detail remains a working hypothesis.

The amount of space which Curtius devotes to this episode, the legal phraseology, and the recurring themes of dissimulation and secret hearings again lend weight to the view that Curtius wrote for those familiar with trials for treason (*maiestas*) in the early Principate.

Cascon Dorada (1990), 257–8 cites this as an example of Curtius' way of dealing at some length with episodes that reflected badly on Alexander, and of further making them appear more real by building in criticisms of Alexander attributed to others.

**1. 22. Parsagada.** The more usual spelling in Latin was Pasargadae (Pliny *HN* 6. 99; *Pasargadai* in Greek: Hdt. 1. 125; A. 3. 18. 10; Strabo 15. 3. 7. 730). It lay in the Dasht-i Murghāb, *c.*80 km. by road north from Persepolis. It was founded by Cyrus and, after Darius I moved the capital to Persepolis, Pasargadae continued to serve as a royal residence (Strabo), and as Badian (1996), 20 puts it, 'the sacred capital', being associated with the mysteries that attended the coronation of the Persian king (Plut. *Artax.* 3. 1). It was dominated by the tomb of Cyrus, in terms of its function, if not in terms of architectural scale. The site is fully described by Stronach (1978): and for more recent work on the site see Briant (2003*b*), 35.

**Orsines.** The name is better rendered as Orxines (as by Heckel (2006), 186). His status was defined by ethnicity (he was Persian), father's name, tribe/clan (cf. Hdt 4. 167; Orxines was of the Pasargadae tribe), and wealth (Briant (1996) 342). Briant also argues that

Orxines was not a satrap in the familiar sense, but a tribal chief or *zantupati (Briant (1996), 483, 768 and 29) and a collaborator (Briant (1996), 870). Alexander had left Phrasaortes as satrap of Persia, and when he died Orxines appropriated the position. Alexander decided, even before he reached Persia, to appoint Stasanor as satrap in place of Orxines (A. 6. 29. 1–2).

**1. 23. He traced his lineage from Cyrus.** Curtius repeats a point made at 4. 12. 8, where Orxines is singled out for special mention as a commander at the battle of Gaugamela. Curtius makes nothing of the point that a descendant of Cyrus was being accused of desecrating his tomb. Curtius' source probably commented on Orxines in the battle order at Gaugamela, knowing that he would feature in the story of Alexander's return to Pasargadae, and Curtius picked up the connecting link. The source could well have been Cleitarchus (Atkinson (1980) 405–6; Pearson (1960), 239).

**amassed . . . during his long tenure of the satrapy.** If satrapy is used in the normal sense, then Orxines could not have been said to have held the position for a long time, as Phrasaortes had died when Alexander was still in India, though Alexander only learnt of the death when he was on his way back to Pasargadae (A. 6. 29. 1).

**1. 24. with all manner of gifts.** The Persian custom was to greet the visiting king with a procession laden with gifts: cf. 5. 1. 21 for gifts of horses, cattle, and wild animals; and 5. 2. 9–10. The list given is obviously meant to suggest extraordinary opulence.

**3,000 talents of silver coin.** This detail is picked up at 1. 34. 3,000 talents would have been enough to pay for approximately 74,000 infantrymen for a year at 4 obols per day (cf. Atkinson (1980), 79).

**1. 25. the eunuch Bagoas, who . . . had gained Alexander's affection through putting his body at his service.** Darius III had had a sexual relationship with Bagoas, and Bagoas then became the property of Nabarzanes, who presented him as a gift to Alexander (Curtius 6. 5. 23). He features again in the account of Alexander's last days in Aelian *VH* 3. 23, where Eumenes appears to be cited as the source. Bagoas was a generic name for eunuchs (Pliny *HN*. 13. 41). Alexander had a sexual relationship with Bagoas, or at least gave that impression at a celebrated occasion in Gedrosia when he gave Bagoas a kiss (Plut. *Alex.* 67. 8; Athenaeus 13. 603a–b, citing Dicaearchus).

The presentation of Alexander's sexual proclivities by the ancient sources, complex and complicated by the variety of agenda of modern commentators, needs to be considered from several distinct angles. Curtius here purports to give via Orxines the Persian point of view, but confuses a Persian noble's disdain for eunuchs at the imperial court with hatred for homosexual relationships with eunuchs. In Athenian society there was a clear distinction between a homosexual relationship between an adult citizen and a youth, and homoeroticism: the former was accepted as a form of social control, the latter was not tolerated (Dover (1978); Ogden (2007), esp. 76–8. Sallares (1991), 160–9 characterizes the Athenian *polis* as an age class system, with a history of institutionalized paederasty). By contrast, the Macedonia of the age of Philip and Alexander accepted bisexualism as the norm, as has been stoutly argued by Kate Mortensen in her thesis (1997) and in numerous seminar or conference papers. And in the Macedonian model, status mattered more than age. Thus Alexander's relationship with Hephaestion would have seemed reasonably natural to a Macedonian (cf. Reames-Zimmerman (1999)), but not so to an Athenian. Ogden (2007), 80–8 explores a different line, arguing that Athenaeus' anecdote about Alexander kissing Bagoas in Gedrosia (13. 603a–b) is evidence of lively debate in the 320s BC about the 'riddle' of the relationship between Achilles and Patroclus in Homer, and shows that this paradigm was then applied to the discussion about Alexander's relationship with Hephaestion, Bagoas being introduced as a contrasting case. Thus Ogden concludes that the passage attests the historicity of the conundrum, but is of limited value on the historical situation with regard to Alexander's relationship with Hephaestion and Bagoas.

Roman attitudes on homoeroticism were different again: the notion of manliness (*virtus*; cf. C. A. Williams (1999), esp. 132–5 on *virtus* and *imperium*, citing i.a. Juv. *Sat.* 8. 13–20; Nepos *Hannibal* 1; Pliny *HN* 7. 130), patrician ideals, and family values reinforced by Augustan legislation tended to incite more homophobic passions. Roman ideals shine through Curtius' account, not least in the way he as narrator emphasizes gender roles in Alexander's relationship with Bagoas.

**1. 26. not the Persian custom to regard as men those who allowed themselves to be sexually used as women.** Through the *persona* of Orxines, as here, and as narrator, Curtius 'draws on the Roman language of sexual insults' (Williams (1999), 143 and 321 n. 70 for the quotation), pouring scorn in particular on a male who played a receptive role: cf. the preceding lemma (where the key phrase in Latin is *obsequio corporis*), and in 1. 29, 'submitting to the shame of the sexual act' (the key words being *stuprum* and *patientia*, the latter linked with the Greek word pathic: Adams (1982), 189 ff., Williams (1999), 174–5. For *patientia* (submission) cf. Sallust *Cat.* 13. 3; Petronius 9. 6 and 87. 7; Tac. *Ann.* 11. 36. 4).

Whatever Persian nobles thought about pathic homosexuals, the reality was that the Persian court accepted eunuchs (Briant (1996), 28–1; (2003*a*), 588). On the Roman side, the employment of eunuchs in the imperial army, administration, and court was a scandal in the eyes of the Roman elite in the Julio-Claudian era, and on through the Flavian period (Suet. *Claud.* 28. 1 of Posides, notorious enough to be mentioned by Juvenal *Sat.* 14. 91; Tac. *Ann.* 14. 59. 2; Dio 67. 2. 1–3; Statius *Silvae* 3. 4. 69–75 with B. W. Jones, *The Emperor Domitian* (London, 1993), 31). In case Fears (2001) is right in arguing that Curtius wrote during the reign of Elagabalus, one should note that the life of Elagabalus in the *Historia Augusta* is full of scandalous tales about eunuchs and the emperor's pathic experiences: notably 6. 3–5; 10. 2–6; 15. 2; 23. 5; 26. 5; 31. 6–7.

**1. 30. fate, whose decrees are inevitable, was approaching fulfilment. It chanced that . . . .** Cf. Livy 5. 19.1. The opening sentence is not of any theological or eschatalogical significance, though Tarn ii. 95 takes it as showing that Curtius believed in fate. The following *forte* (as it happened/it chanced that) rather undercuts the solemn meaning of *fatum.* It means little more than an individual's personal destiny or lot (cf. 3. 12. 6; 6. 4. 12; 10. 5. 35), and in this combination is little more than a narratological device. 'It chanced that' (forte) introduces a *peripeteia*, an unexpected twist in the story.

**Alexander ordered the opening of Cyrus' tomb.** As Aristobulus was commissioned to repair the tomb (A. 6. 29. 10), his account of this episode, as summarized by A. 6. 29. 4–11, ought to be a reliable guide to what happened, or at least to what passed as the official version.

Alexander visited the site and discovered that the tomb had been looted. The Magi who had been acting as guardians of the tomb were tortured and interrogated, but they did not identify the tomb-robbers and there was no proof of their complicity. Strabo 15. 3. 7. 730 confirms Arrian's summary of Aristobulus' account, but Strabo alone explicitly records that Alexander had entered the tomb on his first visit to Pasargadae, and he adds a reference to Onesicritus' fanciful description of the tomb. Curtius did not follow Onesicritus, nor the source followed by Plutarch, who records that Alexander put to death Poulamachos of Pella for vandalizing the tomb (*Alex*. 69. 3).

Clearly Curtius was also not following Aristobulus. Nevertheless, Aristobulus consistently presents an apologetic account of Alexander, and it is therefore quite possible that he suppressed the information that Bagoas exploited the scandal to denigrate Orxines. He may even have concocted the story that he was instructed by Alexander to repair the tomb, since careful analysis of the structure has revealed no evidence of any reconstruction (Shahbazi (2003), 27). The fiction would have been intended to support the record that the tomb had been vandalized.

Badian (1996), 22–4, suggests that Alexander returned to Pasargadae and Cyrus' tomb with specific intent to stage some sort of coronation ceremony. The Magi had every good reason to thwart this plan, and may indeed have desecrated the tomb by throwing Cyrus' remains on the floor to make the tomb unusable for any religious ceremony. If this is so, it might have suited Alexander's purposes to conceal the motives behind the desecration, and to blame instead a greedy official. Aristobulus, as summarized by Arrian and Strabo, states that Cyrus' remains had been disturbed and thrown out of the sarcophagus. The suppression of this detail might also have served Alexander's purposes at the time. But it is no less possible that that this impiety was omitted by Curtius (or his source) in the process of developing the image of Orxines as the blameless victim. Curtius might also have wished to draw a parallel between Orxines and Philotas, found guilty before he even knew he was being charged (1. 37; cf. 6. 9. 26).

**1. 32. Alexander set a golden crown on the sarcophagus in which the body lay.** Augustus was similarly said to have placed a crown at the tomb of Alexander in Alexandria (Suet. *Aug.* 18. 1, with matching

Latin phraseology; Dio 51. 16. 5). The parallel plus the divergence from Aristobulus' account raises doubt about the historicity of Curtius' version.

The term used for a sarcophagus implies that it was fairly simple (*solium*: cf. Pliny *HN* 35. 160). Curtius goes on to have Alexander comment that the burial was surprisingly humble, albeit that he is led to believe that all the wealthy grave objects had been spirited away. Dempsie here suggests that there was some influence from the Roman myth about Romulus' humble life style: Vitruvius *De arch.* 2. 1. 15; Sen. *Controv.* 1. 6. 4 and 2. 1. 5.

**1. 38. innocent.** But, as already noted, A. 6. 30. 2 reports that he was found guilty of plundering temples and royal tombs and of killing people without just cause.

**1. 39. Phradates.** 'Phradates', or rather Autophradates, was the satrap of Tapyria under Darius (A. 3. 23. 7), and was reappointed to this position by Alexander (Curtius 6. 4. 25). In 329/8, or more likely 328/7, Alexander issued orders for his arrest (Curtius 8. 3. 17; A. 4. 18. 2). This suggests that he quickly decided against collaborating, and later led a resistance group (Badian (2000*a*), 91–2; Heckel (2006), 65). Curtius glosses over the case against him.

**quick to order summary execution.** The phraseology echoes Cicero *Har.* 51. There is an abrupt asyndeton in the Latin, as Curtius switches from Phradates to Alexander without signalling the change of subject.

**1. 40–2.** *The corruptive force of success and Alexander's arbitrary decisions*

*Sources:* A. 7. 4. 3; Plut. *Alex.* 42. 2–4.

In closing this section of the narrative, Curtius echoes 6. 2.1–4: but there he refers to Alexander's degeneration into paranoia, a paranoia that was partly justified by the reaction of his officers and troops to his acceptance of oriental culture. In this passage a further stage in the degeneration is marked, as Alexander is now shown as scattering gifts and death sentences at the whim of a eunuch.

**1. 40. Alexander Lyncestes.** Alexander of Lyncestis (Berve (1926), ii. no. 37; Heckel (2006), 19) and his two brothers were accused of complicity in the murder of Philip II, and the two brothers were promptly taken out. Alexander may have been spared because he was prompt to acknowledge his namesake as the new king, and because he was the son-in-law of Antipater (A. 1. 25. 2; son-in-law: Curtius 7. 1. 7; J. 11. 7. 1; 12. 14. 1). Bosworth (1971*b*), 102–3 argues that they were involved in the assassination, but I am inclined to favour the view that they were not involved (so Badian (1963), 248–9), but vulnerable because the family was related to the Macedonian royal family. Still, the Lyncestian Alexander was spared and served with Alexander as commander of the Thessalian cavalry, until he was suddenly removed from his command and arrested, sometime in 333, since he was kept in detention for three years before being brought to trial (Curtius 7. 1. 6; 8. 8. 6 and D.S. 17. 80. 2), late in 330, after the execution of Philotas.

**despite the evidence of two witnesses.** Curtius deals with the trial in 7. 1. 5–9, where he refers back to two witnesses or informers who provided evidence at the time the Lyncestian was first arrested (7. 1. 6): this must be a cross-reference to an episode which he covered in the missing second book. Diodorus 17. 32. 1 says that in 333 Olympias warned Alexander to be on his guard against the Lyncestian, so she may have been one of the two informers. Almost certainly a witness would have been Sisines, a Persian who had defected to Philip and then served Alexander, but turned out to be a double agent, whom Darius used to contact the Lyncestian Alexander, urging him to assassinate Alexander (Curtius 3. 7. 11–12). In Curtius' version the letter from Darius, or rather from Nabarzanes acting for Darius, was intercepted and passed on to test Sisines' loyalty (3. 7. 13–15); in Arrian's version the Lyncestian was no innocent victim of a Persian plot, because he had written to Darius, who responded by sending Sisines to contact the Lyncestian: Sisines was arrested by Parmenion and gave evidence against the Lyncestian (A. 1. 25. 3–10). The two versions are quite different, and the latter suspicious because it puts the Lyncestian so clearly and conveniently in the wrong. The letter *from* the Lyncestian would not have been in Sisines' possession when he was arrested, and could only have been found (or invented) later, perhaps after the capture of the Persian camp at Damascus. This in turn might explain the time gap between the removal of the

Lyncestian from his command early in 333 (the date implied by Arrian and J. 11. 7. 1) and his arrest later in 333 (as implied by the tradition that he was a prisoner for three years before being brought to trial at the end of 330). Of immediate relevance is that Sisines was surely one of the two witnesses, and Parmenion might have counted as the second, unless we take Diodorus to show that Olympias was the other. These issues are examined by Atkinson (1980), 183–7, Bosworth (1988a), 50–1, Baynham (1998), 144–5, who follows Atkinson in noting a Tacitean echo at *Ann.* 2. 42. 2–3, on Tiberius' entrapment of Archelaus.

**1. 41. he had also ... acquiesced in the acquittal of prisoners.** By implication Curtius understood that Macedon had a functioning judicial system. Attempts to impose upon this system the framework of modern *Staatsrecht* have now generally been rejected. The older view was well represented by Granier (1931): there was indeed a Macedonian assembly, and that was an assembly of men-in arms (*Heeresversammlung*), as there was no separate popular assembly (*Volksversammlung*). Briant (1973), esp. 286–90 reviews the debate, listing scholars who followed Granier and assumed that Macedonians had limited constitutional rights as members of the army, and therefore as members of any army assembly convened. The army's constitutional right to function as the final court in capital cases was deduced from the accounts of political trials in Alexander's reign, and from Curtius 6. 8. 25, as emended by Hedicke: *de capitalibus rebus vetusto Macedonum modo inquirebat <rex, iudicabat> exercitus* (in capital cases following the ancient Macedonian way, the hearing was conducted <by the king, the verdict was decided> by the army). But there is no good reason to import these crucial words (Atkinson (1994), 226–8, Goukowsky (1975), 274). Incidentally, Curtius goes on to say that in peacetime that function, sc. of investigating capital cases, was the responsibility of the people, which Briant (1973), esp. 288–92 takes as a serious objection to Granier's case that there was no such thing as a Macedonian popular assembly. The approach of Granier and his followers to Macedonian 'constitutional law' has been challenged in various ways by Errington (1978), 91 and (1986), 197 ff., Lock (1977), Bosworth (1980a), 361–2, and others.

It must be added that just as modern scholars have imposed anachronistic models on the Macedonian system, so too Curtius was capable of seeing Macedonian phenomena through Roman eyes, or at least of presenting those phenomena in a way that would be immediately intelligible to a Roman reader.

O'Neil (1999) reviews the debate on Macedonian judicial practice in the light of what is recorded about political trials under Alexander and the Successors. He comes to the unsurprising conclusion that, as it suited him, Alexander sometimes used a Macedonian army assembly as a court, and sometimes a council of his *hetaeroi*. but he would also try cases himself, or simply liquidate those who offended him.

**1. 42. though earlier possessed of unassailable self-control.** The challenge for Curtius was to breath fresh life into the hackneyed theme that Alexander was invincible in war (*invictus*: as at 5. 3. 22; cf. J. 12. 15.4; Livy 8. 3. 7), but conquered (*victus*) by greed, arrogance and all the other temptations that followed on his victories (cf. 6. 2. 1–5; 3. 12. 18–21; 5. 1. 36–39; 6. 6. 1–3; 10. 5. 33–4; J. 12. 3. 8–12; D.S. 17. 77. 4–7; A. 4. 7. 4; Livy 9. 17–18; Val. Max. 4. 3. ext. 4; Pfister (1964), esp. 39–46; Schepens (1989); Atkinson (1994), 167–9 and 200–4).

**he followed a male whore's judgement to give some men kingdoms and deprive others of their lives.** Curtius rounds off the section by reverting to Bagoas as the *scortum* (whore). There is an echo here of the scene in Persepolis when the camp-follower Thais proposed the destruction of the royal complex by fire. Curtius there uses the same strong term of abuse, *scortum*, of Thais, coupling with it the formula used to describe a senator's delivery of his opinion in the House (5. 7. 4). In Roman history Lucius Quinctius Flamininus (cos. 192) was removed from the Senate by the censors of 184 for charges that included beheading a Gallic nobleman to humour his catamite (Livy 39. 43. 1–4; Livy adds a variant recorded by Valerius Antias, that Flamininus beheaded a man to amuse his prostitute). The tale became a rhetorical topos: Cicero *Sen.* 42; Val. Max. 2. 9. 3; Seneca *Controv.* 9. 2. Curtius echoes the theme.

**1. 43–5.** *Troubles in the west*

*Sources*: J. 12. 1. 4–5 and 2. 16–17; 37. 3. 2; D.S. 18. 14. 2; Macrobius *Sat.* 1. 11. 33.

*Bibliography:* Yardley and Heckel (1997), 196–8.

**1. 43. Alexander received a letter from Coenus.** This is probably the Coenus who was later appointed as satrap of Susiana (J. 13. 4. 14; Dexippus *FGrH* 100, F.8. 6; Berve (1926), ii. no. 440; Heckel (2006), 93), and, as Berve notes, such an appointment implies prior experience as a senior military officer. Thus it is possible that he had been sent back to Macedon with some veterans, perhaps from Media (cf. A. 3. 19. 5), or Hecatompylus (cf. Curtius 6. 2. 15–18), or to collect reinforcements. As argued below, he might well have gone on from Macedon to Thrace, and survived to report on what happened there. Curtius mentions a letter, but at some point he must have rejoined Alexander's camp in time to have been appointed satrap of Susiana before Alexander's death (Berve (1926), i. 262). This may mean that Coenus arrived with reinforcements and delivered a written report.

This convenient reconstruction is however complicated by Curtius' following point that Coenus dealt with events in Europe *and* *Asia*. Possibly this Coenus was able to report on problems in Asia Minor, but scholars have been tempted to think that Curtius, or his immediate source, misunderstood something in a Greek source and turned an adverbial phrase into a proper name: Mützell suggested that the original read *apo koinou* (alike, at the same time): Alexander received reports on events in both Europe and Asia. Heckel (1984), 297 suggests as an alternative that the report came from the Macedonian *koinon* (state). Tarn ii. 96 unconvincingly suggests that Curtius carelessly substituted Coenus for Antipater.

**1. 44. Zopyrion, who governed Thrace.** In 331 Memnon, Alexander's military commander in Thrace, rebelled, but Antipater re-established control and Memnon was left in charge of Thrace (D.S. 17. 62. 4–6; Curtius alludes to these events in 5. 1. 1; Badian (1967), 179–80 and 191–2, with (1994b) for a revised chronological scheme). Later Memnon was ordered to leave Thrace and to lead reinforcements to Alexander, whom he would have reached sometime after September 326 (C.R. 9. 3. 21; Bosworth (1988a), 134 calculates the date from information supplied by Aristobulus, in Strabo 15. 1. 17. 691). Thus Zopyrion may have succeeded Memnon in Thrace sometime earlier in 326, though Yardley and Heckel (1997), 197 argue for replacement in 328. Either way, Coenus could have been back in Macedonia early enough to have been around when Zopyrion initiated his disastrous incursion into Scythian territory. If Justin is literally correct that Zopyrion's entire force of 30,000 was wiped out (12. 2. 17; 37. 3. 2 and Macrobius *Sat.* 1. 11. 33), then Coenus could not have been involved in the incursion, but he might have been operating in Thrace, and thus was able to report on what happened in Thrace and beyond.

The failure of Zopyrion's campaign across the Danube was perhaps a factor in Alexander's decision at Opis to send Craterus to assume control of Macedonia and Thrace, while Antipater was to lead further reinforcements to join Alexander (A. 7. 12. 4). If this is so, and if, as Curtius suggests, Zopyrion failed because of extreme weather conditions, then Zopyrion may have died in the winter of 325/4.

**while... on an expedition against the Getae.** The Getae were concentrated in the Dobrudja, but also stretched further west, either side of the Danube (Strabo 7. 3. 2. 295; A. 1. 3. 5, with Bosworth (1980*a*), 61, dealing with Alexander's campaign against the Getae in 335). But the area north of the Dobrudja across the Danube was known as the Desert of the Getae (Strabo 7. 3. 17. 306), and Zopyrion's campaign was in this direction, as he went on to lay siege to Olbia, on the Bug Liman, and advanced as far as the Borysthenes (the Dnieper) (Macrobius *Saturnalia* 1. 11. 33; *SEG* 32, 1982 (1985), 794–5 provide epigraphical evidence from Olbia of emergency measures that may have been taken when Zopyrion attacked the city). Tarn i. 71 suggests that Zopyrion's campaign was an element in a grand strategy to establish a link between Thrace and Bactria, there being some confusion about the geography and distances that separated the Thracian Scythians and the Scythians of Kazakhstan (cf. Curtius 7. 6. 12–13). Since one group was referred to as the European Scythians (Curtius 7. 6. 12; A. 7. 15. 4), we may have an explanation of Coenus' report on actions in Europe *and Asia.*

**1. 45. Seuthes had driven his subjects, the Odrysians, to rebellion.** The king in Alexander's day is referred to as Seuthes III, but it is not known whether he was related to the earlier king Seuthes II and his successor, Cotys (384–360 BC) (Elvers (1994), 246). On Cotys' death the kingdom was split up, Cotys' son Cersobleptes, Berisades, and

Amadocus each grabbing a portion of the territory (Dem. 23. 8; Tod *GHI* ii. no. 151, now R&O, no. 47). In the 350s Philip annexed the western two kingdoms (cf. J. 8. 3. 14–15), and by the summer of 340 Cersobleptes had also been deposed by Philip (Dem. 12. 8). Alexander took with him into Asia some Odrysian troops, as virtual hostages (D.S. 17. 17. 4), and Sitalces, who may have been a prince of the royal house (Berve (1926), ii. no. 712; J. 11. 5. 3, with Yardley and Heckel (1997), 106; he appears at 10. 1. 1).

Somehow Seuthes III emerged as the new king of the Odrysians and he is credited with founding the city of Seuthopolis, now identified as Kazanlak in Bulgaria. It appears that the tomb-heroon of Seuthes III has been found in the 'Valley of the Thracian kings' near Kazanlak, together with a bronze head (well illustrated Web sites posted by Bulgarian agencies can be readily found). The Odrysian homeland seems to have stretched from the upper Ebros (Maritsa) to the Black Sea, and, despite Macedonian ambitions, the area under Odrysian influence, if not control, extended to the Aegean coast, through the king's power over Pistiros and its harbour, and Maroneia (*SEG* 49, 1999 (2002), 911 with *SEG* 43, 1993 (1996), 486. But the extension of Odrysian rule to the Aegean is rejected by C. Veligianni: *SEG* 45, 1995 (1998), 830, 863 and 875). There is also evidence that Odrysian control extended as far as the Propontis (A. Zournatzi, 'Inscribed silver vessels of the Odrysian kings', *AJA* 104 (2000), 683–706). Thus the manpower resources potentially available to Seuthes were considerable (cf. D.S. 18. 14. 2), and the Odrysians commanded enormous resources of precious metals (Thucydides 2. 97; Hdt. 4. 7. 1–2). Seuthes III rebelled against Macedon, perhaps in 326, and was still able to assert Odrysian independence after Alexander's death; hence the campaign which Lysimachus launched against him (D.S. 18. 14. 2–4), and much later, *c.*313, Lysimachus is again attested as clashing with Odrysian forces, this time in a mountain pass in the Haemus range (D.S. 19. 73. 8; Strabo 7. 3. 8. 302, repeated at 305). Thus armed resistance by the Odrysians was a serious matter. But the nature of Macedonian control over the Odrysians prior to the 'rebellion' should not be exaggerated. As noted above, Alexander appointed a 'general' to watch over Thrace, and Macedonian control was probably not much tighter than had been Persian control from 513 BC, when Thrace was neither a satrapy, nor a semi-autonomous region under a native ruler directly answerable to the king, but rather a 'peripheral territory' for which the closest satrap was responsible in terms of security and the collection of tribute (J.M. Balcer, 'Persian occupied Thrace (Skudra)', *Hist* 37 (1988), 1–21). Seuthes was autonomous enough to have his own eponymous city, and to mint his own coins. Seuthopolis was an instrument of Hellenization (cf. Calder (1996), esp. 169). Thus in the fullness of time, it was not too difficult to downscale what had been labelled a rebellion to a diplomatic spat. In, or more likely after, 306/5 Seuthes followed the Successors in taking the royal title (cf. D.S. 20. 53, though see 19. 73. 8), and Lysimachus married an Odrysian (Pausanias 1. 10. 4). And after Seuthes became incapacitated, his wife Berenice and her four sons are attested as still having authority in Seuthopolis (Elvers (1994); Calder (1996), but not aware of Elvers' edition of *IGBulg* 1731).

An Athenian decree of June 330 records honours for Rhebulas, the son of Seuthes, and brother of Cotys (*IG* ii² 349 = Tod *GHI* ii. no. 193). Tod took this inscription as reflecting Thracian preparation for conflict with the Macedonians and suggested that Seuthes III sent his son to negotiate an agreement with the Athenians. But this interpretation is rejected by Badian (1967), 191–2 and Schwenk (1985), 225–7. The inscription shows that Rhebulas had been granted Athenian citizenship earlier, and thus in 330 he might even have been in exile from his father's court, as Schwenk suggests. But Osborne (1983), 66–7 revives the idea of A. Höck that the father was Seuthes II, who died in 384/3, and Osborne would date the grant of citizenship to Rhebulas to the period 360–342 BC. Furthermore, if Seuthes III only took the royal title after 306, and had young sons when he became incapacitated (*SEG* 42, 1992 (1995), 661), then he can hardly have been old enough to have been the father of Cotys and Rhebulas: they must have been the sons of Seuthes II (Elvers (1994), 247–51).

**and not even Greece.** Curtius next deals with the crisis in Greece created by the appearance in Athens of Harpalus with a large amount of money which he had stolen from Alexander's treasury. The story resumes in 2. 1 after a significant gap in the text.

The missing section presumably included Harpalus' reasons for quitting his post in Babylon and then fleeing from Tarsus to Greece, as 2.1 opens with his arrival off the southern tip of Attica. D.S. 17.

108. 4–6 explains that guilt forced Harpalus to abscond from Babylon, and his case was thus much like that of the corrupt officers and officials mentioned by Curtius in 1. 1–9. By contrast, J. 13. 5. 9 turns the episode against Alexander: Harpalus fled to escape Alexander's cruelty. It is not surprising that there was also a salacious tradition that Harpalus lost touch with reality when he became besotted with his Athenian mistress Pythionice, and, when she died, with another courtesan, Glycera (D.S. 17. 108. 5–6): the story was embellished by Theopompus (in Athenaeus 13. 586c and 595a and d–e). Theopompus was openly hostile to Harpalus (Athen. 13. 595a; Bosworth (1988*a*) 149), and it appears that Cleitarchus took this hostile material over from Theopompus (Athen. 13. 586c with Pearson (1960), 19). We do not know whether Curtius included this detail or chose to ignore Cleitarchus on the point.

However, we can be sure that Curtius did have something on the initial Macedonian reaction to news that Harpalus was heading for Greece, and did refer to a plan by Alexander to assemble a fleet to attack Athens, because at 2. 4 Curtius says that Alexander 'dropped his plan of crossing to Europe'.

## 2. 1–7. *Athens, Harpalus and the return of the exiles*

### 2. 1–3. *Harpalus on the run*

*Sources*: D.S. 17. 108. 4–8, 18. 19. 1–2; J. 13. 5. 7–9; Pausanias 1. 37.5; 2. 33. 4; Plut. *Mor.* 531a–b; 846a–c; Arrian *Succ.* 1. 16 and Frag. 16. More factual information is provided by Plutarch, *Demosthenes* 25–6, *Phocion* 21–2, and in particular in the two speeches written to denounce Demosthenes by Dinarchus (1) and Hypereides (5), and in Dinarchus 3 (*Against Philocles*). Arrian probably covered the flight of Harpalus in the section of text missing after the end of 7. 12. 7.

*Bibliography*: Ashton (1983); Badian (1961); Bosworth (1988*a*), 149–50, 215–20 and 293–4; Goukowsky (1981), 65–77; Jaschinski (1981); Blackwell (1999); Worthington (1992), *passim*, (1999*a*), 7–12 and 188–90, (2004), 178–9 and 192–3; Whitehead (2000), 359–61; 386–92 and *passim*; Heckel (2006), 129–31.

Harpalus had been in charge of the royal treasury in Babylon, and had abandoned his post after Alexander emerged from the Gedrosian desert. Quite apart from what has been lost in the *lacuna*, Curtius' account of Harpalus' flight to Athens is severely abbreviated, but he appears to be in line with the source used by Diodorus: at 2. 1 Curtius mentions 30 ships, and with the usual complement of 200 per ship this fleet would have needed 6,000 men and Diodorus gives the number of mercenaries with Harpalus as 6,000, when he first landed in Attica (17. 108. 6), with which we can associate Curtius' reference to Sunium. Diodorus states that when Harpalus reached Attica the Athenians would not let his party land, so he bribed some Athenian politicians and took his men off to Taenarum, and returned to Athens alone (17. 108. 6–7): Worthington (1986*b*) argues that he would have returned with only one or perhaps two ships. On his second appearance he was allowed to enter the city by the *strategos* (general) Philocles (Dinarchus 3. 15), who held office in the year 325/4. Curtius goes on to say that Alexander heard that Harpalus had indeed (*quidem*) entered Athens, and this may mean that he or his source was well aware that this was the entry into the city after he had initially been refused permission to stay. Curtius then refers to what happened after Harpalus' return to Athens, when he was arrested, held in custody, and escaped to Crete. Diodorus suggests that the 'escape' was really engineered under political pressure from Antipater and Olympias. At the time Demosthenes and others were accused of accepting bribes to let him escape.

*Dating issues*

(A) **The evidence from Ecbatana.** The dating of Harpalus' flight from Babylon is complicated by Athenaeus' references to a satyr play called the *Agen*, probably by Python of Catana. The play was produced for Alexander, or perhaps even by Alexander, says Athenaeus, at a Dionysiac festival at the river Hydaspes (Athenaeus 13. 586c–d; 595e). The play was a satirical attack on Harpalus, clearly after the final break with Alexander, and thus not after Harpalus' first flight in 333 (H. Lloyd-Jones, review of B. Snell, *Scenes from Greek Drama* (1964), in *Gnomon* 38 (1966), 16–17). Thus it is generally accepted that the production was not while Alexander was on the Indian Hydaspes in 326, but rather in the context of the Dionysiac festivities held at Ecbatana in the autumn of 324 (D.S. 17. 110. 7; A. 7. 14. 1; Ephippus at Athenaeus 12. 538a; Plut. *Alex.* 72. 1). There was a Median Hydaspes (Vergil *Georgics* 4. 211; Petronius *Sat.* 123. 239 refers to

Pompey as the discoverer of the Hydaspes, perhaps exploiting the confusion between the Median and Indian rivers). This may refer to the Qareh Chay (so Lloyd-Jones, art. cit., following Beloch). The *Agen* featured Harpalus ensconced in splendour at Tarsus, and thus before he fled to Greece. This, not surprisingly, would have reflected the situation when the play was conceived, rather than when it was produced, in the summer (or autumn) of 324.

In the context of the drama festival at Ecbatana, Ephippus recorded that Gorgus, a Custodian of the Armour, had it announced that as soon as Alexander should lay siege to Athens, he would provide Alexander with 10,000 complete suits of armour, the same number of catapults and enough of the other types of missiles for the war (Ephippus in Athenaeus 12. 538b = *FGrH* 126, F.5; there is epigraphic evidence that Gorgus gave support to the Samians against the Athenians and offered Alexander a crown to celebrate the exiles' decree (*SIG*³ 312), which lends support to Ephippus' story: Pearson (1960), 63–5; Heisserer (1980), 169–203). Thus in Ecbatana Alexander was well aware that Harpalus had fled to Athens, but, if Athens had backed off from a confrontation, Alexander was not yet aware.

(B) **The purge.** The purge of the corrupt, incompetent and disloyal began after Alexander reached the capital of Gedrosia, Pura (A. 6. 27. 1; C.R. 9. 10. 18 ff.; D.S. 17. 106. 1–2), and intensified after he entered Carmania (A. 6. 27. 3–5), at the end of 325. Thus Jaschinski (1981), 35–44, would date Harpalus' flight from Babylon in about March 324, and his first arrival in Athens in August 324, while Badian (1961), 24 and 43, sets the departure from Babylon in February 324, and the entry into Athens in the second or third week of July, which better suits the Athenian evidence. Goukowsky (1981), 65–77 sensibly argues that Harpalus would have wasted no time in moving off once the purge began, and he would therefore date the *Agen* and Gorgus' pledge of armour much earlier than Alexander's stay in Ecbatana. He exploits the fact that the identity of the Iranian 'Hydaspes' is uncertain, and separates the theatrical festival, at which the *Agen* was presented, from what he argues must have been the earlier Dionysiac celebration at which Gorgus made his offer. In Goukowsky's view, the *Agen* was presented at Salmous in Carmania, and the Dionysiac procession would be that staged while

Alexander was *en route* from Pura to Salmous. This brushes aside the clear references in Diodorus and Ephippus to Ecbatana, and seems to attribute to Python, and (if that is what Goukowsky intends) Gorgus, knowledge of events that had not yet taken place. Gorgus also proposed to honour Alexander as the son of Ammon, which would make more sense after Alexander overtly courted deification in the spring of 324. Thus Goukowsky may be right about an early date for Harpalus' departure from Babylon, but hardly right in setting the *Agen* as early as the end of 325, if it featured Harpalus as already in Tarsus. Gorgus' pledge can not be placed earlier than that.

Goukowsky (1981), 76 finds a reason for Harpalus' precipitous departure from Babylon in the fragment of the *Agen* which mocks Harpalus' delivery of large quantities of corn to Athens to impress his mistress Glycera (Athenaeus 13. 596a–b). If this is true, Alexander would not have been amused that Harpalus had sent to Athens grain which he could have sent to the army in Gedrosia.

**(C) The Athenian evidence.** Dinarchus 3. 15 shows that Philocles, was *strategos* with responsibility for Munichia and the dockyards when he admitted Harpalus into Athens; and the naval records appear to show that for the year 324/3 Dicaeogenes had that area of responsibility with the title *strategos* (*IG* ii² 1631c. 380–1), or *strategos* for the Peiraeus, as that was the title he had when he held the same office in 323/2 (*IG* ii² 1631b. 214–15; Develin *AO,* 408 notes that Reinmuth (1971), 67 and 71 erroneously dates this tenure to the year 325/4. Whitehead (2000), 358 appears to invert the dates of the generalships referred to in 1631c. 380–1 and 1631b. 214–15). The title is further confirmed if the ephebic honorific inscription from Oropus does relate to 324/3 (text and commentary in Reinmuth (1971), 58–82). Thus, pace Jaschinski, Philocles was not *strategos* in 324/3, but in 325/4 (so, categorically, Davies *APF,* 539–40; Whitehead (2000), 358), and Harpalus must have reached Athens before 22 July 324.

There is a problem with the Oropus inscription, which attests for the same year Dicaeogenes as *strategos* for the Peiraeus and Philocles as *kosmetes* of the ephebes (on which office see Aristotle *Ath. Pol.* 42. 2, and 3 on the link between the ephebes and the protection of the Peiraeus). This has generally been taken to be the year 324/3, so that

Philocles took this ephebic magistracy in the year after the crucial generalship. But Dinarchus 3. 15 says that after the scandal of Philocles' acceptance of a bribe to admit Harpalus into the city broke, the Assembly voted that he was not a suitable person to hold a position in charge of the ephebes. Dinarchus is imprecise, and it is not clear whether he means that the Assembly disallowed his candidacy, or deposed him from the office to which he had been elected. Thus, if the Philocles honoured in the Oropus inscription was the same man as the general of 325/4, and if he held the position of *kosmetes* in 324/3, then either he entered the latter office before the storm broke, and he was deposed, which seems improbable, or his candidacy was initially disallowed, but later reinstated when his case came to court and he was found innocent, or was given a light sentence and then rehabilitated. But Demosthenes *Ep.* 3. 31 says that he was exiled. Thus the Oropus inscription does not sit well with Dinarchus 3. 15 if both are taken to refer to the year 324/3 (the issues are fully reviewed by Reinmuth (1971), 67–76). Bosworth (1988*a*), 293–4 offers a 'third way', by following those who would rather re-date the Oropus inscription. He argues in favour of dating Philocles' term as *kosmetes* to 329/8.

After all this it remains more probable that Harpalus fled from Babylon in about February 324 (Badian (1961), 24; Blackwell (1999), 13 n. 13 for other references) rather than later, and more certain that he arrived in Athens before 22 July 324 (cf. Schäfer (1887), 307–8; early July: Badian (1961), 42–3), perhaps even in late June (Worthington (1986*a*), 65). Bosworth (1988*a*), 215–220 sets the issues in context.

In compositional terms Curtius uses the Harpalus episode to pick up on Alexander's plans for operations in the west (albeit a different plan) and to provide an explanation for the exiles' decree, though the exiles' decree must have been formulated before Harpalus was admitted into Athens. Curtius puts the focus firmly on Alexander's reactions to news about Harpalus.

2. 1. **with thirty ships.** As noted above, thirty ships would be consistent with there being 6,000 mercenaries, but 5,000 talents of silver (D.S. 17. 108. 6) would have weighed *c.*140 tons, and Blackwell (1999), 13–14 n. 13 therefore argues that the cargo was rather

5,000 talents of gold, at *c.*14 tons, which he also supports by Plutarch's reference to Harpalus as arriving with gold (*Mor.* 846a, where Philochorus is cited as a source. Gold is also mentioned in Dinarchus 1. 89, 3. 7; Hypereides 5. 8).

**Sunium—a promontory in the territory of Attica.** Livy 32. 17. 3 glosses Sunium with the same words.

**2. 2. Harpalus.** First mentioned in what we have of Curtius' *Historiae*, at 9. 3. 21 on troops and armour sent by Harpalus from Babylon to India in 326. He was from the royal house of Elimeiotis, and was the son of Machatas, the brother of Phila, who is assumed to be the Phila from Elimeia whom Philip II married (A. 3. 6. 4; Satyrus in Athenaeus 13. 557c; and in general on Harpalus, Heckel (2006), 129–31). Harpalus had good reason to be nervous about his misappropriation of funds and abuse of power, as he had once before, in 333, absconded from his post as treasurer (A. 3. 6. 6–7), presumably with a share of the treasure he was supposed to be guarding. Past loyalty to Alexander, if not a relationship by marriage, had won him redemption, but he was alas a recidivist.

**a fleet to be mustered for an immediate strike on Athens.** Cf. J. 13. 5. 7, and Ephippus, *FGrH* 126, F.5, from Athenaeus 12. 538b. This is to be linked with Alexander's plans for a Mediterranean fleet (1. 19 above). Whatever Alexander's plans, Antipater, Olympias and Philoxenus sent messages demanding Harpalus' extradition (D.S. 17. 108. 7; Hypereides *Demosthenes* 8; Plut. *Mor.* 531a, and Paus. 2. 33. 4). Philoxenus was presumably the officer who was put in charge of fiscal collections from allied Greek cities in Asia Minor in 331 (Berve (1926), ii. no. 793; A. 3. 6. 4), and who some time later took over control of Caria (A. 7. 23. 1 and 24. 1; Arist. [*Oecon*]. 2. 31. 1351b, giving his title as satrap; Bosworth (1980*a*), 280–2. Berve, Bosworth and Heckel (2006), 220 all distinguish this satrap of Caria from the Philoxenus who was appointed by Perdiccas as satrap of Caria in 321/0: A. *Succ.* 24. 2; J. 13. 6. 16). Hypereides' reference to Philoxenus' demand for the extradition of Harpalus (5. 8) is a guarantee of its historicity and importance (Whitehead (2000), 387–9), but the demands made separately by Olympias and Antipater presented Athens with the opportunity to play for time. All of this raises questions about the nature of the power relationship between Alexander and the Athenians, well reviewed by Blackwell (1999), esp. chap. 2.

**2. 3. won the support of leading citizens by bribery.** The phraseology echoes Livy 21. 20. 8. The scandal that erupted after Harpalus' arrest by the Athenians and subsequent escape involved charges that Athenian politicians had accepted bribes from Harpalus (e.g. Dinarchus 1. 67, 88–9; Hypereides *Demosthenes* 7 and 12; Plut. *Dem.* 25–6; D.S. 17. 108. 7; J. 13. 5. 9; cf. Plut. *Phoc.* 21. 3–4; Athenaeus 8. 341e–342a).

**an assembly of the people . . . which ordered him to leave the city.** Curtius styles the assembly the *concilium plebis*, which gives the episode Roman colouring, and that must be intentional since the phrase is not generally used by Latin writers of non-Roman communities.

As noted in the introduction to this section, Curtius fudges the distinction between the initial decision of the Assembly to refuse Harpalus permission to enter Athens and the subsequent decision to allow him in, followed by the resolution that he be detained. As Demosthenes was accused of being responsible for Harpalus' escape (Hyp. 5. 12), Harpalus' flight probably happened after Demosthenes' return from Olympia in early August (Worthington (1986a), 66–7; Blackwell (1999), 16). Hypereides indicates that Demosthenes proposed that Harpalus be taken into custody, and that Harpalus escaped because the guards became careless (Hyp. 5. 11–12). Thus Demosthenes was not directly responsible for the escape (Whitehead (2000), 397–8), but he could be held responsible for creating a situation in which Harpalus was allowed to escape, and Hypereides was quick to suggest that Demosthenes had been bribed. Demosthenes' proposal that Harpalus be detained can hardly have been an outcome of Demosthenes' dealings with Alexander's agent Nicanor at Olympia, as Harpalus was admitted into Athens sometime before the games, and his detention seems to have happened soon after he entered the city.

**treacherously murdered at the instigation of a friend of his.** Harpalus was allowed to escape from Athens (Hypereides, *Demosthenes* 12), joined his mercenaries at Taenarum and then sailed to Crete where he was murdered by Thibron, one of his officers (D.S. 17. 108. 7–8; 18.

19. 2; A. *Succ.* 1. 16). Pausanias 2. 33. 4 records a tradition that he was murdered by a Macedonian—yet another Pausanias. More reliably, Arrian *Succ.* 1. 16 states that Thibron was a Spartan. After Alexander's death he operated as a warlord in Cyrenian territory till his capture by Ptolemy in 322/1 (D.S. 18. 19–21; A. *Succ.* 1. 16–19, the date provided by the Parian Marble; Heckel (2006), 265–6 reviews his career). The hostile bias in Curtius' reference to the man behind the killing of Harpalus may thus reflect an Alexandrian source, Cleitarchus.

### 2. 4–7. *The Exiles Decree*

*Sources*: D.S. 17. 109. 1; 18. 8. 2–7; J. 13. 5. 2–3; Hypereides 5. 18–19; Dinarchus 1. 82; Tod *GHI* ii. 202 (trans. Harding (1985), no. 122), now R&O no. 101.

*Bibliography*: Badian (1961), 25–31; Bosworth (1988*a*), 220–8; Faraguna (2003), 124–7; Heisserer (1980), 188–93, 205–29; Jaschinski (1981), 62–92; Whitehead (2000), esp. 413–16; Worthington (1992), 251; (2004), 191–4.

**2. 4. Alexander dropped his plan of crossing to Europe.** Again a reference to Alexander's plan for a fleet to operate in the Mediterranean: D.S. 18. 4. 4; J. 13. 5. 7; cf. above on 1.19.

**he ordered the restoration of exiles . . . by all the cities which had expelled them.** Curtius and D.S. 17. 109. 1 seem to be following a common source: probably Cleitarchus, though Hammond (1983), 72–3 argues for Diyllus. Curtius and D.S. imply that the decree enforcing the readmission of exiles by their mother cities was a consequence of the Harpalus affair. Those who accept this sequence, on the grounds that Harpalus defected with a mercenary force and with promises that he could turn satrapal armies against Alexander (Hypereides 5. 19), are obliged to put the order for the disbandoning of the mercenary units well after Alexander heard that Harpalus had fled, and thus well into 324 (Jaschinski (1981), 45–54, who makes the good point that Hypereides implies that the satraps still had mercenaries at their disposal (49); Lane Fox (1973), 413, dating the decree to May 324). But Hypereides 5. 18 states that when Harpalus first arrived in Attica, Greece was in turmoil because Nicanor was already in Greece to announce the decree. The official promulgation was at the Olympic games of July/August 324 (D.S. 17. 109. 1; Dinarchus 1. 81–2; Sealey (1960) argues that the games fell in the period 31 July to 4 August), but what he had to announce was common knowledge, at least in outline, well before that event. Thus it becomes more likely that the decommissioning of satrapal mercenary units was not decided on only after Alexander heard of Harpalus' flight.

After the disastrous march through the Gedrosian desert, and thus from the end of 325, Alexander became more paranoid and began a purge of those who were reported to have been guilty of disloyalty or maladministration (cf. A. 7. 4. 2–3). He believed that some satraps were threatening defiance and were turning their satrapal forces against him. Hence he ordered the satraps to dissolve their mercenary units (D.S. 17. 111. 1; 106. 2–3). The immediate point is that Diodorus sets the order to the satraps before Alexander reached Salmous in Carmania, or while he was in Salmous (17. 106. 3–4, and thus more or less at the same time as he gave orders for the assembling of a fleet to operate in the Mediterranean). In this context the decree on the return of exiles can be seen as a solution to some of the problems of repatriating demobilized troops, even if not all returnees were mercenaries, and not all mercenaries were exiles. Diodorus 18. 8. 2 states that Alexander issued the proclamation to the exiles that they were to be allowed to return to their cities, partly for the glory, and partly to establish in each city a substantial number of individuals favourable to himself and ready to counter revolutionary and secessionary movements. Even if they were less well-disposed to Alexander than D.S. suggests, Alexander presumably hoped that returning mercenaries would focus their attention on recovering their property and rights in their respective cities. But Alexander also had a plan to intercept the columns of demobilized mercenaries before they embarked for their return to Greece. The satraps of Lydia and Caria induced many to enlist again, but this time with Alexander (A. 7. 23. 1; D.S. 17. 110. 2; Jaschinski (1981), 56). He needed Greek mercenaries not only as front-line troops, but also to man garrisons (cf. Curtius 9. 7. 1–11 with D.S. 17. 99. 5; A. 6. 15. 2; D.S. 18. 7), and he had a policy of encouraging veterans and those unfit for active service to settle in Asia (A. 4. 4. 1, 22. 5, 24. 7; Pliny *HN* 6. 138; Bosworth (1988*a*), 247–50).

If Alexander was seriously concerned about the mercenaries, large numbers of whom were now unemployed and stateless, and was concerned about the problems that those who returned to Greece would cause, this would explain why, as noted above, the Decree was addressed to them and presented to a mass meeting of them at Olympia. There were presumably parallel texts for the Greek cities, with more procedural details, and for Antipater, with instructions.

But the issue was not just about stopping returning mercenaries from creating mayhem in Greece. Bosworth (1988*a*), esp. 223 rightly emphasizes that many exiles would have been in exile in Greece for many years, and many would have gone into exile because they had been anti-Macedonian. This was a U-turn, pragmatic in providing a solution to a problem which he had created, and cynical in the way the decree undercut what Antipater had done in his name (Badian (1961), 29–31; Heuss (1938), 139 ff.). Alexander made a point of stressing that he had not been the cause of Greeks being exiled (D.S. 18. 8. 4): exiles could blame the Corinthian League or Antipater for that, and, as Badian suggests, this may have been part of a conscious plan to undermine Antipater. Still, it must not be assumed that foreign policy, or anti-Macedonian activity, was the only reason for individuals being sent into exile (below on 2. 6).

**2. 5. despite their belief that it constituted the first step towards the collapse of their laws.** Even if the decree was placatory in allowing men hostile to Macedon to recover citizenship, Alexander was confrontational in issuing such a decree. The purge that had begun was now extended to affect Greek cities whose attitude to Alexander had been ambivalent. The decree side-stepped the Council of the Corinthian League, and overrode the autonomy which had been guaranteed to member states (Tod *GHI* ii. 177 (now R&O no. 76); 185 (now R&O no. 86.*B*); Dem. 17. 7–8; *OGIS* 223. 22–3; a scholiast's note on Demosthenes 18. 89 (Dindorf, *Demosthenes, Scholia Graeca*, vol. 8 (Oxford, 1851), 293 (or M. R. Dilts, *Scholia Demosthenica*, vol. 1 (Leipzig, 1983), 219), noted by Heisserer (1980), 19 n. 22); Plut. *Alex.* 34. 2; Faraguna (2003), 99–104; Cartledge (2004), 84–93). Hammond's sanitized version of the Exiles Decree was premised on the assumptions that Alexander had no institutional justification for interfering in the internal affairs of member states of the Common

Peace/Corinthian League and respected that limitation of his powers, and secondly that, as the Decree affected exiles of all Greek cities, Alexander was not working within the confines of the Common Peace. Thus, in Hammond's view, Alexander was very conscious of the limits of his authority, and could do no more than make an announcement of his wishes in the matter of the exiles (Hammond (1988), 80–2). Blackwell (1999), 3–4 for one will have none of this.

**they even restored ... property to the condemned men.** The restoration of land to returning exiles was a difficult problem, which Athens had had to confront before, with the restoration of democracy in 403 (Atkinson, 'Truth and Reconciliation the Athenian way', *Acta Classica* 42 (1999), 5–13). Furthermore, land redistribution had negative connotations, at least for the wealthy, as one 'of the "classical features" of the social revolution from the fourth to the second centuries BC' (A. Fuks, *Social Conflict in Ancient Greece* (Jerusalem, 1984), quotation from p. 70, citing i.a. Isocrates *Panath.* 259). More immediate evidence of the legal and administrative problems raised by the Exiles Decree is provided by the version set up by Tegea after negotiation of certain details with Alexander (Tod *GHI* ii. 202 (now R&O no. 101); Heisserer (1980), 205–29, who accepts that the balance of probability favours restoration of the king's name as [Alex]ander, rather than [Cass]ander; L. Dubois, *Recherches sur le dialecte Arcadien* (Louvain-la-Neuve, 1988), Part 2, 61–77). The issues included the restitution of property, with provision for property that was encumbered with debt; the establishment of arbitration procedures; clarification of the property rights of wives and daughters of exiles; the reassignment of liturgical obligations (on Dubois' interpretation of lines 21–2). Dubois concludes that the Tegeans endeavoured to satisfy the spirit of Alexander's decree, but accorded the returning exiles only the minimum of civic dignity (p. 75). Their general support of Alexander in the past did not spare them from having to respect Alexander's ruling. Ironically Tegea must have had to take back those responsible for leading her into an alliance with Sparta in 331, and thus into the war against Antipater (cf. Curtius 6. 1. 20; Heisserer (1980), 221; Blackwell (1999), 150).

**2. 6. Only the Athenians ... were reluctant to tolerate such a mishmash of classes and individuals.** Hypereides 5. 18 indicates that there was general resistance to the decree, but D.S. 18. 18. 6 states that the Aetolians and the Athenians were the only protesters (Dinarchus 1. 82 refers to the crisis in Athens). The Athenians complained because they did not wish to give up control of Samos (D.S. 18. 8. 6; 18. 6 and 9). If, as noted above, Curtius and Diodorus were following a common source on the Exiles Decree, then Curtius chose to focus solely on Athens (Dempsie (1991), 85).

**mishmash.** The Latin, *colluvionem* (almost a cesspool), introduces an intrusive element, hardly appropriate for the return of citizens. It and the following term *purgamenta* ('scum' in 2. 7) reflect Roman antipathy to the migration of aliens into the city (cf. Juvenal *Satires* 3. 62; Livy 26. 40. 17). But there is also a significant link in J. 5. 6. 5, where Justin says that after their defeat in the Peloponnesian War, the Athenians reached such desperate straits that they had to give citizenship to foreigners, freedom to slaves, and impunity to convicted criminals. And with an army raised from this cesspool (*colluvione*) of mankind, the Athenians, who had earlier been the masters of Greece, were scarcely able to defend their liberty (*libertatem*)(J. 5. 6. 5–6; the phraseology appears also at J. 2. 6. 4 and 38. 7. 1). This clearly became a commonplace, echoed for example in Cn. Piso's attack on Germanicus' excessive friendliness towards Athens, that mishmash (to use the less vulgar image) of nations (Tac. *Ann.* 2. 55. 1. Augustus acted to stop Athens selling her citizenship: Dio 54. 7. 2). In another context Laevinus sought to bring peace to Sicily by shipping out from Agathyrna 4,000 from the cesspool of every kind of troublemaker—*exiles*, debtors, men guilty of capital crimes (Livy 26. 40. 17). Thus there are inappropriate Roman resonances here, and Curtius may be echoing a phrase created by Trogus (cf. Yardley (2003), 99).

As noted above, for Athenians the issue of returning exiles was by no means just about demobilized or absconding mercenaries. From 330, thus after the failure of the revolt led by Agis of Sparta, wealthy Athenians were under particular attack (cf. Hypereides 4. 35–6 on mine lessees; Dem. 42. 3; Lycurgus *Leocr.* 139) in a bout of class warfare. The wealthy were vulnerable in that their pragmatism made them opponents of suicidal military action. They had more to gain from an accommodation with Macedon (Atkinson (1981), 40–8). Thus men like Callimedon of Kollytos were bundled into exile

(Davies *APF* 279; mining interests: *IG* ii² 1587, line 12 with M. Crosby, *Hesperia* 19 (1950), 280–1; exile: Plut. *Phoc.* 35, *Dem.* 27; 'enemy of democracy' (*misodemon*): Plut. *Phoc.* 27. 9). Megara became quite a centre of Athenian emigrants and exiles: Lycurgus, *Leoc.* (of 330 BC) 21, 23 and *passim*; Dinarchus 1. 58 and 94.

**laws and ancestral customs.** The adjective 'ancestral' may qualify both nouns: 'the ancestral constitution/laws' emerged as a slogan in Athens in 411 BC, initially calculated to promote reform in an oligarchic direction, under the guise of a return to traditional democracy (Arist. *Ath. Pol.* 29. 3). In the fourth century BC it became something of a cliché, which Isocrates avoided, as a 'perhaps somewhat discredited slogan' (A. Fuks, *The Ancestral Constitution* (London, 1953), 11). Isocrates uses the phrase at 4. 55, and again at 12. 169, but of the traditional law that the dead had to be buried, and not in the political sense that was the slogan of the late fifth century. Whether or not Curtius drew on an authentic tradition on the Athenian reaction to the decree, the Latin phraseology he adopted had contemporary resonances. There was nothing ancestral about the Principate, and a Republican-minded senator might also lament the passing of the ancestral constitution and *libertas*. If Modius was correct in emending the earlier phrase in this sentence to *publicae vindices <libertatis>* (champions of constitutional liberty), Curtius was echoing wording which Augustus used to re-present his acts of high treason as the championing of the basic principle of the Republic (*Res Gestae* 1, and as a coin legend in 28 BC, LIBERTATIS VINDEX: *BMCRE* i. 112. On the use of this ideogram in the early Empire, Ch. Wirszubski, *Libertas as a Political Idea at Rome during the Late Republic and Early Principate* (Cambridge, 1950); E. Lyasse, 'La notion de Libertas dans le discours politique romain d'Auguste à Trajan', *Ktema* 28 (2003), 63–9; cf. Spencer (2002), 194. The phrase was used earlier, e.g. by Caesar, *BCiv.* 1. 22. 5.). So Curtius was either trying to recapture something of the political rhetoric of fourth century Athens, or introducing phraseology that had resonances in his own day.

**2. 7. they barred the exiles from their territory and were prepared to suffer anything rather than admit what was once the scum of their city.** This makes sense with regard to men exiled for political reasons or for their criminal record. It does not make sense with regard to the case of Samos, which Athenian settlers had to vacate so that Samians could return to their land. There is debate whether Samos was directly covered by the Exiles Decree (so Bosworth (1988*a*), 221, Ashton (1983), 62–3, Heisserer (1980), 183–9), or was raised as a separate issue, and at a later date (Errington (1975), 53–5, who argues that Alexander's ruling in favour of the Samians (*SIG*³, 312, translated in Harding (1985), no. 127) was announced in Babylon in 323, whereas most scholars set the proclamation in Susa in 324). But Samos certainly emerged as a special case (Zahrnt (2003), 425). Curtius' formulation here does not suggest that he had the Samos issue in mind. He is in line with D.S. 17. 109. 1, but not with D.S. 18. 8. 7, where Samos is given as the reason for Athenian resistance to the Decree. Thus, if Hieronymus was Diodorus' source for 18. 8. 7, Curtius here and Diodorus at 17. 109 were probably following Cleitarchus.

The Athenians had seized Samos in 366/5 (Demosthenes 15. 9; Nepos *Timotheus* 1. 2. Demosthenes links the occupation with the mission to assist Ariobarzanes, but the date is indicated by D.S. 18. 18. 9: Samos was liberated after 43 years of Athenian occupation). The scholiast to Aeschines 1. 53 links the settlement of Samos with the archon of 361/0, Nicophemos, and less reliably D.S. 15. 90 deals with Samos among events of 362/1. Thus there may have been a gap between seizure of the island and the settlement of cleruchs there. The Athenians drove the Samians off their land to allow Athenian cleruchs to settle there (Aeschines 1. 53; D.S. 18. 18. 9; Arist. *Rhet.* 1384b. 32–5 on Kydias' opposition to the move; *IG* ii² 1437. 20 ff.). An additional group of 2,000 settlers may have been sent out in the 340s (Strabo 14. 1. 18. 638, with G. Shipley, *A History of Samos 800–188* BC (Oxford, 1987), 12–15 and 141). The return of the Samian exiles was facilitated in 322 (D.S. 18. 18. 9), and this would have forced the Athenian settlers to return to Attica. The scale of the problem is indicated by the inscription from Samos of about 352–347, which attests a local Boule with notionally 25 representatives from each of the ten Athenian tribes (the figure is notional because the system was flexible enough to tolerate small deviations: one tribe had 26 representatives). These cleruchs were Athenian citizens and came from at least 87, or *c.*63 per cent, of the Athenian demes (revised text in *SEG*

45: 1995 (1998), 1162). A total of 250 *bouleutae* is half the size of the Boule in Athens. Thus Habicht in his commentary on the inscription suggests that the number of adult male citizens on Samos fell in the range 6,000 to 12,000 (*MDAI (A)* 110 (1995), 286–303, echoing the range suggested by Shipley; Zahrnt (2003), 412). Alexander's edict created a major crisis for Athens, but not in the way imagined by Curtius.

**2. 8–4. 3.** *The discharge of veterans and the settlement of debts provokes a mutiny*

**2. 8–11.** *The settlement of debts*

*Sources:* A. 7. 5. 1–3; D.S. 17. 109. 2; J. 12. 11. 1–3; Plut. *Alex.* 70. 3, *Mor.* 339b–c.

*Bibliography:* for general studies of Alexander's finances see Knapowski (1970), Bosworth (1988a), 241–5, and Le Rider (2003).

A. 7. 8. 1 sets the discharge of the veterans in the context of Alexander's occupation of Opis, which would have been in the summer of 324. But he sets the settlement of the troops' debts in the context of Alexander's stay in Susa, which he reached sometime after the end of March 324 (Pliny *HN* 6. 100 with Brunt (1983), 500). Plutarch *Alex.* 70. 3 likewise sets the debt clearance in the context of the marriage ceremony at Susa. Curtius has the debt settlement and the discharge of veterans in the reverse order, in that the debt settlement arose out of his decision to send the veterans home. Diodorus' highly abbreviated version (17. 109. 2–3) agrees with the outline of Curtius' account, and although he puts these events at around the time of the Olympic games (of 324), and brings in the story of the Opis mutiny, he followed a source which had at least some of these events before Alexander left Susa (17. 110. 3). Curtius and Diodorus both give 10,000 talents as the sum which Alexander advanced (2. 10). They were not following the same source as Justin (12. 11. 2–3), who gives the amount as 20,000 talents, as does A. 7. 5. 3. Plutarch's source was not Curtius', and Plutarch mentions Chares in *Alex.* 70. 2. Curtius and Diodorus were probably both using Cleitarchus.

The sequence of events indicated by Arrian is the more probable. At the end of 325 Alexander ordered the disbandment of satrapal mercenary forces (D.S. 17. 106. 3 and 111. 1; above on 2. 4). It was also clear that the Persian War was virtually over. This may have had a negative effect on the morale of Macedonian troops who were now uncertain about their future. On reaching Susa, Alexander encouraged some sense of permanence about the imperial army by organizing the marriages (presumably in general the recognition of unions already well established) and clearing debts. But the arrival of the 30,000 Persian youths trained in the Macedonian fashion (A. 7. 6. 1; Plut. *Alex.* 71. 1; D.S. 17. 108. 1) added to the tension. It seems logical that Alexander arranged the marriages some time before the discharge of the veterans, whom he instructed to leave behind their Asian wives and children (A. 7. 12. 2; obviously some liaisons predated the Susa marriages). The time gap was filled by the journey down to the Persian Gulf, and then up the Tigris to Opis (A. 7. 7. 1), which he would have reached well into the summer of 324. But Goukowsky (1976), 267 argues for setting the mutiny in Susa immediately after the arrival of the Epigonoi. and thus gives preference to A. 7. 6. 2 and the Vulgate tradition.

**2. 8. ordered a force of 13,000 infantry and 2,000 cavalry to be selected for him to keep back in Asia.** Alexander discharged 10,000 Macedonian veterans (D.S. 17. 109. 1; 18. 4. 1; A. 7. 12. 1; J. 12. 12. 7 gives 11,000 veterans). Goukowsky (1975), 267 assumes that Curtius is here referring to Macedonians alone, and would reduce their value by suggesting that they included men left to protect garrisons as veterans or invalids (cf. 2. 4 above). But, if Alexander discharged more (Macedonian) troops than he retained (2. 19 below), then the figures given here by Curtius must include non-Macedonians (*pace* Hammond (1989*a*), 68).

**2.10. to tell the wastrels from the thrifty.** The Latin term here translated as 'thrifty' was commonly used as an epithet for a section of the Roman plebs, thus *plebs integra* (with *frumentaria*, 'recipient of the corn dole' as an alternative). On one view this had a quasi-legal or sociological definition to denote those who were kept above the poverty line because they were recipients of the corn dole, and/or handouts from their patrons (Chilver (1979), 48–9; Sallust *or. Cottae* 5 and Suet. *Nero* 12. 1), as opposed to the plebs who fell below the category of recipients of the corn dole (the *plebs sordida* of Tac. *Hist.* 1. 4. 4 and 3. 74. 2). But against this interpretation, Z. Yavetz, 'Plebs

sordida', *Athenaeum* 43 (1965), 295–311 argues that the only consistency in the usage of this phraseology is that pejorative expressions are
used where the people as a class, or in a certain situation, are
threatening to the political or social order, and neutral expressions
are applied where the 'plebs' know their station and accept the
benefits of *clientela* with due gratitude. On this view, the plebs
could be *integra* (with visible means of support, respectable) or
*sordida* ('the great unwashed') according to the prejudice or rhetorical purpose of the writer at the particular time. Yavetz does indeed
show that there is such a pattern in the distribution of the pejorative
and more positive expressions in the sources. But at the same time,
Tacitus *Hist.* 1. 4. 4 would seem to reflect the situation that a section
of the Roman population was kept in line by the economic patronage
of the emperor and the elite through the corn dole and other
handouts, and there were others who fell outside the net. This latter
group was potentially, but not necessarily, more difficult to control.
The antithesis marked by Curtius thus does not precisely match the
Roman model, but his use of the term *integra* does have a resonance
that would be immediately obvious to the Roman reader.

**2. 11. what remained was a mere 130 talents.** Thus the total paid out
was 9,870 talents which is the figure given by Plutarch *Alex.* 70. 3.

**took from Asia more prestige than booty.** Curtius highlights the
paradox with the final phrase, since for the Romans Asia denoted
exceptional wealth.

**2. 12–4.3.** *Alexander puts down a mutiny*

*Sources:* A. 7. 8. 1– 12. 3; Plut. *Alex.* 71; D.S. 17. 109. 2–3; J. 12. 11. 4–
12. 7; Polyaenus 4. 3. 7.

*Bibliography:* Tarn ii. 399–449; Badian (1958*b*); Wüst (1953/4*a* and
*b*); Rutz (1983*b*); Carney (1996), and Spencer (2002), 201–3.

Curtius gives as the two main concerns of the troops that all wanted
to be sent home at the same time, and that he was planning to move
the capital of the empire to Asia. The latter is peculiar to Curtius'
account and is an intrusive element borrowed from Roman politics
(unless it was just a circumlocution for the complaint that it seemed
that they were never going to get home). The other sources all present

as a major cause of the trouble the arrival of the 30,000 Epigonoi
(A. 7. 8. 2, with 6. 1–2, confirming that they joined Alexander's army
at Susa; Plut. *Alex.* 71. 1; J. 12. 11. 6, and by implication D.S. 17. 108.
1–3). Curtius was well aware of Alexander's plan for training Persian
youths for service in his army (8. 5. 1; 10. 3. 10), but chose to ignore it
in his reference to the troops' grievances at what we know to be Opis.
Similarly he chose to leave out the troops' disdain for his infatuation
with the cult of Ammon (A. 7. 8. 3; D.S. 17. 108. 3; J. 12. 11. 6).
Curtius also leaves out here their objection to Persian dress, but
alludes to it in Alexander's address to his troops (A. 7. 8. 2; Curtius
2. 23). Clearly the idiosyncrasies of Curtius' account are due more to
his creative intent than to his choice of sources.

The term mutiny is conventionally applied to this incident, but
with the due recognition that it is somewhat anachronistic (Carney
(1996), esp. 19–20, with references).

**2. 12. assumed that Alexander was going to fix the royal seat
permanently in Asia.** But Alexander had already signalled by the
construction of a large fleet (references at 1. 16–19) that he would be
campaigning in fresh areas. The proleptic allusion to the Last Plans in
10. 1. 18–19 shows that Curtius was well aware of this tradition.
Furthermore, this is not the phraseology which Livy uses of similar
situations where Roman troops clamoured to be allowed to return
home (Livy 32. 3. 4–5; 40. 35. 7, passages mentioned by Rutz (1983*b*)
in his discussion of Curtius' debt to Livy in the account of the Opis
mutiny). The phraseology seems rather to echo a theme that resur-
faced periodically towards the end of the Republic and during the
early Empire: would the seat of empire (*sedes imperii* in Cicero *Leg.
Agr.* 1. 18 and 24, 2. 86 ff.) be moved from Rome to some other city?
(the subject is fully reviewed by Ceaușescu (1976*a*)). Julius Caesar
was rumoured to be wanting to settle in Alexandria or Troy (Suet.
*Julius* 79. 3; cf. Nicolaus of Damascus *Caes.* 20. 68); Antony's proclamation of the 'Empire of the Orient' in 34 (Plut. *Antony* 54; Dio 49.
41. 1–4; Livy *Periochae* 131) provided Octavian with valuable material for a campaign of vilification of his rival. In 32 Octavian was
confronting a situation where Antony, with the backing of both
consuls and some 300 senators, had virtually established a government in exile (R. Syme (1939), 278–9; the number of senators

supporting Antony is implied by the reference in Augustus *Res Gestae* 25. 3 to the tally of 700 senators who backed Octavian), and it suited him to claim that Antony planned to move the seat of government from Rome to Alexandria. Two generations later, it was said that Caligula planned to settle in Antium or Alexandria (Suet. *Gaius* 49. 2; Wardle (1994), 322), and, in his first reference to such a move, Suetonius uses the expression 'the seat and domicile of the empire' (*sedem ac domicilium imperii*: *Gaius* 8. 5). Nero too was supposed to have threatened to transfer his base to Alexandria (Dio 63. 27. 2; Plut. *Galba* 2. 1; Aurelius Victor 5. 14; and for a much later episode, Herodian 4. 3. 7). The formulation here thus seems to reflect a theme of the early Empire rather than the concerns of Alexander's Macedonian troops. Furthermore, the Macedonian kingdom was not focused on a city in the same way as was the Roman Empire.

**oblivious of military discipline.** Carney (1996), esp. 24, argues from 3. 8. 23 and 9. 4. 22–23 that Curtius attributed to the Macedonian army a concept of discipline which reflected his own Roman experience rather than Macedonian thinking (cf. Rutz (1983*b*), 401, noting also the influence of Livy, as at 7. 38. 5 and 28. 24. 9). But Carney, p. 31, also notes that in referring to unrest among the troops, Curtius uses the term 'sedition' (*seditio*) at 9. 4. 22 and here refers to seditious voices (cf. 7. 2. 31; 8. 1. 24; 9. 7.1), and at 6. 2. 4 he refers to a *secessio* of troops (literally a walk-out). The Latin term sedition spans both civil and military disturbances, and does not therefore have quite the same connotation as 'mutiny'. Carney argues that Alexander's authority over his troops had been seriously compromised by his capitulation to them on the Hyphasis. That experience may have 'radicalized the army' (p. 31, where Carney goes on (p. 36) to suggest the applicability of the notion of 'collective self-definition', which J. Ober introduced in his discussion of the Athenian revolution of 508/7 [in *Cultural Poetics in Archaic Greece*, ed. C. Dougherty and L. Kurke (Cambridge, 1993), 215–32, esp. 227]. Cf. Badian (1961), 20; Berve (1926), i. 213–17, esp. 214. One can follow Berve on the gradual breakdown of the relationship between Alexander and his troops without necessarily subscribing to his interpretation of the racial issues.) My inclination is to think that the erosion of Alexander's authority began long before the mutiny on the Hyphasis: the systematic destruction of Persepolis was a particularly mindless exercise in team-building which Alexander presumably thought he needed to try (Curtius 5. 7. 3–11; Atkinson (1993)). Curtius 6. 2. 4 says that the rot set in after the death of Darius (on the range of issues associated with this passage, Atkinson (1994), 167–9). Alexander's leadership was further tested when he was wounded at the city of the Malli (A. 6. 12–13).

**they all ... proceeded to demand demobilization as they displayed their scarred faces and grey heads.** Cf. the veterans in Germanicus' army on the Rhine (Tac. *Ann.* 1. 35. 1–2).

### 2.15–29. *Alexander rebukes his troops*

*Sources*: A. 7. 9. 1–10,7 offers a more detailed version of the speech; J. 12. 11. 4–7; Plut *Alex.* 71. 4 says no more than that Alexander angrily heaped abuse on them.

*Bibliography*: Tarn ii. 290–6; Wüst (1953/4*a*), 177–88; Rutz (1983*b*); Brunt (1983), 532–3; Bosworth (1988*b*), 112; Carney (1996), 38.

Arrian sets it in the context of a mutiny at Opis, and not Susa, but at 7. 10. 7 he includes a reference to Susa as the scene of this episode, which must come from the 'vulgate' tradition, and not from Ptolemy and Aristobulus, unless Aristobulus picked this up from Cleitarchus. Either way, this suggests that Arrian worked from more than one source. Then Curtius 10. 2. 24 and Arrian 7. 9. 6 agree on the amount of bullion and debt which Alexander inherited from Philip, and Arrian's source was not Aristobulus (contrast Plut. *Alex.* 15. 2 = *FGrH* 139, F4), and therefore might have been Ptolemy. Another possible source indicator might be the Ammon factor. Curtius, who may have used Cleitarchus, has left out of the story the reference to Ammon (contrast J. 12. 11. 6; A. 7. 8. 3), and the omission of a derogatory reference to Ammon would not be inconsistent with Cleitarchus' following an Alexandrian line. But against that argument is the fact that Diodorus mentioned the troops' mockery of Ammon (D.S. 17. 108. 3), though he surely used Cleitarchus, and Arrian likewise mentions this issue, though Ptolemy was a, if not his main, source for this episode. Thus Curtius may have simply left Ammon out because it did not fit in with what he planned for this book.

Thus there certainly was a tradition that Alexander addressed his troops when plans to send a section of the army back to Macedon provoked a mutiny. Historically this occurred at Opis. Tarn ii. 290–6 takes Arrian to reflect what Alexander actually said, as reported by Ptolemy, albeit with some intrusive elements. More effusively, Kornemann (1935), 164 suggests that the Opis speech was to Ptolemy's history what Pericles' funeral oration was to Thucydides' *History of the Peloponnesian War*. Wüst (1953/4a) in analysing the speech and the structure of Arrian's narrative in relationship to the speech, concludes that Arrian was working with two sources, whose accounts he failed to harmonize properly. His main source provided much of 7. 8, the speech and 7. 11. 1, and could be identified as a source which drew on Cleitarchus' account, and was thus probably Aristobulus. Arrian's secondary source, used for 7. 11. 2–3, would then be Ptolemy. Thus Wüst comes to the contrary conclusion that the speech as recorded by Arrian does not represent Ptolemy's version, and should not be taken as historically reliable.

Whatever the historical worth of Arrian's rendering, Curtius' version is unflattering to Alexander, and indeed to Curtius. It is embellished with borrowings from Livy (Rutz (1983b)), and at 2. 27 he echoes the famous episode when Julius Caesar addressed mutinous legionaries as Quirites (citizens) and not *milites* (soldiers). Tarn ii. 296 considers this a Curtian creation, owing no more to Ptolemy than the number of talents Alexander found in the treasury after Philip's death (2. 24 with A. 7. 9. 6). If so, this is not Curtius at his best, as can be seen by comparing it with Arrian. Alexander, in Arrian's version, begins by reminding the men of the primitive nature of Macedonian society before Philip's programme of economic restructuring and urbanization (A. 7. 9. 2). Then Alexander sets out in chronological sequence the stages by which Macedon emerged as a major power (A. 7. 9. 2–5). This section in Arrian's version offers a eulogy of Philip's achievements, and would have been very appropriate to placate veterans who were complaining that Alexander was losing the plot. By contrast Curtius inverts this sequence of points, omits the record of achievements, mentioning instead the ignominy of the period when Macedonians paid tribute to Illyrians and Persia. The Macedonians are described as only recently emerged from a state of barbarism (2. 23)—no mention of the positive aspects of cultural advancement, and above all the eulogy of Philip is missing.

In Arrian's version the eulogy of Philip provides the introduction to Alexander's proud defence of his own record (7. 9. 6–9). Again the story is taken through in chronological sequence, to show that the progress to the current situation has been ineluctable and fortunate. The strategy in Arrian's rhetoric is clear and compelling. Curtius' version of this section is reduced to the points that he won the resources of the Persian empire, having inherited very little from Philip (2. 24).

In Arrian's account Alexander's next point is that he himself has gained nothing from his victories apart from purple and a diadem, as the spoils of war have gone to his troops (A. 7. 9. 9). This indeed seems to reflect a reality of Macedonian monarchy, that support was bought from the spoils of 'successful military adventures' (A. E. Samuel, 'Philip and Alexander as kings: Macedonian monarchy and Merovingian parallels', *American Historical Review* 93 (1988), 1270–86, quotation from p. 1284). Curtius does not have the point that Alexander has been modest in what he has taken for himself; and instead of emphasizing what the troops have received, Curtius has Alexander mock the men for what they have lost and for the burden of debt (2. 26–7). Arrian later alludes to the settlement of debts, but that is presented rather as one of a string of benefits which the men and their families have received from Alexander's generosity (7. 10. 3–4). The peroration is also different. In Arrian Alexander shames the troops by recapitulating the list of honourable and glorious victories they have won together. By contrast, in Curtius Alexander further taunts his men by emphasizing that he will now favour Asian troops, and promises them that he will be vindictive (2. 29).

Curtius must surely have realized that his version did little credit to Alexander, and, as he clearly read Ptolemy's memoirs, he could well have read a more flattering version of the speech. Although elements of the speech may be echoes of Livian phraseology, it does not appear that Curtius' version has been shaped by a tradition on some Roman situation. It would therefore seem that Curtius consciously wrote this speech to illustrate Alexander's flawed character, and as an episode in the disintegration of his leadership. Curtius does for Alexander what Tacitus does for Claudius by his misrepresentation of Claudius' speech to the Senate on the admission of Gauls as senators as we know it from the Tabula Lugdunensis (Smallwood *GCN*, no. 369, translated in N. Lewis and M. Reinhold, *Roman Civilization. Sourcebook*, vol. 2, 3rd edn.(New York, 1990), 285–8; Tac. *Ann.* 11. 23–5. I am fully aware that others consider that Tacitus improved upon the original, but I persist in the view that Tacitus subverted the logical progression of the original, and introduced extraneous and counter-productive details, on all of which see K. Wellesley, 'Can you trust Tacitus?', *G&R* 1 (1954), 13–35.).

**2. 15. sudden uproar.** Curtius echoes synonymous phrases all with the adjective *repens* (sudden) found in Livy 1. 14. 5; 8. 29. 1; 10. 18. 3 and 21. 26. 1; cf. Rutz (1983*b*), 403, citing Mützell.

**You have openly flouted my authority.** With the Latin expression *rupistis imperium*, Curtius appears to develop phraseology attributed by Livy to Scipio in a similar situation with mutinous garrison forces at Sucro in Spain in 206 BC: How am I to address you? . . . As soldiers? When you have rejected my authority and auspices, and have broken the sanctity of your oath? (Livy 28. 27. 4: *imperium . . . abnuistis, sacramenti religionem rupistis*). Curtius' formulation is in turn echoed by Tacitus *Ann.* 13. 36. 2, and in Seneca *Hercules furens* 79 (though we cannot say whether Curtius wrote before or after Seneca's *Hercules* was produced).

**I am a king on sufferance.** *Precario* in the Latin picks up several occurrences of the word earlier in Curtius, including 4. 7. 1; 5. 8. 12, where Darius disdains the idea of taking the kingship of a single nation at Alexander's whim; 6. 3. 6, where Alexander characterizes his new empire as precarious; 9. 2. 34, in Alexander's speech to the mutinous troops at the Hyphasis. Curtius may have picked the expression up from Livy (as at 3. 47. 2; 8. 35. 5; 39. 37. 13), and Curtius in turn may have inspired Tacitus *Ann.* 1. 42. 4, in Germanicus' speech to mutinous troops on the Rhine in AD 14 (cf. *Hist.* 1. 52. 3, for Galba's precarious rule: *precarium imperium*).

**You have not left me the right of addressing you, encouraging you, advising you, or even watching you.** In modern times autocratic regimes have seen advantage in insisting on the trappings of democracy, with elections, referenda, and legislation by an assembly. This string of 'rights' has the same ominous ring, as Alexander gives the impression that, when the constitutional system works as it should, he is but the servant of the people. The force of the last word in the list 'watching' (*intuendi*) is 'to take one's lead from another' (cf. Sen. *Dial.* 11. 16. 5; Pliny *Ep.* 6. 11. 2). As it happens, Curtius may here be giving a fair description of the ideal of Macedonian monarchy, but one suspects that he had more in mind the way the Principate was presented by true believers and dissemblers. Indeed Curtius' list here is reminiscent, in form if not content, of a less benign clause in the first surviving law conferring the whole package of powers on an emperor, the *Lex de imperio Vespasiani*. The relevant section is the catch-all clause that Vespasian should have the right (*ius*) and power to do and effect whatsoever he should deem to be in the interests of the State and in accordance with the dignity of all things divine and human, public and private (Latin text in M. McCrum and A. G. Woodhead, *Select Documents of the Flavian Emperors* (Cambridge, 1966), no. 1).

**2.19. I have discharged more than I am going to retain.** This indicates, when read with the figures given by Diodorus and Arrian, that Alexander kept fewer than 10,000 Macedonian troops (cf. 2.8 above). This meant that the Macedonians who remained would constitute a significantly smaller proportion of Alexander's army in Asia.

**2. 21. forgetting your wild uproar... I am trying to cure incurables.** Another echo of phraseology in Livy's account of the mutiny at Sucro: Livy 28. 27. 11.

**2. 22. The prosperity all around you has begun to unbalance you.** Rutz (1983*b*), 404 notes the parallel expression in Lucan 5. 324, and goes on to note many other links between Lucan and Curtius' account of the Opis mutiny. Both authors were familiar with Livy's account of Scipio Africanus' dealings with mutinous troops in Spain (cf. 2. 27 below).

**2. 23. Look! Men who a short while ago were tribute-paying subjects of Illyria and Persia.** The interjectional Look! (Latin *en*), the collo-quial expression 'I should dearly like to know' (*pervelim scire*: 2. 17), and the parenthetic 'if I may be forgiven for saying so' (2. 24), are there to suggest the immediacy of oral delivery. D.S. 16. 2. 2 records that Macedon became a tributary of the Illyrians after they won a victory over Philip's father Amyntas III: cf. J. 7. 5. 1, and on the history of that conflict, Borza (1990), esp. 180–9. Then in the aftermath of Darius' abortive campaign against the Scythians of *c*.513, Macedonia effectively became a vassal state of the Persians when Darius left Megabazus in the area to gain control of Thrace (J. 7. 3. 1), and Megabazus sent envoys to Macedonia to demand their submission. The offerings of earth and water were duly made (Hdt. 5. 18. 1), and Alexander I, apparently acting as an envoy for his father Amyntas, offered his sister as a bride to Bubares, the son of Megabazus (Hdt. 5. 21, with Badian (1994*a*), esp. 109–14, countering the line taken by Borza (1990), 100–4 that Macedonia did not enter into a state of vassalage thereby). After the Ionian revolt Mardonius was sent to reassert Persian control of Thrace and Macedonia (Hdt. 6. 42–45). Herodotus says that the Macedonians now became 'slaves' (6. 44. 1), which clearly implies that Macedonia was at this time more firmly established as a tributary state. Persian control was imposed more overtly when Xerxes marched through the territory in 480 (Hdt. 7. 123–7. Further on the range of issues see L. Scott, *A Historical Commentary on Herodotus Book 6* (Leiden, 2005), 186–90 and 198).

**men who recently went half-naked under Philip.** A definite link with Arrian's version (7. 9. 2). This picture matches the tradition on Macedonian society in the early and mid-fifth century (cf. Hdt. 8. 137), but much changed particularly while Archelaus was king (*c*.413–399) (Thuc. 2. 100. 1–2; Borza (1990), 161–79. Curtius and Arrian may be right to suggest that Alexander chose to suppress what had been achieved long before Philip became king.

**2. 24. when I took you on, together with a debt of 500 talents, when the entire royal assets were no more than sixty talents.** A. 7. 9. 6 gives the same figures, and these did not come from Aristobulus, nor from Onesicritus, who give the size of the inherited debt as 70 and 200 respectively (Plut. *Alex.* 15. 2, *Mor.* 327d). The argument in Arrian's account is that Philip achieved great things, and Alexander built on that, and a measure of the scale of difference between these two stages in Macedonian development is that while Philip built up a debt of 500 talents, Alexander needed an advance of a further 800 talents to launch his invasion of Asia. Thus Alexander's point is not to disparage Philip's record, but to mark the magnitude of the growth of the Macedonian economy since 336 (cf. Wüst (1953/4*a*), 180). Curtius' reworking of the material clearly turns this into a criticism of Philip.

**if I may be forgiven for saying so.** The phrase (which means more like 'May I not arouse the ill-will of the gods') is repeated at 10. 9. 6, where it is even clearer that Curtius has in mind Livy 9. 19. 15, who, at the end of a long digression comparing Alexander's record with Rome's long history of military success, boasts of Roman invincibility, with the same parenthetic wish, 'May I not arouse the ill-will of the gods'.

**2. 27. I am keeping no one back.** Possibly an echo of Dido's dismissal of Aeneas (Vergil *Aen.* 4. 380, noted by Dempsie).

**you most ungrateful of citizens.** This is borrowed from Roman history, and the episode in 47 BC when Julius Caesar confronted troops who were clamouring to be demobilized and won them over by dismissing them as Quirites (Suet. *Caes.* 70; Dio 42. 53. 3–4; Appian *BCiv.* 2. 93). Livy wrote up this episode (*Periochae* 113), and borrowed the idea from Scipio's address to the mutineers at Sucro (28. 27. 4; E. Burck, in *Wege zu Livius* (Darmstadt, 1967), 435; cf. in another context Livy 45. 37. 14. A similar ploy is attributed to Septimius Severus in SHA *Sev.* 52). A variant occurs in Germanicus' speech to mutinous troops in Tac. *Ann.* 1. 42.3. Either Germanicus or Tacitus might have adapted Caesar's line (Rutz (1983*b*), 406), but this might also just be added to the list of passages where Tacitus echoes Curtius. The distinction between *cives* (citizens) and *milites* (soldiers) belongs to Roman law rather than the Macedonian system.

**2. 29. I shall triumph over your desertion of me.** The irony is more marked in the Latin as the connotation of triumph was a victory parade to honour a commander for the defeat of an enemy state or tribe (e.g. Livy 3. 10. 4, Cicero *Sen.* 55, and the *Acta Triumphorum* that formed part of the Capitoline Fasti), an honour which in the Principate was almost exclusively reserved for the emperor, an exception being Germanicus' triumph in AD 17 for victories over the Cherusci, Chatti, and other German tribes (Tac. *Ann.* 2. 41. 2).

**2. 30. He leaped down from the dais.** Cf. D.S. 17. 109. 2; J. 12. 11. 8; A. 7. 8. 3; and in a similar scene, Germanicus at Tac. *Ann.* 1. 34. 4.

**Alexander handed thirteen of them over to his bodyguard to be kept in custody.** Curtius agrees with Arrian on the number of ringleaders arrested (7. 8. 3), but he agrees with J. 12. 11. 8 and D.S. 17. 109. 2 in setting the arrests after Alexander's harangue. Their punishment was to be execution (3. 2 and 4). Carney (1996), 27 notes that Alexander rarely used capital punishment, and that the victims were generally senior officers or, as here, men of lower rank whom he could at least plausibly identify as ringleaders.

**3.** *Alexander marginalizes his Macedonian troops*

*Sources*: D.S. 17. 109. 3; A. 7. 11. 1–4; Plut. *Alex.* 71. 4–7; J. 12. 11. 9–12. 6, who, like Curtius, summarizes a speech by Alexander to the Persians.

On the broader issue of Alexander's policies with regard to the incorporation of Persians into his court, officer corps and army see Bosworth (1980*b*), who argues that assimilation developed as a response to new situations and needs, and there was no 'visionary policy of fusion'. Brosius (2003) takes the matter further by arguing that even when Alexander adopted strategies for integrating Persians into his army and administration he had little success because of Persian resistance to assimilation by the conqueror.

**3. 1. paralysed with sudden panic.** Cf. Livy 28. 29. 11 (Rutz (1983*b*), 407, noting that Livy followed Polybius 11. 30. 2, and influenced Curtius); 34. 38. 7. A. A. Lund (1987), 51 compares Tac. *Agric.* 34. 3, as an example of the possible influence of Curtius on Tacitus.

**3. 3. whether from deep respect for the royal name ... or ... for Alexander personally, or ... because of the confidence with which he so forcefully exerted his authority.** In the corresponding passage in Justin's account, Alexander gets away with the execution of the ringleaders because 'fear of the king gave *them* such acceptance of dying, or military discipline gave *him* such determination to exact punishment' (J. 12. 11. 9). It appears that Curtius has picked up Trogus' idea, and developed it with a starker antithesis, as the Latin juxtaposes the key terms 'veneration' and 'self-confidence', without the personal pronouns to signal immediately the switching of subjects from the troops to Alexander.

**deep respect for the royal name.** The semantic range of the Latin word *nomen* (name) would cover the notions of 'title' and 'reputation', but Curtian usage favours the translation here 'name'; cf. 5. 13. 14 (with commentary ad loc.), 5. 10. 2 (of Asian kings), and 10. 5. 37. In Roman thought power might attach to a name: cf. J. 42. 5. 12 on the power of Julius Caesar's name, and I. Lana (1952), 204 ff. on the idea in Velleius Paterculus. Lesser breeds had names that were unknown: 3. 2. 9; 4. 12. 9; J. 41. 1. 4 (of the Parthians in the Persian era).

**because people living under a monarchy regard kings as gods.** Because of the negative associations of the word *rex* (king), Curtius here implies that in his value system the cult of a ruler as a god is unacceptable.

**3. 4. they were the very model of submissiveness.** Lund (1987), 50–1 compares Tacitus *Agricola* 2. 3, and counts this too among the cases of cross-influence, with the likelihood that Tacitus was influenced by Curtius, rather than Curtius by Tacitus.

**3. 6. he had an interpreter called.** Bosworth (1996*a*), 72, 98, and 124–5 raises the important issue of the function of interpreters in the interaction between Alexander and the peoples of the Persian Empire.

**3. 7. I hoped to annex to my empire many famous peoples and large numbers of men.** Bloedow (2003) reasons that in invading Asia Minor Philip and Alexander both started with the notion that a war of conquest was inherent in a war of revenge, and that 'the extent of the conquest would depend on just when the Great King was eliminated' (p. 273). Cartledge (2004), 165 goes even further in suggesting that by crossing the Hellespont and performing the rituals at Troy, Alexander was 'probably' signalling an intent 'to conquer at least the existing Achaemenid Empire as a whole'. The relevance of the ritual at Troy is unclear, and in any case Thucydides 1. 96. 1 shows that while from 479 the Greeks vowed to take vengeance, this did not mean nothing less than the conquest of the Persian Empire. Xenophon's account of the exchange between Agesilaus and Pharnabazus (*Hellenica* 4.1. 29–40) illustrates the point that hostility to Persians was not constant nor universal (cf. J.M. Cook, 'The rise of the Achaemenids', in *CHI* ii. 290–1). Furthermore, while Isocrates wishfully, if not whimsically, advocated a pan-hellenic campaign against the Persians and even spoke of the conquest of 'the whole of Asia' (*Paneg.* 186), he appears to be thinking more realistically of Asia Minor and the western satrapies (*Paneg.* 133–7; 160–6). As for Alexander, the evidence rather shows that his ambitions and expectations grew over time, and in line with his successes.

**3. 9. I had believed everything here to be swamped in luxury.** Curtius has prepared for this not by a series of speeches in which Alexander engages in the 'othering' of Persians, but rather by a sequence of passages in which he is criticized for adopting oriental customs and yielding to luxury: 5. 1. 36–9 and 6. 1–8; 6. 2. 1–5 and 6. 1–9.

**3. 10. I have made a selection of younger soldiers from among you and have integrated you into the main body of my troops.** Alexander had ordered the conscription of 30,000 young Persians, in 327 according to Curtius 8. 5. 1; cf. Plut. *Alex.* 47. 6. These troops, known as the *Epigonoi* (the Descendants), reached Alexander in Susa in 324 (A. 7. 6. 1; D.S. 17. 108. 1; Plut. *Alex.* 71. 1). They are not the same as the men mentioned in J. 12. 12. 4. In the second limb of this sentence, Curtius seems to refer to the integration of Iranian troops into the battalions (*taxeis*) of the Macedonian Companion Infantry, though Arrian 7. 23. 1–3 only attests this later, after Alexander's return to Babylon and the arrival of Peucestas with a contingent of 20,000 Persian troops. But D.S. 17. 110. 1–2 puts these two events in the context of Alexander's stay in Susa, and at 110. 1 Diodorus refers to the selection of 1,000 Persians to join the elite infantry division of Hypaspists, which may link up with Curtius' opening reference to the separation out of a special group of Persians. This suggests that Curtius and Diodorus were following the same source, presumably Cleitarchus.

In all this there is some confusion of four distinct developments. First, the arrival of the *Epigonoi* introduced the establishment of a new counter-force of Persians trained in the Macedonian manner, though Goukowsky (1975), 268–9 takes D.S. 17. 110. 1 to mean that the *Epigonoi* were immediately deployed to fill gaps in the army. Secondly, at Susa Alexander drafted 1,000 picked Persians into the elite infantry corps of Hypaspists, but as a separate battalion

(A. 7. 11. 3; J. 12. 12. 4 and D.S. 17. 110. 1). Thirdly, in the following year, after the arrival of Peucestas with reinforcements, Alexander moved to the full integration of Asian troops into Macedonian units (A. 7. 23. 3–4). Fourthly Alexander provided for the enrolment into the imperial army of the sons of mixed marriages between his Macedonian soldiers and their Asian wives (J. 12. 4. 2–10). The issues are analysed by Bosworth (1980*b*), esp. 9 and 17–19, who emphasizes that Alexander was slow to move to the full integration of Asians into traditional Macedonian units. By contrast, M. J. Olbrycht, *Alekasander Wielki I swiat iranski* (Rzeszow, 2004) (known to me through T. K. Mikolajczak's review, *BMCR* 2006.03.41) returns to the old orthodoxy that Alexander began the process of assimilation with the commissioning of a force of mounted javelineers in 330.

**3. 11. I married the daughter of the Persian Oxyartes.** Alexander married Roxane, the teenage daughter of the Bactrian satrap Oxyartes in 328/7 (A. 4. 19. 5; Plut. *Alex.* 47. 7; *Itinerarium* 45). At 8. 4. 23–30 Curtius says that Alexander was immediately besotted with Roxane when he first saw her, and promptly asked her father for her hand in marriage. Aetion painted a picture of this romantic marriage, which was displayed at the Olympic games (Lucian *Herodotus* 4–7), presumably of 324. This lost painting inspired other artists, and one derivative seems to be the 'Alexander and Roxane' fresco from the Insula Occidentalis at Pompeii (Stewart (2003), 41–2, with figure 6). But in the same passage Curtius adds that Alexander justified his move by explaining the political advantage to be gained by his compacting a marriage with a Persian (cf. Plut. *Alex.* 47. 7). Curtius, unlike Plutarch, treats the marriage as ignominious (cf. 10. 6. 13), and an aberration which scandalized the Macedonians. This was probably a common line, since Arrian makes a point of defending Alexander's decision as a mark of his ethical courage (4. 19. 5–6).

Carney (2003), 245–6 suggests that the marriage probably scandalized the Persians too. In similar vein, Holt (2005), esp. 88–91 imagines the marriage of Alexander to Roxane from the point of view of Roxane by comparing her situation with that of Shurbat Gula, who lost her family and home in Afghanistan, and then, as a nameless refugee, won unsolicited and unwanted fame when a photographer took the iconic picture of her which was to grace the front cover of

*National Geographic,* June 1985. But events after Alexander's death in 323 show the gulf between the two cases. Roxane's first child by Alexander had died in infancy (*ME* 70, which Baynham (1995), 70 finds impossible to deny or verify), but she was certainly pregnant at the time of his death, and the child had a brief existence as Alexander IV (see further on 6. 9, and for her murderous role in protecting her baby, 5. 20 below; Heckel (2006), 241–2 reviews Roxane's life). Her father, Oxyartes, kept his position as satrap after the marriage, and his area of control was later extended to cover the Parapamisadae (Curtius 9. 8. 10), and his position was confirmed after Alexander's death (D.S. 18. 3. 3). Roxane's brother Itanes was one of the Asian nobles enrolled in the royal *agema* of the Companion Cavalry in 324 (A. 7. 6. 4–5).

**3. 12. I took Darius' daughter as a wife.** In the mass marriage ceremony at Susa Alexander took as an additional wife Stateira, Darius' elder daughter (A. 7. 4. 4–8, where Aristobulus is named as the source for detail not in Curtius, and Arrian alone gives her the name Barsine; D.S. 17. 107. 6; J. 12. 10. 9; Plut. *Alex.* 70. 3). A detailed account of the marriages was written by Chares (Athenaeus 12. 538b–539a), who was clearly not Curtius' source. Chares mentioned 92 bridal chambers (90 in Aelian *VH* 8. 7). Curtius mentions Stateira as among the captives taken after the battle of Issus (3. 11. 25), and reports that Darius offered her to Alexander as his bride, when Alexander was at Tyre (4. 5. 1). Carney (2003), 246–7 explains why Alexander put off establishing a marriage link with the Persian royal family: he waited till he had established 'an Asian power base' and could give priority to his role as 'an Asian ruler, not a Macedonian king'. The tradition of his honourable treatment of Darius' wife may be a myth, if there is any truth in the record that she died in childbirth some two years after her separation from Darius (Curtius 4. 10. 18–19; J. 11. 12. 6; Carney (2003), 247, but Atkinson (1980), 392 suggests that Curtius, or his source, may have transposed the death from an earlier context, as is indicated by Plut. *Alex.* 30. 1).

**I set the pattern for my closest friends to have children by our captives.** There was no suggestion that Alexander was going to allow Persian men to marry Macedonian women (Bosworth (1980*b*), 11–12). This tells against the romantic notion of Tarn and others that Alexander wished to promote the fusion of the races (below on 4. 1–3). Brosius (1996), 79 notes that the marriages were enacted according to Persian rites: this may have been a political move at the time to accommodate the Persians, but there may possibly have been an intention on Alexander's part to provide his Macedonians with a formula for disavowing these commitments when it was time to move on. Those returning to Macedon had to leave their Asian wives and children behind, the sons to be trained as soldiers in the Macedonian style (A. 7. 12. 2).

**3. 13. Foreign newcomers though you are, I have made you established members of my force.** This circumlocution represents the pithy *inveteravi peregrinam novitatem.* Strikingly similar phraseology is attributed to Claudius in Tacitus *Ann.* 11. 24. 7, and the thought is there in the archival record of the same speech, which was to the Senate on the admission of Gauls as members of the Senate (the Tabula Lugdunensis, in Smallwood, *GCN*, no. 369). Claudius was arguing that innovation was a Roman tradition, and Rome had from the start been used to expanding the boundaries of citizenship.

**you are both my fellow-citizens and my soldiers.** This salutation contrasts with Alexander's dismissal of the Macedonians in 2. 21 and 27, and is picked up again in 4. 1.

**3. 14. Those who are to live under the same king should enjoy the same rights.** Bourazeli (1988), 258–9 argues that this reflects the rhetoric of the Severan era, which preceded the promulgation of the Constitutio Antoniniana, which, in simple terms, gave Roman citizenship to all free-born inhabitants of the Roman Empire. He compares Aelius Aristides *On Rome* 60–1 and Dio 52. 19. 6 (in a very long speech attributed to Maecenas in an advisory session with Octavian in 29 BC, but written by Dio c. AD 205). Bourazeli assumes that Curtius is giving positive support to an ideal of Septimius Severus. But Curtius attributes this statement to Alexander and this speech includes elements which Curtius did not laud (contrast 8. 4. 21–30). Furthermore the context is a scandalous rejection of the Macedonians by Alexander. Thus one cannot take this sentence out of context to prove that Curtius espoused world citizenship, especially after the way he recasts the Exiles Decree in 2. 6–7. In any case, Rome had a long history of claiming that its imperialism was welcomed because Rome dispensed the rule of law (*iura*; e.g. Vergil *Georgics* 4. 561–2; Atkinson (1994), 130 on 5. 7. 8). Dempsie suggests that Curtius may be echoing Livy 1. 2. 4, who says that Aeneas promoted integration by calling his people and the native population all Latins and having them share one legal system.

**4. 1–3.** *Alexander refuses to compromise*

*Sources*: A. 7. 11. 4: in the context of the mutiny at Opis, the troops at the end were ready to hand over the ringleaders for punishment; Plut. *Alex.* 71. 5–7; D.S. 17. 109. 3; J. 12. 12. 5–6. Curtius' account differs from the other sources in that he introduces a complaint by the Macedonians that Alexander was using Persians as executioners. Curtius, Diodorus, and Justin do not refer to Alexander's ploy of shutting himself up in his headquarters for three days to soften his troops' belligerence: contrast A. 7. 11. 1, and Plut. *Alex.* 71. 7–8.

**4. 1. with such ... executions of a foreign kind ... dragged off to punishment without trial.** Goukowsky (1975), 275 takes this to show that there were some limitations on the powers of the Macedonian kings. Curtius at 6. 8. 25 suggests that when the Macedonian army was mobilized and a capital offence was at issue, the king could not take executive action unless he took direction from a hearing by the army assembly (Atkinson (2000*a*), 441–2 deals with the textual and historical issues). By implication the king took a major political risk if he judged a case in camera or dispensed with a hearing. Curtius shows that Alexander was inconsistent and played by his own rules: cf. 10. 1. 7 and 36–42 above.

**led off ... by their own captives.** Here again Curtius introduces the racial theme. He is not intending the sort of gallows humour that was associated with the killing of those convicted of treason (*maiestas*) in the Principate, as when the Senate obliged Domitian with a guilty verdict, and he then appealed to the senators to grant what he could hardly hope to receive as a favour, that they should grant the convicted men a free choice of how they should die (Suet. *Dom.* 11. 3).

**4. 2. his anger had risen to frenzy.** The phraseology echoes Livy 22. 51. 9.

**4. 3. They offered up their persons to his anger, urging him to slaughter them.** The negative bias which Curtius demonstrates here may be partly a literary device to produce a jarring effect before the scene in Babylon where the troops mourn for their dead king. But the text breaks off at this point and the extent of the *lacuna* is uncertain.

*The lacuna after 4. 3*

If anything like Arrian's account, the missing text would have covered the reconciliation scene, and the feast attended by 9,000 Macedonians and Persians, ethnically ranked, with the Macedonians grouped closest to Alexander. Greek seers and Magi initiated libations, when Alexander prayed that Macedonians and Persians might enjoy harmony (common purpose: *homonoia*) and partnership in empire (A. 7. 11. 8–9). This tight summary of Arrian's account follows Badian (1958*b*), who was concerned to counter the Romantic interpretation offered by Tarn ii. in his chapter on 'Brotherhood and Unity', 399–449. Tarn wished to show that Alexander was preaching the unity of mankind, and strengthened this interpretation of what lay behind A. 7. 11. 8–9 by invoking a lost account of the Opis feast which he inferred by fusing a fragment of Eratosthenes (in Strabo 1. 4. 9. 66–7) with a passage from Plutarch *On the fortune of Alexander* I (*Mor.* 329b–d), which says that Alexander rejected Aristotle's advice that he should treat Greeks as if he were their leader, but barbarians as if he were their master; for Alexander, considering that 'he had a divine mission to unite the world, brought all men together by persuasion or force, and mixed together, as in a loving cup, their ways of life, marriages etc.' (quotation from Badian's summary: (1958*b*), 435). Tarn saw in this metaphorical reference to a lovingcup an allusion to the *krater* which Alexander circulated at Opis. And, as Plutarch and Strabo both open with Aristotle's vision of the Greeks as a master race, Tarn concluded that Plutarch was following Eratosthenes, and found the account of the Opis feast in Eratosthenes. Badian's exposure of the gaps and flaws in Tarn's argument does more than put the record straight on the tradition of a reconciliation feast at Opis, for he undermines Tarn's vision of Alexander as the promoter of the Unity of Mankind (cf. Bosworth (1980*b*), 3–4, supporting Badian and commenting on Curtius and Plutarch). A contrasting view of Alexander's racial policy is provided by Berve

(1938), reflecting his full acceptance of Hitlerian ideals. At Susa Alexander moved from a policy of assimilating talented Persians into the ranks of his military and administrative officers, to a policy of Blutvermischung, to the end that 'the two racially related (!) Herrenvölker would lord it over the rest of the world empire' (Berve (1938), esp. 157 and 162, as summarized by Bosworth (1980*b*), 1). Tarn ii. 434–49 distanced himself from Berve's view of the policy of fusion, which Tarn saw as social engineering which failed, whereas in his view Alexander was pursuing 'an idea...a dream, an aspiration, an inspiration, call it what you will' (434).

Also missing from Curtius' account, and perhaps lost in the *lacuna*, is Alexander's enrolment of Asians in the Macedonian Companion Cavalry (A. 7. 6. 3–4; it is not clear whether the appointments were *ad hominem*, or whole units were incorporated), and a number of high-ranking Persians into the royal guard (*agema*) of the Companion Cavalry (A. 7. 6. 4–5; see on 3.10 above).

**5. 1–6.** *The death scene of Alexander in Babylon*

*Sources:* A. 7. 25–6; Plut. *Alex.* 75–7. 1; D.S. 17. 117; J. 12. 15. 3–16. 1; *LM* 103–12; Ps.-Call. 3. 33. 26–7; Athenaeus 10. 434a–c. Key source passages are translated in Heckel and Yardley (2004), chapter 11.

*Bibliography:* Bosworth (1971*a*), (1988*b*), 171–3; Hamilton (1973), 151–3; Heckel (1988); Samuel (1986), esp. 427–9; Schachermeyr (1973), 556–65; Worthington (2004), 194–6.

A. 7. 25.1–26. 3 and Plut. *Alex.* 76 purport to give an account of Alexander's last days as it was recorded in the *Ephemerides* or Royal Journal. Plutarch claims to offer an 'almost verbatim' version (*Alex.* 77. 1); Arrian implies that he consulted the Journal directly (7. 25. 1 and 26. 1), but he also used Ptolemy and Aristobulus (7. 26. 3), and his account gives prominence to Medeius and Nearchus, both of whom wrote memoirs that Arrian could have consulted (*FGrH* 129 and 133 respectively; Brunt (1983), 289). But Bosworth (1988*b*), 157–70 makes a strong case for believing that Arrian used Ptolemy, from whom he derived a version of the *Ephemerides*, and also worked from Aristobulus. The Journal apparently recorded two days of serious drinking, followed by ten days of sickness, and it would not have suited Aristobulus to follow the line on Alexander's excessive drinking (cf. Plut. *Alex.* 75. 5), hence his divergence from the tradition.

It is of course quite possible that there was indeed a Macedonian royal journal of some sort, and that Eumenes played a role as an archivist (Pearson (1954/5), 434); it also probable that Babylonian priests covered events of Alexander's last days in their records. Something of the nature of Babylonian records can be gleaned from fragments of astronomical diaries for parts of the years 331 and 328 in Sachs and Hunger (1988), nos. 330 and 328. These astronomical diaries are precisely that, with the addition of commodity prices and readings of the river level. References in this collection of texts to historical events are few and terse, and centred on what happened in Babylon itself, and, in particular on events that involved the temples and priestly activities. The diaries show that the priests might record events of successive days in special circumstances. Samuel (1965), 11–12 suggests that a picture of the Royal Journal gradually emerged in the early Hellenistic period from transcriptions and references by various writers (such as perhaps Berossus, and authors mentioned in *FGrH* no. 117). But what we have in Arrian and Plutarch is quite different in style and level of detail from the astronomical diaries.

The supposedly archival based account is problematic for several reasons. The two versions, in Arrian and Plutarch, do not agree in detail (the differences are well set out by Bosworth (1988b), 158–67). Secondly, there is no direct reference to the *Ephemerides* as a source for any other chapter in Alexander's reign, except for fragments of uncertain historical value relating to Alexander's hunting and drinking (Plut. *Alex.* 23. 4; and references in *FGrH*, 117; Bosworth (1988b), 171–2 suggests that the record of mammoth binge-drinking in Aelian *VH* 3. 23 might refer to Alexander's visit to Babylon in October 331, or more likely to his stay in Ecbatana in perhaps November 324, when Hephaestion died). Thirdly, the reference in the account of Alexander's death to the temple of Serapis in Babylon (Plut. *Alex.* 76. 9; A. 7. 26. 2) is considered by some to be anachronistic. But Bosworth (1988b), 168–70 argues that, as the cult of Oserapis, created by a fusion of the cults of Osiris and Apis, is attested at Memphis in the mid-fourth century BC, Egyptian expatriates might have taken the cult to Babylon before 323. Alexander's troops might then have given the temple the name Sarapis, and this popular name could have been taken up when Ptolemy much later established the official cult of Sarapis (see further at 10. 13 below). So this third line of objection is not compelling.

But there is still the more general doubt concerning the *Ephemerides* on Alexander's death, because, as specific allegations were made that Alexander had been poisoned, and as in any case there were bound to be suspicions about the circumstances of his death, those close to him during the final sickness had a vested interest in establishing a record of the sequence of events that would pass muster as dispassionate and official. A sceptical attitude to a record that is 'official' and problematic in detail is therefore not unreasonable. Nevertheless Hammond (1983), 4–11 argues that there was indeed a King's Journal, which Arrian and Plutarch referred to indirectly, and directly respectively, for the account of Alexander's last days. Much earlier C.A. Robinson, *The Ephemerides of Alexander's Expedition* (Providence, 1932) attempted to sketch the state of the *Ephemerides* in which it was available for later writers, and suggested that on events from about 326 to 323 the *Journal* permitted divergent readings because it was no longer under the competent editorship of Eumenes, as Evagoras had taken over as Secretary (72–3; A. 5. 24. 6). But, since Pearson's article of 1954/5, scholars have generally considered the Journal spurious, or at best, with regard to what we have on Alexander's last days, an *ad hoc* compilation fabricated to serve the interests of the officers in Babylon (so Brunt (1983), 289; Hamilton (1969), esp. 59–60; Worthington (2004), 194). Most notably, Bosworth (1971*a*) argues that it was produced within two years of Alexander's death, quite possibly by Eumenes under the direction of all the generals, though it served Antipater's interests as a counter to rumours that he had organized the poisoning of Alexander (cf. Bosworth (1988*b*), 157–84. But Wirth (1986) sees more of the hand of Ptolemy in the establishment of the tradition. Further on these issues, 10. 14 below).

The *Liber de Morte* was more obviously created to serve a political purpose, as it develops the theme that Alexander was killed by poison sent by Antipater with Cassander for Iolaos to administer to the king. Bosworth (1971*a*), 115–6 suggests that this pamphlet was written to serve Perdiccas' purposes after the break with Antipater in 321 BC;

but Heckel (1988) argues that it was produced in Polyperchon's circle, probably by Holkias, and not before about mid-317, as part of a campaign to discredit Cassander and Antigonus. Bosworth (2000) revises his earlier interpretation and makes a more compelling case for dating the *LM* as we have it to 309/8 and recognizing it as a product of the Ptolemaic camp (further at 10. 5 below).

Curtius agrees on the key points with D.S. 17. 117. 3: as Alexander lay dying he gave his ring to Perdiccas, said that he was leaving the kingdom to the best man, and predicted that the funeral games would be on a grand scale (cf. D.S. 18. 1. 4). A. 7. 26. 3 likewise records Alexander's last words, but indicates that these were not recorded by Aristobulus and Ptolemy.

J. 12. 15. 7–13 is close to Curtius in detail and phraseology, but differs on two significant points: J. identifies three possible heirs whom Alexander ignored, and inverts the sequence so that Alexander hands over his ring to Perdiccas after he loses his voice. Trogus or his source, perhaps Timagenes, presumably attached significance to these details which had a bearing on the history of the successors. Thus, if Trogus was dependent on Timagenes, the source shared by Curtius and Diodorus might well be Cleitarchus.

**5. 2. Alexander ... said, 'After my death will you find a king worthy of such men?'** A similar scene occurs in Velleius Paterculus 2. 14. 1–2, where M. Livius Drusus, the controversial Tribune of the Plebs in 91 BC, lies dying, having been stabbed with a knife, and is surrounded by a large crowd of grieving family members and friends. Before expiring he manages to ask, 'My relatives and friends, when will the Republic ever find a citizen like me?' (one has to accept that death scenes in Roman historiography tend to the melodramatic). This is similar to Justin's account of Alexander's last days: when the troops had been sent away, Alexander asked his friends whether it seemed that they were going to find a king like himself (J. 12. 15. 5). Curtius changes this *topos* in two ways: Alexander is surrounded by a crowd of men, and not just his close circle of officers, and secondly his question is whether they could find a king worthy enough for such men. Curtius made Alexander's treatment of the mutineers abusive, and now recasts this scene to imply that the reconciliation is complete.

The Latin term for worthy, *dignus*, reflects a Republican ideal. A noble held office because he was worthy of the magistracy, and a magistracy could be referred to as a *dignitas*, a mark of worthiness.

**5. 3. until he had received the last salute from the whole army.** The Royal Journal, according to Arrian, explicitly stated that Alexander was unable to speak when the troops filed past (A. 7. 26. 1). Plut. *Alex.* 76. 8 puts the file-past on the day before Alexander died.

**as though released from all life's obligations.** The flowery phraseology is borrowed from Roman funerary notices: e.g. *CIL* vi. 25617; ix. 5860. The idea of life as being on loan was a commonplace: Dempsie compares Cic. *Phil.* 10. 20; 14. 31; Sen. *Dial.* 11. 10. 5.

**5. 4. He ... took his ring from his finger and handed it to Perdiccas.** Cf. J. 12. 15. 12; D.S. 17. 117. 3; Nepos *Eum.* 2. 1; *LM* 112; *HE* 1. At 6. 6. 6 Curtius says that Alexander used both his own ring and Darius', the latter just for communications with Asians. The ring is an important element in the following drama (6. 4 below). It does not feature in the account of Alexander's last days in the Royal Journals as summarized by A. 7. 25–6 and Plut. *Alex.* 76. A. 7. 26. 3 implies that Ptolemy and Aristobulus likewise did not mention the handing over of the ring to Perdiccas. Thus it may be fiction (cf. Badian (1987), who at the same time rejects the argument of Hammond (1983), 10 that the incident must be unhistorical for the simple reason that it is not mentioned in the summaries of the *Ephemerides*). A *caveat* is that Ptolemy had an interest in not promoting Perdiccas' claim to the kingship. Another complicating factor is that handing over rings was a feature of Roman death scenes (as in Val. Max. 7. 8. 5, 8 and 9; Dio 53. 30. 2, when Augustus was seriously ill; P. Sattler, *Augustus und der Senat* (Göttingen, 1960), 67).

**gave instructions that they should have his body transported to Hammon.** Cf. J. 12. 15. 7. Arrian *Succ.* 1. 25, Pausanias 1. 6. 3 and Strabo 17. 1. 8. 794 indicate that, when Arrhidaeus left Babylon in mid-321 (D.S. 18. 26.1 and 28. 2) with Alexander's corpse, the party was heading for Macedonia and Ptolemy hijacked the hearse to Egypt. This may represent the version of Hieronymus, who served on the staff of Eumenes and later under Antigonus, both of whom were enemies of Ptolemy. Curtius here and at 10. 10. 20 and D.S. 18.

3. 5 suggest that Ptolemy was simply carrying out Alexander's wishes, and this may derive from Cleitarchus, representing the Alexandrian tradition. A hostile bias in Hieronymus' account would not necessarily make the detail which he offers unhistorical, and Arrhidaeus may indeed have thought he was heading for Macedon.

**5. 5. 'To the best man'.** Cf. A. 7. 26. 3, who implies that this detail was not reported by Ptolemy and Aristobulus; D.S. 17. 117. 4 and 18. 1. 4; J. 12. 15. 8; Ps.-Call. 3. 33. 26.

**but added that he could already foresee great funeral games for himself provided by that issue.** The prolepsis and the silence of Ptolemy and Aristobulus on Alexander's last words indicate that Alexander's prophecy was apocryphal, but not Curtius' creation: cf. A. 7. 26. 3; D.S. 18. 1. 4; J. 12. 15. 6 and 11. Justin says that it was as though Alexander was tossing among them the apple of Discord (J. 12. 15. 11), a reference to the myth of the apple which Eris (Strife) threw in at the wedding of Thetis and Peleus, which led to the judgement of Paris, his abduction of Helen, and the Trojan War. Yardley and Heckel (1997), 292 plausibly suggest that in the Greek tradition followed by Trogus, Alexander's wish to have his kingdom pass to the strongest (*kratistōi*) was a pun on the message on the apple of Discord, 'for the most beautiful' (*kallistēi*). If this is so, I should see this as another case where Curtius removes the mythical and rationalizes.

Funeral games were very much a Roman custom (e.g. Livy 28. 21. 10; 31. 50. 4; 39. 46. 2), even though they were given Greek ancestry (Vell. Pat. 1. 8. 2; Pliny *HN* 7. 205). But Alexander himself held games to honour Hephaestion after his death (A. 7. 14. 4), and Arrian adds that many of the performers in that event participated a little later in the funerary games for Alexander (cf. D.S. 18. 28. 4 and 19. 52. 5; and on the various games organized by Alexander see W.L. Adams (2007)).

**5. 6. When Perdiccas . . . asked when he wished divine honours paid to him, he said . . . when they themselves were enjoying good fortune.** After the reference to Hammon in 5. 4, Curtius introduces two questions, about who should succeed Alexander, and at what point he wanted divine honours to be accorded to him. This would seem to be a conscious echo of Alexander's visit to the oracle of Ammon at

Siwah, when Alexander put questions to the priest, and his friends then asked the oracle whether they were to accord Alexander divine honours (4. 7. 25–8). Furthermore, the question on ruler cult here is not in the other sources, and is possibly a Curtian addition, since ruler cult is a motif running through the *Histories*. Further on Alexander's divine pretensions see 5. 33.

The phrase which Curtius uses here for apotheosis (*caelestes honores*: unfortunately 'celestial honours' looks more like a transliteration than a translation) was an expression used officially for the deification of the deceased Roman emperor (with or without a comet such as marked Julius Caesar's translation to celestial heights: Suet. *Julius* 88). Augustus was accorded 'celestial honours' on 17 September AD 14 by a decree of the Senate, and games in the Circus were thereafter celebrated to mark the anniversary (Fasti Amiternini (*CIL* ix. 4192); Tac. *Ann*. 1. 10); and the same formula was probably used for the deification of Claudius (Tac. *Ann*. 12. 69. 3, where Tacitus makes an ironic comparison between Agrippina and Livia). But in AD 33 the formula was drawn into the charge against Pompeia Macrina that Pompey had been a great friend of her great-grandfather Theophanes, and that Greek flattery had accorded Theophanes 'celestial honours' upon his death (if we can trust Tac. *Ann*. 6. 18; one assumes that there was somewhat more to the case against Pompeia). Thus Curtius might have expected the Roman reader to find the proposal of divine honours for Alexander after his death an acceptable ritual, though such an award for a lesser mortal would have been considered deplorable (Lozano (2007) shows that Greeks, by contrast, were willing to accord divine honours not only to the ruling emperor, but also to members of his family, and in their lifetime).

In this final scene, Curtius makes Alexander temper his earlier demand for recognition as a god (contrast e.g. 6. 11. 23–5; 8. 5. 5–6), with the qualification that they should first have reason to feel happy. The term for 'enjoying good fortune' (*felices*) connotes the success and prosperity that attend an honourable life, success that is a reward (cf. 4. 14. 18; Cicero quoted by Ammianus Marcellinus 21. 16. 13; admittedly the adjective is often used with heavy irony as at Lucan 10. 21, of Alexander, and at Cic. *Phil*. 2. 59, *Nat. D*. 3. 83 of a, if not the, Harpalus). But a more immediate parallel here is Seneca *Clem*. 1. 7, where Seneca says that as Nero is now established as emperor, and has shown what the nature of his rule will be, all the citizens are happy.

Those who favour a Flavian (or later) date for Curtius' *Historiae* might add to their case the fact that Felicitas became an imperial blessing regularly celebrated on coins from the time of Galba (starting with *BMCRE* i. 328–9, and featuring on coins of Titus, Vespasian, Trajan, and Hadrian).

**he died.** Alexander died on 10/11 June 323 according to Babylonian records (Samuel (1962), 46 ff.). Plutarch *Alex.* 75. 6 puts the death on 30th Daisios, but at 76. 9 dates it to the 28th: Samuel *loc. cit.*, explains that the discrepancy occurs because Daisios was a 'hollow month', with the last day being the 29th, and Plutarch cited first Aristobulus, who would have counted the 29th (*qua* the last day or the '30th') as beginning on the evening of the 28th, and then copied the date in the *Ephemerides*, which, following a different calendar system, counted the evening of the 28th as the 28th. The Babylonian date has to take precedence over that of the Alexandrian and later Ps.-Call. 3. 35, Pharmouthi 4 (13 June), and Pharmouthi 14 in the Armenian version, 286.

The main sources on Alexander's death are A. 7. 24. 4–27. 3; Plut. *Alex.* 75. 2–77. 3; D.S. 17. 117. 1–4; J. 12. 13. 7–16. 1; Athenaeus 10. 434a–b. As noted above, the *Journal* recorded two days of heavy drinking, followed by ten days of sickness before death. The sources provided the basis for a fascinating clinicopathological protocol drawn up by Dr D. W. Oldach for the *New England Journal of Medicine* 338, no. 24 (11 June 1998): 1764–9, as part of a report on a clinicopathological conference held at the Maryland School of Medicine in 1996, when Alexander was taken as a case study. The report is reviewed, and expanded, by Borza and Reames-Zimmerman (2000). If, as Livy believed (8. 3. 7), Alexander died of some illness, he may have had a recurrence of falciparum malaria, which was quite possibly the cause of his collapse in Cilicia in September 333 (Engels (1978*b*), 226–7; Curtius 3. 5–6). As Macedonia itself was a malarial area (Borza (1979)), Alexander may even have been first affected long before 333. The effects of malaria can include anaemia and porotic hyperostosis, and Schachermeyr (1973), 563 counts leucaemia as a contributory factor in Alexander's death. Battersby (2007) attempts to identify the immediate cause of death, and, on the assumption that binge drinking was the main contributory factor, he suggests the possibility of acute pancreatitis or a perforated peptic ulcer, but concludes that the most likely cause was 'spontaneous' perforation of the oesophagus, usually referred to as Boerhave's Syndrome.

If there is any historical basis for the tradition that putrefaction failed to manifest itself for several days after Alexander's death (10. 12 below), then other possibilities arise. Methanol toxicity would retard putrefaction, but it is also possible for ascending paralysis in terminal cases of diseases such as typhoid fever to give a premature indication of death (Borza and Reames-Zimmerman (2000), 25; but it is unlikely that typhoid fever would have struck only Alexander, and the sources do not indicate any sort of epidemic). Alexander might indeed have been vulnerable to any opportunistic disease after years of strenuous campaigning, and injuries in battle—most seriously a chest wound with the complication of a pierced lung, hemopneumothorax (A. 6. 10. 1–11.8; Plut. *Alex.* 63. 3–6; Curtius 9. 5. 9–6. 1; D.S. 17. 99. 3; Plut. *Mor.* 341c). To all of which must be added a steady record of what detractors might label binge-drinking. Furthermore, psycho-somatic factors may have increased Alexander's vulnerability. Borza and Reames-Zimmerman (2000), 27–30, claim that there is clinical evidence for a significant correlation between bereavement and the suppression of lymphocyte stimulation, and suggest that the death of Hephaestion further sapped his strength. His grief for Hephaestion is recorded by A. 7. 14. 1–15. 1, Plut. *Alex.* 72. 1–3, and D.S. 17. 114–5 (see also on 5. 20 below). But I am reliably informed that there is no sound scientific evidence that grief contributes to leucopenia.

Of course there remain the possibilities that he was murdered or the victim of pro-active euthanasia (cf. 10. 14 below). But against the conspiracy theories, Badian (1985*b*), 489, followed by O'Brien (1992), 228, concludes that Alexander 'died of disease, undiagnosable to us'. Perhaps.

**5. 7–18.** *An army mourns*

*Sources*: J. 13.1. 1–4; *LM* 113.

*Bibliography*: Lühr (1979), esp. 96–9.

Much of this will be free composition by Curtius, and Dempsie notes the number of inter-textual references to earlier Latin literature,

including, e.g. the combination of superlatives best and bravest in
5. 9, which occurs 20 times in Cicero, and the echo of Vergil in 5. 8.
There may also be echoes here of reactions in Rome to the death of
Germanicus (described in the later account by Tacitus, *Ann.* 2. 82).
But the passage must also depend on a core account which was
eulogistic in bias. Trogus or his source revised the standard account
to give it a hostile bias (cf. J. 13. 1. esp. 7–8).

Curtius develops the picture from the royal quarters to the city, to
the surrounding area and then to Asia (5. 18). He presents a fine
account of conflicting emotions and an understanding of crowd
psychology (cf. Lühr (1979), esp. 96–9), noting the mood changes,
as in 5. 7 and 11, and the switch from mourning Alexander to
concern about themselves (5. 11). The reactions span the emotional,
the ethical (penitence in 5. 11), and the rational (till calculation
about what lay ahead turned to panic).

**5. 7. the royal quarters.** This is generally taken to refer to the
Southern Palace, built by Nebuchadrezzar to the south west of the
Ishtar Gate (Oates (1986), 149–52). Schachermeyr (1970), 49–73 was
particularly concerned to establish the details of the site as a means of
testing the credibility of Curtius' account of the events in Babylon.

**5. 8. The young noblemen who formed his customary bodyguard.**
They are commonly referred to in modern accounts as the Pages.
Curtius deals with the institution at 5. 1. 42 and 8. 6. 2–6; cf. A. 4. 13.
1 and Aelian *VH* 14. 48 (Bosworth (1995), 90–6; Heckel (2003*a*),
205–6; Roisman (2003), 302–3).

**They wandered around like madmen, filling such a large city with
the sound of their mournful grieving.** Dempsie notes here the echoes
of Vergil *Aeneid* 4. 68–9, and [Ovid] *Consolatio ad Liviam* 317 (a text
seen by some as produced under Tiberius or Claudius, or even in the
early period of Nero's reign).

**5. 10. in the bloom of his young life.** The Latin expression generally
refers to those under, or not much older than twenty (Williams
(1999), 73–4, citing i.a. Cic. *Phil.* 2. 3, Livy 8. 28. 3, Suet. *Jul.* 49. 3,
and *CIL* xi. 3163).

**laid siege to cities.** As at Tyre (4. 2. 1 ff.) and Gaza (4. 6. 7 ff.).

**scaled walls.** As at the city of the Malli (9. 4. 30 ff.).

**made presentations for gallantry before the assembled army.** Cf. Curtius 5. 6. 20 and 9. 1. 6; and for the involvement of the troops in identifying merit, 5. 2. 1–5, with Atkinson (1987).

**5. 11. The Macedonians then regretted having refused him divine honours.** Cf. 8. 5. 10–11 and 15–16.

**5. 12. They had passed . . . beyond the Euphrates.** Traditionally the river Halys had been the boundary between the Persian sphere of influence and the Greek world, but in his third exchange with Alexander, and shortly before the battle of Gaugamela, Darius had offered a deal which would have given Alexander control of territory as far as the Euphrates (Curtius 4. 11. 5; D.S. 17. 54. 2; Plut. *Alex.* 29. 7; A. 2. 25.1; the range of problems associated with this tradition are analysed by Atkinson (1980), 271–8 and 395–6).

To the Roman mind this would be significant as meaning into Parthian territory. The Euphrates frontier was a preoccupation of successive Julio-Claudian emperors (the history is economically reviewed by Levick (1990), 158–60), and remained so in the Flavian era (Levick (1999), 155–6 and 163–9), but in Vespasian's reign Rome was developing roads and military installations beyond the Euphrates, with Palmyra as a pivotal point. This tends to support the argument that Curtius completed his work in Claudius' reign, or no later than early in Vespasian's reign.

**enemies who balked at the new regime.** Cf. 4. 1. 5, 5. 7. 2 and 10. 2. 5; Sen. *Suas.* 1. 4. In this section Curtius deliberately echoes many earlier passages.

**Lacking a definite heir.** Roxane was pregnant when he died, and Stateira was swiftly killed (above on 3. 11–12). His infant son Heracles by Barsine was discounted (6. 11–13 below), and the son by Cleophis (J. 12. 7. 10) may be a fiction: Curtius 8. 10. 36 states only that her child was given the name Alexander (cf. Heckel (2006), 90–1).

**5. 14. to win power for someone who might be an obscure henchman.** This does not make much sense in the Macedonian context: Alexander would not have as successor a Bagoas. Curtius possibly

had in mind the way in which non-senators, while similarly having
no chance of becoming emperor, had been able to play a role in
imperial politics beyond their station in Roman society—perhaps
Sejanus, or Macro, as Caligula's Praetorian Prefect, or those involved
in his murder, such as the freedman Callistus (Tac. *Ann.* 11. 29. 1; Jos.
*Ant.* 19. 64 ff.; Suet. *Calig.* 56. 1 and 58. 1), or the Military Tribune
Cassius Chaerea (Jos. *Ant.* 19. 20–3, 45–6, 78 ff., Suet. *Calig.* 56.2 and
58. 2, with Wardle (1994), 355). The term we have translated as
'henchman' (*satelles*) is often used of aides or lackeys of Rome's
enemies and despots (such as Hannibal: Livy 25. 28. 7; Nabis: Livy
35. 35. 11; Perseus: Livy 42. 51. 2; and in Tac. *Ann.* 2. 45. 3 Arminius
attacks Maroboduus as Caesar's henchman).

**5. 16. No one dared to light lamps.** In his account of Alexander's
reaction to the death of Hephaestion, D.S. 17. 114. 4 states that
Alexander issued a decree that throughout the empire the sacred
fire was to be extinguished, though it had been the Persian custom to
do this only upon the death of the king. Tarn ii. 108 takes this as a
reference to a genuine Persian custom, which Diodorus took 'doubt-
less ... from Deinon or Ctesias'. Schachermeyr (1970), 38–48 likewise
lends the Diodorus passage credence in his discussion of Persian fire
altars. But Badian (1985b), 486 makes the reservation that this may
be a later anachronistic fiction, and, in any case, the relevance of
Zoroastrian practice, as described by Diodorus, to what happened in
Babylon in 323 may be questioned. Either way, if Curtius' source was
alluding to the ceremonial extinguishing of the eternal fire upon the
death of the king, he has removed the mystical element, moved the
action to the streets and homes and turned it rather into a crowd
reaction of more political significance.

This section on the Macedonians and Babylonians scrambling
around in the dark may also, or alternatively, be linked with the
commonplace attributed first to the Athenian politician Demades
that, when Alexander died, the army was like the Cyclops after it had
been blinded (Plut. *Galba* 1. 4). The idea was picked up by Posidonius, and repeated by Eunapius (*Posidonius*, ed. L. Edelstein and
I. G. Kidd (Cambridge, 1972), F. 252).

Curtius exploits the image of the darkness that descended after the
demise of the ruler at 9. 3–5.

**5. 17–25.** *Persian reactions and Sisygambis' despair and death*

*Sources*: J. 13. 1. 4–6 and D.S. 17. 118. 3.

*Bibliography*: Lühr (1979); Brosius (1996); Carney (2003), 248–50.

As the story of Sisygambis' suicide also appears in Diodorus, it is likely that Cleitarchus was the common source, from whom Curtius could have picked up the references to Persian customs, as Cleitarchus used the *Persica* of his father, Dinon, and made critical use of Ctesias' *Persica* (Pearson (1960), 221 and 226–31). But Hammond (1983), 78 and 109 prefers to attribute the story to Diyllus. Diodorus and Justin both refer to Sisygambis' suicide, but Curtius differs from them in that he uses Sisygambis' thoughts about Alexander as a preface to his own final assessment of Alexander, and secondly he uses her pessimistic predictions to foreshadow the political chaos as the Macedonians battled over a succession plan. This literary elaboration must represent Curtius' own contribution.

**5. 17. The Persians ... grieved with genuine feelings of regret.** In chapter 5 Curtius refers variously to Persians, barbarians and Babylonians, and Persian here presumably includes Babylonians. Kuhrt (1990) shows that reports that the Babylonians had surrendered to Alexander in 331 willingly, and even jubilantly (Curtius 5. 1. 19–23 and A. 3. 16), were probably somewhat exaggerated. Alexander played out a role as temple restorer or builder, and performer of sacrifices as the Chaldaean priests instructed (A. 3. 16; Badian (1985*b*), 437; Bosworth (1994), 815; Brosius (2003), 185). But a Babylonian text, the *Dynastic Prophecy*, reveals that 'after the fifteen years of devastation suffered by Babylonia at the hands of Eumenes, Antigonus, et al., the period of Persian rule preceding the Macedonian conquest was seen, at least in retrospect, as an almost idyllic one' (Kuhrt (1990), 128; A. K. Grayson, *Babylonian Historical-Literary Texts* (Toronto, 1975), 24–37 presents the text; a translation of the revised text is offered by Sherwin-White (1987), 10–14; Briant (1996), 883). This fragmentary text appears to present Alexander's occupation of Babylon in very negative light, complaining of pillaging, robbery, and taxation.

**had their hair shorn in traditional fashion and wore garments of mourning.** For shaving the head as a sign of mourning cf. Hdt. 9. 24

(Brosius (1996), 99) and Suet. *Calig.* 5; but head shaving was not peculiar to the Persians: cf. Hdt. 2. 36, and of Alexander himself, A. 7. 14. 4, and of his horses, Plut. *Alex.* 72.3. Mourning dress is mentioned with regard to Cyrus' widow, Aspasia, by Aelian *VH* 12. 1, but the tearing of garments is even better attested (Brosius (1996), 99–100, citing the Nabonidus funerary stele, the Harran inscription, 3. 24–31, esp. 28–9).

**5. 19. Darius' mother.** Curtius followed a tradition that after the capture of Darius' mother, Sisygambis, Alexander would address her as mother (3. 12. 17 and 25; 5. 2. 22; D.S. 17. 37. 6). Brosius (1996), 22–3 suggests that he was following Persian protocol, and adapting a royal title for the queen mother, ummi (or amma) sarri.

**5. 20. one of her two granddaughters ... in mourning after the recent loss of her husband Hephaestion.** The two young daughters of Darius are introduced earlier at 3. 11. 25 and 4. 5. 1. In the mass wedding ceremony at Susa Hephaestion was given the honour (or obligation) of marrying Drypetis (D.S. 17. 107. 6; A. 7. 4. 5), while Alexander married her sister Stateira, earlier known as Barsine. Hephaestion died at Ecbatana in 324 (A. 7. 14. 1; D.S. 17. 110. 8). Curtius probably knew that Roxane had the two sisters killed with Perdiccas' complicity (Plut. *Alex.* 77. 6), hence in 5. 21 the proleptic reference to their vulnerability. The implication of the murders is that the Macedonians did not want any *Persian* claimant to the throne, and Roxane had no such royal entitlement for her son (cf. Brosius (1996), 78 n. 69; Carney (2003), 245–6). Curtius omitted the murders as falling outside his narrative, and limited himself to an allusion in Sisygambis' gloomy forebodings.

**5. 23. her eighty brothers had all been butchered on the one day.** It is commonly stated that Sisygambis was married to her brother 'Arsanes' (so Berve (1926), ii. no. 711, citing D.S. 17. 5. 5, where 'Arsanes' must stand for Arsames). But Diodorus does not say that Sisygambis was also Arsames' sister (cf. Bosworth (1980a), 217–18). For the following discussion the family tree in Brosius (1996), 379 may be found helpful. Arsames was the grandson of Darius II, and son of Ostanes, the uncle of Artaxerxes III Ochus. Val. Max. 9. 2. ext.

7, in line with Curtius, states that Artaxerxes (that is Artaxerxes III Ochus) killed his sister Atossa, his uncle and his 100 sons and grandsons (cf. J. 10. 3.1). Badian (2000*b*), 244–5 takes Curtius to mean that Ochus killed 80 sons of a brother of Ostanes. Sisygambis was then either a sister, or more likely a cousin, of the 80 brothers. Badian also notes that Ochus would not have spared the life of 'Darius III' Codomannus, if the family tree attributed to Codomannus had been true. Thus Codomannus probably was of the Achaemenid family, along with thousands of others, but the family tree as indicated by our sources was a construct, invented for propaganda purposes after Codomannus became king and took the title Darius. The official line may have been that he was the son of Sisygambis and Arsames, and thus the great-grandson of Darius II, but the reality was that he was not in direct line to succeed, but a member of the extended family, who was called Codomannus, and who made his mark in the war against the Cadusii and was advanced to the kingship (J. 10. 10. 3–5), since the line of Darius II came to an end with the murder of Artaxerxes Ochus' son Arses in 336 (D.S. 17. 5. 5; Strabo 15. 3. 24. 736).

**only one child remained of the seven she had borne.** But at 3. 11. 8 Curtius mentions the rôle of a brother of Darius in the battle of Issus. In alluding to Ochus and events in Persia that fell outside the history of Alexander's campaigns, Curtius perhaps points to Cleitarchus as his source, since Cleitarchus was the son of Dinon, whose major work was on Persian history, as noted above, and Cleitarchus presumably aimed to carry on his father's work.

**5. 24. withdrew . . . from nourishment. . . . Five days after deciding on death, she expired.** Details as in D.S. 17. 118. 3. Croesus' widow is said to have committed suicide by throwing herself off the city walls: Ctesias *FGrH* 688, F9 (4).

**5. 25. firm evidence for Alexander's gentle treatment of her and his fairness towards all the captives.** Thus Curtius leads into the following obituary.

**5. 26–37.** *The final assessment of Alexander*

*Sources:* A. 7. 28–30; J. 9. 8. 11–21; 12. 16. 7–12 may offer vestigial traces of Trogus' obituary.

*Bibliography*: Baynham (1998), 101–31; Cascon Dorado (1990); Heckel (1984), 12–14; McQueen (1967), 33–9, and the exchange between Holt (1999*a*) and Worthington, most recently (2004), 207–17.

Diodorus was writing universal history and so clearly took the conscious decision to avoid offering an obituary (similarly he says nothing about Darius III, offers only a one line tribute to Pericles (12. 46. 1), and deals with Philip II in a few sentences at 16. 95. 1–5). Historians generally did provide obituaries, as Seneca *Suas.* 6. 21 notes, mentioning as examples Thucydides, Sallust and Livy. Thus this significant omission in D.S. 17 need not mean that Cleitarchus must have chosen not to offer a final assessment of Alexander. And, whether or not Cleitarchus included an obituary, Curtius' presentation is in any case partly derivative, since he adopts the common antithesis between *virtus* and *fortuna* as the framework for his assessment. This rhetorical tradition is reflected in Livy's assessment of Alexander (9. 17–19) and in Plutarch's essays *De Alexandri Magni Fortuna aut Virtute* (*Moralia* 326d ff.). Furthermore, Curtius makes some points as though he has forgotten what is in his narrative (e.g. 5. 30, 'devotion to his parents' [*pietas erga parentes*]); and Tarn ii. 100 goes as far as to declare that Curtius stultifies nearly everything he has said. An explanation for some inconsistency between narrative and obituary may have to do with the political context in which Curtius wrote, and a desire on his part to make this passage serve a purpose. Certainly Alexander's good points include several virtues of the Roman principate, notably generosity (*liberalitas*), and clemency towards the defeated (*clementia in devictos*); and his failings are presented in more generalized terms than they are in Livy's assessment (esp. 9. 18. 1–5). This suggests that the passage has a programmatic function, to indicate what was expected of a good *princeps*. Thus in functional terms this passage has to be coupled with the eulogy of the new emperor in 9. 1–6, and Curtius labels this section a digression (6. 1).

The programmatic purpose of Curtius' final assessment of Alexander can be appreciated by comparison with Arrian's version. In the view of Brunt (1983), 297, in Arrian 7. 28–30, 'Alexander is characterized as the good king and the good general by quite conventional

criteria'. Arrian's lengthy comment is based on direct engagement
with the historical record. He includes items of no programmatic
value, such as Alexander's physical beauty, not mentioned by Curtius. He identifies aspects of Alexander's generalship and diplomacy
which can be exemplified by episodes in his narrative. He addresses
squarely matters that gave offence: in particular the adoption of
Persian dress and the recruitment of Persians into Macedonian
infantry and cavalry units, and attempts to justify Alexander' actions
in political terms (7. 29. 3), whereas Curtius refers to Alexander's
failings more cursorily, and offers only the mitigating circumstances
of youth and the burden of good fortune (5. 33–4). Arrian draws in
a reference to a primary source—Aristobulus, on the subject of
Alexander's social responsibility as a drinker (7. 29. 4), whereas
Curtius does not allude to the sources, though, as Arrian shows,
differences in the sources could be used in defence of Alexander.
Thus in the obituary Arrian engages with the history and the sources
in a way that Curtius does not. But it is worth setting Arrian in the
context of the Second Sophistic movement. Swain (1996), 242–8
briefly introduces Arrian as a representative of this phenomenon.
Thus Arrian proudly asserts his aspiration to be recognized as one of
the masters of the Greek language (1. 12. 5), and in the same passage
signals his championship of classical Greek literature (Homer and
Xenophon are directly mentioned at 1. 12 1 and 3). But of more
immediate relevance is the way Arrian takes the final chapter (7. 30)
to eulogize Alexander as a world ruler, who spanned both continents,
and whose name reached every *polis*, and who was peerless among
mankind, and who was Macedonian—and by that Arrian means that
Alexander was a Greek. This assertion of Greek pride was very much
a feature of the Second Sophistic. Thus, while tackling the obituary as
the conclusion of his history, Arrian still had his own agenda, and
that of course was very different from Curtius' concern.

Arrian was able to keep Alexander back in the historical past, but in
the Roman context and in that earlier Claudian (or possibly Flavian)
era, Curtius was writing when emulation of, or rivalry with,
Alexander was a worrying and recurring theme in the projection of
autocracy. Thus, e.g. after Caligula toyed with imitation of Alexander,
Claudius distanced the Principate from Alexander in one symbolic
way recorded by Pliny the Elder. Augustus had had two friezes created

in an important section of the Forum Augustum, one depicting
Victory and Alexander accompanying Castor and Pollux, and the
other showing Alexander riding in triumph in his chariot alongside
the image of War in shackles; but Claudius had the faces of Alexander
cut out and replaced with images of the deified Augustus (Pliny *HN*
35. 93–4; it is generally assumed that the panels decorated the entry
way into the Sala del Colosso). Beyond that, there was a problem with
autocracy itself, and not just the Alexander paradigm. The death of
Caligula opened the opportunity for some to consider a return to a
Republican system possible; and again after the death of Nero the
Senate was briefly back in business, and after the death of Vitellius in
December 69 senators had to decide how far they could go in assert-
ing senatorial rights (cf. Levick (1999), esp. 81–3). Thus in Curtius'
day, unlike Arrian's, one-man rule was still not fully accepted; there
was still, at least in the mind of the idealist, a serious role for the
Senate to play and republicanism was not just a distant memory (cf.
Spencer (2002), 37–8), even if what characterized most of the senators most of the time was 'apathy and inertia' (Rudich (1997), 252, in
a well-referenced survey of senatorial realities in the early Empire,
pp. 250–3). In his narrative Curtius goes way beyond the historiographical commonplace in dealing with the failings of Alexander's
advisers (Atkinson (1975), 365 with references), but in the obituary
he does not mention their failure in mitigation of Alexander's mis-
deeds. Contrast A. 7. 29. 1, who explains his lapses by reference to his
youth, excessive good fortune, and the evil influence of flatterers in
his circle. Curtius purposely keeps the focus on Alexander: he has
made his point about Alexander's court earlier.

**5. 26. it is obvious to anyone who makes a fair assessment of the
king.** Korzeniewski (1959), 73 notes that this implies that Curtius was
critical of writers who unthinkingly followed the fashion of being
brutally critical of Alexander (compare J. 13. 1. 7; Valerius Maximus
9. 5. ext. 1).

**his weaknesses to fortune or his youth.** Arrian too mentions
Alexander's youth and his perpetual good fortune as factors that
might explain his faults and errors of judgement (7. 29. 1). The
notion that power corrupts can be traced back in historiography at
least to Herodotus 3. 80. 3, and the inevitability of degeneracy

became a starting point for Polybius' theory of *anacyclosis*, according to which, without constructive intervention, there will be a recurring cycle of kingship, aristocracy, and democracy, each of these forms of constitution in turn degenerating into its matching debased form: tyranny, oligarchy, and ochlocracy, respectively, and producing the next pure form by way of reaction. The competing notion of the vulnerability and redeemability of youth was a commonplace: e.g. Cicero *Cael.* 42–3; Sen. *Controv.* 2. 4. 10; 2. 6. 7. A motif running through the *Histories* is that Alexander's relative youth brought him into conflict with officers of an older generation (especially in the tale of the murder of Cleitus: 8. 1. 27, 31 and 52), but that has more to do with the reality of the generational divide than with the idea that Alexander made mistakes because he was young. Curtius makes more of the idea that Alexander started well, until he was overwhelmed by good fortune (3. 12. 18–21; Baynham (1998), 124 ff.): he was not maturing and developing with age, but was degenerating (references at 10. 1. 42). But here by listing first Alexander's strengths and then his lapses, Curtius avoids sketching the stages in his degeneration as Tacitus did in summarizing Tiberius' life (*Ann.* 6. 51. 1–3, on which A.J. Woodman, 'Tacitus' obituary of Tiberius', *CQ* 39 (1989): 197–205 offers worthwhile insights). Thus Curtius is careful to indicate that Alexander's true nature lay in his array of strengths (5. 26).

**5. 27. incredible mental energy.** Cf. 3. 5. 8 and 9. 9. 23. Livy uses the same expression of M. Porcius Cato (39. 40. 4), and the following reference to Alexander's tolerance of toil echoes Livy's praise of Cato's endurance of toil and danger (39. 40. 11).

**courage exemplary not just in comparison with kings.** This is the only place in the *Histories* where the noun courage (*fortitudo*) is applied directly to Alexander: in five other cases it is applied to other characters, and in three it is invoked by Alexander as a challenge (4. 13 12 and 14. 6; 7. 9. 18). Alexander's bravery was demonstrated at the battle of Gaugamela (4. 16. 27), and in particular in the attack on the city of the Malli (Curtius follows the erroneous tradition that the city belonged to the Sudracae: 9. 4. 26 ff., corrected by A. 6. 11. 3), on which Curtius notes that his courage extended to resolute dismissal of omens and superstition (9. 4. 28–9). As for the 'kings', Curtius may have had in mind the rulers with whom

Alexander had clashed in various parts of the Persian empire, or the kings who had featured in the history of the succession of world empires (cf. A. 2. 6. 7; Atkinson (2000*b*), 308–10), but more likely he was thinking of the Hellenistic kings, to whom he alludes in 5. 37.

**5. 28. generosity.** Cf. Suet. *Claudius* 29 and Quintilian *Inst.* 6. 3. 52. As *Liberalitas* it was an official virtue at least by Hadrian's day (coin evidence and *CIL* 6. 972). In key earlier references in Curtius narrative Alexander's liberality is treated as something problematic, as officers and men were quite capable of realizing that the cost of a share in Persian opulence was supposed to be subservience (6. 6. 11; cf. 6. 8. 7–8; Spencer (2002), 231 n. 39, with Cic. *Off.* 2. 53–4). Then in his response to Hermolaus Alexander expresses concern that he might stir up resentment if he offended individuals' self-respect by reminding them of his generosity (this paraphrase does not do justice to the economy of Curtius' formulation at 8. 8. 9). Then again in 8. 12. 17 Alexander's extravagant generosity to Taxiles severely obligated Taxiles, and by the same measure offended Alexander's friends (8. 12. 17). Thus in the body of the narrative this generosity (*liberalitas*) is not presented as a particular merit in Alexander's record.

**clemency towards the defeated.** There are 14 references to clemency in the *Histories* as shown, offered, or approved of, by Alexander (including 7. 6. 17; 7. 9. 18; 8. 14. 41): the highest incidence among the abstract nouns denoting qualities attributed to Alexander apart from 'virtue' (*virtus*, more literally manliness). But of course clemency occupied a semantic field somewhere between an abstract virtue and a diplomatic instrument, rather like good faith (*fides*). At 5. 3. 15 Curtius refers to Alexander's treatment of Medates as illustrating 'the king's self-control and clemency at that time', implying that he was not to remain so self-controlled and inclined to mercy, and yet most of the occurrences of the word occur later in Curtius' narrative. There are nine references to pity (*misericordia*, as at 8. 14. 44) in the text, but fairly evenly distributed between Alexander and others.

Whether *clementia* was shown in the context of a foreign war or internal conflict, it had preconditions and implications: the pardoner had to have unchallengeable power and acceptance of clemency validated the giver's right to rule (cf. 8. 8. 8: clemency depends not just on the character of the king or commander, but also on the character of those under them; Augustus *Res Gestae* 3; the final phrase is an adaptation of Spencer's comment (2002), 170 on Lucan's Caesar). In the Principate, the emperor's mercy was generally more associated with the way the emperor dealt with internal opposition— particularly from senators. Clemency (*clementia*) was an imperial virtue, celebrated by Tiberius on coins and with the establishment of an altar in AD 28 (*BMCRE* i. 132; Tac. *Ann.* 4. 74. 2). Then in 39 Tiberius reintroduced the charge of *maiestas* (treason), which poten- tially covered any show of disrespect towards the present or past emperor, and the imperial house. The nervous senators celebrated the return of stalinist courts with the establishment of an annual celebration of the emperor's clemency (Dio 59. 16. 10). Claudius promised on his accession to govern with clemency (Jos. *Ant.* 19. 246, echoed in Sen. *Cons. ad Polybium* 13. 2), and indeed granted an amnesty for all treasonous acts and talk in the two-day period between Gaius' death and his own accession (Suet. *Claud.* 11. 1). Nero, like Claudius, promised to rule with clemency (Suet. *Nero* 10. 1; Tac. *Ann* 13. 11. 2; cf. Sen. *Clem.* 1. 11. 1–2; M. Griffin, 'Clementia after Caesar', in F. Cairns and E. Fantham (eds.), *Caesar against Liberty? Perspectives on his Autocracy* (Cambridge, 2003), 157–82). It was a coin legend again in the brief period of Vitellius' reign in AD 69, and also in Hadrian's reign. Curtius has in mind these connotations of clemency in the field of the ruler's dealings with his subjects, as opposed to with his defeated enemies, e.g. at 6. 10. 14 and 8. 8. 8.

**returning so many kingdoms.** Beneficiaries included Taxiles and Porus (8. 12. 12–14; 9. 3. 22), and Pharasmanes (8. 1. 8, though Curtius erroneously calls him Phrataphermes).

**or giving them as gifts.** As Sidon was effectively given as a gift to Abdalonymus: 4. 1. 26 (on which episode see now Burstein (2007)). Oxyartes received extra territory to govern (9. 8. 10). In all these cases, what was returned or granted was less than unencumbered royal power, as all these territories fell within the framework of the satrapal administration.

**5. 29. continuous disregard for death.** Demonstrated e.g. at Gaza (4. 6. 14), at Gaugamela (4. 13. 25), at the Mallian city (9. 4. 26 ff.). Linked with bravery by Cicero *Rep.* 5. 9.

a burning desire for glory and fame reaching a degree which exceeded due proportion, but was yet pardonable in view of his youth and great achievements. Cf. 3. 6. 19 on what he achieved despite his youth. A recurring motif in the Alexander sources is his 'burning desire' (*cupido/pothos*) to conquer, explore and go beyond where others had been: so in Curtius 3. 1. 16; 4. 7. 8; 4. 8. 3; 7. 11. 4 and 20; 9. 2. 9 and 12; 9. 9. 1; 10. 1. 16; A. 2. 3. 1; 3. 1. 5; 3. 3. 1; 4. 28. 4; 5. 2. 5; 7. 1. 1: J. 11. 7. 4; 12. 7.13). The term is not used exclusively of Alexander, but occurs so frequently, and in many cases with an almost mystical force, that Ehrenberg (1938), 52–61 and 74–83 posited that the references all lead back ultimately to an idea expressed by Alexander himself. But Montgomery (1965), 208–17 argues that it was little more than a commonplace of Graeco-Roman historiography (cf. Bosworth (1980*a*), 62; Hamilton (1969), 18; Yardley and Heckel (1997), 122).

Glory (*gloria*) was a core element in the value system of the Roman aristocracy (e.g. Cicero *Rep.* 5. 9; *Off.* 2. 45; *Arch.* esp. 26–30; *Leg. Man.* 27; Sallust *[Ad Caes. sen.]* 2. 11. 3; Syme (1939), 26, 70, 145–6; Drexler (1959) and (1962); Brunt (1990), 441–2). At a national level, by the end of the Republic it could be invoked as a justification for war (e.g. Cicero *Leg. Man.* 7, 11, 12, 19 etc.: admittedly, Cicero was not giving glory as the sole justification for war against Mithradates, but as a reason for war it was in conflict with the principles of fetial law, that Rome would only fight in self-defence, and where attempts at peaceful resolution of a conflict had failed. Even Augustus showed some respect for fetial law in his triumphalist *Res Gestae*, 26.).

**5. 30. devotion to his parents.** Not mentioned by Arrian. In the Roman value system devotion (*pietas*) was due to the gods, the fatherland, and one's parents. It was the archetypal virtue ascribed to Aeneas, and Octavian dared to invoke it when going to war against Brutus and Cassius. Successive emperors upon their accession made a show of filial devotion (Suet. *Calig.* 15. 1; *Claudius* 11. 2–3; *Nero* 9). Alexander's respect for his mother is a motif running through the *Histories*, and at 5. 2. 18 Alexander is described as according Sisygambis the devotion one would expect of a son. But with regard to Philip Curtius is here at odds with what he wrote at 8. 1. 24–26; cf. 4. 10. 3; 6. 11. 23; 8. 7. 13. Dempsie *ad loc.* notes that 'these examples match the normal Roman view of the bad relationship between father and son' (p. 157). Still, as Worthington (2004), 218–21 emphasizes, Alexander's rivalry with Philip was a powerful force, for good or ill.

**he had taken the decision to deify Olympias.** Sometime after Alexander was wounded in the attack on the Mallian city, his officers urged him to avoid further unnecessary risks; Alexander replied in a speech, which, as Curtius gives it, was part *apologia* and part mission statement, but ended with his expressing the fear that he was more at risk from conspiracies than enemy action. He calls on the officers to stand by him, and to respect his wish that Olympias should be granted apotheosis on her death (9. 6. 26). This has some support from the fact that Philip II had a statue of Olympias included in the group set up in the Philippeion at Olympia (Pausanias 5. 17. 4, and 20. 9–10; a point emphasized and explained by D. Miron (2000), 51; cf. Carney (2007)). In rhetorical exercises Alexander's relationship with Olympias was presented in a positive way (as in Seneca *Suas.* 1. 4 and 8), as also in some passages in the Alexander sources which reflect on Alexander rather than on Olympias (e.g. Plut. *Mor.* 332f and 340a; Curtius 3. 6. 15; 6. 3. 5; and especially 9. 6. 26, noted above). But the stronger tradition was that she was a malicious force, who created a poisonous atmosphere by plying Alexander with letters in which she made accusations against various of his senior officers and friends, so that even Alexander came to realize the damage she was doing (A. 7. 12. 5–6; on the letters: D.S. 17. 32. 1; 114. 3; 118. 1; J. 12. 14. 3; Plut. *Alex.* 39. 8–11; Curtius 7. 1. 12. J. 9. 7 deals with her role in the murder of Philip and support of Alexander's bid for power.). Furthermore, the other sources are silent about any wish on Alexander's part to have Olympias deified. Thus there is a strong suspicion that Curtius has here introduced an element from Roman ruler cult. Bödefeld (1982), 87–92 suggests that Curtius echoes Claudius' deification of his grandmother Livia in AD 41 (Suet. *Claud.* 11. 2; Dio 60. 5.2; *Acta Fratrum Arvalium*, F. 13, in Smallwood *GCN*, p. 15).

**he had avenged Philip.** At the oracle of Ammon at Siwah Alexander asked if all his father's murderers had been punished. The priest told him that Philip's murderers had indeed paid the price, but that his real father was beyond the reach of mortals (Curtius 4. 7. 27;

Atkinson (1980), 356–7 argues that this exchange should be treated as fiction). Curtius picks the story up again at 7. 1. 6, when the Lyncestian Alexander was brought to trial in late 330, and involvement in the conspiracy to kill Philip was added to the charge sheet. Circumstantial evidence suggests that Pausanias may indeed have been manipulated into killing Philip in 336, hence in part the speed with which he was put to death minutes after the assassination. Bosworth (1988*a*), 25–8, and Yardley and Heckel (1997), 72–83 provide the source references and review the theories about those party to the assassination plot.

**5. 31. kindness towards almost all his friends.** The term for kindness elsewhere in the text is used only of other characters. The qualification 'almost' shows that Curtius has not forgotten Alexander's murder of his friend Cleitus in 328 (8. 1. 19—2. 13; for recent discussions of the episode see Tritle (2003), seeing it as the tragic result of post-traumatic stress disorder, and Alonso (2007)). A rhetorical *topos* was that Alexander killed two of his friends, Cleitus and Callisthenes, and exposed a third, Lysimachus, to a lion, though the lion was killed and Alexander was reconciled with Lysimachus (Val. Max. 9. 3. ext. 1; Cleitus: Sen. *Ep.* 83. 19; *De ira* 3. 17. 1; Callisthenes: Sen. *QNat.* 6. 23. 3; Lysimachus: Sen. *De ira* 3. 17. 2; J. 15. 3. 3–10; Curtius 8. 1. 17 represents the Lysimachus story as apocryphal). Tacitus says that, unlike Alexander, Germanicus was 'kind to his friends' (Tac. *Ann.* 2. 73. 2). Another connotation of the term used by Curtius is generosity, and this can be exemplified by the way Alexander generously bestowed on his friends and troops gifts from the loot that they had pillaged from Persepolis (5. 6. 20), and made further gifts to his friends and troops sometime after the death of Darius (6. 6. 11), and similarly distributed pack animals and animals for meat in Sogdiana in 327 (8. 4. 20).

**goodwill towards the men.** Curtius does not offer much detail on the mundane business of managing the troops, except at 5. 1. 45 on the distribution of bonuses at Babylon, which sheds light on pay differentials (Atkinson (1994), 54–5, but see the objections of Milns (1987), 240 ff.), and 5. 2. 1–5, on a one-off scheme to open up certain posts to competition and to carry this through in an open way (Atkinson (1987)). His concern for ordinary troops in dire situations is illustrated e.g. at 7. 3. 17 and 8. 4. 15–20 (cf. Val Max. 5. 1. ext. 1); and in the early days he was able to lead by exercising, dressing, and behaving much as the ordinary troopers did (3. 6. 19). Alexander's achievement in keeping his men in general well motivated can be appreciated by a consideration of what Engels (1978*a*) reveals and infers about the logistics of the Macedonian army. We can set on the negative side the way Alexander used the sack of Persepolis as a motivational exercise (Atkinson (1993); Curtius' view of this episode was negative: Curtius 6. 7, with Atkinson (1994), 120–33). Then, as Carney (1996) has argued, Alexander never fully recovered the ground which he lost with the mutiny on the Hyphasis (cf. 2. 8–4. 3 above).

**ingenuity.** The noun occurs only once before this reference, and not in the same positive sense: at 4. 13. 8 Alexander says before the battle of Gaugamela that he will not steal a victory in the way Parmenion suggested, for that would be the scheming of bandits and thieves (cf. Silius Italicus 13. 772, in Alexander's advice to Scipio).

**5. 32. control over immoderate urges.** A virtue he would have shared with Cato (Livy 39. 40. 10). In the body of the narrative Curtius mentions Alexander's moderation, but in the context of his dealings with those he had worsted (4. 11. 7; 5. 3. 15; 8. 8. 10, where Alexander says that he has shown moderation by not behaving in an arrogant way towards the defeated). But Curtius' phrase here is closer in sense to what he earlier calls continence, as in 3. 12. 18 and 21 with regard to the Persian female captives. But the key passage is 6. 6. 1, where Curtius introduces the climactic stage of Alexander's degeneration with the line, 'His moderation and continence... degenerated into arrogance and dissipation'. (In his book on moderation, Valerius Maximus introduces the anecdote of Alexander's exchange with Diogenes the Cynic, with the comment that Alexander could not rival Diogenes' continence: 4. 3. ext. 4.) Here Curtius suppresses that basic story-line, and emphasizes the positive element by the following comment on his treatment of women of the Achaemenid royal house.

**a sex-life limited to the fulfilment of natural desire.** Cf. A. 7. 28. 2; this is consistent with all that Curtius has written about the Persian women from Darius' family and the Amazon queen (6. 5. 32), but he produced bastards (6. 5. 32; 8. 10. 36), a point which is given meaning by Tacitus' comment that Germanicus, unlike Alexander, was moderate in his pleasures, and had one wife and legitimate children (*Ann.* 2. 73. 2). Curtius here also glosses over Bagoas (6. 5. 23; 10. 1. 25 ff.). Tarn ii. 93 takes this as Curtius' admission that there was no truth at all in what he had written earlier about Bagoas. But Bagoas cannot be airbrushed out of the history so simply, and Tarn misinterprets Curtius' purpose in this section.

Yardley proposes transposing the final clause in the Latin text to the end of 5.26. On its content cf. 3. 6. 20.

**5. 33. putting himself on a par with gods and assuming divine honours.** See on 5. 6 above and 6. 6. 2. Badian (1996) argues that Alexander had been working towards gaining recognition as *isotheos* (equal to a god; cf. Curtius 6. 6. 2), and that it was only in the last months of his life that he tried to pressure the homeland Greeks into according him full honours as a god (p. 26; cf. Val. Max. 9. 5. ext. 1; Sen. *Suas.* 1. 5). Fredricksmeyer (2003) does not specifically address Badian's arguments, but is less reluctant to accept the historicity of references to Alexander's earlier claims to divine status. Still, there is now general acceptance that Alexander did not communicate to the Greeks at the Olympic Games of 324 an edict enforcing establishment of divine cults of himself (thus Cawkwell (1994) emphasizes that there is no evidence to support this notion, which surfaces again, e.g. in Adams (2007), 125). Nevertheless, Alexander's promotion of ruler cult was clearly an historical reality. Apart from the enforcement of *proskynesis* as part of court ritual, which Macedonians and Greeks chose to interpret as a mark of ruler cult, and the approval he must have given to Greek states which accorded him divine honours, Alexander gave licence to select artists and poets to represent him in ways that blurred the distinction between man and god (for Lysippus, Apelles, and Pyrgoteles: A. 1. 16. 4; Plut. *Mor.* 335a–b; *Alex.* 4. 1; Pliny *HN* 7. 125; Horace *Epist.* 2.1. 239–41; Val. Max. 8. 11. ext. 2; Stewart (2003), 37–9 and 41 on the reliefs in the Shrine of the Bark at Luxor; poetasters: Curtius 8. 5. 8–10; A. 4. 9. 9; Horace *Epist.* 2. 1. 232–8; add perhaps the sophist Anaxarchus who features in the debate with Callisthenes on proskynesis in A. 4. 10. 5–11. 9). Alexander's divine pretensions and his imposition of ruler cult were a rhetorical and literary *topos* (e.g. Livy 9. 18. 4; Val. Max, 7. 2. ext. 11; Sen. *Ben* 1. 13. 2; Gellius 13. 4, citing Varro *Orestes, or On Madness*). The prominence which Curtius gives to this failing here and in the rest of his narrative surely reflects a preoccupation of Curtius' own day. Arrian 7. 29. 3 gives less attention to Alexander's divine pretensions.

**giving credence to oracles which recommended such conduct.** In 332 Milesian envoys went to Memphis to tell Alexander that the oracle of Apollo at Didyma had announced his divine ancestry, and a similar revelation came from the medium at Erythrae (Strabo 17. 1. 43. 814; Curtius refers to the Didymaion at 7. 5. 28). But Curtius must be alluding principally to the oracle of Ammon at Siwah, as he follows the tradition that the oracle assured him that he was of divine parentage: 4. 7. 25–8; cf. D.S. 17. 51; J. 11. 11. 8–10; Plut. *Alex.* 27. 5–11 (A. 3. 4. 5 evades the isssue). This oracular pronouncement was an irritant to Macedonian officers, as Curtius mentions at 8. 1. 42, 7. 13, 8. 14–15.

**reacting with excessive anger to any who refused to worship him.** Curtius has covered the cases of Cleitus (8. 1.42; cf. A. 4. 8. 2–3; Sen. *De ira* 3. 17. 1), Callisthenes (8. 5. 14–20), Polyperchon (8. 5. 22–4, with Atkinson (2000*a*), 499), and Hermolaus (8. 7. 13).

**assuming foreign dress and aping the customs of defeated foreign races for whom he had had only contempt before his victory.** A summary of points made in 6. 6. 1–12. The adoption of 'barbarian' dress is also mentioned by A. 4. 7. 4, 8. 4 and 9. 9; Plut. *Alex.* 45. 1–2; D.S. 17. 77. 5; J. 12. 3. 8. Plut. *Mor.* 330a–c presents a defence of Alexander's dress policy (cf. Roskam (2004), 262). The negative view would have been the standard Roman version, as seen in Livy 9. 18. 3; Val. Max. 9. 5. ext. 1. Thus the prominence given to this 'fault' by Curtius may reflect a Roman preoccupation, but it may also be a reaction against the orientalizing ways of Caligula, who apart from wearing on occasion non-Roman and effeminate garments, also donned the gear of Alexander (Suet. *Calig.* 52; Dio 59. 17. 3–6). Seneca *Ben.* 2. 12. 2 refers to Caligula as 'this creature born for the express purpose of changing the manners of a free state into a servitude like Persia's' (translated by Basore in the Loeb edition).

**5. 34. explosive temperament.** Alexander was notorious for his proneness to uncontrollable anger, particularly after the death of Darius: 6. 2. 4. His anger (*ira*) is mentioned some four times before that passage and at least twelve times later, including 6. 5. 19, and especially 8. 1. 31, 43 and 48–49. It features in the other sources: e.g. J. 9. 8. 14; 12. 6. 5–7; A. 7. 29. 1, but not nearly as prominently as in philosophical texts and rhetorical exercises. Anger is an emotion that is culturally defined, and time and circumstances may determine whether it is a strength or weakness (cf. D. Konstan, 'Translating ancient emotions', *AClass* 46 (2003): esp. 9–19, relating Aristotelian theory to Homer's treatment of anger in the *Iliad*). Although Greek had an extensive vocabulary for the semantic field of anger and there was a wide range of philosophical positions on the subject, Plato and Aristotle allow a distinction to be made between *thymos* and *orge*, where *thymos* was generally seen as a positive force, an emotion driven by righteous indignation or similar justifiable cause, while *orge*, brute anger, was a failing (cf. Harris (2001), esp. 88–98 and 195). Plutarch chose to present Alexander as a man of spirit (*thymoeides*) (Hamilton (1969), pp. lxiii–lxiv), and thus puts less emphasis on Alexander's anger than do the other sources. Under the influence of Stoicism the conventional Roman view was that anger was a weakness, as was any surrender to emotion. Anger is what leapfrogs reason and rushes it off (Seneca *De ira* 2. 3. 4), and thus is to be avoided by the wise man. Anger uses reason to its own violent ends; but where violence has no semblance of rational justification, that is not anger, but savagery (*feritas*: Sen. *De ira* 2. 5. 2). It was allowable for an orator to show anger in a forensic or political context because that was not real anger, but an emotion assumed for a performance, just as an actor might represent an angry person (Sen. *De ira* 2. 17). Another element in the Roman approach to anger related to social status, as anger was considered an emotion that was inappropriate for aristocrats (Seneca *De ira* 1. 1. 2–4; 2. 15–16; 3. 6. 2–3; Roller (2001), 280–1). Epicureans offered a different approach, and it appears that Philodemus virtually inverted the values which Plato and Aristotle attached to *thymos* and *orge*, and defended the exercise of anger (for text and commentary see G. Indelli (ed.), *Filodemo, L'Ira* (Naples, 1988); there is ongoing debate as to whether Vergil was influenced by Epicureanism in the way he dealt with anger and fury (*furor*) in the *Aeneid*: cf. G. Indelli. 'The vocabulary of anger in Philodemus' *De ira* and Vergil's *Aeneid*', in D. Armstrong et al. (eds.), *Vergil, Philodemus and the Augustans* (Austin, 2004): 103–10). But Curtius sticks to what can be described as the conventional Roman, Stoic view of anger, and follows this Roman convention in singling out anger as one of his most serious failings. Curtius does also use the terms *feritas* (savagery) and *furor* (fury) (*feritas*: 3. 8. 15 and 5. 6. 15; *furor*: 10. 1. 5), but of other characters. Curtius' treatment of Alexander's explosive temperament reflects what was clearly a philosophical and rhetorical commonplace: cf., e.g. Livy 9. 18. 5; Velleius Paterculus 2. 41. 1; Val. Max. 7. 3. ext. 4; 9. 3. ext. 1; Seneca *De ira* 2. 23. 3 and 3. 17. 1 and 23. 1; *Ep.* 113. 29; Aelian *VH* 12. 54; and indeed Philodemus *De ira* 43. 25–7.

**fondness for drink.** Cf. 6. 2. 1–5; 8. 1. 22 ff.; J. 9. 8. 15; Plut. *Alex.* 23. 6–8, taking a rather defensive line. Alexander's explosive temper was commonly linked with his excessive drinking (e.g. Livy 9. 18. 4–5; Vell. Pat. 2. 41. 1, contrasting Caesar and Alexander; Seneca *De ira* 3. 17. 1; *Ep.* 83; Pliny *HN* 14. 58; Plut. *Mor.* 454d–e; 623d–624a), and this combination plays an important part in the story of Alexander's killing of his friend Cleitus (8. 1. 43 and 2. 1; the episode is analysed by Tritle (2003), who suggests that Alexander's behaviour was consistent with PTSD, post-traumatic stress disorder). Aristobulus tried to deny that Alexander had a drinking problem (A. 7. 29. 4; cf. Plut. *Mor.* 623d)). Curtius throughout this section seeks to attribute Alexander's failings at least in part to Alexander's youth (26, 29, 31, 34; contrast A. 7. 29. 1, where there is a single passing reference to his youth as a possible factor). If Curtius wrote 10. 9. 1–6 with Claudius in mind, then the allusion here must be to Gaius Caligula, a youthful imitator of Alexander (Suet. *Caligula* 52, with commentary of Wardle (1994), 341).

**5. 35. much though he owed to his own virtues, he owed more to Fortune.** The antithesis appears earlier e.g. at 4. 16. 27; cf. Vell. Pat. 2. 35. 2. On Alexander's consistent good luck see, e.g. 3. 1. 17; 4. 9. 22; 7. 11. 27; 8. 3. 1; 8. 6. 14; 9. 5. 3. At times it was certainly not deserved: e.g. 8. 10. 18 and 9. 10. 27–28. In the Hellenistic period Fortune, *qua* Tyche, developed a range of meanings from the base idea of 'what happens', to a positive notion close to that of fate or providence, and to the negative concept of a fickle force, capable of bringing the mighty low, deservedly or undeservedly (neatly expressed by Manilius *Astron.* 4. 96–7. The history of the idea, and the range of meanings, are reviewed by, among others, A. A. Buriks, *Peri Tyches* (Leiden, 1948), J. Kajanto, *God and Fate in Livy* (Turku, 1957), and Swain (1989*a* and *b*)). But there is little point in attributing to Curtius' concept of Fortune, in its various manifestations, a profundity which is not there. The antithesis here between virtue and Fortune has to mean that good fortune is a matter of chance, or, if providential, good fortune is instrumental in some higher purpose, rather than merited by the individual. The antithesis given here was well established in historiography (e.g. D.S. 16. 1. 6 on Philip; 17. 38. 5, on Alexander; Livy 7. 34. 6; 22. 12 10), and was a stock topic of debate in the Hellenistic schools of rhetoric. It was also an aspect of exercises in counter-history: what would have happened, if Alexander had had to clash with Rome?—the theme of Livy 9. 17–19, on which see Morello (2002). In patriotic Roman literature Fortune was more generally seen as the concomitant of, and just reward for, virtue (Oakley (1998), 336–7 lists examples in his commentary on Livy 7. 34. 6). Baynham (1998) devotes a chapter to the range of issues (pp. 101–31).

**when he had recklessly ridden into danger.** As in his action against the Uxii : 5. 3. 21; at the city of the Malli: 9. 5. 1; and when he explored the lower Indus: 9.9. 2; not to mention his heroic intervention in the battles at Issus and Gaugamela: 3. 11. 7–10; 4. 15. 19–20 and 24–5. In the narrative Curtius plays on the irony of the way Alexander's opponents deluded themselves with the idea that recklessness was his fatal flaw: 4. 14. 13 and 19; 7. 4. 2. His luck against the odds was derided in hostile rhetoric, as at Livy 9. 18. 15 and Lucan 10. 20–21.

**5. 36. The fates waited for him to complete the subjection of the east and reach the Ocean.** See on 1. 17 above. A common theme of rhetoric was that Alexander had ambitions to cross the Ocean: e.g. Sen. *Ep.* 91. 17; 94. 63; 113. 29; 119. 8; *QNat.* 5. 18. 10; 6. 23. 3; *Ben.* 1. 13. 1; 7. 2. 5; Lucan 10. 30–37; and the elder Seneca *Suas.* 1. But the connecting theme of such references to Alexander's plans for world domination was generally that they betrayed his dementia (cf. Cresci

Marrone (1993), esp. 34). Livy 9. 16. 19 speculates that Papirius would have been a match for Alexander, if the latter, having completed the subjection of Asia, had moved his army into Europe. But it was also recognized that Asia might have been conquered by Alexander, but was not pacified (Sen. *Suas.* 1. 4). Tacitus was later to complain that after Agricola's completion of the subjection of Britain, Domitian immediately abandoned those gains (Tac. *Hist.* 1.1. 5). In neither case was the subjugation as total as Curtius and Tacitus respectively suggested. Certainly in Alexander's case the Achaemenid dynasty was terminated, and the material and human resources of the Persian empire were wasted by the pillaging and killing. But there were areas that were not fully pacified, notably Cappadocia and perhaps Armenia; Indian satrapies were given up to indirect rule; Egypt had effectively passed into the control of Cleomenes. Furthermore, there were areas where well-entrenched administrative systems survived the Macedonian occupation and continued to operate with little noticeable change: e.g. Graf (2003), 330 on Idumaean territory, and Burstein (1994) on Egypt.

Heckel (2003*b*) shows that many modern writers have gone beyond the extravagances of ancient rhetoric in describing Alexander's ambition to reach 'the limits of the world', whereas in the east his goal was the *southern* Ocean, and not the *eastern* Ocean. At the Hydaspes in the summer of 326 (A. 5. 9. 4), Alexander had already initiated the construction of a fleet to sail down the Indus (D.S. 17. 89. 4–5; Curtius 9. 1. 4–5; Strabo 15. 1. 29. 698). Arrian conceals this till his reference to Alexander's joining the fleet at the Hydaspes (6. 1. 1). Thus, beyond the Hydaspes, Alexander had a limited objective, for he was planning to sail down the Indus, and not cross to the Ganges (cf. Kienast (1965), 182; Atkinson (2000*a*), 527), and his mission was limited to the incorporation of Porus' kingdom as a buffer zone (Heckel (2003*b*), 173–4; Hamilton (1973), 117).

The reference here to Alexander's reaching the Ocean is not matched in the other sources, and may be another conscious allusion to a link between Alexander and Gaius Caligula (cf. Suet. *Caligula* 46).

**5. 37. The burden was too great to be shouldered by one man.** Tiberius is supposed to have made a similar comment to explain his reluctance to accept the Principate in AD 14 (Tac. *Ann.* 1. 11. 1 and 12. 1; cf. Suet. *Tib.* 25. 2). The key term, *moles* (burden) had been applied earlier by Ovid (*Tristia* 2. 221–2) to the load of responsibility carried by Augustus; and the idea became a commonplace of imperial panegyric: e.g. Vell. Pat. 2. 127. 3 and 128. 4; Stat. *Theb.* 4. 39; Martial 6. 64. 14–15; Pliny *Pan.* 66. 2; Béranger (1953), 175–8. The burden of running an empire had rested lightly on Alexander's shoulders, as he had been preoccupied with conquest and founding an empire. Apart from the reference to *labor* (somewhere between hard work and fatigue) in 5. 27, Curtius has little of the vocabulary which his age associated with the business of running an empire.

**his reputation and the fame of his achievements.** Cf. *Auct. ad Her.* 4. 31. A theme of imperial panegyric was the power of the emperor's *nomen* (name/reputation) to cow other peoples into submission (e.g Vell. Pat. 2. 94. 4, with Woodman's commentary; cf. Curtius 5. 13. 14; 8. 13. 2; J. 12. 13. 2; 42. 5. 12).

**distributed kings and kingdoms . . . throughout the world.** Alexander's successors were to spread to cover the whole world, says Curtius; by contrast it could be said that when Claudius became emperor, he dedicated himself to the whole world (Sen. *Ad Polybium* 7. 2).

**6.1–10. 8.** *The power struggle in Babylon after Alexander's death*

*Sources:* A. *Succ.* (= *FGrH* 156, F.1); Dexippus, *FGrH* 100, F. 8; D.S. 18. 2–4; J. 13. 2–4; Plut. *Eum.* 3. 1–2; *Heidelberger Epitome* 1 (Bauer (1914), 2–3; also at *FGrH* 155, F1. 1); Appian *Syr.* 52; Aelian *VH* 12. 64.

*Bibliography:* Bosworth (2002), chapter 2, and (2003), 177–81; Briant (1973), 121–43; Errington (1970); Fontana (1960); Martin (1987); McKechnie (1999); Schachermeyr (1970); Sharples (1994); Seibert (1969), 27–38.

On the events in Babylon Curtius' account (chapters 6 to 10) is the fullest, and probably depends upon a hard core of historical facts (Errington (1970); cf. Bosworth (2003), esp. 178–9). In Errington's view, Curtius' reliability arose from his use of Hieronymus, which is perhaps supported by the detail on Eumenes at 10. 10. 3, cf. Plut. *Eum.* 3. 2. Briant (1973), 105–7 and 112–16 likewise argues for

Curtius' dependence on Hieronymus, but his case focuses on the quite different matter of Curtius' treatment of Celaenae, which he would link with Seneca *De ira* 3. 22. 4–5, and hence with Hieronymus. Over against Errington, Schachermeyr 1970, 96–104 argues for Cleitarchus as Curtius' main source, and by implication takes Curtius' silence about the rôle of Eumenes in these events as evidence that Curtius did not use Hieronymus (pp. 104–5). Comparison with the other sources (in particular D.S. 18) and the line taken on Ptolemy (see on 10. 20) indeed suggest that Curtius was following Cleitarchus, rather than Hieronymus (cf. Bosworth (2002), 24–6 and 42; J. Hornblower (1981), 87–97). But it does not follow that if Curtius followed Cleitarchus, his account has no historical value. Schachermeyr (1970), 101 argues that Cleitarchus drew on information from officials linked with the royal records. Furthermore, it is quite possible that Cleitarchus was in Babylon in 323 (Badian (1965), 9–11), and thus would have been able to record what he himself witnessed.

Sharples (1994) focuses on sections where Curtius lines up with Justin: in particular at 10. 6. 9–15 (with J. 13. 2. 5–12) and 10. 7. 8 (with J. 13. 2. 14). Sharples then argues that the common source was Hieronymus, and that differences between Curtius' account and Justin's, and inconsistencies in Curtius' narrative arose from his use of a second source—one which presented Arrhidaeus in a positive light.

Duris and Diyllus may have covered these events, and Fontana (1960), 299–310 argues that the idiosyncrasies of Curtius' account arose from his use of Duris, who adapted Hieronymus' account to suit his own purposes. But the general view is that, since Duris and Diyllus were not eyewitnesses, they probably would have had nothing new to add to Cleitarchus' account, and Schachermeyr (1970), 130–3 considers it fruitless to speculate whether either of them could have been an intermediary source between Cleitarchus and Curtius (Hammond (1983), in this case, appears to accept Schachermeyr's judgement).

At the end of his account of Alexander's last days Arrian adds that Aristobulus and Ptolemy offer nothing further (A. 7. 26. 3), which seems to mean that they had no other significant details to add to what Arrian has given in his account (cf. Bosworth (1988*b*), 162).

The alternative interpretation is that Aristobulus and Ptolemy did not carry their story beyond the death of Alexander, but it seems improbable that Ptolemy passed up the opportunity to refer, however briefly, to his role in the succession debate. But there is no evidence to indicate that this could have been substantial enough to form the basis of Curtius' account.

The difference in scale between Curtius' account and other parallel accounts makes it difficult to determine which differences arose from use of divergent sources, and which are compositional. Still, the differences on points of detail between Curtius and Justin (see on 6. 5–24) suggest that Curtius followed a source that was not the main source used by Trogus/Justin.

Schachermeyr (1970) tests the reliability of Curtius' account by two lines of argument which are not compelling: he questions whether Curtius' account matches the archaeological evidence (e.g. the *regia* (6. 2 and 4) was not large enough for a mass meeting of troops, if that is supposed to refer to the Throne Room off the Central Court: pp. 96 and 134–5); and secondly he finds that the characters in Curtius' story do not appear to respect Macedonian constitutional law (esp. 97–8). Schachermeyr lays too much emphasis on non-essential details and a questionable assumption about the nature of Macedonian constitutional law.

On the other hand Curtius includes elements which do not belong to the events of 323. First there are literary allusions—notably in the debate in 6. 5 to 23, echoes of the debate of the Persian conspirators in Herodotus 3. 80 ff. (but this idea is roundly dismissed by Bosworth); and secondly there are the allusions to events in Rome in Curtius' day (9. 1–6 shows that Curtius consciously explored the parallels). Martin (1987) deals fully with the Roman and contemporary allusions in Curtius' account, and McKechnie (1999) takes this even further in arguing that nothing in Curtius' version can be taken as historical unless confirmed by another source, and in concluding that it is substantially 'imaginative fiction' (60). Thus, though he does not make the point, McKechnie believes that Curtius strayed outside the parameters of *narratio* as they were prescribed by rhetoricians. Bosworth (2003), 177–81 strongly argues against McKechnie's line; and the earlier paper by Sharples (1994), in challenging Martin's case point by point, comes to the clear conclusion that there is 'no reason to believe that [Curtius] ever consciously falsified history' (60). Still the point remains that Curtius' account contains elements that are not corroborated by other sources.

**6. 1–4.** *Perdiccas sets the scene for a succession debate*

*Sources:* J. 13. 2. 4; Plut. *Eum.* 3. 1.

**6. 1. Alexander's bodyguards summoned his principal friends and the army officers to the royal quarters.** The group that took the initiative would have been the elite corps of Somatophylakes (Bodyguards; cf. 6. 7. 15; 9. 8. 23), traditionally seven in number, except for a brief period from the winter of 325/4 to Hephaestion's death in 324 when there were eight (A. 6. 28. 3–4; Berve (1926), i. 25–30. Heckel (1978) reviews the list; cf. (2003a), 206–8.). Ptolemy was one of the seven in Arrian's list, which may have some bearing on the question of Curtius' source(s) for this episode, and may be another indication that Cleitarchus was the source.

The 'principal friends' (cf. 9. 6. 4) were probably the Companions (Hetaeroi), a group which at this time numbered about 90 (Ephippus *FGrH* 126, F2 gives the range as 60 to 70, but on the marriages at Susa A. 7. 4. 4–6 indicates that the number had grown to about 90). The title was an honorific one, and holders of the title might be assigned to any military or administrative office (Berve (1926), i. 30–7). The picture was confused by the honorific ranks in the Hellenistic kingdoms, and the Vulgate sources are thus imprecise in referring to the Companions: Curtius variously calls them Friends, Allies (*socii*) and Nobles (*purpurati*): 3. 6. 4, 7. 11, 12. 2 and 7; 8. 1. 44; 9. 6. 4; 10. 3. 12. Hatzopoulos (1996), 331–3 argues that Curtius here refers to a body with a fixed composition, but the formulation suggests rather an *ad hoc* arrangement.

**6. 2. a herald's announcement forbidding access to all except those called by name.** There has been much debate as to whether the meeting to discuss the succession was a council of senior officers, or more of a general assembly of Macedonians. Here and in 6. 4 Curtius implies that ordinary soldiers participated alongside senior officers, and thus it is argued that this was an assembly of troops in Babylon functioning for a Macedonian army assembly (Errington (1970), 50; (1978), 88–9 on the *contio* at 7. 3; Mooren (1983), 234).

Others argue that this was a meeting open strictly only for the Companions, and that their decision was then referred to the cavalry (cf. J. 13. 3.1) and infantry. Thus Briant (1973), 243–4 takes this passage and 6. 12 to mean that ordinary soldiers tried to enter the assembly hall but were blocked from entering (cf. Plut. *Eum.* 3. 2 and A. *Succ.* 1. 2–3). But that is not what Curtius says, and in what follows he clearly imagines that this was a prolonged undifferentiated meeting (cf. 10. 7. 1, 3, 8–10 and 13).

The reality no doubt was that senior officers planned amongst themselves before holding an assembly of the army. There may well also have been subsequent separate meetings of cavalrymen and of the infantry, as is indicated by A. *Succ.* 1. 2–3 and J. 13. 3. 1, the latter putting these separate gatherings after the 'unanimous approval' of Perdiccas' plan to recognize Roxane's child, if a son, and to establish a regency administration (J. 13. 2. 13–14; Briant (1973), 244). The flow of Justin's narrative in 13. 2. 1—3. 1 indicates that 'the unanimous approval' came from a meeting of officers, and not a mass meeting such as Curtius seems to describe.

The Latin expression represented by 'called by name' was one used of summoning senators to attend a curial session: Sen. *Dial.* 10. 20. 4 (though in the Roman context the personal summons tended to connote an obligation or command (Dio 55. 3. 1; Sen. *Brev. vit.* 20. 4), rather than a privilege or entitlement (Gellius 3. 18. 6–8, and perhaps Dio 74. 12. 2–3)).

**6. 4. Perdiccas presented the royal throne in full view of the assembly.** Eumenes tried a similar ploy in 318 BC when he set up Alexander's throne in a royal tent, along with the diadem and other trappings, as a neutral place where he could meet Antigenes and Teutamus (Plut. *Eum.* 13. 3; D.S. 18. 60. 4–61. 2, following a different source; Polyaenus *Strat.* 4. 8. 2; Nepos *Eum.* 7. 2). Tarn ii. 116 assumes that some source—neither Hieronymus, nor Diodorus—transferred the Eumenes episode to Babylon. But there is no compelling reason to reject Curtius' version. If we suppose that the detail is historical, we might still allow that Curtius was aware of the occasion when Caligula was out of town, and, though a meeting of the Senate was not called, senators went up to the Capitol to perform *proskynesis* before Caligula's empty throne in the temple (Dio 59. 24. 4).

On the form of the throne we have Plutarch's description of the scene in 318 when Polyperchon set Philip Arrhidaeus up on a throne to receive two Athenian delegations. Plutarch suggests that the throne would have been in the Persian fashion with a canopy (*ouraniskos*; *Phocion* 33. 8), as portrayed on the late fourth-century Alexander Sarcophagus. But Paspalas (2005) argues that, while Plutarch's account of this episode is tendentious and the invocation of the Achaemenid model serves to discredit Polyperchon, it may be that for a brief period after Alexander's death, his adaptation of the Persian throne was still used to facilitate the transition to the new order (p. 92). But Hellenistic iconography offers no support for the idea that the throne with a golden canopy was used as a symbol of Hellenistic royalty (p. 84).

**Alexander's diadem.** This was the fillet, which could be tied around the royal headpiece, as a distinctive mark of royalty. The general opinion is that this was a Persian custom, which Alexander took over in 330 (Curtius 6. 6. 4 with Atkinson (1994), 202–3, and (1980), 129–30 on Curtius 3. 3. 19; Ritter (1965), 31 ff. and (1984), arguing against the case of Fredricksmeyer (1983), 99–100 that the diadem was a well established Macedonian convention long before Alexander's reign). Fredricksmeyer (1997) returns to the fray and argues forcefully that the diadem was a 'Dionysus-victory band' (106), which Alexander sported when he went into battle at Gaugamela. The diadem was the distinctive mark of kingship from the outset of the Hellenistic kingdoms (D.S. 20. 53. 2–54. 1).

**the ring the king had given him.** Mentioned at 10. 5. 4.

**6. 5–24.** *The succession debate*

*Sources:* J. 13. 2. 5–12.

*Bibliography:* Bosworth (2002), chapter 2, and (2003), 175–81; Errington (1970); Martin (1987); McKechnie (1999); Schachermeyr (1970); Seibert (1969), 27–38, and (1983), 84–9 for discussion of earlier treatments.

The debate was not just a Curtian invention, as J. 13. 2. 5–12 summarizes something similar, and Curtius was not following Trogus, since Trogus differed from Curtius on the rôle of Meleager and on the length of Roxane's pregnancy. In the favour of the historicity of the core narrative is the plausibility of the roles assigned to the participants in the debate. It will be seen that Nearchus would have had good reason to punt the idea that Barsine's son Heracles should be declared the successor (6. 10), and Aristonus' support for Perdiccas (6. 16) is consistent with the rest of his record. The points relating to Nearchus and Aristonus do not depend on evidence provided elsewhere by Curtius, thus this argument is not circular. The same can be said about the Macedonian nationalist line taken by Ptolemy (6. 13–15), which would be consistent with his political campaign from 321, if not 323, to appropriate Alexander's remains and to win control of at least the western half of Alexander's empire.

The debate is generally cast in terms of what was to happen about the dynastic succession, but Goukowsky (1975) argues that in the historical situation in Babylon in 323 the debate had another dimension too, and that concerned the Asian peoples. In taking Alexander's ring, Perdiccas had effectively taken the position of chiliarch, the Greek term used to describe the Macedonian adaptation of the Achaemenid post of *hazarapati*, the king's second-in-command; and in proposing succession by Roxane's child, if a male, Perdiccas was signalling to the Asians that shared rule would continue (Goukowsky (1975), esp. 270–1). Sensitivity to Persian concerns is perhaps not consistent with the tradition that Perdiccas was party to the murder of Darius' daughters, Stateira and Drypetis (Plut. *Alex.* 77. 6; further at 6. 9). Still, it would be true to say that the debate went beyond the succession issue, as, in the absence of a competent heir, they had to address the question of the management of the empire (D.S. 18. 1. 5 and 2.1; Briant (1973), 243), and Diodorus puts in the early days, and before the removal of Meleager, Perdiccas' presentation to the troops of Alexander's Last Plans (18. 4. 2–6), a 'document' not covered by Curtius, but known to him (see on 10. 1. 17–19).

Curtius' version of the debate echoes that of the Persian conspirators in Herodotus 3. 80–4 (cf. McKechnie (1999), 54–5). Perdiccas and Nearchus argue for the retention of hereditary monarchy, even though that would require as an immediate measure the appointment of a regent or a regency council, and the continuance of that arrangement until Roxane's child, if a son, attains adulthood. Then Ptolemy effectively argues for oligarchy (13–15). Aristonus turns the debate towards elective monarchy, but Meleager harangues the troops and urges them to take power in their own hands, and thus to create ochlocracy, a model which Augustus rejected in his 'resignation' speech in 27 BC, when he claimed that he was entrusting the entire administration to the senators (Dio 53. 8. 4–5). Against this interpretation Bosworth (2003), 179 states that he 'cannot find a single hint of alternative constitutions'. He also notes that although Meleager appeals to the troops to loot the treasury, he is no democrat, and is immediately shown as supporting Arrhidaeus to take over the kingship. But if one starts from the position that the debate is something of a construct, then consistency in a character's actions may well be elusive. Scholars who believe that Seneca's tragedies were written for declamation rather than theatrical performance have noted that characters often appear to adopt opposing positions in successive scenes.

**6. 5. I return to you the ring handed to me by Alexander.** It would be difficult not to see a connection between this scene, and the pattern established in January 27 BC when Augustus transferred the state from his power to the control of the Senate and Roman people (*Res Gestae* 34. 1, as rendered by Mason Hammond). Subsequently he routinely expressed reluctance to take new powers offered to him: e.g. Vell. Pat. 2. 89. 5; Dio 55. 6. 1 and 12. 3; 56. 28. 1. Thus refusal of power (*recusatio imperii*) became almost a routine ceremonial in the Principate, starting with Tiberius (Vell. Pat. 2. 124. 2; Tac. *Ann.* 1. 11. 1 and 12. 1; Suet. *Tib.* 24. 1–2, 25. 2; Dio 57. 2. 3; cf. Woodman (1977), 222 who lists later examples. Claudius at least declined the *praenomen* Imperator: Suet. *Claud.* 12. 1). But it does not seem that a profession of reluctance to take power was a feature of Hellenistic monarchy after the Successors first took the royal title in 305 (the dating issue is considered in the Additional Note at the end of this commentary). Thus if there was any contamination here of the record of Perdiccas' bid for power, it was from Roman history rather than Hellenistic.

**6. 6. one could believe that such a great man was merely on loan from the gods.** Perdiccas thus deals first with the issue of apotheosis, but Curtius carefully hedges the statement attributed to Perdiccas so as not to give express support to the idea. The hedging elements include the formula 'one could believe' (having almost the same force as 'one could be forgiven for believing'), the juxtaposition of the Latin words for man and gods, and the idea that the initiative came from the gods. The image of the gods' reclaiming Alexander is also more prosaic than the images in other sources for ascension and the celestial resting place, as found, e.g. in Manilius 4. 57, of Julius Caesar (with whose apotheosis the rot began); Vell. Pat 2. 123. 2 (of Augustus); Manilius 4. 934–5 (of Augustus); Val. Max. 4. 5. 6; Sen. *Cons. ad Polybium* 12. 5 (of Claudius' destiny); and Sen *Ep.* 86. 1 (of Scipio Africanus).

**they might swiftly reclaim him for their family.** Valerius Maximus 4. 5. 6 presents the divine nature of Julius Caesar in a similar way. At the beginning of 6. 7 Curtius returns to what might be characterized as a broadly accepted notion of the Stoics, that a human's soul survives death (Cic. *Tusc.* 1. 42; Sen. *Ep.* 79. 12), and Curtius avoids mentioning the cliché of the heavens as the soul's destination.

**6. 8. Fellow soldiers.** Curtius observes the Latin distinction between soldiers (*milites*) and fellow soldiers (*commilitones*). The latter term was avoided by Augustus as being too popularist and as inappropriate for the maintenance of military discipline (Suet. *Aug.* 25. 1; E. Dickey, *Latin Forms of Address* (Oxford, 2002), 288–92).

**a body without a soul.** Curtius uses the image of the body needing a head at 9. 2 and 4.

**6. 9. This is the sixth month of Roxane's pregnancy.** But J. 13. 2. 5 says the eighth month. Wirth (1967), 281 n. 3 supports Curtius, while Berve (1926), ii. 347 favours Justin's version. Roxane's child was Alexander IV, who nominally ruled as joint-king with Philip Arrhidaeus (*OGIS* iv. 4–5 and 12–13; Arrian *Succ.* 1a. 1).

The story of Alexander's marriage to Roxane is told in Curtius 8. 4. 23–30; cf. Plut *Alex.* 47. 7, and A. 4. 19. 5–6, and 7. 6. 4–5. See the commentary on 10. 3. 11 above on how the marriage was viewed by Macedonians and Persians.

Alexander subsequently married Darius' daughter Barsine/Stateira (Berve (1926), ii. 347; Heckel (2006), 256–7) at Susa, but that marriage produced no child, and she was murdered by Roxane immediately after Alexander's death, with the connivance of Perdiccas, according to Plut. *Alex.* 77. 6. Consistent with that is the tradition in the *Testament* that Alexander indicated before he died, and in his will, that Perdiccas should marry Roxane (*LM* 112 and 118; Heckel (1988), 26–8). O'Neil (2002), 166 notes that there were Macedonian precedents for such a 'levirate' marriage between the royal widow and the claimant to the throne. On the complexities of this issue see Heckel (2001). But there is much to commend the line of Mitchell (2007), 63 that 'the king's power was not institutional, but situational', where Mitchell summarizes the approach of Borza (1990), 236–41. Whether or not Perdiccas actually took Roxane as his wife, the murder of Stateira and her sister Drypetis can hardly have happened without the approval of Perdiccas. He himself soon after took as his wife first Nicaea, Antipater's daughter, and then Alexander's sister, Cleopatra (A. *Succ.* 1. 21 and 26; D.S. 18. 23. 1–3; 25. 3; J. 13. 6. 4–6). Thus, as after the death of Philip, so after Alexander's death, there was some tidying up of the royal family.

Roxane is attested epigraphically in an Athenian inventory of 305/4 BC as a past dedicant to Athena Polias: *IG* ii² 1492A. 45–57. E. Kosmelatou *ZPE* 146 (2004), 75–80 suggests that she may have made the offerings, by proxy, as Alexander's wife, even while he was still alive.

**6. 10. Nearchus.** But J. 13. 2. 6 attributes to Meleager the proposal that the kingship should be offered to Barsine's son, Heracles. Meleager plays a very different role in Curtius' story, and it seems more likely that the reference to Meleager in J. 13. 2. 6 is incorrect. Schachermeyr (1970), 97 argues that Nearchus, as a Cretan, would not have been allowed to attend a session of the supreme council of officers, but there is no proof that the Macedonians were bound by such a precise constitutional law. Nearchus' advocacy of Heracles may derive from Nearchus' memoirs, since Nearchus married a daughter of Barsine, and his wife was therefore a step-sister of Heracles (A. 7. 4. 6; cf. Schachermeyr (1970), 97; Pearson (1960), 116).

Tarn ii. 330 ff., with apologetic intent, argues that Heracles was an impostor who surfaced sometime after Alexander's death: but Alexander did have a liaison with Barsine (Plut. *Alex.* 21. 3), and D.S. 20. 20. 1 and 28. 1, probably following the reliable source Hieronymus, firmly identifies Heracles as Alexander's son (cf. Brunt (1975)).

**6. 13. Yes, a son of Roxane or Barsine really is a fitting ruler for the Macedonian people.** Curtius uses a feminine noun for 'offspring', which produces a feminine adjective as the first word of the sentence, followed by the particle *prorsus*, here with the connotation of sarcasm (Latinists may compare the ironic formulation in Tac. *Ann.* 12. 2. 3). The objection to the idea of a king who was half Asian echoes the Macedonian troops' reaction to the advancement of Persians at Susa, and the grievances which they articulated at Opis (Bosworth (2003), 179, citing A. 7. 6. 2–3 and 8. 2; cf. Bosworth (1996*b*), 143–4).

**6. 15. Those who used to be consulted by him should meet... whenever a decision concerning the common good has to be made.** This may be an echo of the stratagem which Eumenes adopted in 318 BC to set up a council of officers (D.S. 18. 60. 6–61. 2; Plut. *Eum.* 13. 3–4), and Martin (1987), 178 notes that the alternatives to monarchy offered by Perdiccas and Ptolemy have an analogy in the debates in the soldiers' camp and in the Senate after the assassination of Caligula (Jos. *Ant.* 19. 162–86). But J. 13. 2. 12 agrees that Ptolemy's plan was to establish an officers' council, and Errington (1970), 74–5 argues for the historicity of this proposal, and suggests that in 318 Eumenes put into operation an adaptation of the proposal which Ptolemy had not been able to carry. Mooren (1983), 232 takes Ptolemy's proposal to indicate that in Macedonia the state had an existence independent of the king. Mooren goes on to argue that Ptolemy's model was actualized in 279 BC, when Sosthenes declined to take the kingship, but elected to rule as *strategos* (J. 24. 5. 13–14), and Macedon was a *de facto* republic for perhaps two years. Mooren supports the view that Sosthenes saw this as an interregnum, pending the return to monarchy (Mooren (1983), 239–40). But back in 323, Ptolemy must have had in mind a council of the Companions (Hetaeroi), or the smaller, less formalized, circle of 'friends'. As noted at 6. 1 above, the number of Companions had risen to 90 by 324, and, even if allowance is made for those on service away from the royal camp, the number may have been too large for effective decision-making. Furthermore Curtius goes on to imply that the majority of officers were not included. Thus Curtius may well be referring to a smaller group of trusted advisers, such as he presents at 6. 8. 1 in the lead-up to Philotas' trial. This would also be smaller than the group he indicates in 6. 1, and would mean a council less formalized than Mooren imagines.

**6. 16. Aristonus.** The son of Peisaios, from Pella (A. 6. 28. 4), but apparently an Eordaian by birth (A. *Ind.* 18. 5); attested as a Body-guard by 325 (A. 6. 28. 4), but quite possibly already of that rank by 328, if he was the 'Aristophanes' of Plut. *Alex.* 51. 5–6 (Heckel (1992), 275, and (2006), 50, against Berve (1926), ii. no. 133). He was one of those who saved Alexander's life in the Mallian town (C.R. 9. 5. 15 and 18; hence, as Heckel suggests, the award to him of a gold crown at Susa in 324: A. 7. 5. 6)). He was later put to death because of his loyal support for Eumenes (D.S. 19. 50–1. 1). His record from 323 indicates consistent support for Perdiccas, thus the appearance of his name in this context is credible. But as Bosworth (2002), 43 observes, there is nothing in Justin's account to support Curtius' claim that Aristonus went as far as to propose that Perdiccas be appointed king.

**6. 18. wavered between a burning desire to take it and a sense of decency.** The first hint of the sordid role Perdiccas will play in the events leading up to the killing of Meleager. This is reinforced by the following claim that he acted with dissimulation to get what he wanted.

**6. 20. Meleager.** Son of Neoptolemus, attested as an infantry com-mander at the Granicus (A. 1. 14. 3), and first mentioned by Curtius at 3. 9. 7. His career is discussed by Heckel (2006), 159–61. In this speech attributed to Meleager, Curtius uses colloquialisms and irony to give the statement immediacy, and to characterize Meleager as in touch with rank and file troops. He cuts through the rhetoric to attack Perdiccas' ambition, and at the end takes a demagogic line in inciting the troops to raid the treasury. A. *Succ.* has no corresponding refer-ence to Meleager's anarchic stance. But it conforms line with the confrontational style attributed to Meleager in an episode in India, when Meleager passed a racist remark while taunting Alexander about his favouritism towards orientals (Curtius 8. 12. 17–18; cf. Plut. *Alex.* 59. 5 and Strabo 15. 1. 28. 698, but without naming Meleager).

Justin's version is somewhat different: the infantry have met sep-arately, and Attalus and Meleager are sent by the senior officers to calm the men down, but they abandon their mandate and court the favour of the troops, so aggravating the sedition (J. 13. 3. 2). Another point of difference is that in Justin's account, Meleager only emerges as the leader of the infantry after they have hailed Arrhidaeus king. Goukowsky (1975), 272 would emphasize that the historical issue was not the class divide (*pace* Briant (1973)), but a clash of two models of monarchy, and the infantry saw Arrhidaeus as the way to restore the traditional Macedonian kingship, over against the new cross-cultural model that Alexander had created, and Roxane's son would continue. Thus Goukowsky, by implication, gives preference to Justin's account. The difference between the two accounts means that, as Arrhidaeus does not come into the equation in Curtius' version, Meleager in Curtius' account of this debate can more fairly be described as representing an alternative to monarchy, which can be labelled in a negative way ochlocracy.

**those of better birth than this fellow.** But at 7. 8 Curtius shows awareness that Perdiccas was of royal stock.

**6. 23. Well, why not run off and loot the treasure chests?** The seemingly naive formulation emphasizes Meleager's irresponsibility (and not advocacy of traditional Macedonian monarchy).

**7. 1–3.** *The name of Philip Arrhidaeus is raised and commands general support*

*Sources*: J. 13. 2. 6–10.

*Bibliography*: Schachermeyr (1970), 136–7; Martin (1987); Sharples (1994); Bosworth (2002), 35–41.

This incident comes at roughly the same point in Justin's narrative, but a major difference is that Justin attributes the introduction of Arrhidaeus' name to Meleager (J. 13. 2. 8). Arrian and D.S. 18. 2. 2 do not indicate who first proposed Arrhidaeus. Sharples (1994), esp. 55–9, argues that J.'s account was based on Hieronymus, while Curtius blended Hierony-man elements with material taken from some other source, but Sharples also suggests (p. 74) that Justin may have simply transferred the incident to Meleager in the process of compressing his material.

**7. 1. a man of the lowest class, who was unknown to most of the Macedonians.** Schachermeyr (1970), 97 dismisses this episode as fiction because a common soldier could not have addressed such a council of officers, but this argument rests on a dubious assumption, and Curtius is clearly imagining that this episode took place at a general assembly or mass meeting. He has turned the episode into a Roman situation, calling the assembly a *contio* (an assembly met to discuss an issue before the convening of a formal assembly for voting); and referring to the man as of the lowest plebeian rank, where it might have been more appropriate to label him a common soldier (like Vibulenus, the *gregarius miles* of Tac. *Ann.* 1. 22. 1 in the context of the mutiny in Pannonia). While there is no absolute way of determining the sequence of events in this confused chapter in history, it is highly improbable that Arrhidaeus' name first came up only when a common soldier raised his voice: it has the smack of a literary device.

When a minor character was responsible for a twist in the tale, there was perhaps always a narratological tendency to write down his, or her, status, or to make the character anonymous. So, e.g. on the death of Antiochus II in 246 BC, his wife Laodice used a double to conceal the death and to announce a succession plan, and, whereas Val. Max 9. 14. ext. 1 identifies the double as Artemon, a high-ranking officer, the elder Pliny *HN* 7. 53 makes him a commoner. Thus too in Greek tragedy a nameless individual may be the agent of a twist in the story (*peripeteia*), like Phaedra's nurse or the drunk who told Oedipus that he was not Polybus' son (Soph. *OT* 779–80). The *Alexander Romance* includes in the death bed scene an exchange between Alexander and a Macedonian, Peucolaus, who was quite handsome, but of no social standing (Ps-Call. 3. 32. 14; *ME* 105–6).

There is a parallel of more immediate significance in the story of Claudius' accession, when, as Josephus tells the story in *Antiquities* 19. 217, Gratus, a member of the Praetorian Guard, found Claudius hiding in the palace, and called out to those with him, 'Here is a Germanicus, let us make him emperor.' In Suetonius, Gratus becomes a nameless 'common soldier' (*Claudius* 10. 2), multiplied in Dio 60. 1. 2 to appear as 'some soldiers'. Thus Martin (1987), 176–83 suggests that Curtius has here borrowed an element from the story of Claudius' accession. Sharples (1994), 57 rejects Martin's line of argument, but concedes that the unknown soldier (*ignotus*) may be a literary device.

The closer parallel is in Josephus' earlier account of the accession where he has a nameless trooper urge his comrades not to be drawn into a civil war, when they have in Claudius an emperor who is blameless (*Bell. Jud.* 2. 211–12). The bravery and nobility of attitude of this common soldier echo the reasonable, measured line of Curtius' unknown soldier. Curtius brings out the seriousness of his anonymous trooper by casting his statement in an elegant way that contrasts with the colloquial, rabble-rousing style attributed to Meleager. It may be noted that Josephus' trooper was speaking in an assembly dominated by senators, and not just a mass meeting of guardsmen.

**7. 2. Philip's son, Arrhidaeus.** Philip's son by Philinna of Larisa (A. *Succ.* 1. 1; J. 9. 8. 2; 13. 2. 11; Athenaeus 13. 557c etc.), born perhaps *c*.358 (Berve (1926), ii. no. 781, citing Athenaeus 13. 557d and Plut. *Alex.* 10. 1). Plut. *Alex.* 77. 5 says that she was a commoner (cf. Carney (2001), 81) and Ptolemy in J. 13. 2. 11 styles her a Larissan whore. This may be another example of the writing down of the status of a minor character, but more likely reflects the hostile bias of some source (cf. Bosworth (2002), 113 and 274). The sources generally describe him as mentally challenged (see on 7. 5). He held the royal title for over 6 years and 4 months, before he was murdered in 317 (D.S. 19. 11. 2–5; Wheatley (2007), 192). For a summary of his career see Heckel (2006), 52–3.

**he accompanied the king in performing sacrifices and ceremonies.** Briant (1973), 330–1 takes this to mean that by using Arrhidaeus as a co-celebrant, Alexander was designating him as the heir apparent, and also that Macedonian law tolerated association in regnal power. This was rejected by Goukowsky (1975), 272, noting the argument of Fredericksmeyer (1966), 179–82 that this is a reference to the family cult of the Argeads as opposed to the ancestral cults of the Macedonians (Athenaeus 14. 659 f–660a; the point was made earlier, e.g. by Mützell in his commentary *ad loc.*). Thus Alexander marked Arrhidaeus out as his immediate heir only in respect of cultic matters (cf. Schachermeyr (1970), 21). The distinction between family and national cults seems to be glossed over in Fredricksmeyer's more recent study: (2003), 256–7; cf. Badian (1999), 87–8), and Arrhidaeus plays a cultic role in the 'purification' ceremony at 9. 11–19.

**7. 4–7.** *The Macedonians ignore Peithon's negative comments and choose Arrhidaeus as their king*

J. 13. 2. 11–12 attributes the criticism of Arrhidaeus to Ptolemy, and not Peithon. As will be seen, this probably means that Curtius and Justin depend on different sources, and that Curtius was following Cleitarchus (cf. Bosworth (2002), 40–3; Sharples (1994), 158–9 does not identify Curtius' source here, but says simply that it was not Hieronymus, on whom Curtius depended for material he shared with Justin). But with regard to the diplomatic way in which Curtius alludes to Arrhidaeus' mental incapacity, it remains conceivable that Curtius was writing in the early part of Claudius' reign, and did not wish to appear to be mocking Claudius (despite Sharples' bid to demolish the case of Martin (1987)), or wrote later than Claudius and wished to avoid any such association.

**7. 4. Pithon.** Pithon, or in Greek Peithon, son of Crateuas, from Alcomenae in Deuropos (Arr. *Succ.* 1a. 2; A. *Ind.* 18. 6 with Strabo 7.7.8 326–7; Berve (1926), ii. no. 621; Heckel (1992), 276–9, and (2006), 195–6) was a Bodyguard at least as early as 325 (A. 6. 28. 4), and perhaps even from 336 (Heckel). He features in various accounts of Alexander's final illness (A. 7. 26. 2; Plut. *Alex.* 76. 9; Ps-Call. 3. 31. 8). Subsequent events that may have influenced the primary sources' views of him would include his savage suppression of the revolt of Greek colonists in the Upper Satrapies (D.S. 18. 4. 8; 7. 3–9), his support for Perdiccas in the invasion of Egypt, and then the way he turned against Perdiccas (D.S. 18. 36. 5; Heckel (1992), 278 suggests that behind J. 13. 8. 10 lies a source which charged Peithon with the murder of Perdiccas), and his treachery after he joined Antigonus' camp and helped him to secure a victory over Eumenes (D.S. 19. 19. 4 and 8; 20. 2–3; 26. 7; 29. 2–3 to 43. 4). When he plotted against Antigonus, Antigonus retaliated by eliminating him (D.S. 19. 46. 1–4). Grainger (1990), 218–19 suggests that it was someone from Antigonus' circle who was responsible for including Peithon in the list of unsavoury characters who supposedly held a vigil in the temple of Sarapis while Alexander was on his deathbed (A. 7. 26. 2). This group includes Seleucus, who also joined Antigonus against Eumenes (D.S. 19. 18. 1). Thus Grainger (1990), 17 takes Hieronymus, a friend of Eumenes, to have been at least an unreliable, if not hostile source on

Seleucus. This only makes sense because, after the death of Eumenes, Hieronymus threw in his lot with Antigonus, and Seleucus, like Peithon, fell victim to Antigonus, being effectively driven out of his satrapy, Babylonia (D.S. 19. 48 and 55; Bosworth (2002), esp. 211–13). But the immediate point is that there probably was a hostile tradition on Peithon, and Hieronymus may have played a part in developing it (cf. Bosworth (2002), 160–1, who argues that it may have suited Hieronymus' purposes to accept Antigonus' justification for removing Peithon).

But Bosworth (2002), 40–3 offers another approach. In J. 13. 2. 11–12 it is Ptolemy and not Peithon who attacks the proposal that Arrhidaeus should be recognized as the new king. There is no good reason why Curtius should have substituted Peithon for Ptolemy, but in the pattern of events from 318, Ptolemy found himself lined up with Cassander, and therefore also Arrhidaeus, against Polyperchon, and from 315 against Antigonus (D.S. 19. 11. 2; J. 14. 5. 3; D.S. 19. 57. 2; Bosworth (2002), 40–3). Thus Ptolemy might have wished to dissociate himself from the historical record that he had opposed the accession of Arrhidaeus in 323, and Cleitarchus may then have obliged by transferring Ptolemy's role to Peithon (Bosworth (2002), 42, as part of his defence of the historicity of the essentials, if not the details of the debate recorded by Curtius).

**7. 5. his derogatory remarks.** As the text stands Curtius does not spell out the nature of Peithon's complaints about Arrhidaeus, but other sources explain that Arrhidaeus had limited intelligence: D.S. 18. 2. 2; Plut. *Alex.* 10. 2 and 77. 5; J. 13. 2. 11 and 14. 5. 2 (though J. is less specific about the nature of Arrhidaeus' debility); Plut. *Mor.* 337d and 791e. The *Alexander Romance* seems to give support to the tradition that Arrhidaeus was in some way challenged, as Alexander is recorded as stipulating in his will that in the short term the king should be Arrhidaeus, but after the birth of Roxane's child, the kingship should pass to it, if a male, as Alexander's child, and that, if the baby was a female, the Macedonians could choose whoever they wished, if they did not want Arrhidaeus (Ps-Call. 3. 33. 11). The implication is that what might count against Arrhidaeus was not just that he was Philip's son rather than Alexander's.

Carney (2001), esp. 78–82 argues that Arrhidaeus' problem was probably mental retardation, rather than mental illness. She takes Plut. *Phocion* 33. 5–7 to show that Arrhidaeus was capable of taking part in public business, as in the situation when Polyperchon and he gave audience to Phocion and his supporters and a rival group of Athenian leaders: thus she finds him an 'only moderately limited ruler' (Carney (2001), 75 and 81, and we should take Carney to be judging by ideal standards rather than by the standards of many who have held high elective office with disastrous consequences in modern history). But the episode in *Phocion* 33 can be differently interpreted, for Arrhidaeus' initial reaction to the Athenian approach is a maniacal laugh and Polyperchon and the rest of his party carry on as though Arrhidaeus were not there; and when Arrhidaeus leaps up to attack Hegemon, Polyperchon physically restrains him. This is not inconsistent with Plutarch's description of him as no different from an infant (*Mor.* 337d), and like a non-speaking extra on the stage, dressed as a bodyguard, and mocked by those who held the real power (*Mor.* 791e).

Of course, as is noted above, the debate is complicated by the fact that Claudius had a similar reputation (Suet. *Claudius* 3–4), which may explain why Curtius is reticent about the nature of Peithon's complaints about Arrhidaeus, if Curtius was writing this book after Claudius had become emperor. Bosworth (2002), 36 would date Curtius later than Claudius' reign and finds no reason why Curtius should have failed to record Peithon's case and emphasizes the textual crux. In his view a substantial piece of text was lost between *destinabatur* and *inpense*, and the missing section spelt out what were Arrhidaeus' weaknesses. But the text can be repaired with quite minor emendation (as in the Mondadori edition, where I follow Damsté's proposal). Furthermore, in the following narrative there is nothing related to Arrhidaeus' actions which would explain any charge of physical or mental disability; and at 8. 21 Curtius' line is that, as Arrhidaeus had grown up in the shadow of Alexander, the Macedonians had not appreciated his strength of character. Thus what follows does not suggest that we have lost from the text Peithon's charges against Arrhidaeus. It is more likely that Curtius airbrushed them out, whether for narratological, or other more sinister reasons. Still the special treatment of Arrhidaeus suggests that, even if the emperor celebrated in 10. 9 was not Claudius, Curtius wrote after the events of AD 41, and thus later than Claudius' reign.

**7. 7. Out of antagonism and hatred for Perdiccas Meleager brought him into the royal quarters.** Cf. D.S. 18. 2. 2. Plut. *Mor.* 337d likewise attributes the initiative to Meleager. Clearly he was concerned to stop Perdiccas becoming a monarch by means of the regency.

**7. 8–15.** *The (cavalry) officers dictate terms, but Meleager rallies support for Arrhidaeus*

*Sources*: J. 13. 2. 13–3. 1; D.S. 18. 2. 2; A. *Succ.* 2–3.

*Bibliography*: Errington (1970), esp. pp. 49 and 52 labels Peithon's plan 'the proposed settlement', though, as Badian has commented, it was more of an imposed deal. Bosworth (2002), esp. 49–55 on the revised settlement.

Curtius indicates that the mass meeting had chosen Arrhidaeus by acclamation, whereas J. 13. 2. 13 records that the meeting had unanimously voted for Perdiccas's proposal, and it would seem that the meeting included the infantrymen (the men attended in arms, and Meleager was there to put the case for Arrhidaeus: J. 13. 2. 4 and 6; and consensus was reached: 2. 13). There is a further disjunction in that Justin implies that after the acceptance of Perdiccas' proposal the senior officers took an oath of allegiance to what was effectively a regency team, and the cavalrymen did the same (J. 13. 2. 14–3. 1), presumably meeting separately for the purpose, and the infantry-men, certainly meeting separately, complained that they had been left out of the deliberative process, and chose Arrhidaeus king by ac-clamation (J. 13. 3. 1; cf. commentary on 6. 20 above). But Curtius implies that the action developed in a prolonged general meeting: the rank and file noisily acclaimed Arrhidaeus, but the officers won the argument when it came to detailed proposals (7. 8–9), and forced the requirement of an oath of allegiance. The tide had turned because Meleager and his supporters had withdrawn from the proceedings (7. 10), but after they returned with Arrhidaeus, although some stood by the decision to support Perdiccas, the majority took fresh heart and renewed the choice of Arrhidaeus by acclamation (7. 12–14). Justin's statement that the infantrymen complained that they had been excluded from the deliberative process (itself at odds with the preceding apparent reference to a mass meeting) might be reconciled with Curtius' account, if the complaint related to the period after Meleager withdrew from the meeting (7. 10).

**7. 8. proposing Perdiccas and Leonnatus, both of royal blood, as guardians for Roxane's future son.** J. 13. 2. 13–14 likewise indicates that the officers supported only Roxane's son. Perdiccas hoped the plan would be palatable because there was to be shared responsibility, and both were guardians (*tutores*) rather than regents, and both were of royal lineage (Berve (1926), ii. nos. 313 and 232, and Heckel (2006), 197–202 and 147–51 respectively). There had also been the precedent of Philip's regency for Amyntas (cf. Errington (1970), 49–50). Furthermore, the enforced wait till it was known whether Roxane was carrying a son would provide a useful period for political manoeuvring and consolidation, or so it might have been hoped. But it was not long before the idea of a college of guardians faded, and Perdiccas established primacy (10.11–12 below).

Justin adds the names of Antipater and Craterus as proposed guardians, but that makes little sense in context, and we should prefer Curtius' version of what was proposed for them (7. 9).

**7. 9. Craterus and Antipater should direct affairs in Europe.** Craterus, son of Alexander (A. 1. 25. 9; *Ind.* 18. 5), who came from Orestis, was one of the younger group of Alexander's marshals, with a distinguished military record in Asia, and a close friend of Alexander (Plut. *Alex.* 47. 10; Curtius 6. 8. 2; his career is fully analysed by Heckel (1992), 107–33, and (2006), 95–9). At Opis in 324 he had been ordered to lead the veterans back to Macedon and to take over Antipater's command (J. 12. 12. 9; A. 7. 12. 4), but, when Alexander died, Craterus was still in Cilicia (D.S. 18. 4. 1), waiting on events (Badian (1961), 36–7 assumes that he was putting off a confrontation with Antipater, but Heckel (1992), 126 and 129–30 would rather emphasize Craterus' sickness and the military situation in Cilicia and Cappadocia as the factors that kept him in Cilicia). Antipater, son of Iolaos, had been left in Macedonia in 334 as Alexander's viceroy, responsible for Macedonia, Greece and Thrace (Berve (1926), ii. no. 94; Heckel (1992), 38–49; (2006), 35–8). The officers in Babylon

were inviting Craterus and Antipater to fight it out for supremacy in
Macedonia (cf. Errington (1970), 53).

**an oath of allegiance ... was exacted.** Cf. J. 13. 2. 14.

**7. 10. Meleager ... now once more came storming into the royal
quarters, dragging Philip with him.** According to D.S. 18. 2. 2–3 and
J. 13. 3. 2 Meleager was sent by the cavalry officers to consult the
infantry, but he concealed his brief. Justin sets this incident after the
settlement imposed by the officers, and after the infantry had reacted
by giving support to Arrhidaeus. Thus Meleager's mission would
belong at this point in Curtius' narrative, but Curtius chose to
present it in a different way (cf. Briant (1973), 246 n. 9), or was
following a source that did not have Meleager betray a mandate
(which appears to be the view of Bosworth (1971*a*), 128, who thus
takes a more positive view of Curtius' version). Curtius' line that
Meleager had withdrawn with his supporters is not compatible with
the idea in D.S. and J. that the high command used Meleager as an
intermediary. Then there is the detail in Justin's account that Meleager was sent on this mission together with one Attalus. The extra
detail may increase the chances that this episode was historical, and it
would be all the more significant if this Attalus was the infantry
officer who was, or became, Perdiccas' brother-in-law (D.S. 18. 37. 2;
so Schachermeyr (1970), 136–7; Wirth (1967), 291 n. 37), but Bosworth (2002), 44 sees no reason to make that connection. Either way,
it is another detail missed in Curtius' account, which keeps the focus
on the clash between Perdiccas and Meleager.

**7. 11. No deep sea ... produces waves as violent as the emotions of a
mob.** Another echo of Livy 28. 27. 11; cf. on 2. 21 supra. If 10. 9. 1–6
refers to Claudius, then Curtius must here reflect the situation in
January 41, when, according to Josephus, the crowd was initially
fearful and reluctant to believe the news of Caligula's assassination,
then they hailed Chaerea and celebrated their freedom; but then
rejoiced when Claudius seized the Principate (*Antiquities* 19. 127–8,
189 and 228).

**especially if it is luxuriating in the first flush of political freedom.**
Curtius adds oxymoron to Livy's usage of the verb *luxuriare* (1. 19. 4;
23. 2. 1). For what it is worth, the watchword used by the consuls of

41, after the murder of Caligula, was *libertas* (political freedom) (Jos. *Ant.* 19. 186).

**7. 13. Arrhidaeus . . . was called back.** Arrhidaeus appears to enter the royal quarters four times (7. 7, 10, 13 and 17), which Schachermeyr (1970), 99 takes to indicate that Curtius' source, Cleitarchus, failed to harmonize different versions of a single event. But Curtius is dealing in 10. 6–10 with events that happened over seven days (10. 9), and the repetition could equally well arise from Curtius' dramatization of the episode.

**cowed by the authority wielded by the generals.** Curtius imports a Roman constitutional association, as *auctoritas* (authority) in one sense was a resolution of the Senate, which stood as such, even if it was vetoed by tribunes or passed informally (Livy 4. 57. 5, Cic. *Fam.* 8. 8. 6–8, Dio 55. 3. 4–5, Talbert (1984), 185 and 285). Defiance of the collective will of the Senate had its own hazards. In another sense 'authority' was the aura that attached to the power (*imperium*) of a senior Roman magistrate, and so added a level of protection beyond the constitutional provisions.

Sharples (1994), 57 translates the key phrase 'terrified of the authority of the leading men', and argues that this could not have been written in Claudius' reign, for the Emperor would have seen this as an insult if readers might find any allusion to his situation in 41. But a constitutionally minded Roman might have thought it appropriate for an aspirant to the Principate to stand in awe of the Senate until it had formally recognized the new emperor. It may be added that Curtius says that Arrhidaeus had withdrawn (not 'run away') from the meeting, and was called back (not dragged back), and now that the decision had been taken, he actively put on the royal robes.

**7. 15. pleased that the strength of the empire would remain in the same house with the same family.** Curtius is referring to the counter-proposal adopted by the infantry unilaterally, as Justin presents it, by which Arrhidaeus would become king (cf. J. 13. 3. 1).

The troops' pleasure that power would remain in the same house, with the same family, has an echo in the constitutional crisis of 41, when the Praetorian Guard chose Claudius as the new emperor, and so opposed the bids of those who, as Curtius would put it, 'aspired to a throne to which they had no claim' (7. 14). The phraseology anticipates that which he uses in the eulogy of the new emperor at 9. 6. The echo best fits a Claudian date for Curtius, but does not exclude later alternatives.

**7. 16–21.** *A bloody clash leads to the withdrawal of the cavalry from the city*

*Sources*: J. 13. 3. 3–5, D.S. 18. 2. 3–4, Plut. *Eum.* 3. 1.

*Bibliography*: Briant (1973), 246–7, Schachermeyr (1970), 99–101, taking Cleitarchus to be Curtius' source.

The characterization of Perdiccas seems a little inconsistent: terrified (16), then angry (18), and when the older troops appeal to Perdiccas' men to lay down their arms, he is the first to comply (19). He and Leonnatus lead the retreat towards the Euphrates, but as the rest head into the plain to camp, Perdiccas remains behind, hoping to win over the infantry (20), which seems to be a brave gesture. But through these inconsistencies Curtius is creating the image of a leader who was flexible, pragmatic and manipulative, and who could outgun Meleager in dissimulation and the ruthless determination to win, as emerges in the next two chapters. This coheres with what we know about Perdiccas from other sources.

**7. 16. 600 men of proven valour.** Perhaps a reference to the elite infantry corps of Hypaspists that served as a bodyguard in the court (as in D.S. 17. 110. 1). Schachermeyr (1970), 14, and n. 10 links them with the hypaspists whom Diodorus mentions as crack troops in Perdiccas' army when he invaded Egypt (D.S. 18. 33. 6 and 34. 2), but Bosworth (2002), 82–3 argues that Diodorus in 18. 33 and 34 is using the term in the non-technical sense of 'shield bearers'.

**joined by Ptolemy.** Ptolemy was an infantry commander rather than a cavalry officer, and his association with Perdiccas was short-lived (7. 20–1 *infra*): thus Curtius' source may have presented Ptolemy here as a conciliator. The source may also have emphasized Ptolemy's concern to guard Alexander's corpse (cf. 10. 20 *infra*), just as it was concerned to clear his name of any disrespect towards Arrhidaeus (above on 7. 4).

**7. 18. Perdiccas called aside any who wished to protect Alexander's corpse.** Meleager's group had the advantage of the physical presence of Arrhidaeus. Perdiccas does not use Alexander's unborn child as the rallying cry against Meleager, but the protection of Alexander's corpse.

**7. 20. The cavalry, composed of young men from the best families.** Curtius is referring to the Companion Cavalry, on which see Berve (1926), i. 104. The reference to nobility, like the reference to 'proven valour' in 7. 16, is supposed to evoke the reaction that Perdiccas and Leonnatus—both of royal blood (7. 8)—represented the nobler cause. This adds a touch of irony to what is here an inversion of the tradition of the early Roman Republic when plebeian commoners on more than one occasion mounted a secession in their campaign for *libertas* against the intransigence of their patrician masters (the first in 494: Livy 2. 32. 2; the second in 449: Livy 3. 52. 1–4).

**7. 21. Perdiccas...remained in the city.** Plut. *Eum.* 3. 1 says that when the rest of the senior officers left Babylon, Eumenes stayed behind, calmed down a good number of the infantry, and made them readier for a settlement. It is likely that Plutarch was here following Hieronymus (rather than Duris, whom he dismisses as unreliable at 1. 1–2). If, as we have seen, Justin's account was ultimately based on Hieronymus, then Justin, if not Trogus, chose to leave Eumenes out at this point in the narrative. But Curtius alone states that Perdiccas stayed behind in the city, and this detail is necessary to the following episode.

**8. 1–14.** *Perdiccas survives Meleager's plot to destroy him and tightens the siege of Babylon*

*Sources*: J. 13. 3. 7–8.

*Bibliography*: Briant (1973), 247–50; Heckel (1992), 147–9, 169, 180–3 and 381–4; Bosworth (2002), 45–7.

Justin likewise mentions a plot to kill Perdiccas, but features Attalus as the initiator. It may have been Curtius' idea to switch the focus from Attalus to Meleager, and Curtius was surely responsible for the Roman colouring, especially in 8. 6. Briant (1973), 247–50 considers that, apart from Justin's mention of Attalus, his account and Curtius' version are otherwise in agreement on the essentials, and that Hieronymus must have been the common source. But the differences discussed at

8. 2 and 4 allow the possibility that if Trogus' account derived from Hieronymus, Curtius may have followed Cleitarchus.

In the structure of the book Curtius may have intended the scene with Meleager working on Arrhidaeus to balance the drama of Bagoas poisoning the mind of Alexander against Orxines (1. 28–9), in which case the reader is invited to contrast Alexander's gullibility and decisive response with Arrhidaeus' ability to listen without giving a positive response.

**8. 1. no one could give true allegiance to someone he feared.** A rhetorical commonplace found e.g. in Cicero *Off.* 2. 23, with a quotation from Ennius, and *Amic.* 53 (noted by Dempsie; cf. Otto (1890), 252).

**8. 2. Meleager ... sent men to summon Perdiccas.** But J. 13. 3. 7–8 says that Attalus sent armed men to kill Perdiccas. Attalus must be the same as Justin refers to in 13. 3. 2, and despite the reservations of Bosworth noted at 7. 10 above, this must mean Attalus, son of Andromenes (Berve (1926), ii. no. 181; Heckel (2006), 63–4; Schachermeyr (1970), 124–5, 136–7; Wirth (1967), 291 n. 37), rather than some otherwise unknown infantry officer. As Attalus son of Andromenes was married to Perdiccas' sister Atalante, at least at the time of her death (D.S. 18. 37. 2), Schachermeyr and Wirth assume that Justin mentioned him erroneously in this context. Thus Attalus may well have acted as a go-between, but was not involved in any bid to get rid of Perdiccas. But Heckel (1992), 381–4 provides a plausible reconstruction of Attalus' alliances from the time of Alexander's death to about 317 (he last appears in D.S. 19. 16), and suggests that Attalus was indeed one of the conservative infantry officers linked with Meleager in Babylon, whether or not he was the one who initiated action against Perdiccas. There followed the reconciliation between the infantry and the cavalry, and, in Heckel's view, it was only then that Perdiccas sought to win Attalus' support with the offer of marriage to his sister. Attalus supported Perdiccas to the end, and was his commander of the fleet (D.S. 18. 37. 3–4). After Perdiccas' death, he fought alongside Perdiccas' brother, Alcetas, against Antigonus (D.S. 18. 44. 1), and was defeated and imprisoned (D.S. 18. 50. 1 of 319), and was still in captivity in 317 (D.S. 19. 16. 1). Bosworth (2002), 44 n. 58 accepts that the possible context of the marriage was in 323, after the reconciliation between the infantry and cavalry, but he argues that the Attalus mentioned by Justin would have been liquidated at the same time as Meleager, and was therefore not the son of Andromenes. But the immediate point is that either Justin (or his source) made a simple misattribution, or some source, if not Curtius himself, deliberately shifted the responsibility from one to the other: J. Hornblower (1981), 124–5 suggests that Hieronymus may have picked up a hostile line on Perdiccas from Peithon, who had betrayed Perdiccas (D.S. 18. 36. 5), in which case Peithon may also have been hostile to Attalus; on the other hand a motive for making Meleager responsible for this failed action against Perdiccas would have been to provide another justification for his execution of Meleager (cf. Heckel (1992), 169 n. 18).

**8. 4. Perdiccas came with a few friends to Leonnatus.** Schachermeyr (1970), 100 assumes that when Perdiccas chose to remain in the city (7. 21), he must have compromised, and recognized Arrhidaeus as king, and Schachermeyr takes 8. 8 to signify that Perdiccas had surrendered Alexander's ring to Arrhidaeus. There is no suggestion in Justin's account that Perdiccas was forced to leave the city, and at J. 13. 3. 8 Perdiccas marches into a mass meeting of infantrymen to ask what crime is being plotted against him. But Curtius clearly envisages that Perdiccas leaves the city now, for he goes to join Leonnatus, who must have left the city (7. 20), and Perdiccas is next described as operating in the surrounding plains (8. 11).

**8. 6. proceeded to ask him if he had himself given the order for Perdiccas' arrest.** There is some confusion in the text at this point and editors have marked a lacuna, but it appears that the subject of the sentence is Meleager, as the translation has it. Bosworth (2002), 46 suggests as an alternative that the question was put by Perdiccas' brother, Alcetas, whose name would have appeared in the missing piece of the text. This scene matches the one noted above in J. 13. 3. 8, though there it is Perdiccas himself who addresses the troops, and Arrhidaeus is not asked to explain whether he gave any such order. Perdiccas is not present in Curtius' account, hence Arrhidaeus tells the crowd that the uproar is uncalled for, as Perdiccas is still alive.

**The king answered, yes, he had given the order, at Meleager's prompting.** The issue of authorization reflects the constitutional position of the Roman *princeps*, rather than that of the Macedonian king. An occupational hazard of an emperor's agent was that the *Princeps* might subsequently deny to the senators that he had given authority for an action that was criminal or unconstitutional (e.g. Dio 54. 3. 2; Tacitus *Ann.* 1. 6. 3; Suetonius *Claudius* 29. 2). Curtius adds subtlety to this *topos* by making Arrhidaeus accept responsibility—but put the blame on Meleager (*Meleagri instinctu*: cf. 3. 8. 15. The term translated as 'prompting' (*instinctu*) acquired the connotation of incitement to an unlawful or subversive action: Ulpian, *Digest* 47. 11. 5; *Cod. Theod.* 9. 5. 1 pr.). There is admittedly room for debate about how the Latin is to be read, and Dempsie *ad loc.* makes the valid point that the word order allows (Dempsie would rather say 're-quires') the interpretation that 'the king, at Meleager's prompting, said that he had given the order', but the economy of expression leaves open the traditional rendering, and I think that the ambiguity is deliberate, and ambiguity favours irony. Either way, the flow of the narrative suggests that Arrhidaeus was not being devious, but trying to avoid confrontation (cf. 8. 2. 10–11 and even 9. 18), and indeed his retiring, rather naive style works a reconciliation in 8. 14–21. But his vulnerability to pressure made him ineffectual (cf. 8. 22–3).

**8. 7. He spent some three days brooding.** Almost an echo of the three day period which Alexander spent in isolation after the killing of Cleitus ( 8. 2. 10, with A. 4. 9. 4), and the period he brooded after the mutiny on the Hyphasis, which ended on the third day: 9. 3. 19 (with A. 5. 28. 3). Other temporal references are given at 8. 5 and 9. 13, and the events which Curtius relates are all supposed to have happened within seven days of Alexander's death (10. 9), but Aelian *VH* 12. 64 mentions 30 days in the same context of the time lapse before attention was given to the corpse, and Curtius' reference to famine in 8. 12 implies a longer time frame. Thus little trust can be placed in Curtius' chronological scheme.

**8. 10. whose authority and auspices they had followed.** Curtius borrows Roman constitutional terminology (Atkinson (1994), 142; cf. *CIL* vi. 331; Livy 41. 28. 8). Cf. 5. 1. 1; 5. 9. 4; 6. 3. 2; 9. 6. 9, and commentary on 7. 13 above.

**8. 15–23.** *The infantry and the cavalry are reconciled*

*Sources:* J. 13. 3. 9–4. 5; D.S. 18. 2. 4; A. *Succ.* 1. 3.

*Bibliography:* Schachermeyr (1970), 101–2; Errington (1970), 54–6; Briant (1973), 250–2; Bosworth (2002), 47–54; and on the Roman associations, Martin (1987), 171 ff.

The list of names in 8. 15 suggests that this episode has an historical base, and J. 13. 4. 2 alludes to a reconciliation; cf. D.S. 18. 2. 4 and Plut. *Eum.* 3. 1.

The first part of the speech attributed to Arrhidaeus (8. 16–17) echoes lines attributed to Perdiccas by Justin 13. 3. 9 at the matching point in his narrative. Tarn ii. 116 takes the picture of Arrhidaeus in 8. 16–21 to be a fiction that emerged as 'one more offshoot of Cassander's propaganda against Olympias'. Bosworth (2002), 49 likewise notes that credit due to Perdiccas, Ptolemy's enemy, has been denied, and given instead to Arrhidaeus, Cassander's protégé. This all strongly supports the case for Cleitarchus' being Curtius' source.

**8. 15. The Thessalian Pasas, Amissus the Megalopolitan and Perilaus.** Pasas may be an error for Pasias/Paseas. The codices have Amissus, but the reference may be to Damis of Megalopolis, who served with Alexander and was later linked with Eumenes (D.S. 18. 71. 2 and 19. 64. 1 with J. Hornblower (1981), 172–3; Heckel (1992), 148 n. 454, and (2006), 102). A Perilaus is attested in a later context at D.S. 19. 64. 5, and may be the same as the Perillos named in an anecdote by Plutarch, *Moralia* 179f (Berve (1926), ii. no. 630). He would have been a Macedonian. The two Greeks were used because they were neutrals in the conflict. Schachermeyr (1970), 101–2 suggests that they were chosen as members of Eumenes' chancellery staff, and not as mercenary officers.

**the cavalry would lay down their arms only if the king put in their hands those responsible for the rift.** The situation in Babylon was similar to that in Rome in AD 41 in that, although the withdrawal of the cavalry could be described as a secession (8. 7), Arrhidaeus needed the support of the nobles who commanded the cavalry and the young nobles who made up the cavalry squadrons (7. 20), just as Claudius needed to win over the senators if his position was to be legitimated (cf. Jos. *Ant.* 19. 265).

**8. 20. removed the diadem from his head.** On the symbolism cf. 6. 4
and 7. 13, and for a similar later episode, J. 28. 3. 11–12, when
Antigonus gave up the regency only to have his position restored to
him. The Roman reader might be reminded of the episode in the
Lupercalia festival in 44 BC, when Julius Caesar was offered a diadem
thrice and thrice refused to accept it, as he did not wish to claim the
position of king (Plut. *Caes.* 61, *Ant.* 12; Cic. *Phil.* 2. 84–7 etc.); and
in the Principate there would be an allusion to what became an
almost ritual refusal of the imperial office (*recusatio imperii:* see on
6. 5 above, and 6. 18–19; cf. McKechnie (1999), 50–1, who draws in
the reference to Julius Caesar as he would date Curtius to the late
Augustan period, and thus before Tiberius set the pattern of initially
declining the Principate).

**8. 21. high hopes for his character, which until that day had been
eclipsed by his brother's fame.** If this book was written after Claudius'
accession, then this phrase must surely reflect the fact that he was
overshadowed by his charismatic brother Germanicus, and remained
so long after Germanicus' death (cf. Jos. *Ant.* 19. 223; Suet. *Claudius* 7;
Seneca *Consolatio ad Polybium* 16. 3; Tacitus *Ann.* 11. 12. 1; 12. 2. 3).
Furthermore the success attributed to Arrhidaeus' oratory may reflect
the calming effect of Claudius' diplomacy in 41 (cf. Jos. *Ant.* 19. 246).
After his accession, the Romans had high hopes of Claudius, at least
until he liquidated Gaius Appius Silanus in 42 (Dio 60. 15. 1). Curtius
is the only source to present Arrhidaeus as capable of playing an
independent rôle as a political leader. Of course, an association
between Claudius and Arrhidaeus does not necessarily point to a
date of composition in Claudius' reign: the idea might have occurred
to Curtius even if he wrote in a later context.

  This section includes a number of terms that were used of
imperial virtues or blessings (see further on 8. 23). Here Curtius
introduces 'hope', emphasized by repetition: 8. 17, 19 and 21; 9. 7
and 21. Hope (*spes*) had been given definition in the Republican era,
as shrines to this deity had been erected, and ominously one was
destroyed by arson in 31 BC (Dio 50. 10. 3; temple: Nash *PDAR* i
(1968), 418–19; T. F. Scanlon, *Spes frustrata: A Reading of Sallust*
(Heidelberg, 1987), esp. 17–20 reviews the various connotations of
the term). The concept was then developed by the emperors, and

was used as a coin legend by, among others, Claudius (*BMCRE* i. 182 and 191 for coins minted in Rome), and Vespasian (*BMCRE* ii. 112, 124 and 190, for coins minted in Rome and the provinces). Vespasian coupled the legend with the image of his sons: thus Hope had a dynastic connotation, and it is likely that the coins minted by the Senate for Claudius with the legend Hope had a similar dynastic message, being linked with the birth of Britannicus. Such connotations are relevant here.

**8. 22. Arrhidaeus sent the same men back to ask now that they accept Meleager as a third general.** J. 13. 4. 5 records that Meleager and Perdiccas were assigned the guardianship of the camp, the army and the kings, which is a variant of the tradition followed by Curtius. Arrian *Succ.* 1a. 3 appears to represent a more precise tradition that Perdiccas was appointed Chiliarch (the most senior officer under the king) and Meleager his deputy.

This marks the third substantive settlement, in terms of which Arrhidaeus became king, with the proviso that Roxane's child, if a son, would also have a share in the kingship (J. 13. 4. 3). Curtius has alluded to the second in 7. 12–15, when the cavalry had to go along with the proposal to make Arrhidaeus king straightaway, and not to wait for the birth of Roxane's child. The terms of the new ('third') agreement have to be assembled and rationalized from the mix of elements provided by A. *Succ.* 1a. 3; *Succ.* 1b. 3–4 (= Dexippus, *FGrH* 100, F8. 3–4); J. 13. 4. 2–5; D.S. 18. 2. 4.

After the reconciliation of the infantry and cavalry, Meleager was brought in as Perdiccas' deputy (A. *Succ.* 1a. 3; J. 13. 4. 5, less reliably, has them as equals; Errington (1970), 54–6). Leonnatus was dropped as co-regent (the original appointment is noted at 7. 8), and compensated with the important strategy of Hellespontine Phrygia (A. *Succ.* 1. 6; D.S. 18. 3. 1; J. 13. 4. 16; *LM* 116). The troika to which Curtius refers must therefore consist of Perdiccas, Craterus, and Meleager, as is also indicated in the parallel passage at J. 13. 4. 5. The three were not equals, as Perdiccas, as chiliarch, was the Grand Vizier (Errington (1970), 56); Meleager was his subordinate, and Craterus had to come to terms with Antipater and operate in Europe. There is however also the view that Curtius is referring to Arrhidaeus, Perdiccas, and Meleager as the three leaders (Baynham (1998), 210–12).

Certainly the position of Craterus is problematic. He may have been offered the title of *prostates* (A. *Succ.* 1a. 3), which Bosworth (2002), 53 glosses as 'a commission in the vaguest terms to promote the interests of the royal house', but Heckel (1988), 20–1 is more inclined to believe that Craterus was accorded the prestigious title of Guardian of Arrhidaeus, and suggests that this was in part because Meleager promoted his cause. By contrast, Badian (1962), 383–4 dismisses the *prostasia* as a fiction, and suggests that Craterus was, as before, to proceed to Macedonia. The possible historicity of the Guardianship has some backing from D.S. 18. 23. 2, on Perdiccas' later assumption of the *prostasia* (Heckel (1988), 20). Bosworth (2002), 52–3 attaches more weight to J.'s statement that Craterus was to take custody of the royal treasure, as the reality was that there had been a build up of the financial reserves in Cilicia. Another version is offered in the fictional will of Alexander, discussed at 10. 5 below: if Roxane gave birth to a girl, the Macedonians could choose whoever they wanted to be king, and, till such time as they chose a king, Craterus was to be the overseer of the whole of Alexander's kingdom of Macedonia (Ps-Call. 3. 33. 13). Whatever the concessions offered to Craterus, Perdiccas was clearly the *de facto* regent, now as the incumbent of the chiliarchy which Hephaestion had held (A. *Succ.* 1. 3), which roughly equated the position of *hazarapati* in the Persian system (see on 6. 5–24 above). But some argue that Craterus, though absent, had considerable power, and influenced the distribution of the satrapies (K. Rosen, (1967*b*), 98; Briant (1973), 138–9).

The notion of a triumvirate may be a Roman elaboration: the phraseology in 8. 23 recalls Florus' description of the agreement at Bononia in 43 BC, which established 'peace between the three leaders', Antony, Lepidus, and Octavian (Florus 2. 16. 3: *pax inter tres duces*, a parallel seen by Korzeniweski (1959), 56–7 as further support for dating Curtius to the Augustan period, an idea rejected by Baynham (1998), 211–13). It might be added that in the Triumvirate too the principle of equality or collegiality was an illusion.

**8. 23. with harmony and peace.** This phrase echoes a propaganda theme, *pax* and *concordia*, that was much emphasized in the turbulent period of civil war and coups after the death of Nero. Thus Galba made good use of the image of Concord on his coins (e.g. *BMCRE* i.

309, nos. 1–2; 317–18, nos. 54–61, 337, nos. 164–5), and likewise of Pax (*BMCRE* i. 320, no. 76; 329–31, nos. 123–33). Otho claimed to have restored peace (*BMCRE* i. 364, nos. 1–4), and Vitellius' coup could be celebrated as the realization of Concord (*BMCRE* i. 368 ff., nos. 1, 6–7, 20–1, 48, 65), and of course Peace (*BMCRE* i. 380–1, nos. 66–7). But it took another coup and the establishment of the Flavian dynasty to achieve real concord and peace, according to their coins (*BMCRE* ii. *passim*). All this suits the case for dating Curtius to Vespasian's reign, but these images of peace and concord were invoked by earlier emperors when they ran into trouble, as with Nero from 64 (*BMCRE* i. 209, nos. 61–3, with Sutherland (1951), 166). Indeed the combination was a cliché in the late Republic (e.g. Cic. *Phil.* 2. 24, 10. 8; Sall. *Or. Phil.* 13; Livy 9. 19. 17), which Augustus exploited by linking in statuary, and with a festival in March, Public Safety (*Salus*), Concord and Peace (Dio 54. 35. 2 and Ovid *Fasti* 3. 881–2). In January 7 BC Tiberius announced a plan to restore the temple of Concord (Dio 55. 8. 1–2), and here he gave the concept new meaning by linking it with what he presented as successful campaigns by himself and his brother Drusus, now deceased, on the Rhine and Danube frontiers (Dio 55. 8. 1–2; Ovid *Fasti* 1. 645–50). Thus in the Principate the combination Peace and Concord implied a conditionality: Rome's ability to defend and police the provinces depended upon the Romans' acquiescence in the political order of the Principate. Therefore, while the catchphrase used here by Curtius might be adduced as an argument in favour of a Flavian date, it would have had a similar resonance in the earlier context of Claudius' reign.

### 9.1–6. *Eulogy of the new Princeps*

*Bibliography*: arranged according to the emperor believed to be the subject of the eulogy. **Augustus**: Korzeniewski (1959); **Claudius**: Atkinson (1980), esp. 25–35; Béranger (1953), 220–2; Bödefeld (1982), esp. 10–20; **Nero**: Verdière (1966); **Vespasian**: Barzano (1985); Baynham (1998), esp. 205–16; Fugmann (1995); Instinsky (1962); Scheda (1969); **Trajan**: Bosworth (1983*a*), 151–2; **Septimius Severus**: Bourazeli (1988); **Alexander Severus**: Griset (1964).

It is significant that the eulogy comes before the point in the narrative where Arrhidaeus is party to Perdiccas' plot to destroy Meleager. The

eulogy marks the divide between the acceptable (and perhaps fictitious) chapter in Arrhidaeus' political career, and the rest, when he
was merely a pawn in a series of unsavoury events. The uniqueness of
Curtius' account in the matter of Arrhidaeus calls for some explanation, and the influence of contemporary events is at least a plausible
explanation.

Literary influences on Curtius for this passage may have included
Trogus (compare 9. 2 with J. 13. 6. 17: Atkinson (1980), 27), and Livy
(Fugmann (1995), 237, linking 9. 5 with Livy 26. 11. 3, 1. 16. 2 and
30. 38. 11, on the image of the sudden calm after a violent storm).

**9.1. But destiny was already bringing civil wars upon the Macedonian
nation.** This is, as Baynham notes, a forward-looking observation.
The following reference to **several men** aspiring to kingship must
anticipate the assumption of the royal title by Antigonus, Demetrius,
Ptolemy, and the others in and after the Athenian year 306/5; and when
Curtius says 'their forces first came into conflict' (9. 2) he must be
referring to the series of armed conflicts, including Perdiccas' invasion
of Ptolemy's territory in 321/0, and stretching down to the battle of
Ipsus (301 BC) or Corypedon (281 BC) (Baynham (1998), 210). He
alludes to some of these later events in 10. 18–20.

**a throne is not to be shared.** A commonplace: e.g. Cic. *Off.* 1. 26
(citing Ennius, *Trag.* 411–2[V]); Livy 1. 14. 3; Sen. *Agamemnon* 259;
Columella 9. 9. 1; Suet. *Calig.* 22.1, with a reference to Homer, *Iliad*
2. 204–5, and Suet. *Dom.* 12. 3 for another variant in Greek. It has
been suggested that Curtius' formulation here may have inspired
Tacitus, *Ann.* 13. 17. 2: most people condoned the crime [Nero's
murder of Britannicus], considering the age-old friction between
the two brothers and that kingship was indivisible (Wiedemann
(1870), 441 and Verdière (1966), 508, both arguing for a Neronian
date for Curtius).

It is unlikely that Curtius wrote this while the emperor of the day
had a co-regent or had been a co-regent: thus it is unlikely that the
new emperor was Tiberius, Nerva, or Trajan. Similarly, as Vespasian
took his son Titus as his partner in the Principate perhaps as early as
71 (Suet. *Titus* 6. 1, Philost. *Vita Apollon.* 6. 30), if Curtius wrote in
Vespasian's reign he would have had to write this before 71.

**several men were aspiring to it.** The Roman parallel is not explicitly introduced until 9. 3, and thus it is not clear how far one should push the metatextual analysis of 9. 1–2. If indeed this introductory section does refer to the sweep of events beyond the chronological scope of Curtius' book, and if at 9. 3 Curtius moves to a comparison of events in Babylon in 323 with a similar political crisis in contemporary Roman history after the demise of an emperor, then Curtius was writing of a Rome that was spared such a cycle of civil wars, and that is a reason for postulating that Curtius wrote early in Claudius' reign. In AD 41 there were several men with ambitions for the Principate, and some senators advocated the restoration of the Republic (contestants or senators considered appointable, including M. Vinicius, Valerius Asiaticus, L. Annius Vinicianus, and Galba: Jos. *Ant.* 19. 251–2; Suet. *Galba* 7. 1; Levick (1990), 32; republicanism: Cassius Dio 60. 1. 1), but the people clamoured for rule by one man (Suet. *Claud.* 10. 4). Claudius' rivals took some time to plot his overthrow: Dio 60. 14 ff. indicates that it was Claudius' liquidation of Gaius Appius Silanus in 42 that pushed Annius Vinicianus and Furius Camillus Scribonianus into open revolt, but they failed. If Curtius wrote this passage after Nero's accession, he would have known that Nero, with or without justification, was in fear of M. Junius Silanus, Rubellius Plautus, and Faustus Sulla, and in time had them all removed (Verdière (1966), 506, n. 70).

If Curtius was referring to events of 68–69, then the first round of contestants for power would have featured Galba, Clodius Macer, and perhaps Iulius Vindex, and then apart from Otho and Vitellius, Antonius Primus, Mucianus, and Vespasian.

But if Curtius at 9. 3 was not thinking of this episode in Babylon as 'a turning point in history' but was rather still thinking of a broad sweep of events in contrast with which Rome followed the same path, but at some critical point broke out of the cycle, then Curtius may be referring to a new emperor who emerged from a tumultuous period of conflict. This would support the view that Curtius is here referring to the emergence of the Flavian dynasty, or the transition to the Severan dynasty, though Curtius at 9. 5 below gives the impression that civil war has been averted. Against the Flavian and Severan interpretations stands Curtius' point that the Roman empire was in crisis because it was without its head (9. 4), whereas the Macedonian empire of the Successors failed because it had too many heads (9. 2), including those who survived and went on to take the royal title and diadem in or after 306/5. Furthermore at 9. 19 Curtius indicates that in Babylon the turning point, and thus the beginning of the civil wars, was the killing of 300 of Meleager's supporters. This comes beyond the point at which Curtius marks the difference between the Roman and the Macedonian situations. By implication Rome was spared such bloodshed, at least in the city itself.

**9. 2. when they had burdened the body with more heads than it could stand.** The noun 'heads' (*capitibus*) was inserted by Vogel to mend a defect in the text. Curtius has mentioned Perdiccas, Leonnatus, and Meleager, plus Craterus and Antipater (7. 9 and 8. 22). The imagery of the body was commonly used in references to civil unrest (e.g. Cic. *Phil.* 8. 15; Livy 2. 32. 9–12 (in Menenius Agrippa's address to the men who seceded in 494 BC); Vell. Pat. 2. 90. 1; Sen. *Clem.* 1. 12. 3; Tac. *Ann.* 1. 12. 3 and 16. 1; Florus 2. 14. 6), but Curtius may have been influenced by Trogus (cf. J. 13. 6. 17). The imagery of the limbs is further discussed at 9. 4.

**9. 3. with justification.** The Latin phrase (*iure meritoque*) has an echo in Seneca *Clem.* 1. 12. 1.

**they owe their salvation to their emperor.** In eulogies and propaganda the Roman emperor was presented as fighting for the salvation/safety (*salus*) of the people: e.g. *IGRPP* iv. 316 and Vell. Pat. 2. 85.1 (both relating to the battle of Actium); *ILS* 157, re the execution of Sejanus in AD 31; as a coin legend, starting in Tiberius' reign: *BMCRE* i. 131. nos. 81 ff.; Val. Max. 1. *Praefatio*, with Wardle (1998), 68–9; cf. Sen. *Clem.* 1. 13. 1, of Neronian date, and in Tiberius Julius Alexander's eulogistic greeting of the new emperor, Galba, in 68 (*SEG* 15. 873 l. 8, in McCrum and Woodhead (1961), p. 88, no. 328).

**who shone out.** Appropriate phraseology for a new emperor who simply emerged like a *deus ex machina*, like Claudius, and resolved the crisis by his very presence (cf. Amm. Marc. 22. 9. 14), rather than by forceful action or a *coup d'état*. Verdière (1966), 490–4 suggests an alternative interpretation on the grounds that Latin idiom favours the textual variant which gives the relative pronoun in the dative case (*cui*), meaning 'for whom': thus, 'for whom the new star shone out', but the following references do not support this proposal.

**a new star**: in AD 43 Seneca described Claudius as a star (*sidus*) in a similar metaphorical reference to his accession (*Consolatio ad Polybium* 13. 1). Those who think that Curtius was praising Nero cite Calpurnius Siculus (*Ecl.* 1. 77–83) (so Wiseman (1982), 67), and the comet which was supposed to be an omen of Claudius' death (Verdière (1966), 494–5); but it appeared about four months before Claudius' death (P. J. Bicknell, *Latomus* 28 (1969), 1074–5).

If Galba was the emperor, then reference is made to the image of the rising sun in Tiberius Julius Alexander's dedication in *OGIS* 669, line 8, with *SEG* XV 873 (so Milns (1966), 497–8). For Vespasian scholars cite Pliny *HN* 27. 3 and 33. 41 (so Instinsky (1962); Scheda (1969), but Tarn ii. 114 argues that, as Lucan described Alexander as a new star that brought disaster to mankind (Luc. 10. 35), Curtius, if writing in Vespasian's reign, could not have used the image of the new star to refer to Vespasian. Curtius explicitly distinguishes between the emperor as a star (*sidus*) and the sun (*sol*), thus he was not addressing an emperor who thought of himself as a Neos Helios (New Sun). From the time of his visit to Greece Nero cultivated the association of himself with Apollo and the Sun (Suet. *Nero* 25. 2 and 63; inscriptions from Athens and Sagalassus in Pamphylia are dedications to him as the New Apollo and the New Sun: respectively Smallwood *GCN* nos. 145 and 146), and even before his visit to Greece he allowed coin images of himself radiate (*BMCRE* i. 236 ff., e.g. nos. 191–5, 197–206, 214–24, 335, 338, and 359). Thus for a writer in Rome after the demise of Nero it would have been wise not to liken the new emperor to the Sun, and it would have been prudent to stay away from stellar imagery. That is unless one accepts the argument of Fears (1976*b*) that Nero was not the first or only emperor to be styled the New Sun, and secondly that Nero was attested as worshipping, but not identifying himself with, the Sun (Tac. *Ann.* 15. 74. 1), and thirdly that crowds hailed Nero as Apollo (Dio 63. 20. 5), but as Apollo the Lyre-player (Citharoedus) and not Helios. Thus Fears rejects the notion of Nero's 'solar monarchy', and concludes that Curtius' astral symbolism can not be taken as a reference to Nero. Fears leaves open the possibility of a late date for Curtius.

Bosworth (1983*a*), favouring a Trajanic date, finds a fully adequate
parallel in Pliny *Pan.* 19. 1. The new star has even been linked with
the one that was observed at the time of the birth of Alexander
Severus (SHA *Alex. Sev.* 18. 13. 5; Steele (1915), 423; Griset (1964),
163), but that is a tenuous connection, especially when set against the
weight of evidence that favours a Claudian or Flavian date for
Curtius.

Fugmann (1995), 236–7 takes the key word to be 'new', noting that
while Claudius stressed continuity with the past (Suet. *Claudius*
11. 1), Vespasian rescued the empire and established a *new* dynasty
that brought the empire luck and victory (cf. Pliny *HN* 2. 18).
Verdière (1966), 492–3 likewise focuses on the word 'new', to argue
that this differentiates Curtius' eulogy from that of Seneca *Cons. ad
Polybium* 13. 1.

**in the night that was almost our last:** an echo of Livy 6. 17. 4, and
probably an allusion to the night of 24/5 January AD 41 (Suet. *Calig.*
58. 1, *Claudius* 10. 3; Dio 60. 1. 2), when Caligula's assassination
created political chaos in Rome, and the Praetorian Guard was for a
while beyond the Senate's control. Scholars who favour a reference to
some later emperor interpret *noctis* as a metaphorical image. Fugmann (1995), 241 argues that Curtius is referring to events of 69, and
he cites Tacitus *Hist.* 1. 11. 15, on 'the year that was almost Rome's
last' (cf. Scheda (1969), 382 and Grassl (1974), 162). It has also been
argued that the allusion was to the night of 19/20th December AD 69,
when the Vitellians stormed the Capitoline and set fire to the build-
ings (Tac. *Hist.* 3. 71). Thus Köstlin (*Philologus* 51 (1892), 752 (cited
by Korzeniewski (1959), 9), unconvincingly links this passage with
Statius, *Silvae* 5. 3. 195–8 and concludes that both are referring to
that night in 69. But Scheda (1969), 381–2 n. 1 argues that 'the night'
must not be taken literally, as Curtius does not attach a demonstra-
tive pronoun to it as does Livy at 6. 17. 4.

The issue is, however, not as simple as whether Curtius is referring
to a specific night, or is using the term metaphorically, since what
follows in 9. 4 shows that, even if he began with a specific night in
mind, he goes on to a metaphorical usage in alluding to the wider
sphere of the provinces ('the darkened world') over a longer span of
time. Elsewhere Curtius uses the cliché of 'timeless night' as a cover

for manoeuvres and crimes (4. 13. 4 and 7. 6. 18; Atkinson (1980), 414).

When Curtius switches to the first person plural (*habuimus*), represented in the translation by **our**, he may be speaking as a member of the ruling class, since it is likely that the text was intended first for oral presentation before a select group.

**9. 4. It was his rising, I declare, and not the sun's, that brought light back to a darkened world.** Possibly an indirect, and distancing, reference to a claim by the deceased emperor that he was an epiphany of the Sun: Caligula and Nero (above on 9. 3, *pace* Fears) both advertised their links with the sun-god. Ordinary people at the outset of his reign hailed Caligula their *sidus* (star/sun: Suet. *Calig.* 13), and then from 38 he associated himself with various deities, including Apollo (Philo *Leg.* 93, and 103 ff., admittedly not a dispassionate, nor a reliable source on such matters), and Gaius' solar pretensions were well enough known for Seneca to refer to them playfully in hailing Claudius as 'this *sidus*, which has shone again on the world that was plunged into darkness' (*Cons. ad Polybium* 13. 1; a text charged with irony: Atkinson (1985*b*), 872–9). But in favour of a Flavian date for Curtius, Instinsky (1962), 382–3 notes a parallel in Pliny *HN* 27. 3, where Pliny praises the Roman Peace (*pax*), and adds that thereby the Romans appear to have given mankind 'a second source of light' (*alteram lucem*, a second sun), and Instinsky further notes the reference to the restorative rise of the emperor Vespasian in *HN* 33. 41 (*salutaris* [restorative/healing/curative] *exortus*).

**darkened.** The Latin word used, *caliganti*, is possibly an intentional pun on the name of Caligula. It is objected that the differences in quantities between the corresponding first two vowels of Caligula and 'caligans' would not allow a pun, but parallels of forced puns exist (e.g. Suet. *Nero* 33. 1; Quint. *Inst. Or.* 9. 3. 69 ff.; Verdière (1966), 503–4; Herrmann (1929), 222–3). Translation is difficult: perhaps 'a world in hypo*gaean* gloom'.

**when its limbs lacked their head and were out of harmony and in turmoil.** This must mean that Rome had lost an emperor, and thus this passage was written no earlier than AD 14 (pace Korzeniewski). Writing early in Nero's reign Seneca used the same image of the state needing its head (*Clem.* 1. 1. 7 and 4. 3). The 'limbs' (*membra*) could refer to territorial parts of the empire—provinces and client kingdoms (Suet. *Aug.* 48; cf. Cic. *ad Att.* 8. 1. 1), or to the different status groups and functional units that made up the state (Sen. *Ep.* 102. 6), or to all these elements (Vell. Pat. 2. 90. 1).

To accommodate all the other indications of date, the imagery here would best suit either the troubles of 41–2 or the civil war of 68–9. The reference to the absence of an emperor would only strictly refer to 24/25 January, if it belongs to AD 41; and if it is of a Flavian date, Rome might strictly only be considered acephalous in the period between the death of Vitellius, and the arrival of Vespasian in Rome. But no doubt Flavian propaganda treated Vitellius' Principate as illegitimate or a non-event (coins of Titus show that the Flavians chose to recognize of the emperors from 41 to 69, only Claudius and Galba, and the law on the powers to be held by Vespasian cites no precedent beyond Claudius (text in McCrum and Woodhead (1961), pp. 1–2); Vespasian may have claimed Galba or Otho as his predecessor (Suet. *Vesp.* 6. 4; Tac. *Hist.* 3. 7. 2 and 4. 40. 1), but not Vitellius).

The expression 'out of harmony' (*discordia*) contrasts with the expression 'peace and harmony' (*concordia*) in 8. 23 (usage of this antithesis in Tacitus is discussed by R. Hošek, 'Concordia und discordia', *Eirene* 6 (1967), 82 ff. Verdière (1966), 504 notes Calpurnius Siculus' use of the term at *Ecl.* 1. 57 to refer to a phoney peace). The adjectival form is used by Tacitus at *Hist.* 2. 10. 1 of the Roman state in AD 69, before he launches into the account of Otho's move to fight off Vitellius' challenge to his principate. But the phrase 'were in turmoil' (*trepidarent*) better suits the less violent upheaval of 41 (cf. Vell. Pat. 2. 124. 1 on the reaction of senators to Augustus' death, and Seneca *Cons. ad Polybium* 13. 4: since the death of Caligula exiles have lived a quieter life: 'they are not in turmoil (*trepidant*)' waiting every hour for the sword to strike and fearful at the sight of every ship that comes into sight). Furthermore, 'the discordant limbs' could have a limited reference to Rome itself, and so, in the context of 41, could refer to the people, the Praetorian Guard, senators for the continuation of the Principate, and senators who favoured a return to a Republican constitution (as summarized by Baynham (1998), 207; Atkinson (1980), 32). But if, as noted above, the 'limbs' could refer to the provinces (the preferred view of Baynham (1998), 210–11), and a stronger sense is sought for 'being in turmoil', this would fit the situation in 41 in respect of Judaea and Mauretania (Hamilton (1988), 448), and somewhat later Claudius faced opposition from Arruntius Camillus Scribonianus in Dalmatia (Levick (1990), 32, noting that Aulus Plautius in Pannonia and Memmius Regulus in Moesia, Macedonia, and Achaea resisted the temptation to enter the fray: Dio 60. 15. 2). Bosworth (1983*a*), 151, arguing for a Trajanic date, finds a matching situation indicated by Pliny *Epist.* 9. 13. 11 with *Pan.* 6. 3 and 5. 6–9.

Fears (2001), 450–1 maintains his view that Curtius wrote in the Severan era, and in particular after the accession of Severus Alexander, in which case the period in which Rome was without its head would have been after the murder of Elagabalus, but that might be stretched back to the period from the death of Caracalla. But the balance of evidence tells against a date for Curtius as late as the Severan era (Atkinson (1980), esp. 20–5).

**9. 5. torches . . . extinguished.** Arson was very much a Roman night-mare in periods of political unrest, and allegations of planning for arson attacks were richly elaborated against revolutionaries and in the Principate against the emperor's opponents (e.g. Cicero *In Cati-linam* 1. 6, 2. 6 and 10–11, 3. 24–5; *Piso* 5; cf. Sallust *Cat.* 24. 4, 32. 2, 48. 2 and 4, 52. 36; Juv. 8. 233; Tac. *Ann.* 15. 67. 2; Suet. *Vit.* 17. 2).

**How many the swords he sheathed!** The phraseology arguably better suits civil war averted than civil war terminated.

**How violent the storm he scattered, suddenly clearing the skies!** Fugmann (1995), 237 notes the influence of Livy on Curtius (cf. Livy 26. 11. 3; 1. 16. 2, and 30. 38. 11)), and, as part of his case for a Flavian date for Curtius, he emphasizes the strong parallel in Orosius *Hist.* 7. 9. 1, where the same metaphor is used to describe Vespasian's res-toration of calm. Pliny deployed the image in eulogizing Trajan (*Pan.* 5. 8). But it would also have been appropriate after the dark patch of Caligula's reign.

**our empire is not merely recovering, but even flourishes.** In favour of a Vespasianic date Instinsky (1962), 382 notes that Vespasian celebrated on coins ROMA RESURGENS (*BMCRE* ii. 87, no. 425, and

121, nos. 565–6; cf. Weidemann (1970), 85), but the idea was not new, as Galba had used as coin legend ROMA RENASCENS (*BMCRE* i. pp. cxciii and 291, nos. 9 ff.), and Calpurnius Siculus hailed Nero's accession in 54 as the rebirth of the golden age blessed with peace (*Ecl.* 1. 42, cf. 4. 90–2 and 112–21, with Verdière (1966), 505). In support of a Vespasianic date Baynham (1998), 211 notes a parallel in Suet. *Vesp.* 8. 1.

**9. 6. may I not tempt providence.** The same phrase occurs earlier at 10. 2. 24. This prayer that the wish for the dynasty's perpetuity will not incur divine displeasure clearly echoes Livy's opening line at the peroration of his digression on Alexander (Livy 9. 19. 15).

**the line of this same house ... for ever.** The wish may be for the long life of a newly established dynasty, in which case it would fit Vespasian, whose sons were old enough to be honoured with magistracies in 70 (Tac. *Hist.* 4. 3; Fugmann (1995), 237). But the dynastic wish would not fit the elderly Galba in 68 (pace Milns (1966), 494–6), who adopted an heir only six days before his death at the age of 72, nor the childless Trajan, though Bosworth (1983*a*), 152 notes that Pliny prays that Trajan will add perpetuity to the services which he has rendered the empire and will provide an heir, if not by birth, then by adoption, or at least by picking out a suitable candidate for adoption (*Pan.* 94. 1 and 5). In favour of a date in Vespasian's reign, Instinsky (1962), 382 compares a dedication of the Sucusana tribe in Rome of AD 70 or 71: 'dedicated to the eternal peace of the Emperor Vespasian Caesar Augustus and his sons' (*ILS* 6049 = McCrum and Woodhead (1961), no. 513), though this is not quite the same as praying that the dynasty may last for ever, and the dedication is closer to Pliny the Elder's brief paean to the Roman Pax, with the prayer that it might last for eternity (*HN* 27. 3). But Curtius may rather be referring to the restoration or continuation of a pre-existing dynasty, in which case Claudius is the obvious honorand (cf. Seneca *Cons. ad Polybium* 12. 5); and Curtius could wish that the posterity of the same dynasty would be long lasting, if not for all time, as Britannicus was born in 41, and Claudius' daughters Antonia and Octavia were married (to Cn. Pompeius and L Junius Silanus: Dio 60. 5. 7; Suet. *Claud.* 27. 2). Verdière (1966), 497 ff. and 505 notes phrases in Calpurnius *Ecl.* 1. 93 ff. and 4. 150 which echo phrases in Curtius 10. 9. 6, and as

Calpurnius was acting as Nero's praise singer, Verdière argues that Curtius was a contemporary writer, and also eulogizing Nero. But the differences in wording between Curtius and Calpurnius, and more importantly the historical circumstances in which Nero came to power, by comparison with those that Curtius seems to have in mind, do not suggest that the new emperor praised by Curtius was Nero.

The phraseology has precedents in public vows (*vota*) for the well-being of the state, and, e.g. in an inscription honouring Tiberius: To Tiberius Augustus and for the permanent well-being of the divine house (PRO PERPETUA SALUTE DIVINAE DOMUS: *CIL* xiii. 4635). And from the same era, Velleius Paterculus ends his history with a similar prayer for a long continuation of the present peace and happy state of affairs (2. 131), and Woodman (1977), 275 suggests that Velleius was following a convention of panegyric in ending with a prayer (cf. Pliny *Pan.* 94. 1 ff. It may be added that Curtius, Livy 9. 19. 17, Vell. Pat. 2. 131. 1 and Pliny *Pan.* 94. 1 all use the adjective *perpetuus* or the related noun *perpetuitas* in the passages noted).

**of this age.** Curtius uses the term *saeculum* (age/era) in the meaning established by Augustus to mark out his principate as a new chapter in Roman history (Aug. *Res Gestae* 8. 5 with Ramage (1987), 32 and n. 49; cf. Verg. *Ecl.* 1. 4 and Suet. *Aug.* 100. 3; and we are not dealing here with the *saeculum*, qua 'centenary', as celebrated in 17 BC).

**9. 7–21. the destruction of Meleager and his supporters**

*Sources*: D.S. 18. 4. 7; J. 13. 4. 7–8; A. *Succ.* 1a. 4.

*Bibliography*: Briant (1973), 251–4; Martin (1987), 174–6; Bosworth (2002), 54; Sharples (1994), 55, making the point that this episode rules out a Claudian date for Curtius.

Curtius and J. 13. 4. 7–8 represent variants of a single tradition. Curtius differs in detail from D.S. 18. 4. 7, which may mean that Curtius was still following Cleitarchus while Diodorus had switched to Hieronymus. The historicity of the killings is confirmed by Arrian *Succ.* 1a. 4, and Meleager was set up (Bosworth (2002), 54, who discounts the influence of Roman events on Curtius' shaping of the story, and likewise considers that the possible influence of Xenophon's story of Tissaphernes' entrapment of Clearchus (*Anab.* 2. 5. 24–32) offers no grounds for doubting the historicity of this episode). On the sequence of events Arrian and Curtius should be preferred to Diodorus (Errington (1970), 57), which is to say that the distribution of the satrapies occurred after the removal of Meleager, and not before.

What distinguishes Curtius' account is that Perdiccas traps Meleager into sharing in the planning of the arrest of dissidents in the context of the lustral ceremony, and he differs from Arrian, Diodorus, and Justin in giving Arrhidaeus a role in the proceedings (9. 16–18), and in attributing to Arrhidaeus a conscious decision to switch allegiance from Meleager to Perdiccas (Martin (1987), 175).

**9. 7. national prosperity.** The phrase passed from private usage (e.g. Livy 45. 41. 2) to imperial propaganda and rhetoric. It appears first as a coin legend with Galba, and then was a common legend on Flavian coins, starting with issues of 71 (*BMCRE* i. 329; ii. 130, 141, 146, 150, etc.). But this imperial blessing (*publica felicitas*) was celebrated earlier, in the Julio-Claudian era, with Augustus (Suet. *Augustus* 58. 2), Claudius and Nero (*Acta Fratrum Arvalium* for 43–8 and 58, in Smallwood *GCN* p. 15, no. 13 and p. 19, no. 21; for a much later usage see e.g. *CIL* vi. 323261. 20 in a Senatus Consultum of AD 203). Leeman (1963), 468, n. 77, in arguing for a Vespasianic date for Curtius' eulogy, claims to see a parallel here in Tacitus *Dial.* 17, but 'a principate blessed with good fortune' (*felix principatus*) is not the same as the official catch phrase copied by Curtius.

**9. 8. with deep dissimulation.** The following ploy to allay Meleager's suspicions fits a pattern in Curtius' narrative style (cf. 6. 7. 31–5; 7. 2. 16–27). Perdiccas' dissimulation would seem to echo the charge made against the emperor Tiberius (Atkinson (2000*a*), 322–4; cf. Tac. *Ann.* 6. 50. 1 and Suet. *Tib.* 72. 3), but Bosworth (2002), 54 n. 93 sees no reason to think that Curtius is here 'simply imposing Roman *color*'. Rudich (1993 ), 252–3 offers an overview of usages of the term dissimulation in Latin texts of the Republican period and the early Empire, and for dissimulation in practice in Nero's reign see Rudich (1997), *passim.*

**Meleager had been made Perdiccas' equal.** At 8. 22 Curtius refers to the recognition of Meleager as 'the third general', but, as noted above, Meleager was only Perdiccas' deputy.

**9. 12. The customary purification of the soldiers... involved cutting a bitch in two and throwing down her entrails...** Anthropological evidence for a ceremony of marching between two halves of an animal includes a Hittite model (mentioned by O. Masson, 'A propos d'un rituel Hittite pour la lustration d'une armée: le rite de purification par le passage entre les deux parties d'une victime,' *RHR* 137 (1950): 5–25). Lustration of the Macedonian army with a dismembered dog is mentioned in a much later context by Livy (40. 6. 1–3), probably following Polybius (Tarn ii. 106, citing Polybius 23. 10. 17, a fragment which refers to a military purificatory ceremony held to honour Xanthus, presumably in the month of Xandicus [March]). The ritual lustration was followed by the division of the army into two groups for a mock battle (Livy 40. 6. 5), which may have inspired the following scene. The differences in detail on the rites indicate that Curtius was following a tradition different from that represented by Livy (and Polybius).

**9. 13. the king had positioned himself along with his cavalry... opposite the infantry.** Livy says that the Macedonian tradition for this lustral ceremony was for the king to be followed by 'the royal cohort and his bodyguards' (40. 6. 2). He does not mention cavalry, but must mean that they were included (Walbank (1979), 233–4), and in 323 the key units that made up Alexander's bodyguard were predominantly cavalry (Bosworth (1988a), 268–71 and 275–6). Thus there would have been no immediate need for the infantry to be alarmed if Arrhidaeus paraded with the cavalry (Martin (1987), 174).

**9. 15. Fearing that they might be prematurely impugning their comrades' good faith.** The dilemma is something of a leitmotif in Curtius: cf. 3. 6. 6; 5. 12. 4 and 6. 4. 9.

**9. 16. the king... demanded for execution the instigators of the discord.** Lana (1949), 64 suggests that Curtius had in mind Caligula's plan to decimate the Rhine legionaries in the spring of 40 (Suet. *Calig.* 48,1), but a closer parallel might be the episode in 14 when Germanicus incited the killing of those accused of being the instigators of the mutiny of the Rhine legions (Tac. *Ann.* 1. 44. 2–3 and 48). 'Discord' seems to be something of a euphemism if used by a senior army officer or a member of the imperial family to refer to mutiny or rebellion, as here and in Tacitus *Ann.* 1. 34. 4 and 38. 1, cf. *Hist.* 2. 10. 1.

**although he had a personal obligation to protect them**. This reflects an aspect of the Roman institution of *clientela*, which underpinned important elements of private and public law, and foreign policy. The reciprocal obligation to support and protect had been set up when the infantry stood by Arrhidaeus and forced through his recognition as king. Even without any prior benefit, it could be said that a ruler's relationship to his subjects had to be tutelary (Sen. *Clem.* 1. 18. 1).

**9. 18. he picked out . . . some 300 men**. The text may be incorrect as D.S. 18. 4. 7 gives the number of victims as 30. Dempsie accepts the reading and suggests that Curtius exaggerated the casualties in Babylon to mark the difference between that situation and the transition to Claudius' principate in AD 41. But the larger figure perhaps fits better with the description of Meleager's raid on the treasure store at 6. 24 and 7. 1.

**threw them to the elephants**. Elephants had probably been bred in parks in the area of Babylon (and also Susa: cf. Curtius 5. 2. 10) before Alexander's invasion of the territory in 331 (Epplett (2007), esp. 211–12), and there is a reference to a troop of elephants as part of the guard that was stationed in front of Alexander's tent in Babylon (Athen. 12. 539f; Polyaenus 4.3.24, both apparently following the third century writer Phylarchus).

**neither stopped it nor sanctioned it**. Curtius develops a Livian formula (1. 46. 9: *magis non prohibente . . . quam adprobante*). This comment is consistent with Curtius' presentation of Perdiccas as the prime mover (9. 16), and consistent with Arrhidaeus' avoidance of any clear directive to Meleager on Perdiccas (8. 2 above). In Arrian's version Perdiccas claimed to be acting on Arrhidaeus' orders (*Succ.* 1a. 4).

**9. 19. he would claim as his own only those designs of which the outcome demonstrated their soundness**. Seneca writes that the ruler who seeks approval (*approbare*) of his administration from his countrymen will wield power calmly and with the public good (*Clem.* 1. 13. 4), whereas Curtius describes Arrhidaeus as a man who would wait on events and only claim responsibility for what was approved (same verb, *approbare*) by the outcome. With this cynical comment Curtius has reached the point where Arrhidaeus can no longer be treated with respect. The situation is somewhat different from that of Tiberius, who would feign uncertainty about what to advise (Tac. *Ann.* 6. 6, repeated in Suet. *Tib.* 67. 1), but, particularly after the fall of Sejanus in 31, would direct events from Capri through 'edicts, letters public and private, eye-witness reports and rumours' (Levick (1976), 211). Thus Tiberius appears in the main sources as more manipulative, and Arrhidaeus as more the manipulated.

**an omen and the commencement of civil wars.** This echoes the phraseology of Livy 21. 29. 4.

**9. 21. he sought refuge in a temple.** Possibly the temple of Bel Marduk, which Alexander had renovated or had at least undertaken to renovate (A. 3. 16. 5, 7. 17. 1; D.S. 17. 112. 3; Strabo 16. 1. 5. 738).

**he was murdered.** There is no indication in Curtius' version that there was any sort of judicial process, but Diodorus, by contrast, states that Perdiccas punished Meleager, by adopting a private dispute and a formal charge that Meleager had plotted against him (D.S. 18. 4. 7). Diodorus thus implies that Perdiccas attacked Meleager as a litigant and as a prosecutor, and thus that there was some judicial basis for the killing. The charge related to Meleager's role in the disturbances and to his betrayal of the mandate he had been given by the cavalry to negotiate a settlement with the infantry (D.S. 18. 2. 2–3; J. 13. 3. 2), and then there was the personal affront to Perdiccas. Perdiccas used the same strategy when he turned against Antigonus (D.S. 18. 23. 3–4), as Diodorus indicates by using the same terminology (Briant (1973), 253).

**10. 1–4: the distribution of the satrapies**

*Sources*: A. *Succ.* 1a. 5–7, with Dexippus, *FGrH* 100, F.8, 2–7; D.S. 18. 3. 1–3; J. 13. 4. 10–23 (followed by Orosius 3. 23. 7–13); Ps-Call. 3. 33; *HE* 1. 2, stating that more than 24 satrapies were distributed, Appian *Syr.* 52–3.

*Bibliography*: Rosen (1967*a*), esp. 47–9; Seibert (1969), 27–38; Briant (1973), 132–43; Heckel (1988); Klinkott (2000); Bosworth (2002), esp. 57–8; relevant entries in Heckel (2006) (and for earlier treatments, Berve (1926), ii and Heckel (1992)).

Curtius lists only the western satrapies, plus Media, and presents them in a defensible geographical sequence. Except for Cappadocia and Media, the ten newly defined satrapies appear in the same sequence in A. *Succ.* 1a. 5–7 and D.S. 18. 3. 1–2, which suggests that all ultimately derive from a single—probably archival—source. If, as seems most likely, Arrian and Diodorus took their information directly from Hieronymus, then the variation provided by Curtius might be attributed to his use of Cleitarchus. Curtius also differs from Arrian and Diodorus on the role of Perdiccas in the appointment and confirmation of the satraps (see below on 10. 1).

On the list, J. 13. 4. 10–16 differs from Arrian and Diodorus by leaving Eumenes to the end, and by adding in the appointments of Atropates in Media Minor, Coenus in Susiana, and, erroneously, Nearchus in Lycia and Pamphylia. But D.S. goes on to list the arrangements for the eastern satrapies, and client kingdoms (18. 3. 2–3), and we can infer from this and Dexippus' summary of this settlement that Hieronymus covered the eastern as well as the western satrapies (*FGrH* 100, F.8, 5–6, who, incidentally, confirms the appointment of Coenus, if only at a later stage, as the satrap of Susiana), as indeed he must have done for the list dictated by Antipater at Triparadeisus (D.S. 18. 39. 5–6, since in that context Hieronymus is referred to at D.S. 18. 42. 1 and 50. 4). Then, as Justin's list for the Babylon settlement is closer in sequence to Arrian's and Diodorus' than to Curtius', and as he, like Dexippus, refers to Coenus, he too may ultimately depend here on Hieronymus. Appian *Syr.* 52–3 may also depend on Hieronymus (named by Appian as a source on another topic at *Mith.* 8–9: J. Hornblower (1981), 74).

The *Alexander Romance* (Ps-Call. 3. 33. 14–15) and *LM* 115–17 purport to give the instructions which Alexander left in his will for the distribution of the satrapies, and while the former offers only a partial list, there is enough in common between the two in terms of the sequence of satrapies to suggest that they belong to the same tradition, but a tradition different from the one followed by our major sources.

Klinkott (2000), 58 presents a stemma of the sources on the satrapal list, duly showing Arrian and Diodorus as separately dependent on a common authoritative source, but then showing Trogus/ Justin as dependent on Diodorus, and at the next level Curtius as dependent on Trogus. This scheme is at odds with what is suggested above, which is that while Curtius followed Cleitarchus, Arrian, Diodorus, and Trogus were all, whether directly or ultimately, based on Hieronymus. If Curtius here followed Cleitarchus, then his information would not have derived from Hieronymus, since Cleitarchus may have completed his work by *c.*310 (Badian (1965); Schachermeyr (1970), esp. 211–14), whereas Hieronymus carried his history down to cover events at least as late as 272 BC (*FGrH* 154, Frags. 14 and 15; the relative dating of the sources is discussed in the Introduction. There is no real evidence to suggest that Hieronymus published his early books decades before he completed the whole work.).

*Problems of chronology*: reference is made at various points below to events beyond 323, whose dates are a matter of debate. An 'Additional Note' is appended to the commentary on this chapter to explain why these dates should be considered tentative.

**10. 1. Perdiccas ... convened a meeting of the leading Macedonians. It was there decided that the empire should be apportioned as follows.** Curtius implies that there was some measure of debate before agreement was reached (cf. Plut. *Eum.* 3. 3), but Arrian *Succ.* 1a. 5 and Diodorus 18. 3. 1 give a more executive role to Perdiccas, though Diodorus indicates that Perdiccas took this executive action after consultation with the senior officers (cf. *HE* 1. 2). Arrian adds that Perdiccas claimed to be acting on instructions from Arrhidaeus. Rosen (1967*a*), 47–9 thinks that Hieronymus had it right, and that as Chiliarch, the Macedonian equivalent of the Persian *hazarapati*, Perdiccas would have announced the satrapal arrangements by royal edicts (*diagrammata*), and that he was only entitled to do this in respect of territories that were formerly part of the Persian empire. The appointments for the European territories had to be made in a different way as Perdiccas' writ did not cover those areas. Rosen may be right, but the sources do not attest two distinct procedures as he suggests.

**Ptolemy becoming satrap of Egypt and of the African peoples subject to Macedon.** Ptolemy, son of Lagus, is introduced at 6. 13 above, where he first appears in this book. Alexander had divided the former Egyptian satrapy into four administrative regions, putting two Egyptians, Petisis and Doloaspis, in charge of Upper and Lower Egypt, Apollonius in charge of Africa (Curtius 4. 8. 5; A. 3. 5. 4 calls the area Libya), and an Egyptian Greek, Cleomenes, in control of 'Arabia around Heroonpolis' (A. 3. 5. 4). Cleomenes was further charged with overall fiscal responsibility for Egypt as well as Arabia (A.) or for all four territories (Curtius). The traditional interpretation of this settlement is that Alexander paid 'lip service ... to the nationalistic aspirations of the Egyptians' by the appointment of the two Egyptians (Bosworth (1988*a*), 234), but Burstein (1994), esp. 386–7 (and (2000), 154) argues that it was more a case of continuing the pattern of administration set up by the Persians, as Doloaspis was a Persian name, and the man may have been an Egyptianized Persian, and Petisis may be the same as the Pediese apparently attested as having the title satrap on a demotic ostrakon from Memphis. Petisis (perhaps a.k.a. Pediese) soon bowed out (A. 3. 4. 2), and some time before Alexander's death, Cleomenes had effectively turned Egypt into his personal fiefdom (Dem. *Dionys.* 56. 7–8, Arist. *Oec.* 2. 1352a, and A. 7. 23. 6–8, criticizing Alexander for giving Cleomenes virtual indemnity for his crimes), and sources give the impression that he had usurped the satrapal position (apart from Aristotle and Demosthenes, A. *Succ.* 1a. 5 and Dexippus *FGrH* 100, F.8, 2). But Le Rider (1997), 75 argues that Cleomenes remained in the position as defined by Alexander, and notes that there was a Cleomenes among those who kept vigil in the temple of 'Sarapis' when Alexander was terminally ill (A. 7. 26. 2; the deity may rather have been Oserapis, as explained at 10. 13 below). Welles (1970), 507–8 argues that this might well be the same Cleomenes of Naucratis, and that he might indeed have been deemed an expert on the cult of 'Sarapis', and so included in the party that kept vigil for Alexander. Arrian's criticism of Cleomenes at 7. 23 makes this seem unlikely, but if the identification is nevertheless correct, then Cleomenes may have accompanied Ptolemy to Egypt when Ptolemy took up the position of satrap, for in the fuller version of Arrian and Justin, Cleomenes was attached to Ptolemy as his deputy. Ps-Call. 3. 33. 15 and Julius Valerius 3. 58

state that Egypt was given to Perdiccas, but this may be a case of a scribal error giving rise to a deviant tradition (Heckel (1988), esp. 30–3).

**10. 2. Laomedon was given Syria and Phoenicia.** Laomedon (Heckel (2006), 146) and his brother Erigyius, of Mytilene, had settled in Amphipolis (A. *Ind*. 18. 4) and were accepted as Macedonians, but were both forced into exile in 336 because of their friendship with Alexander (A. 3. 6. 6; cf. Curtius 6. 8. 17 and 8. 2. 40 on Erigyius). Because of his language skills, Laomedon was put in charge of the prisoners of war after the battle of Issus (A. 3. 6. 6; elsewhere Peucestas is the only *Macedonian* directly attested as acquiring communicative skills in Persian: A. 6. 30. 3 and 7. 6. 3, with Bosworth (1980*b*), 12). Beyond that episode Laomedon is attested only as a 'trierarch' in the fleet assembled on the Hydaspes (A. *Ind*. 18. 4). After his appointment in Syria, he remained in control of this satrapy until 319, when Ptolemy drove him out (D.S. 18. 39. 6 and 43. 2; Appian *Syr*. 52, with the date in the Parian Marble). Ptolemy's occupation of Laomedon's satrapy may explain why Ps-Call. A 3. 33. 15 and Alexander's *Testament* (*LM* 117) both state that Alexander declared in his will that he left Coele Syria and Phoenicia to Meleager: the point of this fiction would have been to show that Laomedon had no legal entitlement to his satrapy (cf. Heckel (1988), 67).

In the Hellenistic period the territory was more fully labelled Upper Syria and Coele Syria embracing Phoenicia (D.S. 18. 6. 3, probably following Hieronymus), but the usage changed over time, and by the time of the Elder Pliny Coele Syria referred to what had been called Upper Syria (Pliny *HN* 5. 68–9; Bosworth (1974), 48–50 tracks the history of the name changes; cf. my commentary on Curtius 4. 1. 4, and (1994), 51–3 on Curtius 5. 1. 43).

**Philotas was assigned Cilicia.** Balacrus, the satrap of Cilicia, died sometime before Alexander's death (D.S. 18. 22. 1), and Philotas (Berve (1926), ii. no. 804; Heckel (2006), 219) may have been designated as his successor, and thus confirmed in the office in the deal struck in Babylon (cf. Berve (1926), ii. 398; Heckel (1992), 329–30 and (2006), 69 and 219). Against this reconstruction, Bosworth (1980*a*), 219 argues that Balacrus was killed not in 324/3, but rather in the context of Antigonus' operations in Cilica in 332, referred to in

Curtius 4. 5. 13; but the phraseology in D.S. 18. 22. 1 favours the interpretation that Balacrus died not long before Alexander's demise.

The new satrap may possibly have been the Philotas Augaeus mentioned by Curtius at 5. 2. 5, who might in turn be identified with the infantry commander featured in A. 3. 29. 7 and 4. 24. 10 (Atkinson (1994), 60), but Berve (1926), ii. no. 804 finds the evidence insufficient to identify the satrap with any other known Philotas, and Heckel (2006), 216 and 219 distinguishes between Philotas Augaeus and the satrap of Cilicia, but he does allow the possibility that the satrap had served as the commander of light infantry in 335 (A. 1. 2. 1; Berve (1926),'s Philotas no. 805), or was the battalion commander mentioned in A. 3. 29. 7 and 4. 24. 10.

Philotas was said to have been a co-conspirator with Antipater and Antigonus in 323 (Ps-Call. A 3. 31. 8–9; cf. *LM* 98 and Heckel (1988), 36–7), and if, as is indicated, he was in Babylon in 323, then his departure for Cilicia may have been delayed because Craterus was operating there. Nevertheless, Philotas presumably still arrived in Cilicia long before Craterus left for Macedonia (D.S. 18. 16. 4). Perdiccas removed him from this satrapy in 321/0 because of his friendship with Craterus (A. *Succ.* 24. 2; J. 13. 6. 16), when Craterus was actively supporting Antigonus and Antipater.

**Antigonus was instructed to take charge of Lycia, Pamphylia, and Greater Phrygia.** This is Antigonus, son of Philip, born c. 382, and best known as Monophthalmos, the One-Eyed. He was in overall command of the allied forces in 334, but was then detailed to take over as satrap of Greater Phrygia from 333 (A. 1. 29. 3; Curtius erroneously describes him as satrap of Lydia at 4. 1. 35). His command was apparently extended to include Lycia and Pamphylia after Nearchus left the satrapy in 330 (A. 3. 6. 6 and 4. 7. 2 with Curtius 7. 10.12). He was still in Anatolia when Alexander died. The area which he controlled was of great strategic significance, and he was too well entrenched to be easily removed from this command (C. Schäfer (2002), 56, though Briant (1973), 141 argues that the strategic significance of Phrygia had diminished by 323, and greater importance attached to Cappadocia and the rest of the territory to which Eumenes was now assigned). Among the Successors he was the first to take the royal title (D.S. 20. 53; Plut. *Demetr.* 18; J. 15. 2. 10, and

Appian *Syr.* 54; probably early in the Athenian year 306/5: see Additional Note at the end of this commentary). He was killed by troops fighting for Seleucus at the battle of Ipsus in 301 (Plut. *Demetr.* 29. 7–8; Appian *Syr.* 55). Further on his life and career, Berve (1926), ii. no. 87; Heckel (1992), 50–6, and (2006), 32–4, Briant (1973) and Billows (1990). Bosworth (2002), *passim*, offers much, particularly on the chronological problems.

It seems that Lycia and Pamphylia did not constitute a satrapy before Alexander's occupation of the area, and he may have created it, with Nearchus as its first satrap, as part of his grand strategy to counter the Phoenician fleet (Briant (1973), 76, noting A. 1. 24. 4 and D.S. 17. 27. 7).

**Cassander was sent to Caria.** Thus the codices of Curtius, A. *Succ.* 1a. 6 (as rendered by Photius), Justin (followed by Orosius 3. 23.9), and D.S., but A. *Succ.* 1. 37 and F.25. 1, Dexippus *FGrH* 100, F.8. 2and *LM* 117 give the name as Asander. The satrap had a brother called Agathon (D.S. 19. 75. 2), and in January/February 313 the Athenians honoured a Macedonian called Asander, son of Agathon (*IG* ii² 450 = *SIG* I³ 320). This and other epigraphic evidence make it certain that Asander is the correct name (cf. Bosworth (2000), 211). Heckel (1977) and (1988), 64 rejects the line of argument which makes Asander a nephew of Parmenion (thus Heckel is not convinced by Kaerst *RE* 2 (1896), 1516 and Berve (1926), ii. 87, no. 164). He was more likely in some way related to Antigonus the One-eyed (Heckel (2006), 57, citing A. *Succ.* 25. 1). *LM* 97–8 names Asander as one of those at the dinner-party hosted by Medius, but includes him in the list of those who were not privy to the plot to poison Alexander.

To explain this exculpation of Asander it is necessary to consider his record beyond 323. As a kinsman he sided with Antigonus against Perdiccas in 322/1 (A. *Succ.* 25.1), and Perdiccas reassigned his satrapy to Eumenes (J. 13. 6. 14), but when the satrapies were redistributed at Triparadeisus in 320, Asander regained control of Caria (D.S. 18. 39. 6). While Antipater and Antigonus were in alliance, Asander was used by them in a military action against Perdiccan forces, which failed (A. *Succ.* 1. 41). But he was later in the coalition opposed to Antigonus, entering into an alliance with Ptolemy in 315 (D.S. 19. 57. 1 ff.), and his visit to Athens may have occurred while he was on a mission to solicit military support from Cassander against Antigonus' forces (so Wheatley (1998) 269–73, who concedes at p. 269 n. 64 that his chronological scheme would be somewhat weakened if Asander was not in Athens in Jan/Feb. 313, and the honorific decree reflected a visit at some earlier date). Still in the winter of 314/3 Asander sent troops to thwart an invasion of Caria led by Antigonus' officer, Polemaeus, but Asander's men were themselves caught in a trap (D.S. 19. 68. 5–7), and Asander had to surrender to Antigonus, but quickly changed his mind and appealed to Ptolemy and Seleucus for help (D.S. 19. 75. 1–2). Beyond that nothing is recorded. From all this Bosworth (2000), esp. 210–11, concludes that the source of the positive note in *LM* 97–8 should be the Ptolemaic faction, if, as he argues, the tradition of the *LM* was established in 309/8. As Asander fades from the record after 312 the honourable mention in the Romance might thus be seen as a reward for his defection to Ptolemy. By contrast, Heckel (1988), 64–5, dating the original of the *LM* to 318/7, presents the author's intent in this case to reflect a bid to win Asander over to Polyperchon's cause.

**Menander to Lydia.** He was one of the Macedonian Companions (*Hetaeroi*) and served as the commander of the mercenary infantry until he was appointed as satrap of Lydia in 333 (A. 3. 6. 7). He remained in this post till 323 when he set off with reinforcements, arriving in Babylon shortly before Alexander's death (A. 7. 23. 1). He is included in the list of conspirators in *LM* 98 and Ps-Call. A 3. 31. 8–9, which Heckel (2006), 163 takes as an indication that Menander had fallen foul of Polyperchon sometime before 317; but, as noted above, Bosworth (2000) would see the *LM* as a product of Ptolemaic propaganda in 309/8 (Baynham (2000) adds strength to Bosworth's case). At Triparadeisus Lydia was reassigned to Cleitus (D.S. 18. 39. 6 with 52. 5), and Menander joined Antigonus as a military commander (D.S. 18. 59. 1; Heckel (1988), 39; (2006), 163).

**Lesser Phrygia...they designated as the province of Leonnatus.** Leonnatus, son of Anteas, last mentioned at 10. 7. 20 and 8. 4, was of royal blood (10. 7. 8 above; first introduced in the surviving books of Curtius at 3. 12. 7), and later had plans to seize Macedonia (Plut. *Eum.* 3. 5 ff.). He was sent to Lesser, that is Hellespontine, Phrygia to replace Demarchus (A. *Succ.* 1a. 6). In leaving Babylon he lost parity of power with Perdiccas, but he probably chose, or accepted, Helle-spontine Phrygia as compensation because of its strategic position on the line of communication between Macedonia and Asia. Bosworth (2002), 58 takes it that Leonnatus had to do as he was told, and Heckel (2006), 150 takes it that the assignment 'must have disap-pointed him'. He could console himself by parading his royal pre-tensions, and copying some of Alexander's trappings of power (A. *Succ.* 12). But he had no wish to take orders from Perdiccas, and in 322 responded to Antipater's appeal to give him support against the Greeks (D.S. 18. 14. 4–5), for he had plans to lay claim to Macedonia (Plut. *Eum.* 3.9, which is supported by J. 13. 5. 15 on Antipater's joy at Leonnatus' death). That was not to be, for he was killed in action in a battle, presumably somewhere in the vicinity of Lamia (D.S. 18. 15. 1–3; J. 13. 5. 14; Strabo 9. 5. 10. 434).

**10. 3. Cappadocia and Paphlagonia fell to Eumenes.** Eumenes, a Greek from Cardia, introduced at 9. 1. 19, was the subject of lives by Nepos and Plutarch. He served Philip, probably as a secretary, for that was his role under Alexander (A. 5. 24. 6 and 7. 4. 6; Plut. *Eum.* 1. 4 and 6; *LM* 116). But his duties were not limited to administrative matters, as he appears in 326 on a special mission beyond the river Hydraotes (Ravi) in charge of a cavalry force (Curtius 9. 1. 19; A. 5. 24. 6). Then, after Hephaestion's death in 324 and Perdiccas' pro-motion to replace him as the hipparch or officer in charge of the first unit of Companion Cavalry, Eumenes took over the command of Perdiccas' unit (Plut. *Eum.* 1. 5; Nepos *Eum.* 1. 6). Further on his career under Alexander, Berve (1926), ii. no. 317, Heckel (1992), 346–7 and (2006), 120–1.

After Alexander's death, when the cavalry moved out of Babylon, Eumenes stayed behind in the city and acted as mediator between the cavalry and the infantry, according to Plut. *Eum.* 3. 2, though as noted above at 7. 21 Curtius transfers the credit for this intervention from Eumenes to Perdiccas. With the distribution of the satrapies, Eumenes was now given an unenviable task, as Cappadocia was only notionally a Macedonian satrapy (D.S. 18. 16. 1; Plut. *Eum.* 2. 2; Appian *Mithr.* 8; Atkinson (1980), 135–6), but Perdiccas must cer-tainly have trusted Eumenes to stand up to Antigonus and to guard his interests (cf. C. Schäfer (2002), 65). Leonnatus and Antigonus were instructed to assist Eumenes in the war against Ariarathes (Plut. *Eum.* 3. 2–3), and this was probably Perdiccas' way of trying to deflect the energies of two powerful rivals (Billows (1990), 56–7 explores the politics of this move further). But Antigonus ignored Perdiccas' instruction, and only Leonnatus moved to help Eumenes (Plut. *Eum.* 3. 3–5). In the end Perdiccas had to tackle Ariarathes himself (D.S. 18. 16, and 22. 1, linking Philip Arrhidaeus with Perdiccas in this campaign; J. 13. 6. 1; Plut. *Eum.* 3. 12–13, and Lucian *Macr.* 13, quoting Hieronymus as his source).

Diodorus 18. 60. 1 would have the reader believe that Eumenes was all too aware that as a Greek he was at a permanent disadvantage in dealings with the Macedonians, and so was suitably restrained (cf. D.S. 18. 62. 7; 19. 13. 1; Plut. *Eum.* 3. 1 and 8. 1; Nepos *Eum.* 1. 2–3, all probably derived from Hieronymus. The tale in Plut. *Eum.* 2. 4–8 of Alexander's burning of Eumenes' tent to see if he was hoarding silver may derive from the same tendentious tradition.). But the following narrative in D.S. 18. 60. 3–63. 6 illustrates how Eumenes was perfectly able to command the support of Macedonian troops, as in other situations, and shows that he was highly manipulative and had great ambitions. Thus scholarship has moved away from treating Eumenes as decisively disadvantaged by being Greek. So, e.g. Westlake (1954), esp. 319 criticizes the Hieronyman line taken by A. Vezin, *Eumenes von Kardia* (Tübingen, 1907); C. Schäfer (2002) presents Eumenes as having ambitions and being quite able to win support from Macedonians and to use the card of being foreign when it suited his purposes (esp. 54); Bosworth (2002) concludes a long chapter on the campaign in Iran (pp. 98–168): 'Eumenes was under threat the whole time, not merely or principally because of his nationality' (167); and Anson (2004) takes the strongest line that race was not the major determinant in Eumenes' demise.

Although it has no direct bearing on this passage, it should be added that Hadley (2001) argues for the existence of a lost '*apologetic encomium*' to Eumenes, written c. 318, which was used at various points by Diodorus (including 18. 60. 4–63. 6) and Plutarch (as at *Eum.* 1. 4–5, 12. 2–4 and 6–7). It served to demonstrate that Eumenes was unfailingly loyal to the dynasty, enjoyed the full support of his Macedonian officers and troops, and was without personal ambition. Hadley's case does not *per se* undermine the presentation of Eumenes developed by Anson and others, but it does counsel caution against attributing every positive comment on Eumenes to Hieronymus.

**10. 4. Pithon was ordered to take command of Media**. Peithon son of Crateuas, the Bodyguard (A. 6. 29. 4), has been introduced at 7. 4 above. His appointment was a little more restricted as Media was divided into two satrapies: Peithon, s. of Crateuas (A. 6. 28. 4), had given Perdiccas great support (7. 4 ff. above) and was now rewarded with control of Media Maior, while Atropates, who had formerly been satrap of the whole of Media (A. 4. 18. 3; 7. 4. 5, with 3. 8. 4; the name is incorrectly transmitted at Curtius 8. 3. 17), was restricted to control of Media Minor/Atropatene (D.S. 18. 3. 3; J. 13. 4. 13, with Strabo 11. 13. 1. 523). Perdiccas had married a daughter of Atropates (A. 7. 4. 5; J. 13. 4. 13). Thus Media was important in Perdiccas' scheme of things. At 7. 4 above it is noted that after the death of Perdiccas, Peithon became a supporter of Antigonus, but he gave good cause for Antigonus not to trust him, and in 316 Antigonus had him arrested and executed (D.S. 19. 46. 1–4; cf. Heckel (1988), 38–9; (2006), 195–6). Peithon's clash with Eumenes and his disloyalty to Antigonus would explain Hieronymus' hostile attitude to Peithon reflected in Diodorus, especially at 19. 14. 1–2.

**Lysimachus of Thrace and the Pontic tribes adjoining it**. Lysimachus, son of Agathocles, was one of Alexander's seven Bodyguards (A. 6. 28. 4; Pausanias 1. 9. 5). The father may have been a Thessalian, rewarded by Philip II with Macedonian land and status (*FGrH* 115, F. 81 (Theopompus) and Porphyry, *FHG* iii. 698, F.4. 4 with H. S. Lund (1992), 2; J. 15. 3. 3). Curtius introduces him at 8. 1. 14, with the tale of a hunt in Sogdiana in 328, when Lysimachus angered Alexander by bravely moving to protect him from a charging lion, as though Alexander needed someone else's assistance. Curtius dismisses as apocryphal the tale that Alexander exposed Lysimachus to a lion as a punishment (8. 1. 17; variants of the story in Plut. *Demetr.* 27. 3 and J. 15. 3. 7–9): the tale was a *topos* used by rhetoricians on the subject of anger (Sen. *Ira* 3. 17. 2 and Val. Max. 9. 3. ext. 1). Then at 8. 1. 46 he features as one of those who tried to prevent Alexander from killing Cleitus, which likewise angered Alexander at the time. The myth was extended to provide another clash between Lysimachus and Alexander when, in 327, Lysimachus

slipped Callisthenes a poisonous drug to spare him death by torture
(J. 15. 3. 6–8; Curtius 8. 8. 21 does not mention Lysimachus).

As a Bodyguard he may well have been in the deathbed scene in
Babylon in 323 which is described by A. 7. 26; cf. Curtius 10. 5. 8. *LM*
103 expressly states that Lysimachus was one of those summoned by
Alexander to his bedside, but he was not among those who were
party to the conspiracy to kill him (*LM* 98), a detail that is of more
use to the study of the political background to the composition of the
*LM* than it is to the study of what really happened in Babylon. Like
Eumenes, he had to fight to establish control over as much of his
satrapy as he could (D.S. 18. 14. 2–4). Justin 15. 3. 15 adds the
eulogistic comment that he was assigned the fiercest tribes because
he was the bravest of men (cf. above on Seuthes at 10. 1. 45). The title
given to him in 323 is uncertain: Lund (1992), 54 suggests that he was
styled *strategos* rather than satrap. Later, probably in 305/4, he set
himself up as an independent king (D.S. 20. 53. 4; Plut. *Demetr.* 18. 3;
Ael. *NA* 6. 25 and 15. 2). This may explain why the territory originally
granted to him is carefully delineated, especially by A. *Succ.* 1a. 7. He
died in battle against Seleucus in 281 (Appian *Syr.* 1. 55 and 64; Ael.
*NA* 6. 25; Pliny *HN* 8. 143, citing Duris). Further on his career,
Heckel (1992), 267–75 and (2006), 153–5; Berve (1926), ii. no. 480,
Lund (1992), and Stewart, in Roisman (2003), 50–1.

**The governors of India, the Bactrians and Sogdians … should all
retain command of their … territories.** The other sources all identify
the eastern satraps, thus it was Curtius' choice to focus only on the
western satrapies, and to omit the names of Asians. His list covers the
major role-players in the following power struggle, which was fought
out mainly in the west, and so Curtius has marked out how he would
have continued the story. The arrangements for the Indian satrapies
are discussed at 1. 20–1 above.

**peoples living by the Ocean or the Red Sea.** As 'the Ocean' must refer
to the Indian Ocean, Curtius is here using 'the Red Sea' to refer to the
Arabian Sea and the Persian Gulf (references at 10. 1. 13 above).

**Perdiccas was to remain with the king and command the troops
following him.** Cf. D.S. 18. 2. 4. Initially Perdiccas was responsible for
Arrhidaeus as sole king, but when Roxane produced a son, Alexander

IV, the baby was made co-ruler with Arrhidaeus (A. *Succ.* 1a. 8; J. 13. 4. 3. Habicht (1973) notes that while literary sources often ignore the infant Alexander and refer to Philip after September 323 as sole king, there is epigraphical evidence to confirm that Philip III and Alexander IV were strictly joint kings: so *OGIS* i. 4, and an inscription from Samothrace published by J. McCredie, *Hesperia* 37 (1968), 222. But, as Bosworth (1993), 423–6 argues, there probably was a time gap between the birth of the infant and his recognition as a king. Alexander IV had the royal title by the autumn of 322 (D.S. 18. 18. 6), and Bosworth argues that Perdiccas acted in this matter in the aftermath of his successful campaign against Ariarathes of Cappadocia, to strengthen his own position politically while Antipater was still embroiled in the Lamian War).

**10. 5–8.** *The ambitions and strategic thinking of the Successors*

*Sources*: LM 114–23 and Ps-Call. A 3. 33.

*Bibliography*: Heckel (1988) and Bosworth (2000).

Again Curtius departs from his narrative, now to explain why he does not accept the tradition that Alexander left a will spelling out how the satrapies were to be distributed, and then Curtius adds some further authorial comment.

**10. 5. Alexander's will.** A version of the document to which Curtius refers is preserved in the *LM* 114–23 and in Ps-Call. A 3. 33. Heckel (1988) argues that the forged will was produced by someone in Polyperchon's camp, *c.*317, and he suggests that the author was Holcias, a Perdiccan supporter, who was defeated by Antigonus in 319 and then sent to Macedon (Pausanias 4. 6. 6), where after the death of Antipater he sided with Polyperchon (Heckel (1988), 79–81). Heckel's approach and conclusions were questioned in reviews by G. Wirth in *Phoenix* 44 (1990), 200–1 and J. Seibert, in *Gnomon* 62 (1990), 564–6. Heckel was reacting against the common view that it was a propaganda document produced for Perdiccas in about 321 BC (cf. Bosworth (1971*a*), esp. 115–16, who offers a critique of the case for 321, and recognizes the presence of later interpolations). It contains elements of Rhodian propaganda and points that suited Ptolemy (Alexander's wish that he marry Cleopatra; suppression of Cleomenes' name; Meleager and not Laomedon mentioned as the satrap of Syria):

thus the will was not genuine. But the debate is not just about the prosopographical details, as Seibert (1990) questions Heckel's ready assumption that these texts are to be treated as political documents of the early period after the death of Alexander, and not as 'a late (literary) composition' (Heckel (1988), 2). Against this Bosworth (2000) convincingly argues that whatever the amount of fiction in the LM, it contains too much 'detail, tendentious and misleading, anchored to historical personages' (241) to be fiction without political intent. Thus Bosworth returns to Heckel's view of the *LM* as propagandistic, but contextualizes it in events of 309/8, and argues that it emanated from Ptolemy's camp (this line is supported by Baynham (2000), with more comment on the literary elements of the *LM*, and indeed Seibert (1990) points to 308 as a more probable context for the document than 317, if he had to accept that it had a political purpose). Heckel (2006), 228 defends his case for the earlier context of c. 317. The issues are further considered at 10. 14 below and 5. 1–6 above.

Tarn ii. 94 gives Curtius credit for identifying the will as a fiction, but the debate about its genuineness had a long history, since D.S. 17. 117. 5 sides with those who questioned the historicity of the tradition on Alexander's death in which the will features.

**10. 6. In fact, whatever possessions each held after the division of the empire, he would have firmly established as his own dominion.** The connotation of the verb *fundare*, rendered here as 'firmly established', covers more than the simple act of establishing a state or kingdom. It has more of the force of consolidating, and establishing all the institutions required by the new dominion (Cic. *Balb.* 31, *Paradoxa* 1. 10; Ovid *Met.* 14. 583, and *ILS* 1118).

**10. 7. any pretext for conflict was removed, since they all belonged to the same race.** Here the point of comparison will not be the Roman Empire, unless perhaps Curtius was writing under Trajan, who hailed from Spain, or Septimius Severus, who was of North African stock. It is more likely that Curtius is contrasting the wars of the successors with the history of the kingdoms that made up the Persian Empire.

**10. 8. initial possessions are disdained when there is hope of greater things.** Similar phraseology has been noted at Calpurnius Siculus *Ecl.*

7. 45–6. This point is not noted by Verdière (1966), though his article argues that Curtius read, and wrote soon after, Calpurnius Siculus.

**10. 9–13.** *the corpse embalmed*

*Sources:* LM 113, and Plut. *Alex.* 77. 5, who indicates that most sources commented on the absence of decomposition as evidence that Alexander had not been poisoned; Aelian *VH* 12. 64.

**10. 9. It was now the seventh day that the king's body had been lying in the coffin.** Previous markers of the passage of time appear at 8. 5 and 7. Aelian *VH* 12. 64 refers to a tradition that the corpse lay unattended for 30 days. The problem is discussed by Bosworth (2002), 55, who suggests that 'the seven day period at most covers the initial mutiny and its resolution'. Thus Aelian may be closer to the mark.

**10. 12. What I report now is the traditional account rather than what I believe myself.** Cf. 5. 6. 9 and 9. 1. 34. The section 10. 10. 5–18 is peppered with references to rumours and traditions ($5^2$, 12, 18), what is believed or not believed (5, 12, 14, 15, 18), the appearance of normality (7 and perhaps 13), concealment (11), and general acceptance of what purports to be a scientific fact ($16^2$). Contentious material is couched in indirect speech (5, 14–15). All this must be intentional to signal how much was uncertain about the circumstances of Alexander's death, and, in the aftermath, how reality could be obscured by pretence, posturing, and rumour-mongering.

But if it is accepted that there is a literary plan behind this section, it does not follow that the content is without serious historical purpose. Modern debate on Curtius' historical methods has found it convenient to start from the extreme position adopted by Tarn in a comment on a parallel fuller statement at 9. 1. 34, where Curtius states that he will pass on more than he believes, for he can not bear to be dogmatic on points on which he has doubts, and he can not suppress material that he has picked up. Tarn pours scorn on this: 'One may search the histories of the world in vain for any similar pronouncement; cynicism can go no further' (Tarn ii. 92), for in the *Histories* as a whole Curtius demonstrates an 'entire lack of historical principle' (p. 93). And yet on the next page Tarn takes passages that include 10. 10. 5 as evidence that Curtius 'had the making of a critic, if he had taken his history seriously'.

Historians who have worked in societies where for certain periods textual evidence is scarce, and more reliance has to be placed on oral tradition, praise singers (in South Africa, imbongi/ababongi) and oral evidence, will have less difficulty in appreciating Curtius' approach to unsubstantiated traditions. It is also clear that, whatever the degree of sincerity in Curtius' formulation, he was following a line that was well established and respected. Thus Baynham (1998), 86 sees Curtius as consciously echoing Herodotus (especially 7. 152 (*pace* Tarn); cf. 2. 123.1 and 4. 195. 2). And in this regard Herodotus' influence might also be noted at Pausanias 2. 17. 4 and 6. 3. 8, and even Tacitus *Hist.* 2. 50. 2 (cf. Bosworth (2003), 177–8, Wiseman (1993), 141). The issues are further considered in the Introduction, section 8.

In the immediate context it may be significant that Curtius opted for the tradition that the corpse lay without treatment for only seven days (10. 9), and we have noted in Curtius a general tendency to rationalize where possible and to omit the more outlandish traditions. This tells against Tarn's judgement that Curtius' stated approach to unsubstantiated tradition was the ultimate in cynicism.

**no decay had set into it and…there was not even the slightest discoloration.** So too Plut. *Alex.* 77. 5. Hammond (1989*b*), 305 n. 174 suggests that, if there was any historical basis for the claim that the corpse showed no sign of putrefaction despite the heat and humidity of Babylon, then Alexander might have lived on in a deep coma for some time after he was thought to have died, and such a coma could happen if his death was due to *malaria tropica* (better known as blackwater fever), which can arise as a complication after malignant tertian malaria (*plasmodium falciparum*). There has been more general support for the idea that Alexander died from tertian malaria (Engels (1978*b* and references at 5.6 above), but the duration of a coma in this case is indicated as usually only two to four days, and not seven, and certainly not thirty days. Other medical suggestions of what might have retarded putrefaction are noted at 5. 6 above, but none satisfies the time gap indicated by our sources. Thus this detail was more likely created to support the myth that Alexander had a divine nature (cf. 10. 13). Otherwise the comment on the absence of discolouration might have been produced to counter the rumour or tradition that Alexander had been poisoned. But against this idea it must be noted that the *LM* and Romance do not claim that his remains showed the signs of poisoning (no suggestion of, for example, cyanosis, which can arise from strychnine poisoning).

Lucian in the *Dialogues of the Dead* has Philip taunting Alexander about his pretensions to divinity which were mocked when people saw that his corpse began to decompose like that of any mortal (Lucian *Dial.Mort.* 12. 5 [OCT edition]). Dempsie here appears to suggest that Lucian reflects a tradition that Curtius also followed, but it would be unwise to build on an element in a fictional dialogue, and the Lucian passage should rather be reserved for the discussion of the treatment of Alexander in texts associated with the Second Sophistic Movement.

**10. 13. the Egyptians and Chaldeans ... cleaned out the body.** Egyptian seers in Alexander's camp feature in the story of the eclipse of the moon before the battle of Gaugamela (4. 10. 4–7). But the Egyptians mentioned here should be linked with the tradition that some of Alexander's officers mounted a vigil in a temple of 'Sarapis' in Babylonia when Alexander was dying (A. 7. 26. 2). As the Sarapis cult is generally considered a Ptolemaic creation (Fraser (1972), 246–50, citing Tac. *Hist.* 4. 83–4 and Plut. *De Is. et Os.* 28 = *Mor.* 361f–362b; cf. 984a), Goukowsky (1978) 199–200 suggested that the temple was not of Sarapis but rather of Oserapis, the deity who had been created by the merger of Osiris and Apis. Thus the suggestion is that Egyptian migrants had brought this cult to Babylon long before 323, and the shrine was accepted as a centre for healing (Bosworth (1988*b*), 168–70). Consequently the Egyptians mentioned here would rather be priests or embalmers linked with a shrine of Oserapis. The Chaldeans were Babylonian priests of Bel, known for their skill in astronomy (Curtius 3. 3. 6 and 5. 1. 22). They feature in the story of events leading up to Alexander's death as having warned Alexander not to return to Babylon (D.S. 17. 112; A. 7. 16. 5–6; Plut. *Alex.* 73. 1–2; J. 12. 13. 3).

Persian practice was to coat the corpse with wax before burial, to protect the fertile soil from contamination by the dead body (Hdt. 1. 140; 4. 71. 1; Strabo 15. 3. 20. 735; cf. Plut. *Agesipolis* 40. 3), but the Magi were left exposed to the elements to be eaten by birds or dogs (Hdt. 1. 140). Chaldean and Egyptian practice however was to embalm or mummify so as to preserve the human remains for eternity (Hdt. 2. 86 ff.; D.S. 1. 83. 5 and 91; Briant (1996), 539; on the technical aspects of embalming see e.g. J. H. Taylor, *Unwrapping a Mummy* London, British Museum, 1995).

**A golden sarcophagus.** Perhaps an anticipatory reference to the coffin which, together with the enormous, elaborate hearse, took nearly two years to complete (D.S. 18. 26–8; Erskine (2002), 168–71 deals with the hearse and its journey to Egypt).

**10. 14–20.** *the assassination theory and the fate of Alexander's remains*

*Sources*: A. 7. 27. 1–2; J. 12. 14; Plut. *Alex.* 77. 2–5; D.S. 17. 117. 5–118. 2; 19. 11. 8; *LM* 88 ff.; Ps-Call. 3. 31. 2 ff. Arrian, Plutarch and Diodorus, like Curtius, doubted the historicity of this story, and Pausanias 8. 18. 6 is agnostic, while Pliny *HN* 30. 149 reports the tradition of the poisoning in a chapter written mainly in indirect speech to indicate his scepticism (W. H. S. Jones, Loeb edition (1963), *ad loc.*). But Plut. *Mor.* 849f reports Hypereides' proposal to honour Alexander's poisoner, which shows that the story, whatever its historical value, became an element in Athenian politics not long after Alexander's death.

*Bibliography*: Mederer (1936), 140 ff.; Bosworth (1971a), and (1988b), 175–9 and 182–4; Heckel (1988); O'Brien (1992), chap. 5 (especially useful for the bibliographic references); Bosworth (2000), 16–17; Badian (2000a), 76–7.

The space given to rumours about Antipater's responsibility for Alexander's death may seem disproportionate to their historical significance, and then there is the forward-looking reference to his appropriation of Macedon and Greece. But in the structure of the *Histories* this section rounds off the second pentad by returning to the figure of Antipater. Book 6 opens with Agis' revolt and Antipater's campaign against the allied Greek forces, and Book 10 ends with an anticipatory reference to Antipater's victory in the Lamian war; and to make the balance work, Curtius held back the matter of Agis' revolt from its chronological position in the story till after his account of the death of Darius, so that he could focus on Antipater at the beginning of Book 6. For the contrast Diodorus dealt with Agis' revolt at the end of the first half of Book 17, and before Darius' flight after the battle of Gaugamela (D.S. 17. 62. 6–63. 5). Admittedly Justin, like Curtius, deals with Agis' revolt after the death of Darius (death: J. 11. 15. 13–15; Agis' revolt: J. 12. 1. 4–11); but Justin does not use this sequencing to focus on Antipater in 330 and again after

Alexander's death. Furthermore, neither Diodorus nor Justin comments on the politics of Antipater's victory over Agis and Antipater's
concern to avoid antagonizing Alexander (Curtius 6. 1. 17–19). Thus,
although Curtius indicates that he does not seriously believe the story
that Antipater used his sons Cassander and Iollas to get poison to
Alexander, he makes a good effort to add some credibility to the
conspiracy theory. It is also significant, and, perhaps coincidentally,
to his credit, that he omits the tradition that Aristotle was the
initiator of the plot, and so again he keeps the focus on Antipater
(below on 10. 17). The second pentad ends with a conscious echo of
its opening.

**10. 14. Many believed his death was due to poison.** Plut. *Alex.* 77. 2
indicates that the poisoning charge was first raised only in the 'sixth'
year after Alexander's death; but Hypereides is reported to have
proposed that Athens should honour Iollas for having given poison
to Alexander ([Plut.] *Vitae X Orat.* 849f), and his proposal must
have predated Antipater's victory over Athens at the battle of Crannon in late August or early September 322 (Plut. *Camillus* 19. 8;
Bosworth (1988b), 175–6). Soon after Alexander's death rumours
spread in Greece, and no doubt in Asia, that Alexander had been
murdered. Long after Curtius' day the murder of Alexander could be
regarded as a matter of fact (as in SHA *Alex. Sev.* 62. 3, and likewise in
texts based on the Alexander Romance, as at Julius Valerius 3. 56).

**administered . . . by a son of Antipater called Iollas.** This Macedonian
name is a hypocoristic form of the Aeolo-Doric name Iolaos (Kallèris
(1954), 292–3). Iollas first appears only in the context of events in
Babylon in 323 (cf. Berve (1926), ii. no. 386). Hypereides' proposal,
referred to above, indicates that Antipater was hailed as the initiator
of the plot, but Antipater was not in Babylon, and among those who
were in the Macedonian camp suspicion must have fallen upon those
who were there. To counter these rumours the *Ephemerides*, or Royal
Diary, was produced, with what purported to be a detailed account of
Alexander's last days, to show that he died of natural causes (above,
introduction to 5. 1–6; Bosworth (1988b), esp. chap. 7). In the latter
part of 317 Olympias gained control of Macedonia, with the help of
Polyperchon, and arranged the killing of Arrhidaeus (Wheatley
(2007), 192 puts this in the period mid-October to December, 317).

She revived the charge that Iollas delivered the poison to kill Alexander, destroyed his tomb to avenge the murder of Alexander, and killed Nicanor, the brother of Iollas and Cassander (D.S. 19. 11. 8). The tradition represented by the *Liber de Morte* and Ps-Call. 3. 31 elaborated a story implicating the supporters of Antipater and Antigonus in the conspiracy to kill Alexander (Heckel (1988)). This hostile tradition probably originated in Perdiccas' circle, but in its developed form as we have it, it is now linked with circle of Polyperchon in c. 317 (Heckel (1988)) or the court of Ptolemy in 308 (Bosworth (2000); see further at 10. 5 above and the introduction to 5. 1–6).

Ptolemy and Aristobulus seem to have claimed that they were following the version of the *Ephemerides* (A. 7. 26. 3–27. 1; P. *Alex.* 75. 5), which indicates that they wrote later than the production of the *Ephemerides*, but does not prove that the latter tells the whole story. Plutarch and Arrian likewise chose to follow the 'official' version, but there were obviously various editions of the *Ephemerides*, and we can not be sure how many traditions are represented by our two primary and two secondary sources (Badian (1987), esp. 610–18). Furthermore, as noted above, Plutarch was fully aware of the conspiracy stories, and at *Alex.* 74. 2–6 deals with Alexander's fear of Antipater's sons, Iollas and Cassander, and Cassander's enduring fear of Alexander.

Bosworth (1971*a*), esp. 134–5 argues that there was indeed an agreement between Perdiccas and Antipater, negotiated by Cassander, before the death of Alexander (Bosworth emphasizes D.S. 18. 23. 2). The death of Alexander was then engineered, and as Bosworth concludes, 'Paradoxically the Alexander Romance [with the murder story] is nearer to the truth than the Royal Ephemerides' (136). But Bosworth has now softened his line, emphasizing rather the vulnerability of Alexander's officers to charges of murder, and concluding that the evidence is too thin to sustain any such charge (Bosworth (1988*a*), 171–3; (1988*b*), 157–84).

**Alexander had often been heard to remark that Antipater had regal aspirations.** Cf. 6. 1. 17–19. Olympias had encouraged Alexander to distrust Antipater: A. 7. 12. 5 ff.; D.S. 17. 118. 1; J. 12. 14. 3; Plut. *Alex.* 39. 11–13; Blackwell (1999), 72.

**he was conceited after his famous Spartan victory.** Antipater had defeated the army of Agis and his allies at Megalopolis in 330 BC, thus ending a serious bid by the Greeks to reclaim their independence from Macedon (on Curtius' treatment of this war Atkinson (1994), 164–7). The significance of Antipater's victory over Agis has been duly acknowledged by Badian (1967), 183–4 and 190, cf. Blackwell (1999), esp. 69–73. But Alexander displayed his resentment at Antipater's personal achievement by passing a disparaging remark about the battle of Megalopolis (Plut. *Ages.* 15. 4; cf. Curtius 6. 1. 17–19 noted above).

After 330 Antipater's management of affairs in Greece may have given Alexander increasing cause for concern. For what it is worth, Plutarch says that after the death of Parmenion Antipater particularly was in fear of Alexander, and entered into secret negotiations with the Aetolians (*Alex.* 49. 14–15), who were to play a significant role in the events leading up to the Lamian War. Blackwell (1999) deals with the negative effects of Olympias' hostility to Antipater, as from 330 she and Antipater operated in Greece 'apart from one another, if not necessarily at cross-purposes' (102). Bousquet (1988), 132–3 draws on his work on the financial records from Delphi to comment on what was for Macedon the deteriorating situation in Greece in the period 327–4. In the autumn of 325 Antipater made a gift of five talents to Delphi (*CID* ii. 110),[1] presumably to buy some support, but it appears to have brought little benefit, for relations between

---

[1] Blackwell (1999), 114 concludes from the relevant line item in the Delphic financial records that Antipater was moving to act independently of Alexander, for the donation is listed under the rubric '[M]acedonians', and not Alexander (revised text and notes in Bousquet (1988), 179–84, text on p. 183 [and now in *CID* ii. 110]). Blackwell here follows the lead of Hammond (1988), 89, who likewise notes that the donation is not in the name of Alexander, and includes this episode in a section headed 'Tendencies towards disunity'. Antipater may indeed have arranged the contribution (Bousquet (1988), 133), but in the line item, 'Macedonians' precedes the names of the two religious envoys (*hieromnemones*), Archepolis and Agippus (Column 2, line 10), whose names probably appeared earlier in the document, as the text is restored at Col. 1, lines 2–3 to read 'From Alexan]der, [through the agency of Archepolis and Agippus]' (the supplementation of the text is justified by the appearance of their names at *CID* ii. 32. 42–3 and ii. 99B, lines 13–14). Thus Antipater probably did deal with Delphi in the name of Macedon, but, *pace* Blackwell, not necessarily with intent to supplant Alexander (cf. Lefèvre (2002*b*), 80 n. 32).

Delphi and Macedon were deteriorating: Delphi was among the Greek states and ethnic leagues (*ethne*) which sent envoys to Alexander in 324 with (peace-?) offerings or petitions (D.S. 17. 113. 3–4); and the Delphic records for autumn 324 specifically mention the absence of *hieromnemones* from Alexander (*CID* ii. 102, lines 5–6 as explicated by Bousquet with J. Pouilloux, *BCH* 75 (1951), esp. 269; and Arnush (2000), 302); in the year that Macedon was not represented on the Amphictyonic Council Delphi honoured Promenes of Thebes *FD* iii. 1. 356). Furthermore, whereas the Amphictyony had voted in 327 to honour Olympias with three golden crowns (*CID* ii. p. 205), the amount seems not to have been spent as it is shown as still a credit in the accounts of 324/3 (*CID* ii. 97, lines 5–6, and 102, Column II A, 6; Bousquet (1988), 243–8; Arnush (2000), 302–3); and relations between Aetolia and the Delphic Amphictyony appear to have grown friendlier (Arnush (2000), 299–302; references at *SEG* 50, 2000 (2003), no. 503).

The death of Lycurgus in 324 removed a restraining influence from the Athenian political scene (Atkinson (1981)). The hostile reaction to the decree on the return of exiles (2. 4–7 above), the concentration of returning mercenaries in the Peloponnese and the mission of Leosthenes to the Aetolians (D.S. 17. 111. 3) posed a challenge to Macedon. With all this Alexander would not have been pleased, and Antipater could be blamed for his failure to control events in Greece.

In any case, if Alexander had perished at any point, particularly from 327, Antipater was the most senior Macedonian officer in the territory and would have taken over there at least as regent. Like any tyrant whose position is not guaranteed by dynastic succession, Alexander felt threatened by any contingency plan whether tacit or hatched in secret. In the absence of a constitutional provision or clear directive from Alexander, Antipater was at least a regent in the wings: Alexander's commission to Craterus to summon Antipater to his court upset that comfortable arrangement.

**10. 15. a belief current that Craterus had been sent... to murder Antipater.** A. 7. 12. 3–4 and J. 12. 12. 9–10 agree that Craterus was to lead the veterans back to Macedonia, and was to take over Antipater's command, while Antipater was to conduct the newly levied troops to Alexander's camp. Curtius alone states that Craterus had orders to kill Antipater. Curtius may have invented this detail for literary effect: the intended victim becomes the suspected assassin; and Alexander fails to strike down Antipater as he had done Parmenion. But Heckel (1988), 7 sees it rather as a line of defence invented to counter the charge contained in the tradition represented by the *LM* that Antipater was party to regicide. But in any case the formula of introduction, an unsubstantiated rumour, was a familiar device by which an historian brought in a tale which he did not believe, and did not expect the attentive reader to believe.

D.S. 18. 4. 1 simply states that Craterus had written instructions from Alexander, which Perdiccas effectively nullified by getting the army to reject the list of projects, known as the Last Plans, which Alexander left behind among his papers. Craterus had been sent off with the veterans in about August 324, but after Alexander's death he was still no further than Cilicia (D.S. 18. 4. 1 and 12. 1). Either Craterus was waiting in Cilicia in accordance with plans given to him by Alexander (so Bosworth (1988*b*), esp. 207 ff.; Griffith (1965), 12–17 suggests that Craterus was simply instructed to wait until Antipater had left Macedonia with the reinforcements), or Craterus was hesitant about Antipater's reaction, and so chose to ignore Alexander's orders, or at least to procrastinate (cf. Badian (1961), esp. 37 ff.), which seems more likely. On the mandate given to him after Alexander's death cf. 10. 9 above.

**10. 16. the power of the poison.** The Latin phrase (*vim... veneni*) echoes a Livian phrase (26. 14. 5) found also in Tacitus *Ann.* 15. 64. 3. There may be here an echo of the rumours that Germanicus was poisoned: cf. Tacitus *Ann.* 2. 69. 3, taken as a fact by Dio 57. 18. 9. Murder by poison was something of a Roman preoccupation, enough for them to have established a special standing court to deal with poisoners, sometime before 92 BC (*ILS* 45, with E. S. Gruen, *Roman Politics and the Criminal Courts, 149–78* BC (Cambridge [Mass.], 1968), 261–2, and on the Sullan law, Cic. *Pro Cluent.* 148). This preoccupation is also reflected in the fact that Tacitus uses the term poison (*venenum*) some 47 times, all but three of them in the *Annals*.

**10. 17. Styx.** The Styx was a river near Nonacris in northern Arcadia, notorious for the toxicity of its water (Pausanias 8. 17. 6–18. 6;

Strabo 8. 8. 4. 389; Pliny *HN* 31. 26–27; Plut. *Alex.* 77. 4; Aelian *NA*
10. 40; Vitruvius 8. 3. 16). The poisonous water from this river could
only be carried in the hoof of a horse or mule (same sources plus
Pliny *HN* 30. 149). The reputation of this river was thus well established, and independent of the Alexander legend, but nevertheless
scientifically ill-founded (Hamilton (1969), 215).

**This, it was believed, was brought by Cassander, passed on to his
brother Iollas, and by him slipped into the king's final drink.** On
Cassander's supposed role in the killing of Alexander cf. A. 7. 27. 1–2;
J. 12. 14. 6 (the only source in this list accepting the tradition), and
Val. Max. 1. 7. ext. 2. Diodorus reports that people said that after
Alexander's death historians did not dare write about the poisoning
of Alexander while Antipater and Cassander were in power, but that
Cassander's murder of Olympias and his reconstruction of Thebes
demonstrated his hostility to Alexander (17. 118. 1–2). Clearly Diodorus uses this third-hand speculation to distance himself from the
conspiracy theory. By contrast, the story of Cassander's arrival and
briefing of Iollas is treated as historical in *LM* 96 and Ps-Call. 3. 31. 4,
discussed by Heckel (1988), 10.

  According to one tradition it was Aristotle who devised the method
of poisoning (Plut. *Alex.* 77. 3; A. 7. 27. 1, who gives Aristotle's
supposed motive as fear because of Callisthenes' death; Pliny, *HN*
30. 149). T. S. Brown (1949), 225–6 sees the anti-Peripatetic element
in this myth as another extension of the propaganda produced by
Olympias and her supporters. But the myth of Aristotle's involvement
had a life of its own, showing up, for instance, as a reason for
Caracalla's repression of the Peripatetic philosophers in Alexandria,
and his wish to have all their texts burnt (Dio 77 (78). 7. 3).

**10. 18. Whatever credence such stories gained, they were soon
scotched by the power of the people defamed by the gossip.** This is
not an original observation, since it is matched by D.S. 17. 118. 2 and
J. 12. 13. 10, but it suited Curtius' style to switch from an historical
puzzle which he could not solve, to a political observation, and, as
Bosworth (1971*a*), 123 notes, Curtius' formulation is worthy of Tacitus.

**Antipater usurped the rule of Macedon and of Greece as well.**
Similarly Diodorus says that after Alexander's death, Antipater

gained the most powerful position in Europe (17. 118. 2). He re-established Macedonian control over Greece through his victory in the Lamian War, which began as soon as a number of Greek states learnt of Alexander's death and decided to fight for the liberation of Greece (D.S. 18. 8. 1 ff.; Plut. *Phocion* 23–6; J. 13. 5). Hostilities began when in early September 323 Leosthenes set off with a fleet to occupy Thermopylae (D.S. 18. 11. 5; Dem. 18. 32). Antipater was roundly defeated at Heraclea Trachinia, and then took refuge in Lamia. A counter-offensive was launched, and, with the support of Craterus, Antipater won a major victory at Crannon in late August or early September 322 (Plut. *Phocion* 26. 1; Dem. 28. 1; Paus. 10. 3. 4, and for the date, Plut. *Cam.* 19. 8).

**10. 19. he was succeeded by his son, after the murder of all who were even distantly related to Alexander.** Cassander took control of his father's territory, the Macedonian kingdom (*regnum*), when Antipater died in 319 BC, but he only took *regnum*, in the sense of the royal title or kingship, in 305/4, some time after Antigonus set the fashion (D.S. 20. 53. 2–4 putting it in 307/6, or 306/5. The following additional note argues that there probably was a time gap between Antigonus' action, and the adoption of the royal title by Ptolemy and others.).

Curtius was clearly following the same source as D.S. for 17. 118. 2, but, whereas D.S. limited the reference to the killing of Olympias, Curtius exaggerated this to cover all surviving relatives of Alexander. The exaggeration is probably Curtius' own work, as other sources record that Cassander married Alexander's step-sister, Thessalonice: D.S. 19. 52. 1, 61. 2; J. 14. 6. 13, and Pausanias 9. 7. 3. Cassander arranged the murder of Roxane and Alexander IV in 311/0 (D.S. 19. 105. 2; J. 15. 2. 3–5; but the Parian Marble puts it in 310/309). This should mean that if Curtius here and D.S. at 17. 118. 2 were both following Cleitarchus, Cleitarchus did not complete his work before 311/310. But this argument is complicated by the fact that the dynasts lived with the fiction that Alexander IV was still alive, at least down to 306/305 (e.g. Sachs and Hunger (1988), no. 308; Green (1990), 747 n. 37; Boiy (2002)), while Cleitarchus is now generally believed to have written no later than 310 (cf. Bosworth (1980*a*), 30 n. 52 for references). On the other hand, the corresponding passage in Diodorus falls within a digression (D.S. 17. 117. 5–118. 2). Thus if the main narrative comes from Cleitarchus, then the reference to Cassander did not, and Curtius may have followed Diodorus in diverging from Cleitarchus. It is also possible that, if the exaggeration was not Curtius' own elaboration, the line that Cassander liquidated all surviving members of Alexander's family may have had its origin in Roman propaganda justifying the series of wars against the Macedonians. The point would have been that Rome was, or had been, entitled to contest any claim by any pretender to the Macedonian throne.

Having shown that he could continue the story into the period of the Successors, Curtius switches the focus back onto Alexander for the final paragraph of the work.

**10. 20. Alexander's body was taken to Memphis by Ptolemy.** Cf. D.S. 18. 28. 2, which must mean that the hearse left Babylon in the latter part of 321 BC. Furthermore, the Parian Marble dates the burial of Alexander in Memphis in the year 321/0. The funeral carriage was no less grandiose and monstrous than befitted a 'world conqueror', as we can judge from Hieronymus' description (Athenaeus 5. 40. 206d–e, cf. D.S. 18. 26. 3–27. 5). There is no trace here, nor in D.S., of the tradition that the corpse was to be taken to Macedonia, but was hijacked to Egypt (A. *Succ.* 24. 1 ff.; Pausanias 1. 6. 3; Strabo 17. 1. 8. 794; Aelian *VH* 12. 64). Ptolemy's opportunism may further be confirmed by the provision in Alexander's fictitious will that Ptolemy was to take the body to Egypt (*LM* 119), and at 10. 5. 4 Curtius includes a death-bed injunction that his corpse should be taken to Siwah (represented by Ammon). Thus Curtius seems to be following an Alexandrian tradition.

**Memphis.** Cf. Pausanias 1. 6. 3 and Ps-Call. 3. 34. 4–6. Schmidt-Colinet suggests that Alexander's tomb in Memphis was associated with the complex at Saqqara featuring a lengthy *dromos* leading eastwards to a temple of Nectanebo II. The *dromos* was flanked on the south by a frieze depicting Dionysus with animals reflecting his triumphs in the east, and towards the end of the *dromos* an *exedra* with statues representing giants of Greek poetry and philosophy, since at the time of their discovery Pindar's name could be read on one of the statues (J-P. Lauer, *Saqqara: the Royal Cemetery of Memphis*

(London, 1976), 23). The figures in the *exedra* may have included members of the Ptolemaic dynasty. The Dionysus frieze would have reflected Alexander's 'triumphs' in the East. Nectanebo II was the last of the Pharaohs, and in the revisionist version of the Alexander Romance was Alexander's biological father. All the elements in this group served Ptolemaic claims to legitimacy and authority as rulers of Egypt.

**transferred from there a few years later to Alexandria.** The expression 'a few years later' suits the tradition that it was Ptolemy I who moved the remains to Alexandria (D.S. 18. 28. 3; Strabo 17.1.8. 794; Ps-Call. 3. 34. 6). Though neither D.S. nor Strabo makes reference to a temporary mausoleum in Memphis, Memphis was nevertheless Perdiccas' objective when he invaded Egypt (D.S. 18. 34. 6). The choice of Memphis as the place where Alexander was to be entombed initially may have been for strategic and practical reasons: Alexandria was as yet only being developed as Ptolemy's capital, and the inland site would have been less vulnerable to a recovery mission by Perdiccas. But there were also political considerations: Ptolemy claimed it was Alexander's wish to be buried at Siwah (D.S. 18. 3. 5; 28. 2–3, which must reflect the Ptolemaic tradition, and thus not derive from Hieronymus' account). The satrapal capital was an appropriate resting-place for Alexander's remains, as Ptolemy could claim to be acting as the legitimate satrap of Egypt. After Perdiccas' death in May/June 320 (indicated by the Babylonian Chronicle, BM 34, 660 Vs 4), Ptolemy's control over Egypt, from a Macedonian point of view, was more firmly established, and his position as a Reichsmarschall of the Macedonian empire was strengthened. When he was able to take over Alexandria as his capital, he was presumably also able to move Alexander's remains there, and thus to make the tomb an element of his dynastic palace complex. The myth was generated that Alexander wished to be buried in Alexandria: the *Alexander Romance* (Armenian version) 93.

The Alexander Romance shows that Egyptian revisionists developed the story with oracular pronouncements that Memphis should not be Alexander's resting place, but he should be moved to Rhacotis (Ps-Call. β 3. 34. 4). The idea was to remove him from Memphis, which had been reserved for pharaohs, and by calling Alexander's city

Rhacotis, the revisionists wished to take from Alexander the credit for having founded Alexandria (J. Dillery, 'Alexander's tomb at 'Rhacotis', Ps-Call. 3. 34. 5 and the Oracle of the Potter', *ZPE* 148 (2004): 253–8).

J. Hornblower (1981), 41 sets the transfer to Alexandria after the agreement at Triparadeisus (late 320; Schober (1981), 49–51; Boiy (2007)) and the departure of Antipater and the kings (D.S. 18. 39. Ptolemy had made an agreement with Antipater, back in 323/2: D.S. 18. 14. 2; but Antipater subsequently allowed his daughter Nicaea to marry Ptolemy's enemy, Perdiccas: D.S. 18. 23. 1. Then that relationship in turn went sour, and Antipater was able to think of making a fresh approach to Ptolemy: D.S. 18. 25. 3–4, on events of 322/1.).

Another tradition appears to have been that Ptolemy II effected the transfer (Pausanias 1. 7. 1). It is not impossible that it was Ptolemy II Philadelphus who moved the remains to Alexandria. The expression 'a few years later' is not a compelling objection if one compares Livy's usage of the same phrase, which can refer to a period of about ten years (Livy 4. 16. 4; 37. 43. 1), and perhaps up to forty years (Livy 6. 37. 9). Thus this temporal reference is not fatal to the tradition about Ptolemy II. Furthermore, Curtius uses the passive construction (transferred to Alexandria), and thus does not explicitly state that Ptolemy I was the agent: he may have used this construction to avoid judging between rival traditions. Chugg (2002), 14–15 and (2004/5), 76–8 argues that as the removal of the remains from Memphis to Alexandria is not mentioned in the surviving portion of the Parian Marble, it must have happened after 299/8, but it could have happened in the period 290–280 BC, which would explain why the transfer was variously attributed to Ptolemy I and Ptolemy II, who ruled jointly with his father from 285 to 283/2. Still it seems unwise to prefer the unclear reference in Pausanias to the clear statement of other sources that Ptolemy I transferred Alexander's remains to Alexandria.

The site of Alexander's tomb in Alexandria is unknown and the subject of lively controversy. In Greek the mausoleum could be referred to as a *mnema* or a *sema* (given as the official name by the second-century AD sophist Zenobius 3. 94, quoted by Fraser (1972), ii. 33 n. 80), but was apparently known popularly as the Soma (Strabo 17. 1. 8. 794; Ps.-Call. 3. 34. 6, and also in the Armenian

version of the *Alexander Romance* §284 (Wolohojian (1969), 158).
The manuscript readings which give Soma are defended by Erskine
(2002), 166–7). Another complication is that the mausoleum known
to our main sources would have been part of the royal tomb complex
developed by Ptolemy IV Philopator (222–205) (Zenobius 3. 94).
In Philopator's scheme Alexander's mausoleum may, or may not,
have been on the site of the original mausoleum (Fraser (1972), i. 16;
Erskine (2002), 165–6). Fraser (1972), i. 14–17 and ii. 36–40 argues
for siting the Soma to the north side of the city, where it would have
been vulnerable to the erosion of the embankments. But Chugg
(2003) and (2004/5), 237–53 now argues that the enclosure, which
he takes to have been known as the Soma of Alexander, was further
inland and on the line of the Canopic Way. The Soma, in Chugg's
view, may have measured *c.*600 × 800 m., and the tombs of the
Ptolemies and the actual mausoleum of Alexander would have been
within this area. It would thus have been to the west of the Rosetta
Gate, and a kilometre or so to the east of the Nebi Daniel mosque.
Chugg further argues that there is no archaeological evidence to
support the legend that the tomb lay beneath the Nebi Daniel
mosque, a legend which Mahmoud Bey El Falaki misguidedly followed when he drew his plan of ancient Alexandria in 1866. Chugg
(2004) offers a popular, but critical review of the history of the search
for Alexander's remains.

The mausoleum was visited by Augustus in 31 (Suet. *Aug.* 18. 1).
He is supposed to have damaged the nose of the mummified
Alexander (Dio 51. 16. 3–5), and so must have entered the subterra-
nean chamber mentioned by Lucan 8. 694–7, and 10. 14–20. In 200
Septimius Severus locked up the tomb so that no one could view
Alexander's corpse (Dio 75 (76). 13. 2). The last attested sighting was
in 215, when Caracalla visited the city (Herodian 4. 8. 9). But there is
some uncertainty about this because it is not confirmed by Dio. Dio
77 (78). 7–8 treats Caracalla's great admiration for Alexander, and
consequent detestation of the Peripatetics because of Aristotle's supposed link with the plot to kill Alexander, but on Caracalla's visit to
Alexandria, Dio deals only with his massacre of Alexandrians, and
does not mention any visit to the tomb (77 (78). 22–3; Erskine
(2002), 178). The site may have been abandoned because of coastal
erosion or destruction in the riots of *c.*273 (Ammianus Marcellinus

22. 16. 15 with Fraser (1972), ii. 35). But Chugg (2004), 24–5 uses numismatic evidence to revive Hogarth's idea that the tomb of Alexander was associated with the temple of the Genius of Alexandria, as the Patriarch Georgius complained *c.* AD 361 (Amm. Marc. 22. 11. 7, though Fraser (1972), ii. 35 n. 84 takes the term *sepulcrum* (tomb) to be a rhetorical embellishment and not a literal usage). Thus Chugg suggests that the mausoleum was destroyed by the earthquake and tidal wave that struck Alexandria in AD 365 (Amm. Marc. 26. 10. 15–19; Sozomenus *Eccl.hist.* 6. 2). Either way, by the late fourth century the site was described as no longer identifiable (John Chrysostom *Orat.* 26. 12).

There are those who believe that Alexander was entombed at Siwah, but attempts to identify certain archaeological remains at Siwah as elements of Alexander's tomb have contributed little but entertaining material for the study of media hype and one brand of Greek nationalism (T.R. Stevenson, 'The 'discovery' of the 'Tomb' of Alexander the Great', *Classicum* 23 (1997), 8–15; cf. Chugg (2004/5), 233–4 on excavations conducted at Siwa).

**every mark of respect continues to be paid to his memory and his name.** Erskine (2002), esp. 175–8 argues that for the Alexandrians Alexander's tomb and remains symbolized the Ptolemaic dynasty, and after the demise of the dynasty they served as the symbol that the city was still Alexander's foundation; but they were taken by Romans as symbols of world-power, and the emperors saw themselves as his successors. Thus it suited imperial propagandists to honour Alexander. On the notion in Curtius of the power of the name references are given at 3.3 above.

After a long section in which Curtius magnifies the uncertainties concerning the traditions on what led up to Alexander's death and its aftermath (see on 10. 12), Curtius now cleverly finishes with a platitudinous certainty and brings the story down to his own day.

# Appendix: Additional Note on Problems of Chronology

As noted above there are numerous problems concerned with dating events in the period of the Successors, not least because Diodorus is erratic and unreliable in the way he assigns events to Athenian archon years. Thus dates assumed in this commentary for the following events should be considered tentative. The issues are only briefly identified, as more detailed debate would go beyond the scope of this commentary.

1  The battle of Crannon, when Antipater gained a decisive victory over the Greeks in the Lamian War—late August or early September 322 (Plut. *Phocion* 26. 1, *Dem.* 28. 1, Paus. 10. 3. 4). Plut. *Cam.* 19. 8 gives the precise date as 7th Metageitnion, the anniversary of the battle of Chaeronea. The Julian equivalent is variously given by modern writers as late July (Bosworth (1993), (2002), 10), 2 August (Hamilton (1969), 23), late August (Hammond (1988), 113), and 5 Sept. (http://www.livius.org/am-ao/antipater).

2  The death of Perdiccas—May/June 320 (indicated by the Babylonian Chronicle, BM 34 660 Vs 4; Errington (1970), 75–6; Boiy (2007), 207; Anson (2003), who defends the 'low' chronology, against the case for the 'high' chronology advocated by Bosworth (1992*b*), 80–1 and (2002), 279–81, setting the assassination in late summer, 321). The following section in the chronicle may even mean that his death came as late as November 320 (as suggested by R. van der Spek in his commentary on the preliminary revised version which he has made available at http://www.livius.org/cg-cm/chronicles/bchp-diadochi).

3  The settlement at Triparadeisus (D.S. 18. 39. 3–7)—late 320; Schober (1981), 49–51 and Anson (2003), contra Bosworth (1992*b*), who puts it in the autumn of 321.

4  The assumption of the royal title by Antigonus—306/5. This followed upon the victory of Demetrius' forces in the naval battle at Salamis and the expulsion of Ptolemaic forces from Cyprus, which D.S. 20. 53. 1–4 and the Parian Marble B21 indicate happened in the archon year 307/6, and Pausanias 1. 6. 6 states that Demetrius had sailed to Cyprus after the winter was over. Thus the campaign would have begun in the Spring of

306. The initial land battle, followed by the siege of Salamis might well have taken a couple of months, and it would have taken time for Ptolemy to receive Menelaus' appeal for assistance and to mobilize a fleet to take to Cyprus. Thus the decisive battle might indeed have taken place as late as June, towards the very end of the archon year, as Wheatley (2001), 139 n. 22 suggests (cf. Samuel (1962), 6). Diodorus and Plut. *Demetr.* 18. 1 present Antigonus' assumption of the diadem and royal title as part of the celebration of that victory. What follows makes more sense if Antigonus did not take the royal title before the beginning of the Athenian year 306/5 (thus Müller (1973), 83 would put the assumption in July rather than June 306, though the new year is introduced by D.S. only at 20. 73. 1. Antigonus' adoption of the title is not mentioned by the Parian Marble.). Certainly he is attested as king in the Athenian honorific decree proposed by Stratocles of Diomeia in May 305 (*IG* ii² 471, with 469). Diodorus and Plutarch indicate that Ptolemy followed suit (Plut. *Demetr.* 18. 1–2), and was duly followed by Lysimachus and Seleucus. But the Canon of Egyptian rulers, the Parian Marble B23 and Egyptian documents (*PLouvre* 2427 and 2440) point to 305/4 as the year of Ptolemy's assumption of the royal title, and late 305, from about November, as the most probable period in the year (Samuel (1962), 4–11). Thus there are two possibilities: Ptolemy did not copy Antigonus immediately, and in the aftermath of a humiliating defeat, but at least after the failure of Antigonus' bid to invade Egypt towards the end of 306 (D.S. 20. 73–76), and perhaps 16 months later than Antigonus styled himself king (cf. Müller (1973), 95–9; Gruen (1985), esp. 257–8 allows a gap of nearly two years); or, *pace* Diodorus, Plutarch and Appian *Syr.* 54, Antigonus' more formal assumption of kingship was not part of the celebration immediately after the victorious action in Cyprus, and happened perhaps only in 305: but this seems less likely. To close the gap between Antigonus' and Ptolemy's appropriation of the title, and to accommodate the Egyptian dates for Ptolemy's action, one might be tempted to put the date of the battle of Salamis in 305, a year later than Diodorus indicates. But this possibility seems to be ruled out by the Parian Marble, and by the continuation of the narrative in Diodorus, as he indicates that the victory in Cyprus encouraged Antigonus to stage an invasion of Egypt, and this operation was under way at the time of the setting of the Pleiades, *c.*1 November 306 (D.S. 20. 73. 3 and 74. 1).

# Bibliography

## Ancient Sources and Collections of Primary Source Material

A. *Succ.* = Arrian *De historia successorum Alexandri*, or rather *Events after Alexander's Death*, as summarized by Photius. The Greek text is given in A. G. Roos, *Flavii Arriani quae exstant omnia*. Vol. ii: *Scripta Minora*; 2nd edn. rev. G. Wirth (Leipzig, 1968).

Alexander Romance/Ps-Call. For the Armenian version see Wolohojian (1969).

Dexippus *Events after Alexander's Death*, as summarized by Photius. References are to the text as given in Jacoby *FGrH* 100, F. 8. The text is also given alongside the corresponding section of A. *Succ.* by Roos/Wirth.

Harding, P. (1985) = *From the End of the Peloponnesian War to the Battle of Ipsus* (Translated documents of Greece and Rome, vol. ii) (Cambridge).

*HE* = *The Heidelberg Epitome* (available in G. Bauer, *Die Heidelberger Epitome* (Leipzig, 1914), and in *FGrH* no. 155).

Heckel, W., and Yardley, J. (eds. ) (2004), *Alexander the Great: Historical Sources in Translation* (Oxford).

*Itiner.* = *Itinerarium Alexandri Magni.*

*LM* = *Liber de morte testamentoque Alexandri Magni.*

*ME* = *Metz Epitome.*

(Texts of *LM* and *ME* available in *Epitoma rerum gestarum Alexandri Magni et Liber de morte eius*, ed. P. H. Thomas (Leipzig, 1960).

Parian Marble. The Greek text in *FGrH* 239; translation in M. M. Austin, *The Hellenistic World from Alexander to the Roman Conquest: A Selection of Ancient Sources in Translation* (Cambridge, 1981), 8–9 and 39–41, with the cautionary note of Bosworth (2002), 226.

## Editions of Curtius

Atkinson, J. E. (1998a and 2000a) *Storie di Alessandro di Curzio Rufo*. 2 vols. (Milan, Fondazione Lorenzo Valla/ Mondadori).

Bardon, H. (1961 and 1965), *Quinte-Curce 'Histoires'*, 2nd edn. 2 vols. (Paris, Les Belles Lettres).

Dosson, S. (1912), *Q. Curti Rufi Historiarum Alexandri Magni*, rev. R. Pichon. (Paris).

Giacone, A. (1977), *Q. Curzio Rufo, Storie di Alessandro Magno* (Turin).

Hedicke, E. (1908), *Q. Curti Historiarum Alexandri Magni libri qui super-sunt*, 2nd edn. (Leipzig, Teubner). First edition, Berlin, 1867.

Lemaire, N. E. (1822–4), *Q. Curtius Rufus ad codices Parisinos recensitus*, 3 vols. (Paris).

Müller, K. and Schönfeld, H. (1954), *Q. Curtius Rufus. Geschichte Alexanders des Grossen* (Munich).

Mützell, J. (1841), *Q. Curtii Rufi de gestis Alexandri Magni Regis Macedonum libri qui supersunt octo* (Berlin).

Rolfe, J. C. (1956), *Quintus Curtius: History of Alexander*, 2 vols. (Cambridge (Mass.), Loeb).

Siebelis and Koch (2007–), *Q. Curtius Rufus, Geschichte Alexanders des Grossen, lateinisch und deutsch.* 2 vols. Translated by J. Siebelis; introduction and commentary by H. Koch (Munich).

Koch, H. (2000), 4–8 lists some 52 texts, critical editions, and translations of Curtius. Atkinson (1998*b*), 3448–51 reviews the history of scholarship on the text of Curtius; cf. (1998 *a*), pp. xxxi–xxxiv.

## References

Adams, J. N. (1982), *The Latin Sexual Vocabulary* (Baltimore).

Adams, W. L. (2007), 'The games of Alexander', in W. Heckel, L. Tritle, and P. Wheatley (eds. ), *Alexander's Empire: Formulation to Decay* (Claremont, Calif.), 125–38.

*Alexandre le Grand: image et réalité* (Geneva, Fondation Hardt, 1976).

Alfonsi, L. (1967), 'Nota Tacitiana', *Aevum* 41: 154.

Alonso, V. (2007), 'Alexander, Cleitus and Lanice', in W. Heckel, L. Tritle, and P. Wheatley (eds.), *Alexander's Empire: Formulation to Decay* (Claremont, Calif.), 109–23.

Altheim, F. (1948), *Literatur und Gesellschaft im ausgehenden Altertum* (Halle), i. 153–64.

Anson, E. M. (1985), 'Macedonia's alleged constitutionalism', *CJ* 80: 303–16.

—— (2003), 'The dating of Perdiccas' death and the assembly at Triparadeisus', *GRBS* 43: 373–90.

—— (2004), *Eumenes of Cardia: A Greek among the Macedonians* (Leiden, Boston).

Arnush, M. (2000), 'Argead and Aetolian relations with the Delphic polis in the late 4th C BC', in R. Brock and S. Hodkinson (eds.), *Alternatives to Athens: Varieties of Political Organization and Community in Ancient Greece* (Oxford), 293–307.

Ashton, N. (1983), 'The Lamian War—a false start?' *Antichthon* 17: 47–63.

Atkinson, J. E. (1975), 'Curtius Rufus' Historiae Alexandri and the Principate', in *Actes de la XIIe Conférence Internationale d'Études Classiques 'Eirene'. . . . . 1972* (Bucharest and Amsterdam), 363–7.

—— (1980), *A Commentary on Q. Curtius Rufus' Historiae Alexandri Magni, Books 3 and 4* (Amsterdam/Uithoorn).

—— (1981), 'Macedon and Athenian politics in the period 338–323 BC', *AClass* 24: 37–48.

—— (1985a), Review of N. G. L. Hammond *Three Historians of Alexander the Great* (1983), in *JHS* 105: 216.

—— (1985b), 'Seneca's *Consolatio ad Polybium*', in *ANRW* Teil II, Band 32. 2, ed. W. Haase (Berlin), 860–84.

—— (1987), 'The infantry commissions awarded by Alexander at the end of 331', in W. Will and J. Heinrichs (eds.), *Zu Alexander d. Gr. : Festschrift G. Wirth*, vol. i (Amsterdam), 413–35.

—— (1993), 'Troubled spirits in Persepolis', in *Charistion: Festschrift C. P. T. Naude* (Pretoria, UNISA), 5–15.

—— (1994), A *Commentary on Q. Curtius Rufus' Historiae Alexandri Magni, Books 5–7, 2* (Amsterdam).

—— (1998b), 'Q. Curtius Rufus' "Historiae Alexandri Magni"', in *ANRW,* Teil II, Band 34. 4, ed. W. Haase and H. Temporini. (Berlin), 3447–83.

—— (2000b), 'Originality and its limits in the Alexander sources of the Early Empire', in A. B. Bosworth and E. J. Baynham (eds.), *Alexander the Great in Fact and Fiction* (Oxford), 307–25.

—— (2007), 'On judging Alexander: a matter of honour', *AClass* 50: 15–27.

Badian, E. (1958a), 'The eunuch Bagoas: a study in method', *CQ* 8: 144–57.

—— (1958b), 'Alexander and the Unity of Mankind', *Hist* 7: 425–44.

—— (1960), 'The death of Parmenio', *TAPA* 91: 324–38.

—— (1961), 'Harpalus', *JHS* 81: 16–43.

—— (1962), Review of M. J. Fontana, *Le lotte per la successione di Alessandro Magno* (1960), in *Gnomon* 34: 381–7. (Reprinted in Badian (1964), 262–70.

—— (1963), 'The death of Philip II', *Phoenix* 17: 244–50.

—— (1964), *Studies in Greek and Roman History* (Oxford).

—— (1965), 'The date of Clitarchus', *PACA* 8: 5–11.

—— (1967), 'Agis III', *Hermes*, 95: 170–92.

—— (1968), 'A king's notebooks', *HSCP* 72: 183–204.

—— (1975a), Review of K. Kraft, *Der 'rationale' Alexander* (1971), in *Gnomon* 47: 48–58.

—— (1975b), 'Nearchus the Cretan', *YCS* 24: 147–70.

—— (1985a), Review of Hammond, *Three Historians* (1983), in *EMC* 29: 454–68.

Badian, E. (1985*b*), 'Alexander in Iran', in *The Cambridge History of Iran*, vol. ii: *The Median and Achaemenian Periods* (Cambridge), 420–501.

—— (1987), 'The ring and the book', in W. Will and J. Heinrichs (eds.), *Zu Alexander d. Gr. : Festschrift G. Wirth*, vol. i (Amsterdam), 605–25.

—— (1994*a*), 'Herodotus on Alexander I of Macedon', in S. Hornblower (ed.), *Greek Historiography* (Oxford), 107–30.

—— (1994*b*), 'Agis III; revisions and reflections', in I. Worthington (ed.), *Ventures into Greek History* (Oxford), 258–92.

—— (1996), 'Alexander the Great between two thrones and Heaven', in A. Small (ed.), *Subject and Ruler: The Cult of the Ruling Power in Classical Antiquity* (Ann Arbor), 11–26.

—— (1999), 'A note on the Alexander mosaic', in F. B. Titchener and R. F. Moorton (eds.), *The Eye Expanded* (Berkeley), 75–92.

—— (2000*a*), 'Conspiracies', in A. B. Bosworth and E. J. Baynham (eds.), *Alexander the Great in Fact and Fiction* (Oxford), 50–95.

—— (2000*b*), 'Darius III', *HSCP* 100: 241–68.

Ballesteros-Pastor, L. (2003), 'Le discours du Scythe à Alexandre le Grand (Quinte-Curce 7. 8. 12–30)', *RhM* 146: 23–37.

Balzer, R. (1971), *Der Einfluss Vergils auf Curtius Rufus* (Diss., Munich).

Bardon, H. (1947*a*), 'Quinte Curce', *LEC* 15: 3–14.

—— (1947*b*), 'Quinte Curce historien', *LEC* 15: 119–37.

—— (1947*c*), 'La valeur littéraire de Quinte Curce', *LEC* 15: 193–220.

Barrett, A. A. (1989), *Caligula: The Corruption of Power* (London).

Barzano, A. (1985), 'Curzio Rufo e la sua epoca', *MIL* 38: 71–165.

Battersby, C. (2007), 'What killed Alexander the Great?' *ANZ J. Surg.* (Journal of the Royal Australasian College of Surgeons) 77: 85–7.

Baynham, E. J. (1994), 'Antipater: manager of kings', in I. Worthington (ed.), *Ventures into Greek History* (Oxford), 331–56.

—— (1995), 'An introduction to the Metz Epitome: its traditions and values', *Antichthon* 29: 60–77.

—— (1998), *Alexander the Great: the Unique History of Quintus Curtius* (Ann Arbor).

—— (2000), 'A baleful birth in Babylon: the significance of the prodigy in the *Liber de Morte*', in A. B. Bosworth and E. J. Baynham (eds.), *Alexander the Great in Fact and Fiction* (Oxford), 242–62.

—— (2003), 'The ancient evidence for Alexander the Great', in *Brill's Companion to Alexander the Great* (Leiden), 3–29.

Béranger, J. (1953), *Recherches sur l'aspect idéologique du principat* (Basel).

Berve, H. (1926), *Das Alexanderreich auf prosopographischer Grundlage*, 2 vols. (Munich).

—— (1938), 'Die Verschmelzungspolitik Alexanders des Grossen', *Klio* 31: 135–68.

Billows, R. A. (1990), *Antigonos the One-eyed and the Creation of the Hellenistic State* (Berkeley).

Blackwell, C. W. (1999), *In the Absence of Alexander: Harpalus and the Failure of Macedonian Authority* (New York).

Blänsdorf, J. (1971), 'Herodot bei Curtius Rufus', *Hermes* 99: 11–24.

Bloedow, E. (2003), 'Why did Philip and Alexander launch a war against the Persian Empire?' *AC* 72: 261–74.

Bödefeld, H. (1982), *Untersuchungen zur Datierung der Alexandergeschichte des Q. Curtius Rufus* (diss. Düsseldorf).

Boiy, T. (2002), 'Early Hellenistic chronology in cuneiform tradition', *ZPE* 138: 249–55.

—— (2007), 'Cuneiform tablets and Aramaic ostraca: between the low and high chronologies for the early Diadoch period', in W. Heckel, L. Tritle, and P. Wheatley (eds.), *Alexander's Empire: Formulation to Decay* (Claremont, Calif.), 199–207.

Bolaffi, E. (1949), *Sallustio e la sua fortuna nei secoli* (Rome).

Borza, E. N. (1979), 'Some observations on malaria and the ecology of Central Macedonia in antiquity', *AJAH* 4: 102–24.

—— (1990), *In the Shadow of Olympus: The Emergence of Macedon* (Princeton).

—— and Reames-Zimmerman, J. (2000), 'Some new thoughts on the death of Alexander the Great', *Anc. W* 31: 22–30.

Bosworth, A. B. (1970), 'Aristotle and Callisthenes', *Hist* 19: 407–13.

—— (1971*a*), 'The death of Alexander the Great', *CQ* 21: 112–36.

—— (1971*b*), 'Philip II and Upper Macedonia', *CQ* 21: 93–105.

—— (1974), 'The government of Syria under Alexander the Great', *CQ* 24: 46–64.

—— (1980*a*), *A Historical Commentary on Arrian's History of Alexander,* vol. i: *Commentary on Books I–III* (Oxford).

—— (1980*b*), 'Alexander and the Iranians', *JHS* 100: 1–21.

—— (1983*a*), 'History and rhetoric in Curtius Rufus', *CP* 78: 150–61.

—— (1983*b*), 'The Indian satrapies under Alexander the Great', *Antichthon* 17: 37–46.

—— (1985), review of W. Will, *Athen und Alexander* (Munich, 1983), in *Gnomon* 57: 431–6.

—— (1988*a*), *Conquest and Empire: The Reign of Alexander the Great* (Cambridge).

—— (1988*b*), *From Arrian to Alexander* (Oxford).

Bosworth, A. B. (1992*a*), 'History and artifice in Plutarch's *Eumenes*', in P. A. Stadter (ed. ), *Plutarch and the historical tradition* (London and New York), 56–89.

—— (1992*b*), 'Philip III and the chronology of the Successors', *Chiron* 22: 55–81.

—— (1993), 'Perdiccas and the kings', *CQ* 43: 420–7.

—— (1994), 'Alexander the Great', in D. M. Lewis, J. Boardman, S. Hornblower, and E. M. Harris (eds. ), *The Cambridge Ancient History*, 2nd edn., vol. vi (Cambridge), 791–875.

—— (1995), *A Historical Commentary on Arrian's History of Alexander*, vol. ii: *Commentary on Books IV–V* (Oxford).

—— (1996*a*), *Alexander and the East* (Cambridge).

—— (1996*b*), 'Alexander, Euripides and Dionysos: the motivation for apotheosis', in Wallace, R. W. and Harris, E. M. (eds.), *Transitions to Empire: Essays in Honor of E. Badian*. (Oklahoma), 140–66.

—— (1996*c*), 'The historical setting of Megasthenes' *Indica*', *CP* 91: 113–27.

—— (1997), Review of Prandi *Fortuna* (1996), in *Histos* (electronic journal) 1.

—— (2000), 'Ptolemy and the will of Alexander', in A. B. Bosworth and E. J. Baynham (eds.), *Alexander the Great in Fact and Fiction* (Oxford), 207–41.

—— (2002), *The Legacy of Alexander* (Oxford).

—— (2003), 'Plus ça change: ancient historians and their sources', *CA* 22: 167–98.

—— (2004), 'Mountain and molehill? Cornelius Tacitus and Quintus Curtius', *CQ* 54: 551–67.

Bourazeli, K. (1988), 'Imperium floret: *Η εποχή του Σεπτιμίου Σεβήρου και το έργο του* Q. Curtius Rufus', *Ariadne* 4: 244–66. (in Greek)

Bousquet, J. (1974), 'Le compte de l'automne 325 à Delphes', in *Mélanges Helléniques offerts à G. Daux* (Paris), 21–32.

—— (1988), *Études sur les comptes de Delphes* (Paris)(BEFAR 267).

—— (1989), *Corpus des inscriptions de Delphes. Tome II: Les comptes du 4e et du 3e siècle* (Paris).

Braccesi, L. (1987), 'Livio, Curzio Rufo e Petrarca', *Athenaeum* 65: 237–9.

—— (1991), *Alessandro e la Germania* (Rome).

Briant, P. (1973), *Antigone le Borgne* (Paris).

—— (1996), *Histoire de l'Empire Perse de Cyrus à Alexandre* (Paris) (available in English as *From Cyrus to Alexander*, trans. P. T. Daniels (Winona Lake, 2002)).

—— (2003*a*), *Darius dans l'ombre d'Alexandre* (Paris).

—— (2003*b*), 'New trends in Achaemenid history', *AHB* 17: 33–47.

Brosius, M. (1996), *Women in Ancient Persia* (559–331 BC) (Oxford).

—— (2003), 'Alexander and the Persians', in Roisman (2003), 169–93.

Brown, T. S. (1949), 'Callisthenes and Alexander', *AJP* 70: 225–48.

Brunt, P. (1962), 'Persian accounts of Alexander's campaigns', *CQ* 12: 141–55.

—— (1975), 'Alexander, Barsine and Heracles', *Rivista di Filologia* 103: 22–34.

—— (1976), *Arrian*, vol. i: *Anabasis Alexandri Bks. I–IV* (Cambridge, Mass., and London).

—— (1983), *Arrian*, vol. ii: *Anabasis Alexandri Bks. V–VII, Indica* (Cambridge, Mass., and London).

—— (1990), *Roman Imperial Themes* (Oxford).

Buraselis, see Bourazeli.

Burke, E. M. (1985), 'Lycurgan finances', *GRBS* 26: 251–64.

Burstein, S. M. (1994), 'Alexander in Egypt: continuity or change', in H. Sancisi-Weerdenburg, A. Kuhrt and M. Cool Root (eds.), *Achaemenid History*, vol. viii: *Continuity and Change* (Leiden), 382–8.

—— (1999), 'Cleitarchus in Jerusalem: a note on the Book of Judith', in F. B. Titchener and R. F. Moorton (eds.), *The Eye Expanded: Life and Arts in Graeco-Roman Antiquity* (Berkeley), 105–12.

—— (2000), 'Prelude to Alexander: the reign of Khababash', *AHB* 14. 4: 149–54.

—— (2007), 'The gardener became a king, or did he?' in W. Heckel, L. Tritle, and P. Wheatley (eds.), *Alexander's Empire: Formulation to Decay* (Claremont, Calif.), 139–49.

Calder, W. M. (1996), 'The Seuthopolis inscription, *IGBR* 1731', in R. W. Wallace and E. M. Harris (eds.), *Transitions to Empire. Essays in Greco-Roman History, 360–146 BC, in Honor of E. Badian* (Norman, Okla., and London), 167–78.

Carney, E. (1996), 'Macedonians and mutiny: discipline and indiscipline in the army of Philip and Alexander', *CP* 91: 19–44.

—— (2001), 'The trouble with Philip Arrhidaeus', *AHB* 15: 63–89.

—— (2003), 'Women in Alexander's court', in Roisman (2003), 227–52.

—— (2007), 'The Philippeum, women and the formation of the dynastic image', in W. Heckel, L. Tritle, and P. Wheatley (eds.), *Alexander's Empire: Formulation to Decay* (Claremont, Calif.), 27–60.

Cartledge, P. (2004), *Alexander the Great: The Hunt for a New Past* (London).

Cascon Dorado, A. (1990), 'La labor desmitificadora de Curcio Rufo en su Historia de Alejandro Magno', in *Neronia IV* (Brussels), 254–65.

Casson, L. (1971), *Ships and Seamanship in the Ancient World* (Princeton).

Cawkwell, G. L. (1963), 'Eubulus', *JHS* 83: 47–67.

—— (1994), 'The deification of Alexander the Great; a note', in I. Worthington (ed.), *Ventures into Greek History* (Oxford), 293–306 (repr. in Worthington (2003a), 263–72).

Ceauşescu, P. (1976*a*), 'Altera Roma: histoire d'une folie politique', *Hist* 25: 79–108.

—— (1976*b*), 'La double image d'Alexandre le Grand à Rome', *Studii Clasice* 16: 153–68.

Chilver, G. E. F. (1979), *A Historical Commentary on Tacitus' Histories I and II* (Oxford).

Chugg, A. M. (2002), 'The sarcophagus of Alexander the Great?', *G&R* 49: 8–26.

—— (2003), 'The tomb of Alexander the Great in Alexandria', *AJAH* n.s. 1. 2 (2002 [2003]): 75–108.

—— (2004), 'Alexander's final resting place', *History Today* 7: 17–23.

—— (2004/5), *The Lost Tomb of Alexander* (London).

Courtney, E. (1993), *The Fragmentary Latin Poets* (Oxford).

Cresci Marrone, G. (1993), *Ecumene Augustea: una politica per il consenso* (Rome).

Dempsie, A. (1991), *A Commentary on Q. Curtius Rufus Historiae Alexandri, Book X.* (Diss. St Andrews, available in microfilm).

—— (1995), 'Curtiana', *Philologus* 139: 265–73.

Devine, A. M. (1979), 'The Parthi, the tyranny of Tiberius and the date of Q. Curtius Rufus', *Phoenix* 33: 142–59.

Dosson, S. (1886), *Étude sur Quinte Curce, sa Vie et son Oeuvre* (Paris).

Dover, K. J. (1978), *Greek Homosexuality* (London).

Drexler, H. (1959), 'Potentia', *RhM* 102: 50–95.

—— (1962), 'Gloria', *Helikon* 2: 3–36.

Egge, R. (1978), *Untersuchungen zur Primärtradition bei Q. Curtius Rufus: die alexanderfeindliche Überlieferung* (Freiburg).

Ehrenberg, V. (1938), 'Pothos' ( = chapter 2 of his *Alexander and the Greeks* [Oxford]), repr. in Griffith (1966), 73–83.

Elvers, K-L. (1994), 'Der "Eid der Berenike und ihrer Söhne": eine Edition von *IGBulg.* III 2, 1731', *Chiron* 24: 241–66.

Engels, D. (1978*a*), *Alexander the Great and the Logistics of the Macedonian Army* (Berkeley).

—— (1978*b*), 'A note on Alexander's death', *CP* 73: 224–8.

Epplett, C. (2007), 'War elephants in the Hellenistic world', in W. Heckel, L. Tritle, and P. Wheatley (eds.), *Alexander's Empire: Formulation to Decay* (Claremont, Calif.), 209–32.

Errington, R. M. (1970), 'From Babylon to Triparadeisos: 323–320 BC', *JHS* 90: 49–77.

—— (1975), 'Samos and the Lamian War', *Chiron* 5: 51–7.

—— (1978), 'The nature of the Macedonian state under the monarchy', *Chiron* 8: 77–133.

—— (1986), *Geschichte Makedoniens* (Munich).

Erskine, A. (2002), 'Life after death: Alexandria and the body of Alexander', *G&R* 49: 163–79.

Faraguna, M. (1992), *Atene nell' età di Alessandro* (Rome).

—— (1998), 'Aspetti amministrativi e finanziari della monarchia macedone tra IV e III secolo a. c.', *Athenaeum* 86: 349–95.

—— (2003), 'Alexander and the Greeks', in Roisman (2003), 99–130.

Fears, J. R. (1974*a*), 'Parthi in Q. Curtius Rufus', *Hermes* 102: 623–5.

—— (1974*b*), 'The Stoic view of the career and character of Alexander the Great', *Philologus* 118: 113–30.

—— (1976*a*), 'Silius Italicus, *cataphracti* and the date of Q. Curtius Rufus', *CP* 71: 214–23.

—— (1976*b*), 'The solar monarchy of Nero and the imperial panegyric of Q. Curtius Rufus', *Hist* 25: 494–6.

—— (1981), 'The cult of virtues and imperial Roman ideology', in *ANRW*, Teil II, Band 17. 2, ed. W. Haase and H. Temporini (Berlin), 827–948.

—— (2001), Review of Baynham (1998), in *AJP* 122: 447–51.

Fontana, M. J. (1955), 'Il problema delle fonti per il xvii libro di Diodoro Siculo', *Kokalos* 1: 155–90.

—— (1960), *Le lotte per la successione di Alessandro Magno* (Palermo).

Forsythe, G. (1999), *Livy and Early Rome* (Stuttgart).

Fraser, P. M. (1972), *Ptolemaic Alexandria*, 3 vols (Oxford).

—— (1996), *Cities of Alexander the Great* (Oxford).

Fredericksmeyer, E. A. (1966), 'The ancestral rites of Alexander the Great', *CP* 61: 179–82.

—— (1983), 'Once more the diadem and barrel-vault at Vergina', *AJA* 87: 99–102.

—— (1997), 'The origin of Alexander's royal insignia', *TAPA* 127: 97–109.

—— (2003), 'Alexander's religion and divinity', in Roisman (2003), 253–78.

Fugmann, J. (1995), 'Zum Problem der Datierung der "Historiae Alexandri Magni" des Curtius Rufus', *Hermes* 123: 233–43.

Gissel, J. A. P. (1995), 'The Philotas affair in Curtius' account of Alexander (VI. 7–11): a rhetorical analysis', *C&M* 46: 215–36.

—— (1999), 'The siege of Tyre in Curtius (IV. 2–4) compared with other sieges in Roman historiography', *Analecta Romana* 26: 69–83.

Goukowsky, P. (1975), 'Antigone, Alexandre et l'Assemblée macédonienne', *RPh* 49: 263–77 (a review article on Briant *Antigone* (1973)).

—— (1976), *Diodore de Sicile, Bibliothèque Historique, Livre XVII* (Paris).

—— (1978)/(1981), *Essai sur les origines du mythe d'Alexandre*, 2 vols. (Nancy).

Graf, D. F. (2003), 'Arabs in Syria: demography and epigraphy', *Topoi*, Suppl. 4: 319–40.

Grainger, J. (1990), *Seleukos Nikator: Constructing a Hellenistic Kingdom* (London).

Granier, F. (1931), *Die makedonische Heeresversammlung: ein Beitrag zum Antiken Staatsrecht* (Munich).

Grassl, H. (1974), 'Zur Datierung von Curtius Rufus', *Philologus* 118: 160–3.

Green, P. (1979), 'Caesar and Alexander: aemulatio, imitatio, comparatio', *AJAH* 3 (1978 [1979]), 1–26.

—— (1990), *Alexander to Actium: The Historical Evolution of the Hellenistic Age* (Berkeley).

Griffith, G. T. (1965), 'Alexander and Antipater in 323 BC', *PACA* 8: 12–17.

—— (ed. ) (1966), *Alexander the Great: The Main Problems* (Cambridge).

—— (1968), 'The letter of Darius at A. ii. 14', *PCPS* 14: 33–48.

—— (1979), in N. G. L. Hammond and G. T. Griffith, *A History of Macedonia*, vol. ii: 550–336 BC (Oxford).

Grilli, A. (1976), 'Il "saeculum" di Curzio Rufo', *PP* 31: 215–23.

Griset, E. (1964), 'Per la interpretazione di Curzio Rufo x, 9. 1–6 e la datazione dell'opera', *RSC* 12: 160–4.

Gruen, E. (1985), 'The coronation of the Diadochoi', in J. E. Eadie and J. Ober (eds.), *The Craft of the Ancient Historian* (Lanham, Md., and London), 253–71.

Gunderson, L. L. (1982), 'Quintus Curtius Rufus: on his historical methods', in W. L. Adams and E. N. Borza (eds.), *Philip II, Alexander the Great and the Macedonian heritage* (Washington), 177–96.

Habicht, C. (1973), 'Literarische und epigraphischer Überlieferung zur Geschichte Alexanders und seiner ersten Nachfolger', in *Akten des VI. Internationalen Kongresses für griechische und lateinische Epigraphik, München 1972* (Munich), 367–77.

—— (1996), 'Athens, Samos and Alexander the Great', *PAPhS* 140: 397–405.

Hadley, R. (2001), 'A possible lost source for the career of Eumenes of Cardia', *Hist* 50: 3–33.

Hamilton, J. R. (1969), *Plutarch, Alexander: A Commentary* (Oxford).

—— (1973), *Alexander the Great* (London).

—— (1977), 'Cleitarchus and Diodorus XVII', in K. Kinzl (ed.), *Greece and the Eastern Mediterranean in Ancient History and Prehistory. Studies presented to F. Schachermeyr* (Berlin), 126–46.

—— (1988), 'The date of Q. Curtius Rufus', *Hist* 37: 445–56.

Hammond, N. G. L. (1983), *Three Historians of Alexander the Great: The So-Called Vulgate Authors, Diodorus, Justin and Curtius* (Cambridge).

—— and Walbank, F. W. (1988), *A History of Macedonia*, vol. iii: *336–167* BC (Oxford).

—— (1989*a*), 'Casualties and reinforcements of citizen soldiers in Greece and Macedonia', *JHS* 109: 56–68.

—— (1989*b*), *Alexander the Great, King, Commander and Statesman* (London), reprinted with corrections 1994.

Hansen, M. H. (1999), *The Athenian Democracy in the Age of Demosthenes*, trans. J. A. Crook. 2nd edn. (London). (Reviewed by Atkinson, *Scholia* 2001 [electronic edition].)

Harris, W. V. (2001), *Restraining Rage: The Ideology of Anger Control in Classical antiquity* (Cambridge, Mass.).

Hatzopoulos, M. B. (1996), *Macedonian Institutions under the Kings*, vol. i (Athens).

Hauben, H. (1976), 'The expansion of Macedonian sea-power under Alexander the Great', *Anc. Soc.* 7: 79–105.

Heckel, W. (1977), 'Asandros', *AJP* 98: 410–12.

—— (1978), 'The Somatophylakes of Alexander the Great', *Hist* 27: 224–8.

—— (1979), 'One more Herodotean reminiscence in Curtius Rufus', *Hermes* 107: 122–3.

—— (1980), 'Alexander at the Persian Gates', *Athenaeum* 58: 168–74.

—— (1984), *Quintus Curtius Rufus: The History of Alexander*, trans. J. Yardley, with an introduction and notes by W. Heckel (Harmondsworth).

—— (1988), *The Last Days and Testament of Alexander the Great* (Stuttgart).

—— (1992), *The Marshals of Alexander's Empire* (London and New York).

—— (2001), review of D. Ogden, *Polygamy, Prostitutes and Death in the Hellenistic Dynasties* (1999), *BMCR* 2001. 03. 02.

—— (2003*a*), 'Kings and "Companions": observations on the nature of power in the reign of Alexander', in Roisman (2003), 197–225.

—— (2003*b*), 'Alexander the Great and "the limits of the civilised world",' in W. Heckel and L. A. Tritle (eds.), *Crossroads of History: the Age of Alexander* (Claremont, Calif.), 147–174.

—— (2006), *Who's Who in the Age of Alexander the Great* (Oxford).

—— (2007), 'The earliest evidence for the plot to poison Alexander', in W. Heckel, L. Tritle, and P. Wheatley (eds.), *Alexander's Empire: Formulation to Decay* (Claremont, Calif.), 265–75.

Heisserer, A. J. (1980), *Alexander the Great and the Greeks* (Norman, Okla.) (reviewed by Hornblower, *JHS* 102, 1982: 271–2).

Helmreich, F. (1927), *Die Reden bei Curtius* (Paderborn).

Herrmann, L. (1929), 'La date de l'histoire d'Alexandre le Grand par Quinte Curce', *REA* 31: 217–24.

Heuss, A. (1938), 'Antigonos Monophthalmos und die griechische Städte', *Hermes* 73:133–94.

Higgins, W. E. (1980), 'Aspects of Alexander's imperial administration: some modern methods and views reviewed', *Athenaeum* 58: 129–52.

Högemann, P. (1985), *Alexander der Grosse und Arabien* (Munich).

Holt, F. L. (1988), *Alexander the Great and Bactria* (Leiden).

—— (1999a), 'Alexander the Great today: in the interests of historical accuracy?' *AHB* 13: 111–17 (repr. in Worthington (2003), 319–25).

—— (1999b), *Thundering Zeus: The Making of Hellenistic Bactria* (Berkeley).

—— (2005), *Into the Land of Bones: Alexander the Great in Afghanistan* (Berkeley).

Holzberg, N. (1988), 'Hellenistisches und Römisches in der Philippos-Episode bei Curtius Rufus (III, 5. 1–6. 20)', *WJA* 14: 185–201.

Hornblower, J. (1981), *Hieronymus of Cardia* (Oxford).

Hornblower, S. (ed. ) (1994), *Greek Historiography* (Oxford).

Instinsky, H. U. (1962), 'Zur Kontroverse des Curtius Rufus', *Hermes* 90: 379–83.

Jaschinski, S. (1981), *Alexander und Griechenland unter dem Eindruck der Flucht des Harpalos* (Bonn).

Kaerst, J. (1927), *Geschichte des Hellenismus*, 3rd edn., vol. i (Leipzig; repr. Darmstadt, 1968).

Kalleris, J. N. (1954), *Les anciens Macédoniens: étude linguistique et historique*, vol. i (Athens).

Kaster, R. A. (1995), *C. Suetonius Tranquillus, De grammaticis et rhetoribus* (Oxford).

Kebric, R. B. (1977), *In the Shadow of Macedon: Duris of Samos* (Wiesbaden).

Kienast, D. (1965), 'Alexander und der Ganges', *Hist* 14: 180–8.

Klinkott, H. (2000), Die Satrapienregister der Alexander- und Diadochen-zeit (Stuttgart).

—— (2005), *Der Satrap: ein Achaimenidischer Amsträger und seine Handlungsspielräume* (Frankfurt).

Knapowski, R. (1970), 'Die Finanzen Alexander's des Grossen', in F. Altheim and R. Stiehl (eds.), *Geschichte Mittelasiens im Altertum* (Berlin), 235–47.

Koch, H. (2000), *Hundert Jahre Curtius-Forschung (1899–1999): eine Arbeitsbibliographie* (St Katharinen).

Kornemann, E. (1935), *Die Alexandergeschichte des Ptolemaios I* (Berlin).

Korzeniewski, D. (1959), *Die Zeit des Quintus Curtius Rufus* (Cologne).

Kuhrt, A. (1990), 'Alexander and Babylon', *Achaemenid History* 5: 121–30.

Lana, I. (1949), 'Dell'epoca in cui visse Quinto Curzio Rufo', RFIC 27: 48–70.

—— (1952), *Velleio Patercolo o della propaganda* (Turin).

Lane Fox, R. (1973), *Alexander the Great* (London).

Launey, M. (1949–50), *Recherches sur les armées hellénistiques*, 2 vols. (Paris).

Leeman, A. D. (1963), *Orationis ratio*, 2 vols. (Amsterdam).

Lefèvre, F. (2002*a*), *Corpus des inscriptions de Delphes*, vol. iv: *Documents amphictioniques* (Paris and Athens).

—— (2002*b*), 'Alexandre et l'Amphictyonie en 336/5', *BCH* 126: 73–81.

Le Rider, G. (1997), 'Cléomène de Naucratis', *BCH* 121: 71–93.

—— (2003), *Alexandre le Grand: monnaie, finances et politique* (Paris).

Levi, M. A. (1977), *Introduzione ad Alessandro Magno* (Milan).

Levick, B. (1976), *Tiberius* (London).

—— (1990), *Claudius* (London).

—— (1999), *Vespasian* (London).

Lock, R. A. (1977), 'The Macedonian army assembly in the time of Alexander the Great', *CP* 72: 91–107.

Lozano, F. (2007), '*Divi Augusti* and *Theoi Sebastoi*: Roman initiatives and Greek answers', *CQ* 57: 139–52.

Lühr, F-F. (1979), 'Zur Darstellung und Bewertung von Massenreaktionen in der lateinischen Literatur', *Hermes* 107: 92–114, esp. 96–9.

Lund, A. A. (1987), 'Lexikalische und kritische Bemerkungen zu Tacitus und Curtius Rufus', *Gymnasium* 94: 50–6.

Lund, H. S. (1992), *Lysimachus: A Study in Early Hellenistic Kingship* (London).

Martin, T. R. (1987), 'Quintus Curtius' presentation of Philip Arrhidaeus and Josephus' accounts of the accession of Claudius', *AJAH* 8 (1983 [1987]), 161–90.

McCrum, M., and Woodhead, A. G. (1961), *Select Documents of the Principates of the Flavian Emperors AD 68–96* (Cambridge).

McGushin, P. (1992, 1994), *Sallust, the Histories*, vols. i and ii (Oxford).

McKechnie, P. (1999), 'Manipulation of themes in Quintus Curtius Rufus Book 10', *Hist* 48: 44–60.

McQueen, E. I. (1967), 'Quintus Curtius Rufus', in T. A. Dorey (ed.), *Latin Biography* (London), 17–43.

Mederer, E. (1936), *Die Alexanderlegenden bei den ältesten Alexanderhistorikern* (Stuttgart).

Mensching, E. (1963), 'Peripatetiker über Alexander', *Hist* 12: 274–82.

Milns, R. D. (1966), 'Curtius Rufus and the "Historiae Alexandri"', *Latomus* 25: 490–507.

Milns, R. D. (1987), 'Army pay and the military budget of Alexander the Great', in W. Will and J. Heinrichs (eds.), *Zu Alexander d. Gr. : Festschrift G. Wirth*, vol. i (Amsterdam), 233–56.

Miron Perez, D. (2000), 'Transmitters and representatives of power: royal women in ancient Macedonia', *Anc. Soc.* 30: 35–52.

Mitchel, F. W. (1973), 'Lykourgan Athens', in *Lectures in Memory of L. T. Semple* (Norman, Okla.), 163–214.

Mitchell, L. (2007), 'Born to rule? Succession in the Argead royal house', in W. Heckel, L. Tritle, and P. Wheatley (eds.), *Alexander's Empire: Formulation to Decay* (Claremont, Calif.), 61–74.

Montgomery, H. (1965), *Gedanke und Tat: zur Erzählungstechnik bei Herodot, Thukydides, Xenophon und Arrian* (Lund).

Mooren, L. (1983), 'The nature of the Hellenistic monarchy', in van't Dack et al. (eds.), *Egypt and the Hellenistic World* (Louvain), 205–40.

Morello, M. R. (2002), 'Livy's Alexander digression (9. 17–19): counterfactuals and apologetics', *JRS* 92: 62–85.

Mortensen, C. (1997), 'Olympias: royal wife and mother at the Macedonian court', unpublished diss. (University of Queensland, Brisbane).

Mossé, C. (1973). *Athens in Decline 404–86 bc* (London).

Müller, O. (1973), *Antigonos Monophthalmos und das 'Jahr der Könige'* (Bonn).

Müller, S. (2003), *Massnahmen der Herschaftssicherung gegenüber der makedonischen Opposition bei Alexander dem Grossen* (Frankfurt).

Nagle, D. B. (1996), 'The cultural context of Alexander's speech at Opis', *TAPA* 126: 151–72.

*Neronia IV: Alejandro Magno modelo de los emperadores romanos*, ed. J. M. Croisille. (Brussels, 1990).

Oakley, S. P. L. (1997, 1998, 2005), *A Commentary on Livy Books VI–X*, 4 vols. (Oxford).

O'Brien, M. (1992), *Alexander the Great: The Invisible Enemy. A Biography* (London).

Ogden, D. (2007), 'Two studies in the reception and representation of Alexander's sexuality', in W. Heckel, L. Tritle, and P. Wheatley (eds.), *Alexander's Empire: Formulation to Decay* (Claremont, Calif.), 75–108.

O'Neil, J. L. (1999), 'Political trials under Alexander the Great and his Successors', *Antichthon* 33: 28–47.

—— (2002), 'Iranian wives and their roles in Macedonian royal courts', *Prudentia* 34: 159–77.

Osborne, R. (1983), *Naturalization in Athens*, vols. iii and iv (Brussels).

Otto, A. (1890), *Die Sprichwörter und sprichwörtlichen Redensarten der Römer* (Leipzig, repr. Hildesheim, 1962).

Parroni, P. (1978), Review of Giacone, *Curzio Rufo, Storie di Alessandro Magno* (1977), *RFIC* 106: 444–6.

Paspalas, S. A. (2005), 'Philip Arrhidaios at court—an ill-advised Persianism? Macedonian royal display in the wake of Alexander', *Klio* 87: 72–101.

Pearson, L. (1954/5), 'The diary and letters of Alexander the Great', *Hist* 3: 429–55.

—— (1960) *The Lost Histories of Alexander the Great* (New York).

Pédech, P. (1984), *Historiens compagnons d'Alexandre* (Paris).

Pfister, F. (1964), 'Alexander der Grosse: die Geschichte seines Ruhmes', *Hist* 13: 37–79.

Pichon, R. (1908), 'L'époque probable de Quinte Curce', *RPh* 32: 210–4.

Pinkster, H. (1990), *Latin Syntax and Semantics*, trans. H. Mulder (London and New York).

Porod, R. (1987), *Der Literat Curtius: Tradition und Neugestaltung. Zur Frage der Eigenständigkeit des Schriftstellers Curtius* (Graz).

Potts, D. T. (1989), 'Seleucid Karmania', *Archaeologia Iranica et Orientalis* 2: 581–601.

Prandi, L. (1996), *Fortuna e realtà dell'opera di Clitarco* (Stuttgart).

Ramage, E. (1987), *The Nature and Purpose of Augustus'* Res Gestae (Wiesbaden).

Reames-Zimmerman, J. (1999), 'An atypical affair? Alexander the Great, Hephaestion Amyntoros and the nature of their relationship', *AHB* 13: 81–96.

Reinmuth, O. W. (1971), *The Ephebic Inscriptions of the Fourth Century* BC (Leiden).

Ritter, H. W. (1965). *Diadem und Königsherrschaft* (Munich).

—— (1984), 'Zum sogennanten Diadem des Philippsgrabe', *Archäologischer Anzeiger*, 105–11.

Rives, J. B. (1999), *Tacitus: Germania* (Oxford).

Roisman, J. (1984), 'Ptolemy and his rivals in his history of Alexander', *CQ* 34: 373–84.

Roisman, J. (ed. ) (2003), *Brill's Companion to Alexander the Great* (Leiden), which includes Roisman, 'Honor in Alexander's campaigns': 279–321.

Roller, M. B. (2001), *Constructing Autocracy: Aristocrats and Emperors in Julio-Claudian Rome* (Princeton).

Rosen, K. (1967*a*), 'Political documents in Hieronymus of Cardia', *AClass* 10: 41–94.

—— (1967*b*), 'Die Reichsordnung von Babylon', *AClass* 10: 95–110.

Roskam, G. (2004), 'Plutarch on self and others', *Anc. Soc.* 34: 245–73.

Rudich, V. (1993), *Political Dissidence under Nero* (London).

—— (1997), *Dissidence and Literature under Nero: The Price of Rhetoricization* (London).

Rüegg, W. (1906), *Beiträge zur Erforschung der Quellenverhältnisse in der Alexandergeschichte des Curtius* (Basel).

Rutz, W. (1981), Review of Atkinson (1980), in *Gnomon* 53: 646–54.

—— (1983*a*), Review of Costas Rodruguez, *Aspectos del vocabulario* ... (1980), in *Gnomon* 55: 166–8.

—— (1983*b*), 'Seditionum procellae—Livianisches in der Darsetellung der Meuterei von Opis bei Curtius Rufus', in. E. Lefèvre und E. Olshausen (eds.), *Livius, Werk und Rezeption: Festschrift für E. Burck,* (Munich), 399–409.

—— (1984), 'Das Bild des Dareios bei Curtius Rufus', *WJA* 10: 147–59.

—— (1986), 'Zur Erzählkunst des Q. Curtius Rufus', in *ANRW*, Teil II, Band 32. 4 (Berlin), 2329–57.

Sachs, A. J., and Hunger, H. (1988), *Astronomical Diaries and Related Texts from Babylonia,* vol. i: *Diaries from 652 BC to 262 BC* (Vienna).

Sallares, R. (1991), *The Ecology of the Ancient Greek World* (London).

Salles, J-F. (1990), 'Les Achéménides dans le golfe Arabo-persique', in *Achaemenid History IV: Centre and Periphery,* ed. H. S-Weerdenberg and A. Kuhrt. (Leiden), 149–75.

Salviat, F. (1986), 'Quinte Curce, Les Insulae Furianae ...', *Revue archéoloque de Narbonnaise* 19: 101–16.

Samuel, A. E. (1962), *Ptolemaic chronology* (Munich).

—— (1965), 'Alexander's "Royal Journals" ', *Hist* 14: 1–12.

—— (1986), 'The earliest elements in the Alexander Romance', *Hist* 35: 427–37.

Schachermeyr, F. (1954), 'Die letzten Pläne Alexanders des Grossen', *Jahreshefte des österreichischen archaeologischen Institutes* 41: 118–40; repr. in Griffith (1966), 322–40.

—— (1970), *Alexander in Babylon und die Reichsordnung nach seinem Tode* (Vienna).

—— (1973), *Alexander der Grosse: das Problem seiner Persönlichkeit und seines Wirkens* (Vienna).

Schäfer, A. (1887), *Demosthenes und seine Zeit,* 2nd edn., vol. iii (Leipzig).

Schäfer, C. (2002), *Eumenes von Kardia und der Kampf um die Macht im Alexanderreich* (Frankfurt). (Reviewed by Bosworth, *Gnomon* 77, 2005: 684–8.)

Schanz, M. and Hosius, C. (1935), *Geschichte der römischen Literatur, 2. Teil,* 4th edn. (Munich).

Scheda, G. (1969), 'Zur Datierung des Curtius Rufus', *Hist* 18: 380–3.

Schepens, G. (1989), 'Zum Problem der "Unbesiegbarkeit" Alexanders des Grossen', *Anc. Soc.* 20: 15–53.

Schmidt-Colinet, A. (1996), 'Das Grab Alexanders d. Gr. In Memphis?', in M. Bridges and J. Ch. Bürgel (eds.), *The Problematics of Power* (Bern), 87–91.

Schmitt, O. (1992), *Der Lamische Krieg* (Bonn).

Schober, L. (1981), *Untersuchungen zur Geschichte Babyloniens und der oberen Satrapien von 323–303 v. Chr.* (Frankfurt).

Schubert, R. (1922), *Beiträge zur Kritik der Alexanderhistoriker* (Leipzig).

Schwartz, E. (1901), 'Curtius Rufus (31)', *RE* IV, 2, 1871–91 (repr. in his *Griechische Geschichtschreiber* (Leipzig, 1957), 156–86).

Schwenk, C. J. (1985), *Athens in the Age of Alexander: The Dated Laws and Decrees of the 'Lykourgan Era' 338–322 b.c.* (Chicago).

Sealey, R. (1960), 'The Olympic festival of 324 BC', *CR* 10: 185–6.

—— (1993), *Demosthenes and his Time* (Oxford).

Seel, O. (1956), *Pompei Trogi fragmenta* (Leipzig).

Seibert, J. (1969), *Untersuchungen zur Geschichte Ptolemaios' I* (Munich).

—— (1983), *Das Zeitalter der Diadochen* (Darmstadt).

—— (1990), review of Heckel, *The Last Days and Testament of Alexander* (1988), *Gnomon* 62: 564–6.

Shahbazi, A. Sh. (2003), 'Irano-Hellenic notes, 3: Iranians and Alexander', *AJAH* n. s. 2. 1: 5–38.

Sharples, I. (1994), 'Curtius' treatment of Arrhidaeus', *Meditarch* 7: 53–60.

Sherwin-White, S. (1987), 'Seleucid Babylonia', in A. Kuhrt and S. Sherwin-White (eds.), *Hellenism in the East* (London), 1–31.

Spann, P. O. (1999), 'Alexander at the Beas: fox in a lion's skin', in F. B. Titchener and R. F. Moorton (eds.), *The Eye Expanded: Life and Arts in Graeco-Roman Antiquity* (Berkeley), 62–74.

Spencer, D. (2002), *The Roman Alexander: Reading a Cultural Myth* (Exeter).

Steele, R. B. (1915), 'Quintus Curtius Rufus', *AJP* 36: 402–23.

—— (1919), 'Curtius and Arrian', *AJP* 40: 37–63 and 153–74.

Stewart, A. (2003), 'Alexander in Greek and Roman art', in Roisman (2003), 31–66.

Stronach, D. (1978), *Pasargadae* (Oxford).

Stroux, J. (1928/9), 'Die Zeit des Curtius', *Philologus* 84: 233–51.

Sumner, G. V. (1961), 'Curtius Rufus and the Historiae Alexandri', *AUMLA* 15: 30–9.

Sutherland, C. H. V. (1951), *Coinage in Roman Imperial Policy 31 BC–AD 68* (London).

—— (1987), *Roman History and Coinage 44BC–AD69* (Oxford).

Swain, S. C. R. (1989a), 'Plutarch: chance, providence and history', *AJP* 110: 272–302.

—— (1989b), 'Plutarch's *De Fortuna Romanorum*', *CQ* 39: 504–16.

—— (1996), *Hellenism and Empire* (Oxford).

Syme, R. (1939), *The Roman Revolution* (Oxford).

—— (1958), *Tacitus*, 2 vols. (Oxford).

Syme, R. (1982), 'The career of Arrian', *HSCP* 86: 181–211.

—— (1986), *The Augustan Aristocracy* (Oxford).

—— (1987), 'The word *opimus*—not Tacitean', *Eranos* 85: 111–14.

—— (1990), *Roman Imperial Themes* (Oxford).

Talbert, R. J. A. (1984), *The Senate of Imperial Rome* (Princeton).

Tarn, W. W. i/ii = *Alexander the Great*, 2 vols. (Cambridge, 1948).

Therasse, J. (1973), 'Le jugement de Quinte Curce sur Alexandre: une appreciation morale indépendante', *LEC* 41: 23–45.

—— (1976), *Quintus Curtius Rufus: index verborum, relevés lexicaux et grammaticaux* (Hildesheim).

Tritle, L. A. (2003), 'Alexander and the killing of Cleitus the Black', in W. Heckel and L. A. Tritle (eds.), *Crossroads of History: The Age of Alexander* (Claremont, Calif.), 127–46.

Verdière, R. (1966), 'Quinte-Curce, écrivain Néronien', *WS* 79: 490–509.

Walbank, F. W. (1970/9), *A Historical Commentary on Polybius*, vol. i [original edn. 1957]; vol. iii (Oxford).

Walter, F. (1887), *Studien zu Tacitus und Curtius* (Munich).

Wardle, D. (1994), *Suetonius' Life of Caligula: A Commentary* (Brussels).

—— (1998), *Valerius Maximus. Memorable Deeds and Sayings, Book 1* (Oxford).

—— (2005), 'Valerius Maximus on Alexander the Great', *AClass* 48: 141–61.

Weidemann, U. Vogel (1970), 'Bemerkungen zu den Curtii Rufi der frühen Principatszeit', *AClass* 13: 79–88.

—— (1974), 'The Curtii Rufi again', *AClass* 17: 141–2.

—— (1982), *Die Statthalter von Africa und Asia in den Jahren 14–68 n. Chr.* (Bonn).

Welles, C. B. (1963), *Diodorus of Sicily*, vol. viii: *Books XVI. 66–95 and XVII* (Cambridge, Mass.).

—— (1970), 'The role of the Egyptians under the first Ptolemies', in D. H. Samuel (ed.), *Proceedings of the 12th International Congress of Papyrology* (Toronto), 505–10.

Westlake, H. D. (1954), 'Eumenes of Cardia', *BJRL* 37: 309–27.

Wheatley, P. V. (1998), 'The chronology of the third Diadoch War', *Phoenix* 52: 257–81.

—— (2001), 'The Antigonid campaign in Cyprus, 306 BC', *Anc. Soc.* 31: 133–56.

—— (2007), 'An introduction to the chronological problems in early Diadoch sources and scholarship', in W. Heckel, L. Tritle, and P. Wheatley (eds.), *Alexander's Empire: Formulation to Decay* (Claremont, Calif.), 179–92.

Whitehead, D. (2000), *Hypereides: The Forensic Speeches* (Oxford).

Wiedemann, Th. (1870), 'Über das Zeitalter des Geschichtschreibers Curtius Rufus', *Philologus* 30: 241–64 and 441–3, contd. in (1872), *Philologus* 31: 756–68.

Wilhelm, F. (1928), *Curtius und der jüngere Seneca* (Paderborn).

Wilhelmy, H. (1968), 'Verschollene Städte im Indusdelta', *Geographische Zeitschrift* 56: 259–64.

Williams, C. A. (1999), *Roman Homosexuality: Ideologies of Masculinity in Classical Antiquity* (New York and Oxford).

Wirth, G. (1967), 'Zur Politik des Perdikkas, 323', *Helikon* 7: 281–322.

—— (1972), 'Nearchos der Flottenchef', in *Acta Conventus "Eirene" 1968* (Warsaw), 615–39 (repr. in his *Studien zur Alexandergeschichte* (Darmstadt, 1985), 51–75).

—— (1976), 'Alexander und Rom', in *Alexandre le Grand* (Geneva), 181–210.

—— (1986), 'Ephemeridenspekulationen', in H. Kalcyk et al. (eds.), *Studien zur Alten Geschichte Siegfried Lauffer ... dargebracht*, vol. iii. (Rome), 1051–75.

—— (1988), 'Nearch, Alexander und die Diadochen', *Tyche* 3: 241–59.

Wiseman, T. P. (1982), 'Calpurnius Siculus and the Claudian civil war', *JHS* 72: 57–67.

—— (1993), 'Lying historians: seven types of mendacity', in C. Gill and T. P. Wiseman (eds.), *Lies and Fiction in the Ancient World* (Exeter), 122–46.

Wolf, R. (1964), *Die Soldatenerzählungen des Kleitarch bei Quintus Curtius Rufus* (Vienna).

Wolohojian, A. M. (1969) *The Romance of Alexander the Great by Pseudo-Callisthenes, trans. from the Armenian version* (New York).

Woodman, A. J. (1977), *Velleius Paterculus*, vol. i: *The Tiberian Narrative* (Cambridge).

—— (1983), *Velleius Paterculus. The Caesarian and Augustan Narrative (2. 41–93)* (Cambridge).

—— (1988), *Rhetoric in Classical Historiography* (London).

Worthington, I. (1986a), 'The chronology of the Harpalus affair', *SO* 61: 63–76.

—— (1986b), '*IG* ii² 1631 and 1632 and Harpalus' ships', *ZPE* 65: 222–4.

—— (1992), *A Historical Commentary on Dinarchus* (Ann Arbor).

—— (1999a), *Greek Orators II: Dinarchus and Hyperides* (Warminster).

—— (1999 b), 'How great was Alexander?', *AHB* 13/2: 39–55 (reprinted in Worthington (2003 a), 303–18).

—— (ed.) (2003a), *Alexander the Great: A Reader* (London).

—— (2003b), 'Alexander, Philip and the Macedonian background', in Roisman (2003), 69–98.

Worthington, I. (2004), *Alexander the Great, Man and God* (Harlow).

Wüst, F. (1953/4a), 'Die Rede Alexanders des Grossen in Opis, Arrian VII 9–10', *Hist* 2: 177–88.

Wüst, F. (1953/4b), 'Die Meuterei von Opis (Arrian VII, 8; 11, 1–7)', *Hist* 2: 418–31.

Yardley, J. C. (2003), *Justin and Pompeius Trogus: a Study of the Language of Justin's Epitome of Trogus* (Toronto).

—— and Heckel (1997), *Justin, Epitome of the Philippic History of Pompeius Trogus, Books 11–12*; trans. J. C. Yardley, with comm. by W. Heckel (Oxford).

Zahrnt, O. (2003), 'Versöhnen oder Spalten: Überlegungen zu Alexanders Verbanntendekret', *Hermes* 131: 407–32.

# Index